INDIGENOUS

DEVELOPMENT

IN THE ANDES

.

INDIGENOUS DEVELOPMENT IN THE ANDES

■

Culture, Power, and Transnationalism

ROBERT ANDOLINA, NINA LAURIE,
AND SARAH A. RADCLIFFE

DUKE UNIVERSITY PRESS

DURHAM AND LONDON

2009

© 2009 Duke University Press
All rights reserved
Printed in the United States
of America on acid-free paper ∞
Designed by Amy Ruth Buchanan
Typeset in Minion by Achorn International
Library of Congress Cataloging-in-
Publication Data appear on the last
printed page of this book.

CONTENTS

.

MAPS AND TABLES

•

ACKNOWLEDGMENTS

∎

Multisited ethnographies generate complex itineraries of obligations and debts of gratitude. First we must thank those whose belief in our project from the start made it possible to begin: the Economic and Social Research Council program on Transnational Communities, and its director, Steve Vertovec. Manuel Castells gave ongoing support, and Fiona Wilson encouraged us unstintingly with good suggestions at conferences.

The research for this book would not have been possible without the interest and assistance of institutions and individuals in the field. We are very grateful to everyone who took the time to be interviewed or provide primary documents, but a few deserve special mention. In Bolivia, former members of the Andean Oral History Workshop, especially Carlos Mamani and Maria Eugenia Choque, enthusiastically embraced our project. They willingly offered interviews, facilitated contacts with indigenous leaders, and invited us to meetings and other events as participant observers. Esteban Ticona and Ricardo Calla of the Universidad de la Cordillera in La Paz also provided invaluable insight, as well as access to important documented materials. Maria Ester Udaeta of the Campesino Promotion and Information Center in La Paz was especially helpful with information and her views on water politics and policy. We are also grateful to the National Council of Ayllus and Markas and the Indigenous Confederation of the Bolivian lowlands, who provided primary documents, invited us to workshops and assemblies, and gave in-depth interviews. Likewise, we thank leaders of the Confederation of Bolivian Peasant Workers, who took time out to be interviewed. Members of international development organizations operating in Bolivia, especially Hans Hoffmeyer, David Tuchschneider, and Liz Ditchburn, deserve thanks for their interest in and support of our research. In the Cochabamba region, Pablo Regalsky, Maggie Anderson, Pamela Calla, Maria Esther Pozo, and Carlos Crespo provided invaluable support by way of interviews, feedback, and criticism, contacts for further research, and invitations to meetings and conferences on water issues and intercultural education. The Center for Andean Development was also very helpful in facilitating our participation in meetings with indigenous leaders on local development plans and related water policies.

In Ecuador, the help of Luis Macas and Paulina Palacios at the Scientific Institute of Indigenous Cultures in Quito was invaluable for all aspects of our project. Excellent visiting-researcher facilities were provided by the Universidad Andina, and Catherine Walsh's guidance and support was valuable. Fernando García at the Facultad Latinoamericana de Ciencias Sociales (FLACSO) was extremely helpful in offering interviews, documents, and access to meetings on FLACSO's Indigenous Affairs programs. Faculty and administrators at the Universidad Salesiana were also forthcoming with information on their pedagogy, curriculum, and student body. Liz Lilliott and Pilar Larreamendy provided excellent research assistance, while Oswaldo Sánchez at the Andean Community Development and Ecology Institute in Cayambe offered crucial information and contacts on irrigation policy and practice in Ecuador. We are also indebted to indigenous leaders of ECUARUNARI and the Cayambi People's Council, as well as Arturo Cevallos of Ibis-Ecuador, for interviews, documents, and invitations to workshops and meetings. Finally, Oxfam America's Lima office graciously facilitated information about their work in Ecuador and Bolivia through interviews and access to their archive.

Various chapters of the book have been presented to conferences and seminars, where we received great feedback. Parts of the introduction were presented in the 2002 Society for Latin American Studies conference. We thank Rosaleen Howard for the invitation to speak at the session on indigenous peoples. Sections from chapter 2 were presented at the 2001 American Association of Geographers conference, to which Tom Perreault had invited us, and where Arturo Escobar and Tony Bebbington provided insightful comments. The same transpired at the 2002 European Council of Latin Americanist Researchers (CEISAL) conference, where Tony invited us to speak at the session on "Transnational Civil Society and Rural Change in the Andes." In addition to offering many superb comments and providing camaraderie during field research in Boliva, José Antoonio Lucero graciously invited us to participate in the 2001 conference, "Indigenous Movements and the Transformation of Development and Democracy in Latin America," at Princeton University. Parts of chapter 3 were also presented at the Institute of Latin American Studies, University of Liverpool, at Cambridge University's Scott Polar Research Institute discussion group on "Indigenous Governance," and at the University of California, Berkeley, at the symposium on transnational informality. We are grateful to Nezar Al Sayyed and Ananya Roy at Berkeley for their invitation and hospitality. Meeting Orin Yiftachel and Jai Sen at this symposium contributed to our work's engagement with a wider set of issues than we had originally envisaged. Parts of chapter 4 were presented at the 2001 Society for Latin American Studies, the 2002 Ecuadorianists conference in Quito, as well as the International Studies Association 2003 conference. Sections of chapters 5 and 6 were presented at the 2001 Latin American Studies Association meeting, on the invitation of Amy Lind, and where Mary Weismantel gave excellent comments. After a redraft, the chapter was represented at the Department of Geography, Dartmouth College. Sarah Radcliffe would like to thank Pam Martin and the staff there for their welcome and useful suggestions.

A large number of people receive our deepest thanks for the time and interest they showed in our work by offering helpful commentary. In alphabetical order, we wish to thank Richard Black, Into Goldschmidt, Gerry Kearns, Guillermo O'Donnell, Laura Rival, and Peter Wade. We received comments from a dedicated group of readers on written drafts of the chapters. On chapter 2, Simon Grimble, Fiona Wilson, and Rachel Silvey each had unique and useful things to say, while Tony Bebbington tightened our conception of social capital. Michelle Bigenho, Gail Fondahl, and Deborah Yashar have all had inputs into chapter 3 at different stages of the process. Vicky Lawson—as always—gave a thorough and inspiring critique of chapter 6. Phil Stickler and Owen Tucker of the Cartography Unit in the Department of Geography, University of Cambridge, prepared the maps and diagrams.

While the authors are listed in alphabetical order for the book as a whole, the individual chapters list various orders of authors according to leadership taken on those chapters. However, all three authors worked on every chapter, and the overall contribution to this work is equal among the coauthors.

Parts of this book have appeared previously in print. Pages 140–46 and 151–54 of chapter 4 amend pages of N. Laurie, R. Andolina, and S. A. Radcliffe, "The excluded indigenous? Implications of multiethnic policies for water reform in Bolivia," which appeared in Rachel Sieder, ed., Multiculturalism in Latin America (Palgrave Macmillan, 2002) and which is reproduced with permission of Palgrave Macmillan. Various parts of chapter 5 appeared in N. Laurie, R. Andolina, and S. A. Radcliffe, "Indigenous professionalization: Transnational social reproduction in the Andes," Antipode (Blackwell) 2003; and in N. Laurie, R. Andolina, and S. A. Radcliffe, "Ethno-development: Social movements, creating experts, and professionalizing indigenous knowledge in Ecuador," Antipode (Blackwell) 2005. Various passages in chapter 6 are drawn from S. A. Radcliffe, N. Laurie, and R. Andolina, "The transnationalization of gender and reimagining Andean indigenous development," Signs: Journal of Women in Culture and Society 29, no. 2, 2003 by the University of Chicago.

INTRODUCTION

Indigenous Development in the Andes

One morning in the Ecuadorian capital of Quito, an indigenous woman trained in development issues walks to the offices of the national indigenous peoples' confederation. Here she has a meeting with Afro-Ecuadorians about a multiethnic development program in rural villages, and then she will take a conference call from staff at the Norwegian bilateral agency to coordinate responses to the latest United Nations statement on indigenous rights. In La Paz, Bolivia, a mestizo man working at the World Bank coordinates a meeting with representatives from the continental Fondo Indígena, while responding to a U.S.-based advocacy NGO. Taken together, these stories suggest the increasingly transnational, multiethnic, and institutionalized character of contemporary indigenous movements. Mass mobilizations still matter, but the lines of struggle are drawn increasingly within agencies of power, not just at their doorsteps. These changes in indigenous politics signal a need for new approaches to its study. Developing such an approach is a primary objective of this book.

Over the past twenty years, indigenous peoples in Ecuador and Bolivia have moved from political obscurity to political centrality through a combination of national and transnational activism. They have done so by redefining the meanings of dominant discourses, by mobilizing to pressure national governments, and by taking advantage of opportunities and alliances (Albó 1994; Santana 1995; Radcliffe and Westwood 1996; Patzi 1998; Van Cott 2000a; Selverston-Scher 2001; Lucero 2002; Andolina 2003; Yashar 2005). Their achievements include public acceptance of cultural diversity, legal recognition of multiple indigenous rights and territories, political recognition of representative indigenous organizations, and the creation of institutions to manage indigenous affairs, which are often directed or influenced by indigenous representatives. Indigenous movements have also participated in popular coalitions that have challenged donor-led development initiatives and removed corrupt and unresponsive elected officials.

Indigenous movements have projected identities and information effectively through transnational networks as a means to overcome local limitations on their political possibilities. Transnational action has enabled these movements to amass resources for local organizing and gain leverage over national governments; it has also generated international visibility, legitimacy, and reform (Stavenhagen 1998; Brysk 2000). Guatemalan indigenous leader Rigoberta Menchú, for instance, won the Nobel Peace Prize in 1993, and the UN declared 1995–2004 the International Decade of Indigenous Peoples. More concretely, indigenous rights and agendas hold a firm, if secondary, position within multilateral institutions such as the United Nations and the Organization of American States and are now incorporated within development policies and projects of the World Bank, the Inter-American Development Bank, the European Union, and numerous bilateral aid agencies. Such gains have been well documented and represent significant feats of global struggles against marginalization and racism.

Taking these breakthroughs as a point of departure, we ask two sets of questions in order to extend our understanding. First, how are development policy and practice reconfigured once ethnicity and cultural difference are inserted explicitly into development thinking? While cultural assumptions have always underpinned development, the intentional incorporation of ethnicity as an object of policy represents a significant turn in the relationship between development and culture. Based on this concern, our second set of questions examines the broader character of transnationalism in times of multiculturalism and globalization. How does *multi*ethnic transnationalism—in contrast to the singular ethnic experiences assumed to prevail among transnational communities comprising diaspora migrants or global business expatriates—emerge and sustain itself? How have indigenous movements' advances in visibility and policy reform, and the transnational networking crucial to them, reflected back to affect indigenous peoples and organizations? Linking geographical concerns over space and scale to political-science accounts of networks and anthropological theories of policy, we interrogate a transnationalism that works across ethnic lines, state borders, community boundaries, and continental divides. Through cases of indigenous development in Bolivia and Ecuador, we investigate the enabling and constraining implications of a more culturally and ethnically aware type of development, which has both academic and policy relevance.

Central to our exploration of these issues is the consolidation of expectations about indigeneity within transnational networks and the institutionalization of indigenous agendas within official development policy.[1] Following Margaret Keck and Kathryn Sikkink's model of transnational networks, financially poor and politically disadvantaged indigenous organizations throw "boomerangs" from the Andes, which circumvent local and national obstructions by making connections to organizations outside or parallel to the nation-state. These connections garner transnational support as the boomerang returns to discipline Andean states according to international norms concerning indigenous peoples (Keck and Sikkink 1998; see also Brysk 2000; Perreault 2003).

Without dismissing this dimension of transnational indigenous politics, we show how such boomerangs are also "reloaded" through the forging of transnational governmentalities. This reloading has comprised an appropriation of indigenous rights and their articulation with agendas favoring neoliberal economics, decentralization, and citizen responsibility.[2] In the cases of Ecuador and Bolivia, governments adopted a multicultural discourse formalized through models of pluralist decentralization, while development agencies adopted notions of social inclusion in devising projects targeting the indigenous grassroots (Assies, Van der Haar, and Hoekama 2000; Davis 2002). From the standpoint of many indigenous organizations and pro-indigenous advocates, this "glocalization" (localization processes that are informed or driven by globalization processes) should generate culturally appropriate development that conforms to their agenda and self-identification. The results, however, may approximate developmentally appropriate culture.

In short, this book examines how indigenous policy and advocacy networks intersect to define a transnational but grounded frontier between culturally appropriate development and developmentally appropriate culture. We speak of "indigenous development" as an issue area around which concerned networks and circuits form and discuss "ethnodevelopment" or "development-with-identity" as the policy paradigms that specifically address the issue of indigenous development. The ostensible goal of these paradigms is for development to be culturally appropriate, but actors often differ on what that means. Such differences in meaning constitute one reason for the complexity of indigenous development; another reason is the context dependence of concrete policies and practices. From our perspective, the situated overlap or conflict between neoliberal, grassroots, and indigenous-movement discourses is just as consequential as any core features of different strands of ethnodevelopment policy.

The intersection between transnationalism, culture, and development comes to the fore concretely in Bolivia and Ecuador, where strong indigenous movements, multicultural state reforms, and neoliberal structural adjustments converged. Some indigenous development policies in these countries have been held up as examples among international agencies and thereby acquired significance beyond the immediate area. Our empirical focus on the highland region departs from most previous works on indigenous transnationalism in Ecuador and Bolivia, which dealt primarily with the Amazonian lowlands (Heijdra 1996; Sawyer 1997; Martin 2003; Conklin and Graham 1995; Egan 1996). In this way we not only provide a distinct substantive contribution to understandings of regional indigenous politics but also illuminate the recent reconfiguration of development, indigenous politics, and culture. How so? The Amazonian lowlands in Ecuador and Bolivia were transnationalized earlier and in a discrete—and arguably more profound—manner compared with the highlands. The Amazon region has long been targeted by multinational companies for raw material extraction, by environmentalists for ecological protection, and by cultural rights advocates for highly distinct (or "exotic") indigenous cultures. The highlands, in contrast, has fewer marketable raw materials and is seen as less fragile ecologically, while its indigenous population is viewed as more integrated with the national society. The rural development paradigm dominant in highland areas, furthermore, was largely tied to a state-led modernization agenda focused on national economies.

In the past fifteen to twenty years, however, the highlands in Ecuador and Bolivia have become transnationalized in ways that reflect important shifts in global political economies and development thinking. Such changes result from ongoing dialogue between various indigenous groups and their allies, from new state legislation and constitutional reform, and from the transformation of rural development under neoliberalism. First, neoliberal agrarian reform laws have marginalized indigenous small producers within rural development policy, while indigenous people increasingly find themselves subjects of "social," "local," and "ethno" development rubrics. Second, indigenous organizations in the Ecuadorian and Bolivian highlands have increasingly localized their political identities while globalizing their links with anti-neoliberal movements fighting for secure food and water, and against reforms rooted in promarket orthodoxy. Some of these changes are relevant for the Amazonian lowlands as well, but their dynamics in the highlands brings the novel and transnational character of them to the fore. Maps 1 and 2 illustrate our primary research sites in Bolivia and Ecuador, respectively.

Commonalities across three important but seemingly independent fields of indigenous development reveal that the scope of transnational connections transcends specific policy areas, even as it shapes them in particular ways.

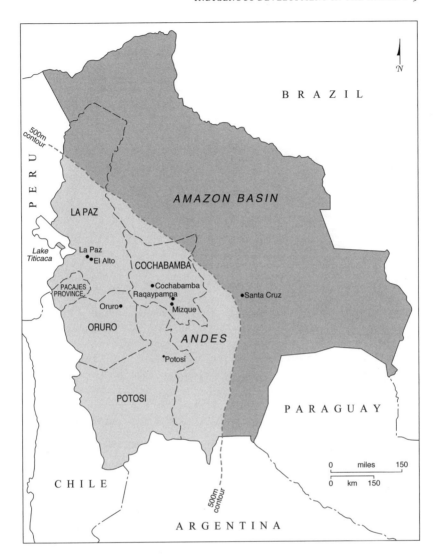

MAP 1. Primary research sites in Bolivia.

Bolivia has been divided administratively into departments, provinces, municipalities, cantons, and parishes. Our research sites are towns and cities marked by dots and by the boundary of Pacajes province in the southwestern part of La Paz department, where we attended workshops in small towns and villages. As these sites are almost entirely in the highland (Andean mountain) region of Bolivia, we have only labeled those administrative departments with substantial territory in the Bolivian highlands.

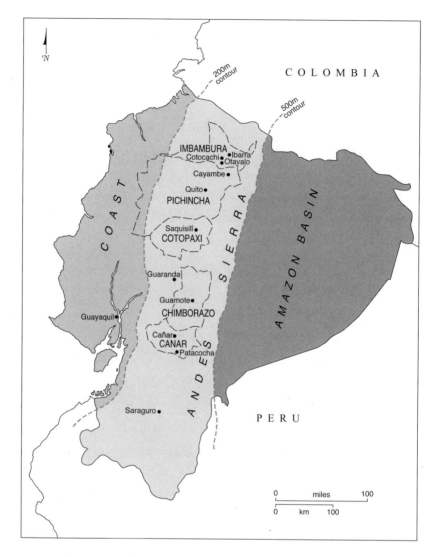

MAP 2. Primary research sites in Ecuador.

Ecuador is administratively divided into provinces, cantons, municipalities, and parishes. The dots in and around towns and cities mark our research sites. As these sites are entirely within the highland (Andean mountain or *sierra*) region of Ecuador, we only labeled the provinces of the region where we researched.

Whether in the governance of local spaces, the politics of water and irrigation, or in indigenous professionalization, we find that development discourses enroll indigenous peoples as stakeholders and that key decisions occur within transnationalized institutional settings and policy forums. The multiethnic complexion of these processes is less visible but equally relevant. Network relations—and the representations of indigenous people in them—are gendered, cultured, and racialized, such that some subjects gain prominence over others. Further examination of these intricacies provides a means of understanding how a common language on indigenous development may smooth out tensions or entrench them further, as illustrated in networks permeating the professionalization of indigenous affairs.

By analyzing these cases we seek to contribute to a poststructuralist research agenda for understanding the geographies of globalization and the politics of multiracial societies. While transnational actors—indigenous or otherwise—have often been viewed as moving in a frictionless world, we echo Anna Tsing's (2005) work on friction through a multiscalar picture of transnationalism. This refocuses attention on how spaces and scales can intersect to block *or* channel subaltern networks and transnational practices. In their engagement of development policy, indigenous organizations negotiate, contest, or collude with powerful forces and actors; however, the consequences of doing so return to impact on the agendas and positions of indigenous social movements, as transnational networks increasingly move from coordinating to governing. Indigenous organizations and leaders therefore grapple with diverse and sometimes unanticipated consequences of their movements' political gains.

Our work also extends Charles Hale's (2002) elucidation of neoliberal multiculturalism. Like Hale, we see official multiculturalism in much of Latin America as a cultural project of neoliberalism that responds to indigenous movement demands while containing them in a broader neoliberal order.[3] Ethnodevelopment policies are posed as solutions to what Hale identifies as a "paradox of simultaneous cultural affirmation and economic marginalization" (493). We also concur with his argument for balancing Foucauldian emphases on the discipline of social subjects with Gramscian concepts of articulation and subaltern struggles. Finally, our approach echoes Hale's call to maintain a "distinction between the cultural project of neoliberalism and the socio-political consequences that follow as this project is deployed" (498). We do so not only to acknowledge the effects of subaltern action and the unintended consequences of interaction but also to indicate how aspects of neoliberal multiculturalism are transmitted to a "post-neoliberal" turn in some parts of Latin America.[4]

Unlike Hale, however, we consider neoliberal multiculturalism within a broader paradigm that we call "social neoliberalism," which responds to multiple social concerns, including but not limited to cultural difference. We find that neoliberal multiculturalism is produced in a more transnational and networked fashion than Hale's analysis suggests. While his study includes international organizations, it focuses largely on national-scale state-society relations. Neo-liberal multiculturalism, in the form of ethnodevelopment policy, is deployed spatially, even as it crosses or transgresses previously acknowledged boundaries. Official multiculturalism in Latin America should be conceptualized as a racial project rooted in regional histories, as well as a cultural project tied to the recent neoliberal order.

We expand on these points through an interdisciplinary theoretical framework that draws on Foucauldian, social constructivist, and political process approaches in conceptualizing the changing relationship between indigenous development and culture. We then adapt theories and concepts of transnational networks and political and economic scales to visualize the wide-ranging institutional and spatial character of Andean indigenous development. By synthesizing and innovating on these theoretical approaches, we seek an understanding of transnational social and political fields that attributes equal significance to discourse, identity, multiscalar interaction, and political and economic contexts.

Repositioning Multiethnicity: Development Rediscovers Culture

While waiting for an interview with the regional director of a major indigenous development project in Ecuador, we spoke with a young indigenous woman filling in a computer-based form. She explained that she was calculating the "social capital index" of each indigenous organization in the region.[5] Ostensibly a measure of the cultural density and infrastructure that indigenous communities may draw on for development, the index determined how much funding each organization received from this World Bank–financed project.

In order to apprehend such realities, we consider how indigenous cultures and communities are "locate[d] on a larger landscape of developmental political economy . . . under the sign of governmentality and rule" (Watts 2003, 11). This landscape consists of forms of thought and knowledge, along with mechanisms and tactics for establishing authority, creating subjects and actors, and representing objects (Dean, as cited in Watts 2003, 14).[6] We approach this panorama in a tripartite manner: examining how indigenous actors are included as development interlocutors or excluded as development obstacles, situating indigenous identities and agendas between being made by others and being elaborated by indigenous people themselves (Hall 1996; Ong 1996), and studying how indigenous people become beneficiaries and objects of intervention. Actual indigenous people may therefore experience external norms and criteria "as constitutive and liberating" or as "illiberal and despotic" (Shore and Wright 1997, 30; Dean 1999, 204–5). Our approach has certain implications for the politics of indigenous development and identity.

Development Policy Discourses and Representations
Because our framework locates development reasoning and practice in a transnational social field, it challenges views of development politics as a series of battles between wholly distinct paradigms (Klarén and Bassert 1986; Nederveen Pieterse 2001) or between incommensurable forms of knowledge (Jameson 1991; A. Escobar 1995). In our view, policies emerge in and through multiple institutions, making apparent the sometimes fragmented character of development thinking.[7] A close analysis and interpretation of the assumptions, concepts, expectations, and representations within development paradigms illustrates how they enable or constrain terminological overlap, agenda bridging, and other interactions across scales and social differences. Ethnodevelopment policy paradigms are produced through complex reformulations of modernization, neoliberal, and grassroots frameworks and are therefore open to various, though not infinite, arrangements.

Ethnodevelopment policies derive, in part, from what we call "social neoliberalism." It counters what Drainville (2004) refers to as "no society neoliberalism" (233), in which narrowly technocratic, structural-adjustment policy concerned itself with paring down the state to remove fetters on the market and barriers to competition and innovation. In contrast, social neoliberalism sees cultural difference, environmental protection, gender equality, and popular participation as necessary ingredients in development and accordant with capitalist markets or self-help agency. Rooted in the notion of social inclusion, it is at once a critique of the "no society" archetype—for having a limited view of what development is and having limited means to achieve it—and a rediscovery of society as a site of development needs and development potential.[8] At a time when society was, in many countries, being reconfigured by new actors—such as women's groups, indigenous peoples, citizens' associations, and environmentalists—social neoliberalism emerged out of a dialogical partnership between neoliberalism, feminism, environmentalism, multiculturalism, and the ideals of grassroots democracy.[9] Its discourse therefore places terms like *diversity, inclusion, sustainability,* and *stakeholders* alongside terms such as *efficiency, self-management, productivity,* and *capacity.* In sum, social neoliberalism is a key component of what Fine (2001) describes as a "post-Washington consensus."

Social neoliberalism also presumes that market-based managerial and technical skills are compatible with, if not optimal for, nonmarket or noneconomic organizations and institutions. It is thereby consistent with good-governance development norms aimed at bringing the state back in while reducing corruption and increasing accountability. Akin to what governmentality theorists refer to as advanced liberal government, good governance "endeavors to not only work through the . . . freedom and agency of individuals and collectives but also to deploy indirect means for the surveillance and regulation of that agency" (Dean 1999, 149). In order to achieve and practice development that is at once inclusive, efficient, and productive, good governance deploys technologies of agency (empowerment, facilitation) and performance (regulation, monitoring): these include spaces of dialogue between civil-society associations and other stakeholders, methodologies such as participatory development planning, systems of accounting and auditing, and training programs, and measures to strengthen institutions and build capacity.[10]

While social neoliberalism embraces criteria of economy, efficiency, and transparency, it is not reducible to them. Social inclusion and its various components, such as education, health care, income equity, cultural diversity, and gender balance, are valued as developmental ends in their own right. They are not just means to achieve growth or abet markets. Likewise, the inclusion of indigenous organizations and other civil-society associations is viewed as a way of achieving greater voice, representation, and dignity in development; it is not perceived exclusively as a means to optimize government by tapping the information and expertise that such organizations possess. That said, social neoliberalism is not a seamless paradigm: tensions arise between various economic and social criteria, and contests ensue over the prioritizing and precise definition of such criteria.

Social neoliberalism is linked to indigenous subjects most directly through ethnodevelopment or development-with-identity programs. Although they take various forms, they share the general goal of including indigenous beneficiaries in the fruits and processes of development while allowing them to retain and draw upon their distinct identities and cultures. The incorporation of indigenous rights into development policy is one key ethnodevelopment strategy; applying the concept of social capital to indigenous culture is another. In Andean

contexts, cultural features like extended-family networks, norms of reciprocity, dense associations, close relationships to land, and consensual communal
governance have been redefined as social capital. As social capital is envisaged
as a basis for participation in markets and governance, indigenous culture is
redefined as an asset to development rather than an obstacle.[11] Indigenous
people are conceptualized, in this respect, as financially poor but rich in social
capital, while development organizations cast their own role as providers of
what indigenous people lack in the struggle to accumulate social capital and
overcome exclusion from political and economic opportunities.

   This recasting of development assumptions permits Andean indigenous
groups to renegotiate their relationship to development as subjects who contribute and participate. But it also makes indigenous peoples and their cultures
into objects of intervention and remains largely silent about key concerns of indigenous organizations, such as racism, national inequalities, and international
dependencies. At the same time, indigenous movements are unstable dialogic
partners with social neoliberalism and the ethnodevelopment policies based on
it. As outlined by Yashar (1999), indigenous movements in Latin America have
generally embraced human rights, citizenship rights, and political localization;
they have also asserted that society is heterogeneous, critiquing state structures
and agents for being unresponsive to the diverse needs of indigenous peoples. To
this extent, they may be well positioned to negotiate and appropriate neoliberal
governmentalities. Yet indigenous movements remain committed to notions
of broader social solidarity and insist on state obligations to meet basic needs
and redress class inequities. Likewise, they construct and represent subjects
like indigenous "nationalities" and "peoples," which they envisage as cultural
wholes irreducible to either the individuals or the associations that comprise
them (Andolina 1999; Selverston-Scher 2001). These more communitarian subjectivities enable indigenous movements to maintain some critical distance from
neoliberal development agendas and generate a continuous risk of disrupting
neoliberal-style governance, whether social or more orthodox.

   The consequences of this ambiguous relationship range from the formation
of alternative modernities, where indigenous people become ethnically distinct
managers, entrepreneurs, and professionals, to a grassroots epistemology where
indigenous actors evoke radically distinct territorialities, concepts of water use,
forms of learning, and notions of gender.[12] However, leaders and members of
indigenous organizations do not always fully agree on goals or the best pathways to reach them; the same can be said for nonindigenous NGOs and other
development organizations. Such disagreements are consequential.

Identity in Racial Formation

Development policy and practice has intervened perennially in intercultural relations, whether those framed by colonialism (Blunt and McEwan 2002; Power 2003) or by more recent sociopolitical regimes (White 2002). We therefore historicize indigenous identities—and their relation to current governmentalities—within Latin America's racial formations, and in the diverse racial projects that compose them (Wade 1997; Hall 1989; Omi and Winant 1994).[13] Until recently, Latin American elites have largely controlled racial projects, based on narratives that were embedded in transnational notions of modern progress but which informed Latin American national identities. Substantively, Latin American racial projects have exhibited a tension between "homogeneity and diversity," which has allowed "equality and inequality to be imagined and experienced" by various social subjects (Wade 2004, 264).[14]

The slippery distinction between race and ethnicity is important for grasping racial formations and projects. While they refer to supposedly self-evident differences based on phenotype and culture, respectively, the two terms have been used interchangeably in Latin American history. Today, indigenous movements and development-policy networks use the term *ethnicity* more than *race*. A shared commitment to cultural recognition—although formulated in very diverse ways—makes sense of this use of the term *ethnic*. However, just as ethnicity has become a historically specific way of talking about race since the mid–twentieth century (Omi and Winant 1994; Wade 1997), phenotypic features are regularly evoked as markers of indigeneity in the Andes and in transnational circuits linked to the region. The racial projects inherent in indigenous development policy therefore rework and extend the process of identity construction within racial hierarchies and contested patterns of racism.

Although the reconfiguration of indigenous identities that we examine in this book has taken place largely in the last twenty years, indigenous subjects have been institutionalized purposely many times in the past, starting in the colonial era. This tended to follow on crises or uncertainties of governance influenced by materialist ambitions and ideological beliefs.[15] For example, once the predictions of social Darwinism (e.g., that Indians were "unfit" and would disappear in the course of evolution) proved to be unfounded, *indigenista* experts and nationalists glorified indigenous traditions and incorporated them into national symbols and myths (including the hybrid mestizo as a "national race"). In the early to mid–twentieth century, indigenista institutes were set up to study indigenous cultures and social conditions and to recommend policy solutions to "the Indian problem." The nationalism of the second half of the twentieth century viewed indigenous peoples and cultures as obstacles to development and as a problem to be handled through public administration. Development policies of the period operated not only to generate economic growth but also to integrate indigenous people into modern institutions and the national market. That such incorporation meant becoming "less Indian" through contact with whites and exposure to Western health care and education went largely unquestioned (Wade 1997, chaps. 3–4; de la Cadena 2000; Garrard-Burnett 2000; Stern 2004).

In much of the Andean highlands, this meant transforming Indians into peasants. Yet "peasants" were constantly reminded of their Indianness through quotidian discrimination that reinforced racial hierarchies and limited access to material resources and institutional opportunities. Land-reform measures passed in Bolivia (1953) and Ecuador (1964, 1973) had real potential to improve indigenous peasant livelihoods, but they were undermined by assumptions that white-owned large landholdings would be more efficient and productive. The result was a halting implementation of agrarian reform in Ecuador and the promotion of commercial agribusiness in the Bolivian lowlands, coupled with developmental neglect in the highlands (K. Clark 1998; Albó 2002).

Such discrimination and unfulfilled promises motivated indigenous social movements from the 1970s onward to make indigenous identities and cultures visible, in ways more empowering and equitable than were available within dominant racial formations (Radcliffe and Westwood 1996; Weismantel 2001; Pallares 2002). These movements, in turn, compelled national governments and international development agencies to explicitly embrace indigenous identities and agendas, which has given more "official space" to "the possibility of combining universalistic citizenship with particularistic rights" (Wade 2004, 276). In this regard, arguably the most significant shift of recent years has been an explicit attention to ethnicity and culture as a related response to indigenous-movement agendas (Rao and Walton 2004; Radcliffe 2006). However, this has also bureaucratized indigenous identities and agendas in multicultural and ethnodevelopment frameworks and institutions, while entangling them with transnational networks and neoliberal discourses.

To further study this ongoing identity formation, we complement the governmentality theory discussed above with a combination of social-constructivist and political-process approaches. Political-process theory, located primarily in the literature on social movements, focuses on how structural political changes open up niches for reconfiguring identity categories. It also emphasizes claims making among political actors and the role of the state in validating different claims (see Hanagan, Moch, and te Brake 1998; Tilly 1998; Tilly 1999). This approach helps us to consider how the identity category of *indigenous* is locked into current Latin American political regimes and institutions as a result of the recognition of indigenous collective rights and organizations. Yet political-process theory remains too rigid to account fully for the shifting content and boundaries of indigenous identity and culture. In the context of multiple and competing racial projects, representation of indigenous people resists full standardization or universal agreement, despite national and transnational niches for such identities. The precise delineation of "indigenous" varies between different educational programs, development projects, and advocacy organizations. In one Bolivian higher education program, indigenousness is formally defined as speaking a precolonial language such as Quechua, but some indigenous students in the program pointed more to a largely oral (vs. book-based) tradition of learning as an indigenous identity marker.[16]

By incorporating social-constructivist currents that stress linguistic, narrative, and ideological foundations of identity (Hall 1989; Somers and Gibson 1994; Alvarez, Dagnino, and Escobar 1998; also see Finnemore and Sikkink 2001), we grapple with this flexibility and analyze political process more contingently in relation to the Andes. This includes interpreting the substantive content that gives intelligibility and meaning to identities and demonstrating how discourses and actors within and outside the state shape these meanings. As such, we offer a more nuanced account of how subjectivities are formed as multiple actors negotiate and contest neoliberal development and governmentality.

Resituating Transnationalism:
Scale, Space, and Social Difference

Driven by the uneven operations of capitalist and other political economies (Harvey 1989; Gibson-Graham 1996), development is imagined and enacted in uneven ways according to particular global-local linkages, colonial and post-colonial histories, and changes in development paradigms. As such, a complex geography of globalization—multiscalar, multiethnic, and inter-institutional— enables us to conceptualize how development paradigms and policies operate through scattered hegemonies and diverse authorities. Crucial to this framework is an understanding of how actors connect across boundaries to administer, negotiate, and contest indigenous development while also inscribing territorial spaces as units of intervention and containers of subjects (see Watts 2003, 13–15).[17]

This spatial approach to globalization contributes to theories on political transnationalism. Risse-Kappen defines transnationalism as "regular inter-actions across national boundaries when at least one actor is a nonstate agent or does not operate on behalf of a national government or intergovernmental organization" (1995, 3). We complement his border-crossing view of trans-national politics by accounting for the reification of spaces as transnational networks converge on specific geographies. We show how these assemblages take place at diverse scales and not only national ones.[18] When a Latin American network supports "indigenous municipalities" in Ecuador, when international donors promote Bolivia as an exemplar country within educational institu-tions, when a European NGO holds an Andean-area strategy meeting, or when protestors from various countries rally in Washington to challenge the Inter-national Monetary Fund's (IMF) worldwide reform recipes, they are transnation-ally acting upon and (re)producing local, national, regional, and global scales respectively.

Another crucial scale involved in transnationalism is the body. Informed by feminist work that demonstrates the body's socially and spatially specific construction (Butler 1993; Grosz 1994), by accounting for the body we avoid reducing actors to "generic . . . or invisible practitioners" (Freeman 2001, 1010). Instead, we can analyze how bodily images and actions play a constitutive role in the emplacement of—and meanings around—the global sphere. Gendered and racialized bodies inform the practices, meanings, and discourses of development for indigenous people. One or two scales out from the body, gendered spaces of reproduction (such as the household and community) are often excluded from mainstream accounts of globalization, yet they are highly relevant for understanding globalization's social and spatial transformations (Marston 2000; Mitchell, Marston, and Katz 2003).

Geographical theory defines scale as an arena—the city, the local, the state, or the global—where social relations fulfill (re)productive functions (McDowell 2001, 229). Accordingly, globalization is produced, in part, through the trans-formation and reproduction of various scales, to which structural shifts and network flows contribute (Lefebvre 1991; Ong 1999; Harvey 2000; Marston 2003, 173; N. Smith 2003). Taking scales as socially produced, we see transnational-ism not as a distinct level of action or analysis but as linked interactions that traverse and reinforce boundaries simultaneously. This conceptualization of transnationalism, furthermore, views scales in globalization less as a sandwich of separate layers and more as of a set of mutually influential arenas over differing geographical expanses.

Our approach to transnationalism and globalization also intervenes in the geography literature on networks and flows (Castells 2000; Appadurai 1996), as well as the "global civil-society school" in political science (Lipschutz 1996; Rosenau 2000; also Brysk 2000).[19] Manuel Castells's distinction between spaces of flows (a circuit of primarily electronic exchanges rooted in scattered nodes and hubs serving the interests of globalized managerial elites) and spaces of places (a composite of mainly personal interchanges within a physically contiguous space serving everyday needs) is a good starting point for our consideration of Andean indigenous development. However, the contrast between these two types of spaces is overdrawn, where "flow" is a global space of elite power and knowledge and "place" is a space of popular experience and meaning (Castells 2000, 458–59). In Castells's model, therefore, concrete place is absorbed by or subsumed under network flow, in which international (global) business dominates and disarticulates (local) civil society. This, of course, does occur, but such a framework obviates the analytical possibility of a global civil society or local elite, as well as quotidian domination through logics of place. Our multiscalar and multiactor framework allows us to explore flows and places in less linear and less deterministic ways. For example, it can account for nonelite actors such as indigenous peoples "jumping scales" into global civil society, as well as the use of global funds and support in defining meaningful places (including indigenous territorialities) as alternatives to the crudest logic of national or international capital.

From the perspective of constructivist international relations theory in political science, transnational groups can "shape human behavior through changing . . . dominant discourses, moral codes, and knowledge" (Betsill and Bulkeley 2004, 476).[20] Whether by way of altering viewpoints within epistemic communities (Haas 1990) or by means of transnational advocacy of political norms (Keck and Sikkink 1998), the impact of transnationalism is presumed to fall primarily on the nation-state. In "moving away from state-centered analyses to consider the multiplicity of actors and institutions that influence [how] issues are addressed across different scales" (Betsill and Bulkeley 2004, 475), global civil society theory improves on Castells's model by expanding society, conceptually, to global political dimensions. By recognizing the multiple scales affected by transnational activity, this theory also moves beyond impact on the state, thereby transcending previous limitations of epistemic community and transnational advocacy network theories.

As such, our take on transnationalism engages global civil society theory while supplementing it with attention to the production of spaces and governmentalities. First, we loosen the distinctions between state and nonstate actors, exploring how diverse actors combine into one institution, or how NGOs and IGOs might "see like states" (Scott 1998) as they identify subject "beneficiary" groups and bureaucratize their identities. Doing so also assists in identifying the role of the state vis-à-vis other actors in transnational relations and governance. Following those who caution against envisioning a full retreat of the state or an evacuation of sovereignty, we find that the state redefines its role and place through flexible and innovative practices (Joseph and Nugent 1994; Risse-Kappen 1995; Ong and Nonini 1997; Sorenson 2004). In the Andes, these include decentralization, mixed-actor decision making, and graduated sovereignty.[21] Ecuador and Bolivia have adapted to neoliberal adjustments in property ownership, governance, and service provision while adjusting to indigenous-movement demands for collective rights and self-determination. A "capable state" is commonly viewed as crucial for executing neoliberal reforms, and indigenous organizations insist that the state guarantee their rights and resource access.

The state thus remains an important actor, and its territory persists as a salient domain of rule, albeit less than before as transnationalism embeds the state in new connections and relations. Transnational networks recruit and enroll new organizations, thereby expanding membership and spatial coverage as well as forging new institutional combinations. Whereas previous studies have explored well-defined networks focused on specific issues, such as human rights networks (e.g., Sikkink 1993), the transnational networks formed around indigenous development often demonstrate more complex circuitries, adjusting to the way "development" is flexible enough a concept to incorporate many otherwise discrete issues into its remit. As a result, ad hoc partnerships, consortia, and coordinators create contingent yet consequential links with states and indigenous organizations, but do not always establish sustained networks. In some cases, they come together in specific places, for specific purposes, and for delimited time periods, while authoritatively defining subjects, recognizing interlocutors, and allocating resources.

Second, we explore subtle interactions of power within transnational relations rather than adopt a model of horizontal networks. At the same time, we assume that these relations follow no predetermined logic of scale in terms of power, process, or form.[22] We approach transnational hierarchies through a diverse social field, which includes class, profession, location, gender, and linguistic distinctions. Because these fields are situated in uneven geographies, local relations with wider scales are constituted through both public and private spaces, visible and hidden workspaces, and formal and informal politics.[23] This means that actors have differentially situated knowledge(s) and powers, constituted at the intersection of unequal social forces (Spivak, as cited in Grewal and Kaplan 1994, 352; see also Katz 2001, 1,214; Slater 1997; A. Escobar 2001). These social and spatial divides create hierarchies and inequalities that shape relative authority and legitimacy within development programs and projects.

Third, we view the configuration of place and scale as a constitutive part of transnational processes and practices and not limited to pregiven sites of politics. Although scales are grounded in material relations that facilitate decision making, production, reproduction, and distribution (McDowell 2001, 229), they also function as metaphors that are deployed as a "way of framing/reframing reality" (Leitner 2003, 239). Persuading others to adopt a particular mental map of the world is central to the discursive power of scales (Delaney and Leitner 1997, 94). Globalization itself is often portrayed as inevitable in a way that may dismiss or delegitimate political projects at other scales (Kelly 1997). In political agendas contesting global capitalism, nonglobal scales may offer other visions of future relations of production and reproduction. For instance, Andean indigenous movements base their transnational connections on local indigeneity and regional territories, defined as spaces of cultural reproduction and as buffers against governmental and market discipline. In each case, local areas—the environs of an indigenous settlement or an NGO patch—comprise "extroverted places" (Massey and Jess 1995). These do not confine, but rather provide routes for engagement with actors and institutions at or from other scales and assert that indigenous knowledge has universal as well as local relevance (Cox 1998).

Finally, our framework speaks to the transnational identities literature, which is dominated by discussions of migrants who attempt to balance the need for income with national and ethnic ties to a homeland. Although many transnational migrants hail from the Andean region, among them indigenous people (Jokisch and Pribilsky 2002; Colloredo-Mansfeld 1999), this book focuses on indigenous peoples adopting *non*migrant transnational strategies. Here they adjust to a series of political and economic changes set in motion by a combination of their own social movements and forces beyond their influence. The result is a multiethnic transnational community that converges around an interest in indigenous cultural specificities and development. It builds on and reproduces networks of policymaking institutions, advocacy organizations, and indigenous social movements. "Indigenous people" as a category is effectively transnationalized through this interaction, but the policies and strategies are designed for nondiaspora indigenous subjects imagined to stay in their country or town of origin.

In contrast to ethnically defined business transnationals who work primarily through private-sector institutions and deal with the market allocation of resources (Ong 1999), the Andean indigenous actors that we describe in this book interact with official and nonprofit institutions and cope with the public allocation of resources. In these interactions, connections with global capitalism and flexible accumulation are indirect and mediated by development and indigenous organizations in their interpretations of those economic forces through specific ideologies and strategies.[24] In addition, since Andean indigenous movements stake their identities on anticolonial struggles, cultural distinctiveness, and territorial integrity, their subjectivities are more self-consciously identified with specific scales and places than those of many diaspora transnationals.

The relations that emerge over indigenous development operate through practices such as setting agendas, forming political strategies, distributing funds, promoting examples or models, sharing information, and exchanging personnel across institutions and scales. All of these involve narratives and representations of the goals, histories, and subjects of development, which are manifest in documents, communications, and face-to-face discussions. Although indigenous leaders often take part in these practices, administrative demands of policy design and implementation has called forth a new professional class of anthropologists, sociologists, educators, and policy experts drawn from various ethnic and racial groups. Indigenous and nonindigenous professionals with knowledge of indigenous and multicultural affairs are increasingly in demand, and programs to form these professionals have sprouted throughout the Andes.[25] By examining the "situated cultural practices" (Ong 1999, 17) within multiple policymaking and social-movement activities, we explicate a politics of transnationalism in terms of the contextualized construction of subjects, spaces, and identities.

To summarize, our view of transnational relations emphasizes agency and multiscalar complexity but does not presume excess voluntarism or assume that globalization processes are random or free floating (e.g., Appadurai 1996). We envision "a local that is constitutively global" and consider countertopographies that challenge the politics of globalization through a "grounded but translocal politics" (Katz 2001, 1214, 1230–31). We also conceive of actors as situated but not predetermined (i.e., both enabled and constrained) by power-laden institutions, projects, and subject positions. Development and culture are reframed through neoliberal governmentalities, multiscalar networking, and social protest. We analyze and appraise the effects of these processes on the possibilities and limitations that indigenous peoples face.

Plan of the Book

Chapters 1 and 2 provide an overview of the discursive, institutional, and spatial character of indigenous development affairs. Chapter 1 builds on the introduction's theoretical treatment of multiscalar relations by examining how the intersection of policy paradigms, movement agendas, and diverse actors redefines and rescales indigenous development. A combination of social and neoliberal development criteria emerged through these intersections, creating a social neoliberalism that has offered points of articulation for indigenous-movement agendas while imposing disciplinary constraints. Chapter 2 illustrates how international discourses are grounded through regional imaginative geographies. It examines the conceptual foundations of the entanglement between social neoliberalism and indigenous rights, which brings development and culture together in new policy frameworks. Policy narratives combine global concepts such as social capital with regional Andean concepts of indigeneity. These combinations—and their particular meanings—constitute indigenous development policies as racial projects.

The case studies of different issue areas in chapters 3, 4, and 5 reveal common patterns in the way that transnationalism works through Ecuador and Bolivia, including the ways in which negotiation and contest may entrench *and* unsettle ongoing political and economic restructuring in the Andes. Chapter 3 analyzes the production of local spaces within transnational relations, as international development projects, state decentralization, and indigenous subjectivities jointly inform a common focus on local scales. Within this local emphasis however, negotiation and struggle take place according to different assumptions and distinctive purposes. These processes demonstrate the ability of states, indigenous movements, and development agencies to extend their influence through the local, but they also reveal disciplinary effects and limits to this influence.

Chapter 4 provides an account of transnationalized water politics operating through development paradigms and indigenous-movement symbols. National water legislation and local irrigation projects are bound up in globalized coalitions and discourses, leading to overlapping agendas, complex inter-institutional relations, and the mobilization of cultural imageries. These intersect to validate or marginalize certain actors and subjectivities, albeit with varying impacts at different scales, depending in part on the kind of neoliberal governmentality in effect. The new programs in higher education and graduate training examined in chapter 5 show how neoliberal development and human-capital concerns can be combined with transnational emphases on multiculturalism and indigenous affairs. Institutionalized in a series of universities and research institutes in Ecuador and Bolivia, such programs exchange personnel and transform curricula as they train a new generation of indigenous and nonindigenous professionals. These programs make some headway in reducing tensions between globalized notions of expertise and representation of Andean indigenous peoples; yet they also downplay or exclude some kinds of knowledge, pedagogy, bodily markers, and performances, while generating new hierarchies.

Focusing on embodiment and subjectivity around gender, the analysis of the intersection and disjuncture between ethnicity, race, and gender in chapter 6 extends our discussion of transnationalism in multiscalar terms—from the body to the global—in order to examine the cross-cutting social categories and hierarchies in transnational relations. Successful integration of women and indigenous components of development policy has been limited, despite transnational guidelines on the need to do so effectively. The concluding chapter discusses the theoretical and practical ramifications of transnational Andean indigenous development. It highlights the need for and usefulness of interdisciplinary theoretical syntheses in capturing the growing complexity of indigenous politics. It recommends more flexible indigenous development frameworks and calls for egalitarian policymaking. These conclusions also show that elements of social neoliberalism analyzed in this book are incorporated into policies and practices of the recent post-neoliberal turn in Bolivia and Ecuador.[26]

CHAPTER 1

SARAH A. RADCLIFFE, NINA LAURIE, AND ROBERT ANDOLINA

Development, Transnational Networks,
and Indigenous Politics

> No longer is it merely anthropologists, romantic idealists or support groups
> which take an interest in indigenous cultures, but also governments, UN
> agencies, the European Community, and the Nobel Peace Prize committee.
>
> **LYDIA VAN DE FLIERT**

In 1992, a group of twenty-four indigenous representatives from around the world gathered in Amsterdam to carry out a symbolic "discovery of Europe" by peoples who had been marginalized by Western conquests (van de Fliert 1994, 7). Five centuries after Columbus's arrival in the Americas, indigenous people overcame the frictions of distance and domination to proclaim their arrival on the world stage and claim a stake in emerging global politics. The articulation between indigenous politics and shifts in development thinking and networks generated a transnational social field (Vertovec 2001; Portes, Guarnizo, and Landolt 1999) in which a policy community crystallized around "ethnodevelopment" or "development-with-identity." This policy community's ideas rest on assumptions of indigenous poverty and cultural distinctiveness, and it proposes a strategy of community development that will erase this poverty while maintaining distinctiveness. Its institutional nodes comprise offices of indigenous social movements, state agencies, NGOs, multilateral organizations, and hybrid institutions that bring together members of each. The policy community's practices include project formulation, evaluation, and reporting, as well as document circulation, informal personal exchanges, conference presentations, and the allocation of funds. This chapter highlights patterns of discourse and practice concerning indigenous development and the complex relations that produce them.

International social development has been the primary arena for conceiving and debating indigenous development as a matter of policy. During the 1990s this arena was infused by notions of a neoliberal nature, joined by ideas on multiculturalism, environmentalism, and grassroots development. Contributing to this intellectual pluralism was the embedding of indigenous development in mixed-actor networks comprising a multiethnic social field in which indigenous leaders, development consultants, national NGO staff, and government officials have moved regularly across scales and borders. This transnational social field is also political, as these actors both engaged in advocacy and established policy, sometimes entangling the two. The very connectivity among ideas and organizations that inserted indigenous and cultural criteria into mainstream development also underpinned the formation of governmentalities that shaped the design and administration of specific programs.

An overview of indigenous-movement organizing and agendas in Bolivia and Ecuador provides a substantive example of what we mean by "nondiaspora transnationalism" and "reloaded boomerang." Multiscale networking takes place between actors who advocate and formulate policy for indigenous development. A genealogy of social-development thinking allows us to see the ways in which indigenous issues are incorporated into development policy. And by examining the inter-institutional administration of ostensibly pro-indigenous development policies, we can see how this administration appropriates and deploys altered notions of the relationship between development and culture. Such administration opens spaces for indigenous participation and innovative development practices but also fixes such spaces in potentially constraining ways.

Indigenous Movements in Bolivia and Ecuador

Indigenous people have long been significant in processes of nation and state building in the Andes, but only recently have they overcome the "ventriloquism" of more powerful actors to sustain their own kinds of agency.[1] Indigenous movements in Ecuador and Bolivia have placed indigenous peoples at the political forefront through widespread organizing, ideological contest, and public protests. These actions, in turn, created new possibilities for influencing elections, policy agendas, and constitutional reform. In response, Ecuador and Bolivia have recognized collective indigenous rights, established indigenous-run education and development councils, adopted national constitutive principles based on multiethnicity and participatory democracy, and instituted accountability mechanisms such as recall referenda on elected officials (Van Cott 2000; Andolina 2003).

In Bolivia and Ecuador, nationwide indigenous organizing began in the 1970s, conditioned by corporatist political regimes and a statist development model. In each country, government policy toward indigenous groups was ambivalent. On the one hand, agrarian reform and the registration of indigenous communities provided legal support for their claims to land and communal forms of governance (Ibarra 1992; Wray 1989; Albó 1987) and in some cases led to the redistribution of landholdings to indigenous peasants. On the other hand, government policy was underpinned by racist assumptions about the inferior contributions of indigenous people to national development and the need for indigenous people to adopt national mestizo culture. This tension was replicated by the traditional Left, which sought to bring Indians into their unions and political parties. The Left advocated for Indian land and labor rights but often resisted efforts at cultural revival, as it envisioned indigenous people largely as the rural sector of a modernizing working class. Such racism and ethnocentrism was also widespread in society at large, as indigenous people faced quotidian discrimination in schools, markets, and workplaces even as they gained individual citizen rights and recognition (Andolina 1999; Pallares 2002; S. Rivera 1987; Patzi 1998).

In the wake of the Bolivian Revolution in 1952, the government forged a national confederation that incorporated indigenous people into the regime and bequeathed a template for future organizing. The National Federation of Peasant Workers of Bolivia (CNTCB) recognized indigenous people officially as "peasants" or "rural farmers" who would form a smallholding class to bolster national agricultural development. The CNTCB was also a mechanism of state control over Indians, especially under the "military-peasant pact" established at the outset of military rule in 1964. The current indigenous movement in Bolivia began when dissident activists appropriated these unions in the 1970s and created the Sole Union Confederation of Bolivian Peasant Workers (CSUTCB) in 1979, rupturing state control over peasant organizations. The Kataristas and the CSUTCB forged an anticolonial ideology that tied indigenous ethnicity—defined at the time by the Aymara and Quechua languages and generic cultural tradition—to a class-based peasant identity around the symbol of the colonial-era indigenous rebel Tupaj Katari (Hurtado 1986; Hahn 1996).

Since then, the CSUTCB has gained affiliates in all departments of Bolivia, but it mainly represents indigenous people in the highland region. However, many highland indigenous people are now organized into federations and councils affiliated with CONAMAQ, the National Council of Ayllus and Markas of Qollasuyu (Bolivia), created in 1997. This council rivals CSUTCB for indigenous representation (see chapter 3).

Lowland Indians in Bolivia organized separately from those in the highlands. Activists from the Guaraní and Ayoreo indigenous groups founded the Indigenous Center of the Bolivian Lowlands (CIDOB) in 1982. Its principal adversaries were white ranchers, logging and mining companies, and the Santa Cruz departmental development agency. Its main allies were local and international NGOs working in the areas of cultural advocacy, environmental protection, and grassroots development (Brysk 2000). As CIDOB moved from being a "center" to a representative "confederation" in 1988, it identified and represented over thirty groups in lowland Bolivia according to language use, local territories, and traditional authority systems of *capitanías*. Its platform and agenda downplayed class discourse, which is one reason why the lowland CIDOB has never united with the highland CSUTCB to form a single national organization. However, they have joined forces at certain moments, and their representations of indigenous groups—taken together—informed commonsense cultural geographies in Bolivia (see map 3).

Map 3 is a representation of such cultural geographies. Produced in 1991 by the Center for Campesino Research and Promotion (CIPCA)—a grassroots development NGO in Bolivia that has long been an ally of indigenous and campesino organizations—this map adopted precolonial language as the constitutive marker of indigenous identity in Bolivia. As a result, it located numerous indigenous groups in the lowland areas of Bolivia (to the north, west, and southwest) but identified only two indigenous groups in the highland areas of the country: speakers of Aymara and Quechua. Accepted features of highland indigenous identities grew more diverse by the late 1990s, however, leading to a proliferation of named highland indigenous groups, even though their members all spoke Aymara or Quechua.

In Ecuador, indigenous peoples did unite across the lowland-highland divide in 1986. The establishment of the Confederation of Indigenous Nationalities of Ecuador (CONAIE) in that year cemented a unification process underway since 1980 through a highland-lowland indigenous coordinator. During the 1960s and 1970s, however, indigenous activists in each region organized separately,

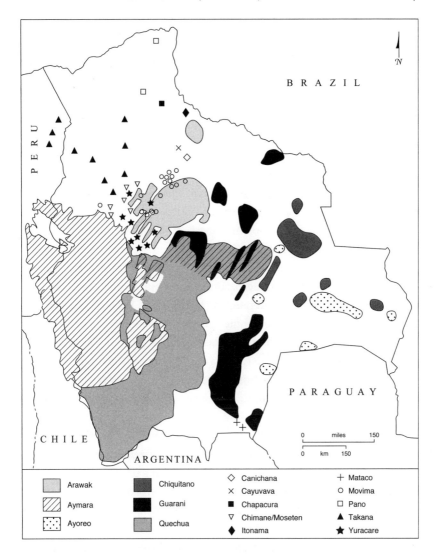

MAP 3. Indigenous ethnolinguistic groups in Bolivia.

This map labels Bolivian indigenous groups according to language use, an identity criterion promoted by indigenous movements and advocates, and largely accepted by the Bolivian state. As discussed in chapter 3, however, a set of nonlinguistic identity categories have become visible among Aymara and Quechua speaking groups, who together form a slight majority of the Bolivian population. The Bolivian state and international development agencies have likewise responded to these recent identity shifts by accounting for them in the administration of multicultural policies and programs.

although budding organizations in both regions received support from the same international NGOs, such as Oxfam America and the Inter-American Foundation. With additional local help from the Catholic Church and some government funds, indigenous activists in the highland created Awakening of Ecuadorian Indigenous People (ECUARUNARI) in 1972 to fight racial discrimination and recuperate or fortify indigenous cultures. As it grew in strength, ECUARUNARI organized and incorporated federations in all provinces of the highland region of Ecuador, which were composed of second-tier, local federations. These, in turn, were made up of first-tier, village-level organizations.

Indigenous activists in Ecuador's Amazon basin created the Confederation of Indigenous Nationalities of the Ecuadorian Amazon (CONFENIAE) in 1980. Unlike ECUARUNARI, whose members are almost all Quichua speaking, CONFENIAE's membership was multilingual: Shuar, Achuar, Quichua, Huaorani, Cofán, Siona, and Secoya.[2] CONFENIAE is made up of provincial organizations established in the 1970s, such as the Organization of Indigenous Peoples of Pastaza (OPIP) and the Federation of Indigenous Organizations of Napo (FOIN). It is also composed of ethnic-specific associations such as the Shuar Federation and the Secoya Indigenous Organization of Ecuador. The Amazonian Quichua and Shuar are the two largest linguistic groups in the region, and most CONFENIAE leadership comes from these two groups. CONFENIAE's formation was motivated in part by the intrusion of "outside" forces that intensified during the 1960s and 1970s.

The National Coordinating Council of the Indigenous Nationalities of Ecuador—CONACNIE—was created in 1980 to mitigate differences between highland and lowland indigenous activists in Ecuador. In doing so, it abated ethnic and class tensions, staged campaigns against religious control of bilingual education, and acquired new allies in the form of human rights groups, environmental activists, and academics. In light of these activities and growing indigenous consciousness, CONACNIE was replaced by a full-fledged indigenous confederation, CONAIE in 1986 (CONAIE 1989). In 1988, the Ecuadorian government recognized CONAIE as representing approximately 70 percent of Ecuador's indigenous people (Selverston-Scher 2001).[3]

Protests, lobbying, and electoral participation throughout the 1990s made indigenous organizations and agendas politically central in both countries. Lowland indigenous marches to La Paz, Bolivia, and Quito, Ecuador, sparked profound national discussions concerning nationalism, territory, and indigenous rights (Van Cott 1994; Sawyer 1997). These were reinforced by a nationwide indigenous uprising in Ecuador (1990) and by the Bolivian anti-quincentenary campaign in 1992, both spearheaded by highland-lowland indigenous coalitions. In the wake of this mobilization, press statements and public opinion increasingly acknowledged indigenous proposals for pluricultural and multiethnic societies, and in some cases showed support for them (CIPCA 1991; López 1993; Nieto 1993).

Indigenous movements further raised the profile of their issues by gaining elected seats and appointed posts in government. In Bolivia, indigenous leader Víctor Hugo Cárdenas was vice president from 1993 to 1997, while indigenous leader Evo Morales was runner-up in the 2002 presidential elections and won the Bolivian presidency in 2005.[4] In Ecuador, the social movement's political wing (which includes indigenous and nonindigenous members), Pachakutik, has held an average of 10 percent of the seats in the national congress since 1996. The controversial appointment of indigenous advisors and ministers by the governments of Sixto Durán Ballén (1992–1996) and Abdalá Bucaram (1996–1997) did not prevent the more consensual choice of Nina Pacari as vice president of congress in 1998. Indigenous leaders in Ecuador have also held prominent cabinet positions in agriculture, foreign relations, and social welfare, while in Bolivia they have comprised over half of Evo Morales's cabinet. In addition, Ecuadorian and Bolivian indigenous leaders have occupied hundreds of local government positions since they began running candidates en masse in 1995 and 1996. In some cases, they have been able to restructure local governmental institutions and practices to ensure more grassroots control over elected officials and augment their influence in local policymaking.

Participation in elections has complicated, but not terminated, indigenous protest politics. The Ecuadorian indigenous movement peacefully took governmental power in January 2000 through a "popular coup," in alliance with a large faction of the military and other social-movement organizations. While their stay in power lasted only a few hours, it was a watershed in Ecuadorian politics and led to their co-governance of Ecuador with President Lucio Gutiérrez's political party in 2002 (see Lucero 2001; Whitten 2003). After a period of decline for CONAIE, due in part to its association with an unpopular Gutiérrez government, it led a successful national campaign in 2006 to reject a U.S.-Ecuador free trade agreement. In Bolivia, highland and lowland indigenous activists in Bolivia led a broad popular front that forced the resignation of then-president Gonzalo Sánchez de Lozada in 2003. This also compelled incoming president Carlos Mesa to authorize the convocation of a constitutional assembly, which was ultimately realized in 2007 after the election of Evo Morales as president.

Through these various political tactics, indigenous organizations in both countries launched postliberal challenges based on anticolonial ideologies and platforms for plurinational states (Andolina 1999; Yashar 1999; Brysk 2000). Although there is some variation among indigenous organizations in this respect, most of their platforms have demanded ethnic autonomy and direct participation, the promotion of indigenous languages and cultures, reduction of racial discrimination, greater socioeconomic equity, and self-directed development. These agendas appropriated some elements of liberal rights discourses, while reformulating them along collective concepts of rights, identity, and territory in ways that challenged liberal democracy's individualizing and homogenizing proclivities (Yashar 1999). In other respects, the indigenous movement's concerns with equity, autonomy, and grassroots livelihoods have articulated with anti-neoliberal thinking. In Ecuador, for example, indigenous movements opposed agrarian-reform proposals that promoted free markets and export-oriented production. Stressing land rights and aid for small farmers together with indigenous identity, they created a development agenda in anti-neoliberal language (Collins 2000). In campaigns against then-president Durán's agrarian bill (1993–1994), CONAIE and its allies mobilized for production centered on national consumption, small-farmer participation in decision making, fair distribution of land, and respect for communal landholding traditions. This mobilization forced the government into negotiations, which led in turn to incorporation of the indigenous movement's demands for credit, water rights, and land tenancy into the new agricultural legislation (Selverston 1997, 184–86; Collins 2000).

These indigenous movement agendas overlapped conceptually and historically with concrete grassroots development efforts, such as those pioneered in Latin America by the Inter-American Foundation (IAF). From the 1970s on, the IAF supported socioeconomic improvements via cultural strengthening in order to create sustainable and equitable development.[5] Funding over two hundred projects totaling US$20.9 million, the foundation supported diverse groups (including ethnic federations, agricultural cooperatives, folklorists, artists, and radio communicators) to create more viable, productive, and efficient local organizational capacity.[6] Projects in Ecuador and Bolivia included bilingual-education and adult-education projects, indigenous radio programming, theater, craft production and marketing, and indigenous leadership training. Guatemalan experiments in grassroots development echoed those in the Andes to some degree. They sought to enhance indigenous cultural control over resources, decision making, and project design via labor exchange, communal solidarity, and collective regulation of wealth accumulation (Palenzuela 1999).

Indigenous Development and Transnational Networking

As the actions of the Inter-American Foundation suggest, contemporary indigenous movements and issues were never exclusively national. But their transnational dimensions have expanded over time. Indigenous development has been established firmly on global and local scales through complex "itineraries of connection" (Ong and Nonini 1997). These were crafted out of new methods of communication, indigenous leaders' "scale jumping," and advocacy strategies by diverse types of organizations, from NGOs to multilaterals. They increasingly entangled indigenous-rights advocates with development practitioners and elicited changes in the goals, strategies, and architectures of the various institutions composing indigenous development networks.

Transport and communication technologies have arguably provided building blocks for contemporary transnationalism (Cohen and Rai 2000; Castells 2000), which indigenous peoples have rapidly exploited (Larreamendy 1996; Havemann 2000; Ginsburg 1997). Indigenous consultants and the INGO Cultural Survival initiated a computerized database to facilitate conversation among indigenous organizations (Fox 1998, 136), while the UK-based Catholic Institute for International Relations financed payment for a communications specialist to work with the Ecuadorian highland confederation, ECUARUNARI. Linking indigenous organizations across the world via new information technologies, the Red Indígena (Indigenous Network) was initially housed within the World Bank, which provided institutional and staff support, and later transferred to the Americas-wide Fondo Indígena (see below). The national and regional indigenous confederations that we focus on in this book have web sites, although they vary in quality and quantity of information.[7] However, indigenous organizations continue to rely heavily upon nonelectronic communication, due to insufficient resources and a preference for oral communication. Face-to-face conferences, workshops, and meetings have dominated their networking, while electronic networks serve to reinforce such ties. While indigenous use of new information technologies reduced states' control of information (Brysk 2000), these technologies are often insufficient in themselves to create meaningful pressure on governments, multilateral donors, and INGOs (Keck and Sikkink 1998).

Communication between indigenous groups across national borders and continental gaps is one key aspect of transnational networking (Brown 1993; Brysk 2000). Most of this has centered on framing, publicizing, and codifying indigenous rights. Building on earlier international conferences, such as those held in 1977 and 1981 (Van de Fliert 1994, 91), indigenous organizations across the Americas coordinated protests against celebrations of the 1992 quincentenary, thereby challenging the legitimacy of the European conquest of the Americas. Since then, indigenous representatives from Latin America and elsewhere have met in continental summits to exchange ideas and cultural practices and to draft regionwide political platforms. One such summit in Ecuador was held in 2004, just prior to the Americas Social Forum in Quito, in order to create an autonomous indigenous-movement platform that could contribute to broader popular agendas set during the Social Forum.[8] In an earlier and even more extensive initiative, indigenous peoples from various continents formed the International Alliance of Indigenous and Tribal Peoples of the Tropical Forests (1992), connecting Latin American regional organizations with counterparts from Rwanda, the Philippines, and other Asian countries.[9]

These associations among indigenous peoples were supplemented by concrete human rights work. Indigenous representatives from Latin America and elsewhere attended sessions of the United Nations Working Group on Indigenous Populations and later participated in the UN Permanent Forum on Indigenous Peoples. With up to six hundred people attending to draft UN policy, indigenous leaders familiarized themselves with international discourse and bureaucracy (Van de Fliert 1994; Stavenhagen 2002b). After more than a decade of refinement and lobbying by indigenous people and their allies, the UN finally approved a global indigenous rights declaration in 2007.[10] Although the Organization of American States has yet to approve a parallel declaration, it has worked on a draft declaration for nearly ten years, and negotiation for completion and approval is intensifying in the wake of the recent passage of the UN declaration.[11] Indigenous groups have also collaborated across boundaries to defend indigenous rights on legal grounds. For example, indigenous people brought the Nicaraguan government before the Inter-American Court in 2000 for breaching domestic and international law—by failing to guarantee indigenous use of ancestral lands against a Japanese logging company working on the north Nicaraguan coast. Reflecting continentwide organizational and legal-assistance networks, a Canadian indigenous organization submitted the Nicaraguan case to the court when the Nicaraguan government proved resistant to local efforts in this respect. The indigenous organizations won the case (Macklem and Morgan 2000; Stavenhagen 2002a).

This transnational networking among indigenous organizations was supported by numerous advocacy NGOs, who altered their own strategies over time. Some of them funded indigenous development projects in the 1980s, well before the issue of indigenous development was taken up by governments or multilateral agencies. The Inter-American Foundation, for example, was an early advocate of grassroots perspectives in development and began supporting local and national indigenous federations in the late 1970s.[12] The development NGO Oxfam America has focused its South America policy on indigenous people since 1985, and it sustains links to Oxfam Australia's work on aboriginal issues.[13] The Dutch NGO International Humanist Institute for Cooperation with Developing Countries (HIVOS) was another early advocate of indigenous development, coordinating with the Bolivian lowland indigenous organization CIDOB starting in 1987. The German Christian Democrat foundation Hanns Seidel has supported indigenous organizations in Ecuador since 1989.[14]

These and other NGOs also made an effort to bolster transnational linkages among indigenous organizations and facilitate indigenous presence in international policy venues. A case in point is the Indigenous Coordinating Body for the Amazon Basin (COICA), which coordinates among Amazonian regional indigenous confederations in multiple South American countries, including CIDOB (lowland Bolivia) and CONFENIAE (lowland Ecuador). Oxfam America abetted the formation of COICA in 1985; the Amazon Alliance later built on Oxfam America's efforts to provide links between COICA and U.S.-based NGOs, responding in part to Indian movement demands for more coherent and equitable "north-south" coordination. Based in Washington, D.C., the alliance has an indigenous-majority steering council.[15]

Until recently, this kind of transnational activity was less common with respect to highland regions of South America. It was only in 2005 that an organization analogous to COICA was created.[16] Part of this discrepancy derived from greater political differences among highland indigenous confederations and to the perceived absence of a sufficiently representative highland federation in Peru (Lucero and Garcia 2007). But it was also because highland areas were viewed as less ecologically and culturally fragile, making transnational support for them seem less urgent (Andolina, Radcliffe, and Laurie 2005). This regional imbalance began to shift in the late 1990s. In the wake of the major protests and campaigns concerning the quincentenary, INGOs like IBIS from Denmark and

Norwegian People's Aid actively supported highland indigenous organizations in the Andes.[17] IBIS has worked in Bolivia, Ecuador, and Peru and has financed exchanges among highland activists from the three countries as of 1998. Oxfam America cosponsored some of these exchanges as well, which laid some of the groundwork for the formation of the Coordinator of Andean Indigenous Organizations (CAOI) in 2005.[18]

A key motive behind NGO support for transnational indigenous organizing was the belief that indigenous people should represent themselves and procure a voice within policymaking forums. While Oxfam America's overall goal has been grassroots empowerment in the global South, it increasingly advocated change within the international centers of power, and set up a Washington, D.C., office in part for that purpose (Fox 1998, 118–24). The Bank Information Center, also located in Washington, D.C., serves civil-society organizations by providing "citizens' guides" for campaigns against multilateral projects, thereby "opening a wedge" for action on international development issues.[19] Similarly, Cultural Survival has argued that indigenous peoples and their advocates must work together to build a "climate of informed opinion powerful enough to change the policies of the US government and international institutions" (Fox 1998, 154–55). In the 1990s, the indigenous coordinating body for the quincentennial protests approached the World Bank about the possibility of creating specific indigenous development programs (Lucero 2002, 107). Such a move was unprecedented at that time and reflected an emergent transnational field where indigenous movements were increasingly confident of the recognition of their concerns, of their own international capabilities, and of the support flowing from a growing number of nonindigenous advocates of indigenous rights.

Overlapping with this largely nongovernmental transnational advocacy was a discursive shift that enabled official agencies to conceive development policy for indigenous people. Linkage between human rights and poverty reduction was a crucial foundation of this. In 1989, International Labor Organization (ILO) Convention 169 codified the idea of culturally appropriate development, recognizing indigenous decision making and collective rights in development projects that affect them. While stopping short of sanctioning indigenous peoples' power to veto projects, it affirmed rights to consultation by indigenous representatives and facilitated the construction of new development subjects of a collective ethnic character. In a like manner, the United Nations Working Group on Indigenous Populations emitted a 1994 draft declaration, arguing forcefully that indigenous people "have a right to development in accordance with their own needs and interests" (Van de Fliert 1994, 6).

Responding to the increased lobbying for and legitimacy of indigenous rights, numerous bilateral development agencies drew on ILO Convention 169 to redefine their policies. The Netherlands (1993), Belgium (1994), Denmark (1994), Britain (in its 1999 White Paper), and, to a lesser extent, the United States (1994) incorporated concerns for culturally appropriate development into policy frameworks.[20] The Netherlands, Belgium, and the United States have supported numerous development projects in both Ecuador and Bolivia, while Denmark and Britain have concentrated mainly on Bolivia. Countries without an explicit pro-indigenous policy (e.g., France, Germany, Spain, Switzerland, Sweden) have nonetheless furnished considerable financial and political support for the continental indigenous development fund. In addition, the German, Spanish, and Swiss bilateral agencies have extensive operations involving indigenous peoples in the Andean region.[21]

Multilateral agencies have made similar policy adjustments. In 1992, the European Union's economic policy on Latin America called for "special attention" to be given to indigenous groups "through measures designed to improve their living conditions while respecting their cultural identity" (Van de Fliert 1994, 31), an attention that intensified in the wake of oil pollution that threatened indigenous groups in Ecuador (Van de Fliert 1994, 34).[22] One result of these statements was the European Commission's funding of the Latin America–wide Fondo Indígena, with participation and partnership as guiding concepts (see below). In 1991, the World Bank released Operational Directive 4.20 (OD 4.20) on indigenous peoples, which required projects to consult with ethnic group representatives and mitigate negative impacts on those groups. Procedurally, "indigenous people's development plans" became mandatory for projects affecting indigenous people. Between 1992 and 1999, over 50 percent of World Bank loans to Latin America included such indigenous-specific plans (Davis 2002, 234–35). In the mid-1990s, the World Bank formed the "Indigenous Peoples Thematic Team," an interdepartmental body of personnel from different regional programs and environmental departments. The thematic team increased awareness and acceptance of the importance of cultural diversity among bank staff and borrowers and oversaw revisions to OD 4.20. These revisions involved discussion within the bank and consultation among borrower country governments, NGOs, and indigenous peoples' organizations.[23] The World Bank's indigenous-issue team also initiated an Indigenous Peoples Working Group, which networked between UN agencies, government ministries, and indigenous professionals in order to improve delivery of "culturally appropriate . . . social services to indigenous communities" (Davis 2002, 245). Finally, it designed and

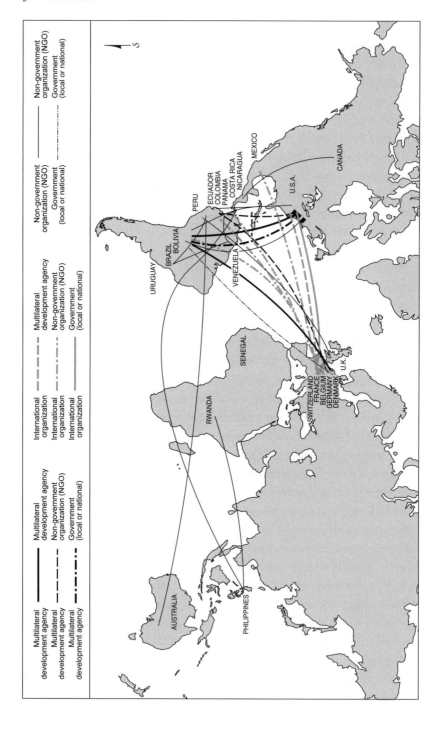

negotiated a series of ethnodevelopment projects in various Latin American countries, together with national government officials and indigenous organization representatives (Davis 2002, 235).

Although the Inter-American Development Bank (IADB) did not approve an operational policy on indigenous peoples until 2006, it began accounting for indigenous issues in the 1990s. By 1994, the bank's Committee on Environmental and Social Impact was required to review projects for their impact (positive or negative) on indigenous people and internationally defined indigenous rights. The IADB then established the Indigenous Peoples and Community Development Unit to open space for indigenous peoples in relevant bank policy areas and to locate projects that met the needs and demands of indigenous peoples. In 2001, it established a fund of US$250 million for indigenous and Afro–Latin American projects as part of its plan to mitigate racial exclusion in the region. By 2002, about 20 percent of IADB loans included indigenous peoples as beneficiaries (Inter-American Development Bank 2006, 27–28).

The processes we have outlined thus far have two interrelated general consequences. First, we can point to a "positive boomerang effect." Indigenous organizations were able to extend their influence spatially and institutionally in the international arena, while official development agencies adjusted procedures and allocations in favor of indigenous peoples and their concerns about culturally appropriate development (see map 4 and table 1, respectively). Both of these changes, in turn, produced requirements or incentives for national governments to improve treatment and inclusion of indigenous people in their own development practices (Brysk 2000). Second, we can speak of an indigenous development network that enrolled multilateral, bilateral, nongovernmental, and indigenous organizations. Such enrollment, moreover, entangled organizations advocating for indigenous rights with those focusing on development policy, creating a hybrid policy/advocacy network. As this chapter progresses,

---

◄ MAP 4. Transnational connections around indigenous development discussed in chapter 1.

These networks all cross national boundaries but vary in the scales of interaction and types of organizations linked. This map represents only some the complexity of the connections pertinent to Andean indigenous development networks. Other features of such connections include but are not limited to their multiethnic and gendered character. (Our purpose in changing the orientation of the world map here, and elsewhere in the book, is to prompt an understanding of transnationalism from a non-dominant perspective.)

TABLE 1. International frameworks for indigenous development

Organization	Framework	Date	Type of Development
UN Working Group on Indigenous Population	Established to elaborate standards for indigenous rights' protection	1982	Uses term *indigenous peoples* beginning in 1988
UNESCO World Decade for Cultural Development	To acknowledge cultural dimensions of development; to affirm cultural identities	1988–1997	Intercultural dialogue; culture's increasing importance in development; rights.
International Labor Organization	ILO Convention 169 on indigenous rights	1989	Special projects; indigenous control over economic, social & cultural development
World Bank	Operational Directive 4.20 on indigenous participation in development	1991	Culturally appropriate development with beneficiary consultation
Asian Development Bank	Guidelines on indigenous populations	1991	Need for economic advancement and social, cultural, and community development
European Commission (EU)	Increase in pro-indigenous projects and programs	1991–	Human rights and environmental concerns in development
Council of European Union	Regulation #443/92 on development with respect for cultural identity	1992	"Ethnic minorities warrant special attention . . . while respecting their cultural identity."
Amnesty International	Program on Indigenous Peoples of the Americas	1992	Collective social and economic rights

TABLE 1. *Continued*

Organization	Framework	Date	Type of Development
Conference on Security and Cooperation in Europe (CSCE)	Provision 29 on indigenous development, in Helsinki II	1992	Focus on European ethnic minorities
Ibero-American Summit	Establishes Fund for the Development of the Indigenous Peoples of Latin America and the Caribbean	1992	Rights and entitlements. Indigenous self-development, strengthening indigenous culture
United Nations	Year of World's Indigenous Peoples	1993	"Recognition of indigenous peoples' values, traditional knowledge and resource practices [for] sustainable development."
	International Decade of World's Indigenous Peoples	1995–2004	
		2007	
	Declaration on indigenous rights		
Dutch government	Policy on indigenous rights and representation	1993	Cultural identity protection, pluralism, rights
Organization of American States	Draft Declaration on indigenous rights	2002	Rights; development "in accordance with their own traditions, needs and interests [&] values, objectives, priorities and strategies."

Sources: Van de Fliert (1994); www.unesco.org/culture/development; Van Schaik (1994, 203–6); Amnesty International (1992); www.oas.org/indigenous.

we emphasize policy but acknowledge that advocacy and mobilization remain important.

New Ideas: Development Paradigms of Neoliberalism and Social Difference

According to Siddarth, "The social agenda, including gender, participation, human rights, governance and the diversity of civil society has gained prominence in international development institutions" (1995, 31). Indeed, the connection of indigenous thematic units with social-development departments reflected an implicit consensus that "social development" is the policy area where indigenous issues fit.[24] This linkage created institutional space for indigenous development within influential agencies but also embedded it within a complex conceptual nexus. Just as indigenous issues were embraced within development networks, development paradigms were altering in ways that crafted what we described in the introduction as social neoliberalism. Neoliberal development thinking was infused with old and new social criteria, while social development was increasingly neoliberalized, as capitalist markets and efficient governance were defined as social development solutions.

The term *social development* has existed as a basis for assessing national progress since at least the early twentieth century, although it did not gain a central place within international development discourse until the 1960s. At that time, the United Nations was the main institution promoting and discussing social development. Building on the International Covenant of Economic, Social, and Cultural Rights, the UN "developmentalized" these rights by passing the Declaration on Social Progress and Development in 1969 and renaming the Social Commission as the Commission on Social Development (UNDESA 2005, 73). As in the 1960s, social development gained policy importance in the 1990s in a kind of rediscovery of society after a decade of narrowly economic development thinking. In the 1950s, emphases on productive investments and technology inputs predominated; in the 1980s, macroeconomic stabilization and structural adjustment prevailed. During both periods, progress for developing countries was measured largely through economic and financial indicators such as GDP, investment capital, inflation rates, and budget deficits. The concept and discourse of social development thus predates neoliberalism, and recent changes in social development policy agendas are not wholly reducible to orthodox neoliberal influences. Concerns such as health, education, housing, pensions, poverty reduction, integration, income equity, and popular mobilization have remained fairly standard components of social development since the 1960s; gender equity, multiculturalism, environmental protection, good governance, and social inclusion are more recent additions to the lexicon.[25]

The World Bank and IADB have driven the neoliberalization of social development discourse, but NGOs and other international agencies—like the UN and ILO—have been participants in what became a hegemonic, "post-Washington" consensus (Fine 2001) that also "socialized" neoliberal development discourse. According to Grindle (2000), some economists and public-sector reformers in the World Bank and IADB came to view markets—taken in isolation—as too limited for conceiving and achieving development; they combined social and neoliberal criteria to overcome such limits. In this view, social services, social capital, and institutional reform might contribute to development in various ways: building human capital as a correlate of economic growth, stimulating local entrepreneurship, providing infrastructure to regulate and correct market deficiencies, and forging a fiscally disciplined state for positive macroeconomic performance. These criteria were also embraced by NGOs interested "in demonstrating the worth of their activities," advocating "for participation and mobilization of civil society," and stressing "attention to the quality of government services" (Grindle 2000, 39). Although other IGOs like the UN and the Economic Commission for Latin America and the Caribbean (ECLAC) promoted equity and redistribution, they linked these concerns positively to free-market globalization, labor flexibility, consumerism, privatization, and competition—stressing the need to correct market failures and mitigate negative impacts on vulnerable groups, if not on the poor more broadly (World Summit for Social Development 1995, 13–14; ECLAC 1997; ECLAC 2004, 242–43).

The making of social neoliberalism was furthered by positing social integration as an antidote to the problems of social exclusion. Within social-neoliberal thinking, exclusion is seen as impoverishing and unjust in itself, as it denies full participation in the community and obstructs access to employment and other income-generating activities. However, such exclusion is also marked as a lost opportunity with respect to the success of concrete development policies and projects. First, the participation of beneficiaries in partnerships with public, private, and civic agencies—viewed as crucial in initial design and implementation—would provide legitimacy and needed information and would bypass undemocratic centralized procedures (Garland 2000). Second, projects and policies would only generate lasting improvements—it was believed—if participants had a stake in economic change (Edwards 2001). Based on these assumptions, for example, the World Bank increased civil-society participation in its development procedures and projects (Nelson 1996, 626), and citizen action moved into "the center of international policy debates and global problem solving" (Edwards 2001, 1). Given these understandings of exclusion, social-integration policy may consist of anything from nondiscrimination and tolerance of diversity, to widening access to education and health services, to enhancing democracy and rule of law, to increasing civil society participation, to reforming institutions in order to improve efficiency and transparency of social services or public policy (see Sen 2000; Garland 2000; UNDESA 2005, 47–52).

In short, social neoliberalism became hegemonic in tying together various agendas and actors, while allowing a modicum of ideological heterodoxy. This heterodoxy was also significant in forging an ethnodevelopment policy that dovetailed with indigenous-movement agendas and with prior experiences in grassroots development focused on empowerment. Consider the adoption of concepts like social capital and community development. From policymaker standpoints, tapping indigenous peoples' social capital would provide a possible solution to flagging economic growth and perceived social splintering. In the words of two architects of the World Bank indigenous development policy, "The vision of development with identity . . . builds on the positive qualities of indigenous cultures and societies, including a sense of ethnic identity, close attachments to ancestral land, and the capacity to mobilize labor, capital and other resources to promote local employment and growth" (Van Nieuwkoop and Uquillas 2000, 4).

Adding on to indigenous cultural infrastructure would therefore be a way of including indigenous people in development while strengthening—rather than weakening—the social fabric. This approach is distinct from the concepts of popular mobilization that characterized 1960s thinking on social development, in which the fabric of "traditional" groups like indigenous people had to be *broken down* to make development successful.

Most indigenous movements in the Andes (as elsewhere in Latin America) have decried the longstanding discrimination and marginalization of indigenous people, and they have demanded active participation and government responsiveness as remedies (see CONAIE 1994b; CSUTCB 1992; CIDOB 1993b). Their agendas have also pressed for secure titles to land, access to markets, and recognition of Indian contributions to national economies (Pacari 1996). These demands may articulate with social-neoliberal emphases on partnership and stakeholding, the potential and capability of diverse cultures, and efficacious delivery of social services. Grassroots development approaches also sought to

counter discrimination and alienation while buttressing participation and organization; these criteria are included in current social-development policy. Thus,
institutions as seemingly disparate as CONIAE, Cultural Survival, and the World
Bank may share a belief that indigenous and tribal peoples are "productive
participants in multiethnic states" (Fox 1998, 279).

However, indigenous organizations retain the ability to negotiate or contest these paradigmatic shifts. Many of them view "integration" with considerable suspicion, as continuing a history of assimilation that effaces indigenous
cultural differences and exploits their labor or natural resources. From this
standpoint, they see relative autonomy as part of a development solution and
press for a kind of "interculturality" where indigenous peoples are equal players
in defining the terms of interaction (see chapter 5 for in-depth consideration
of interculturalism). Similarly, indigenous movements may be uncomfortable
with social-development concepts that define indigenous people as a "vulnerable" group.[26] In the counter-quincentenary campaigns of the early 1990s, indigenous organizations took pride in a narrative of five centuries of resistance
to—and sometimes outright rebellion against—domination and exclusion
(S. Rivera 1987; Andolina 1999). Grassroots development organizations with an
empowerment agenda might also be unenthusiastic about including indigenous
people on the grounds of their vulnerability, or may balk at ethnodevelopment
policy that does not ensure regular access to credit or allow local control over
external funding sources (Kleymeyer 1993; Palenzuela 1999). Finally, indigenous
organizations and some grassroots development agencies may question social
inclusion and participation that is limited to specific projects. For instance,
the World Bank has not mandated participatory development in relation to
macroeconomic policy, where technocracy is favored over broad participation
(P. Nelson 1996, 621); yet the presence of indigenous leaders at Ecuador's Paris
Club discussions in late 2000 demonstrates their ability to participate in high-
level economic discussions (Collins 2000; Espinosa 2000).[27]

In sum, social neoliberalism offers a basis for ethnodevelopment policy that
articulates with key parts of indigenous-movement agendas and grassroots
development principles but clashes with others. In this way, social neoliberalism effectively reloaded the transnational indigenous advocacy "boomerang"
with principles and assumptions that were only partly shared by indigenous
peoples' movements or pro-indigenous NGO advocates. This reloaded boomerang bounced back to the Andes through the administration of social and
indigenous development programs.

New Institutions and Practices:
Indigenous Development Administration

Transnational networks and connections provided channels for placing indigenous issues on international and global development agendas. Such connections also created avenues for diverse transnational groups of stakeholders to
design, implement, and evaluate programs and projects. These practices enact
policy paradigms through governmentalities that combine a participatory impulse emerging from various social movements with a disciplinary inclination
arising from a neoliberal "audit culture" to ensure technical, rather than political, governance.[28] Thus, carrying out indigenous development has comprised
greater numbers of social scientists, NGOs, and hybrid development institutions
operating at the border of state and civil society (Fox and Starn 1997). It has
also opened spaces for indigenous participation in policy implementation while
shaping such spaces—both institutional and geographical—in ways not entirely
controlled by indigenous participants.

In its adaptation to social neoliberalism, ethnodevelopment policy combined
with new notions of citizenship to create the poor discursively as "partners in
development." At the same time, ethnodevelopment has been infused with
neutral, legal-rational idioms that promote efficiency and effectiveness (Shore
and Wright 1997, 6). One manifestation of this is the increasing administration
of development through civil society by means of NGO project execution and
implementation, in large part due to international perceptions of their flexibility,
social embeddedness, and professional staffs. A second indication of this combination was the appointment of social scientists as development administrators,
in order to tap cultural diversity and civil-society potentialities (Eyben 2000).[29]
Like the feminists who were appointed in earlier decades to administer women-
in-development, anthropologists and other social scientists specializing in culture have attempted to reformulate the organizational cultures and priorities
of their institutions, often entangled with lobbying groups or grassroots organizations. As a result, consultants, agency staff, indigenous representatives,
and project beneficiaries have all become attuned to and embodied within
administrative practices (Stirrat 2000).

What we call *hybrid institutions* constitute a third expression of these new
forms of development governance. Actors who historically would have operated
in distinct spheres—the state, grassroots organizations, or NGOs—have recently
come together in these new apparatuses, which further reconfigure boundaries between state and civil society. Hybrid institutions are often established

in order to oversee specific programs and projects, and they invent a space for various stakeholders to interact in a nominally horizontal manner. They may therefore include members of international development agencies, quasi-governmental departments, expert consultants, NGOs, private-sector companies, and beneficiary representatives or advocates (Radcliffe 2001a).[30] In Ecuador, the hybrid institution Training System for Management of Renewable Resources (CAMAREN) was created to train indigenous and other actors in natural resource management; labeled a consortium, it brings together staff and projects from a French NGO, a Dutch NGO, the Ecuadorian Ministry of Environment, three Ecuadorian NGOs, and numerous civil-society associations.[31] Although hybrid development institutions permit knowledge, resources, and personnel to move across borders and scales, they usually act upon and reinforce one or more scales according to the remit of the program or project they administer.[32]

At the Latin American regional scale, the Fondo Indígena is one example. Created at the Madrid 1992 Ibero-American Summit at the suggestion of the Bolivian government, the fund's mission is to promote indigenous rights in development and facilitate indigenous peoples' control over their development processes.[33] Following the 1991 Ibero-American Summit in Mexico, the Bolivian government and the Inter-American Development Bank met over the course of four meetings with the World Council of Indigenous Peoples, COICA, and supranational agencies such as the United Nations Development Programme (UNDP), ILO, and International Fund for Agricultural Development (IFAD) to negotiate the constitution of the fund. At the 1992 Madrid meeting, twenty-one countries signed on to the fund; by 1993, it had a secretariat based in the Bolivian capital, La Paz. At the outset, finances flowed largely from the IADB, but other multilateral agencies and national governments contributed monies later on.[34] Most recently, representatives from Portugal and Spain described their donations to the fund as a "contribution to social capital" (as cited in Fondo Indígena 2007a). Technical support came from the European Union, German bilateral agencies, and the World Bank. Transnational connections among indigenous groups furthered this support, as when Scandinavian Saami and the Canadian First Nations offered technical assistance.

The Fondo Indígena operates through a participatory and multiple-stakeholder decision-making structure. Indigenous delegates occupy half the seats in the assembly and one-third of the seats on the executive council. Latin American government delegates make up the other half of the assembly, while Latin American and extraregional government delegates make up the other two-thirds of the council. Reinforcing both regional and national scales, the fund contributed to

8 regional projects and 280 country projects by 1998.[35] To enhance its technical capacity and efficiency, the fund has created a system of social indicators for the design of policy or projects, among them a "development-with-identity indicator" and spatial indicators using Geographical Information Systems (GIS) technologies (Fondo Indígena 2007b).

Assessments of the fund's influence have been mixed: fund ex-president Víctor Hugo Cárdenas argued that it made great strides in the 1990s, while a former IBIS director in Bolivia suggested that it was underfunded and insufficiently transparent.[36] Ecuadorian Shuar professional Ampam Karakras shared IBIS's view on the financing but was more concerned about the fact that the fund's technical secretariat consisted almost entirely of nonindigenous people. He quipped, "The problem with the Fondo Indígena is that it is without funds and without *indígenas*."[37] Regarding the "funds" issue, the US$100 million endowment anticipated was not achieved; the actual total was closer to half that. Indigenous control over financing is also limited, as the Inter-American Development Bank presides over the fund's board of trustees. Regarding the matter of indigenous presence in technical bodies, the fund has established professional training programs for indigenous individuals, in both traditional and online formats.[38]

A similar institutional framework governed a two-scale project in Ecuador known as the Development Project for Indigenous and Afro-Ecuadorian Peoples of Ecuador (PRODEPINE).[39] A World Bank flagship program, PRODEPINE was funded to the tune of US$50 million for a five-year period.[40] The project provided monies and technical assistance for participatory development projects that could strengthen cultural identity and indigenous social cohesion (van Nieuwkoop and Uquillas 2000). As the project's remit was national, its governing board was made up of World Bank personnel, central government officials, and representatives of national indigenous and Afro-Ecuadorian organizations. Yet it operated by providing development inputs to local organizations, working largely with *organizaciones de segundo grado* (OSGs), second-tier organizations that agglutinate multiple, village-scale indigenous associations in a given locale. Drawing on previous experiences of projects supported by the Inter-American Foundation and certain Ecuadorian NGOs, OSGs were chosen as the optimal organization and scale for indigenous development by the national governing board.[41] Like the continentwide Fondo Indígena, many viewed PRODEPINE as an exemplary model of culturally sensitive development. The World Bank favored this project, highlighting its semiautonomous administration, high degree of local participation, intercultural assembly of personnel, and strong team spirit.[42] The national Ecuadorian Indigenous Development Council welcomed PRODEPINE's participatory methodology, viewing it as a forerunner of what one project director called "Andean community planning."[43]

From our standpoint, PRODEPINE constituted a paradigmatic example of social neoliberalism and a governmentality that sought to work through local cultural differences *and* international development mandates. On the one hand, it promoted participatory methods aiming to include and empower indigenous beneficiaries. Each OSG was allowed to create its own development plan in a series of participatory assemblies comprised of delegates from each of its constituent indigenous communities. Financing and technical assistance was then channeled from the national project office to help local organizations implement the development plan they designed. On the other hand, PRODEPINE adopted tightly audited and technically defined terms of reference, which ordered the otherwise "free" indigenous participation. It staffed the national and regional administrative offices with a mix of professionals from diverse ethnic backgrounds and specializations (management, engineering, social sciences), it utilized measures like a social capital index to determine local indigenous capacities and regulate funding flows, and it employed standard reporting and recording procedures for local development plans.[44]

Far from seamless, however, PRODEPINE exhibited strains concerning culture, gender, and autonomy. We explore these in later chapters, but note one such tension here: the project was premised, in part, on fomenting local and cultural diversity in development (enacted through local development-with-identity planning), but it imposed national uniformity by standardizing its technical and administrative practices (Radcliffe and Laurie 2006). Moreover, PRODEPINE's consequences were varied, and its results ambiguous. Reasons for this include tensions in strategy and vision between the numerous actors involved at multiple scales, contradictory implications for indigenous identities through the kinds of programs and interlocutors it funded, and uneven on-the-ground implementation of specific local projects. These differences filtered into post-project assessments. They became so marked that, in 2005, the national indigenous federation CONAIE decided not to continue with a second PRODEPINE in Ecuador, even as the World Bank championed it internationally.[45]

Although no direct analog to PRODEPINE was implemented in Bolivia, the World Bank supported indigenous development there through its participatory Rural Community Development Program. This program sought to appropriate the participatory and surveillance mechanisms contained in Bolivia's 1994 Law of Popular Participation, which incorporated local indigenous organizations through reformed municipal governance and embodied principles similar to those of Ecuador's PRODEPINE project. Later, the World Bank implemented a more limited ethnodevelopment project outside of Bolivia's decentralization scheme. Called the Innovation and Learning Project, it sought to tie indigenous cultural knowledge to active free-market participation. The program was co-governed by World Bank personnel, national indigenous confederation representatives, and government delegates from the indigenous-affairs ministry.[46]

In parallel with their execution of specific programs, Bolivia and Ecuador encompassed indigenous affairs within social-development discourse, institutionalized them through new bureaucracies, and professionalized them through recruitment of experts with academic or NGO backgrounds.[47] Bolivian president Gonzalo Sánchez de Lozada (1994–1997) established the Secretariat of Gender, Ethnic, and Generational Affairs within the Ministry of Social Welfare. Under Hugo Banzer (1997–2001), indigenous and ethnic affairs were overseen by the Vice-ministry of Indigenous and Aboriginal Peoples' Affairs (VAIPO) segregated from gender and generational issues and later promoted to a ministry.[48] In 1998, VAIPO adopted "development-with-identity" as its explicit mandate and formed consultative committees with indigenous representatives (VAIPO 1998; Van Cott 2000a, 206–18). Echoing social neoliberalism, the former head of VAIPO proclaimed in 2000, "Our government's policy is to use economic policies to create citizens of the indigenous peoples, and participation is the key" (Postero 2000, 7). Transnational resources and models of social development were crucial: governmental policy was strongly influenced by the German development agency's strategy to combine antipoverty, ethnicity, and gender initiatives (Paulson and Calla 2000), while the UNDP and the Danish government stepped in to finance office space, equipment, and salaries of state personnel working in indigenous affairs (Van Cott 2000a, 194).

In Ecuador, the Sixto Durán government established a national indigenous affairs secretariat in 1994 as it implemented a largely neoliberal policy agenda; the short-lived Abdalá Bucaram presidency appointed Rafael Pandam, then the head of CONAIE, to a newly created indigenous ministry in late 1996. After Bucaram was forced out of office by popular protests and congressional maneuvering, the interim government implemented CONAIE's demand to create an indigenous development council whose members would be appointed by indigenous organizations in civil society. Originally called the Development and Planning Council of Indigenous and Black People (CONPLADEIN) in 1997, this council was renamed CODENPE, again at CONAIE's request, in 1998.[49] Its director is effectively named by CONAIE; assemblies of delegates from CONAIE's constituent federations select the members of its executive council (Andolina 2003; Lucero 2003).[50]

Also based on the mantra of development-with-identity, CODENPE has focused on defining appropriate development policies for indigenous peoples, strengthening ethnic identification, and coordinating with other state bodies on these matters. It has stressed the need for integrated rural development and the reconstitution of indigenous areas through local-scale development plans that can be joined together. Staffed by indigenous intellectuals and development professionals, the council offers Indians a unique political space, defined by one staff member as "a public institution of indigenous people within the state."[51] Seeking local sustainable development, CODENPE has debated how to organize rural indigenous development, seeing PRODEPINE as only one among a number of possible projects.[52] Orienting indigenous development toward questions of cultural expression and intercultural education, CODENPE bases its vision on territorially defined, locally autonomous ethnic communities, a vision that is struggling to gain hegemony within a more classically defined development model based on preexisting associations.[53] Much like the continental Fondo Indígena, CODENPE also seeks technical discipline by promoting the training of indigenous professionals and by streamlining policymaking through a matrix of indicators that would measure various dimensions of indigenous living conditions.[54] Overall, the council has acted as a significant node within a network, galvanizing resources and validity for development-with-identity in diverse political arenas, inside and outside of the state. One of its major programs involved supporting municipalities redesigned by indigenous-movement leaders elected to local office; this program was financed primarily by Spanish bilateral aid with a supplement from the Ecuadorian central government. Other CODENPE activities have received external support from the Inter-American Development Bank and the Danish NGO IBIS.

It is worth remembering that these institutional changes responded to a combination of global and local forces that reconfigured the national state in the Andes. Influenced by Colombia's 1991 constitutional reforms and ILO Convention 169, the 1994 Bolivian constitution defined the country as a multicultural and pluriethnic state and recognized indigenous rights that included communal land and justice systems (Article 171).[55] The 1994 Bolivian educational reform pressed for the establishment of national-level bilingual, intercultural curricula, while the Law of Popular Participation aimed to diversify local politics by recognizing local indigenous organizations as participants.[56] Bolivia's 1996 agrarian reform law (the Ley INRA) provided for the legalization of indigenous community lands yet also aimed to firm up Bolivia's land market, which in some ways threatened small agricultural producers (many of them indigenous). Formalizing its own status as a multiethnic state, Ecuador's 1998 constitution recognized indigenous rights to collective territory, autonomy, and indigenous justice systems. While establishing the rights of indigenous people (and Afro-Ecuadorians) to formulate their own development plans, this constitution made the Ecuadorian state responsible for providing adequate financial support for these ends (Article 84, point 13). Previously, Ecuador's National Directorate of Bilingual Intercultural Education (DINEIB)—in place since 1989—built on seed money from the German Development Agency (GTZ) to push for culturally appropriate education for indigenous people (Abram 1992; Krainer 1996). Afterwards, new social-development paradigms became central in the Ministry of Social Welfare, which in 2001 was headed by Luis Maldonado, an Indian leader who had previously directed the national indigenous development council, CODENPE (Lucero 2002, 203).

These second-generation reforms addressed indigenous demands to some degree and reconstituted the Ecuadorian and Bolivian states in terms of their scope (more market oriented, less corporatist), territoriality (decentralization, constitutional recognition of indigenous territories), and identity (multicultural and pluriethnic). Moreover, in international policy circles, Bolivia and Ecuador became global exemplars of multicultural democratization, thereby legitimating multilateral and bilateral agendas, despite local contradictions and indigenous movement criticisms (see appendix 2). According to a high-ranking official, "the [World] Bank has more per capita investment in Bolivia than any other country at this time [mid to late 1990s]," and Bolivia became a test bed for a new comprehensive development framework.[57]

The Rise of Indigenous Development Policy

Over the past fifteen years there has been a profound shift in development policy that corresponds to intersecting paradigms, actors, and institutions. Compared with the 1960s and 1970s, indigenous issues and agendas are firmly included in broader policy. Development-with-identity is viewed as both a problem and solution for the transnational indigenous development community and is often represented as compatible with a neoliberalism revised along social lines. The transnational field of indigenous development is embedded in various inter-actions that interweave local villages, multilateral development agencies, the national state, and nongovernmental organizations. These players interact in arenas as diverse as the UN's headquarters in Geneva, a highland community in northern Bolivia, and World Bank offices in Quito; each site acts as a node in networks of variable duration and purpose.

If this illustrates a "globalization [that] both situates and besieges indigenous people" (Llorens 1999, 152), we have traced these effects through the metaphor of a "reloaded boomerang." Like an original transnational boomerang defined by Keck and Sikkink (1998), globalization has situated indigenous people centrally in new advocacy and communications networks that assist in spreading their demands for culturally appropriate development across the world and into emerging social-development policies. As indigenous development became both "a cultural category and a political technology" (Shore and Wright 1997, 12), this boomerang was reloaded, such that indigenous peoples experienced a globalization that besieged them with complex challenges: they have been en-rolled in policy paradigms and project administration more than ever before, but the policy principles and administrative norms entailed are only partially of indigenous peoples' own making.

From the perspectives of critical policy studies and governmentality theory, the indigenous development agenda exemplifies the worldwide governance mode of "advanced liberalism," which sees in individuals a capacity for self-regulation (Hyatt 1997). In postwelfare societies like those in the United States and Europe, self-regulation involves governance of the poor by the poor, draw-ing on their local knowledge to implement technically defined projects. Britain's neoliberal housing policy, for example, involved poor tenants in their own empowerment, governing themselves through citizenship technologies like ten-ant committees and housing-repair oversight. Although such programs aimed to instill active citizenship and reduce dependence on the state, "any discus-sion of poverty as inequality or disadvantage [was] effaced from the discourse" (Hyatt 1997, 219).

The social neoliberal mode of government we explicate here modifies some of this. For instance, it does situate inequality in the lexicon of development problems and holds it partly responsible for poverty in many circumstances. It also views the social fabric, and the social capital derived from it, as potent in its own right and not simply a framework or instrument for individual action. On the other hand, social neoliberalism largely elides consideration of capitalist markets or structural factors as problems for development or as major causes of poverty and exclusion. In addition, it embraces "advanced liberal" faith in technical administration and the widespread viability of self-help agency. Although certainly an improvement over strictly top-down models of development, participation and inclusion run the risk of becoming part of an inflexible orthodoxy rather than genuinely empowering practices (Cooke and Kothari 2001; Hickey and Mohan 2004).

Finally, new social and indigenous development policies have not resulted in unequivocal economic gains. Many indigenous small farmers and rural dwellers struggle to rely upon a combination of income sources (e.g., urban migration, crafts) under conditions of income and monetary insecurity (Hentschel and Waters 2002; Bebbington 2000). Despite a formal commitment to distributing resources to indigenous communities (via Bolivia's decentralization legislation or Ecuador's constitutional provisions), insufficient political will and contradictions between market-oriented reforms and multiculturalism hamper efforts to create substantial improvements for indigenous people (Van Cott 2000a). Some government measures actually threaten agricultural livelihoods, such as the removal of state extension services in Bolivia and neoliberal agrarian reform in Ecuador (Bojanic 2001; Martinez 2003). A March 2007 international seminar organized by the Fondo Indígena concluded that, in spite of recent political and policy gains, "indigenous living conditions have not changed significantly, while inequality increases. Nor have racist . . . practices been overcome" (Fondo Indígena 2007c). As such, indigenous development policy may be deterritorialized—to some degree—through transnational circuitry and bureaucratic discourse, but it is far from being "dematerialized" (Nonini and Ong 1997, 18). The following chapters on racial projects, community place making, water usage, indigenous professionalization, and gender issues consider how these changes shape indigenous development possibilities in diverse arenas.

CHAPTER 2

SARAH A. RADCLIFFE, NINA LAURIE, AND ROBERT ANDOLINA

Development-with-Identity: Social Capital

and Andean Culture

Having traced the transnational networks and paradigms concerned with indigenous development in chapter 1, here we unpack their discourses further in order to examine the specific representations of indigenous people within them. These representations are significant because they inform policy rationales, development indicators, subject/beneficiary identities, and administrative strategies.[1] Development policy directed at indigenous people is not free floating, as some interpretations of globalization would suggest (e.g., Mato 1998) but arises from and takes meaning in particular places. When we explore the articulation of international concepts like social capital and culture through the prisms of Andean racial politics and geographies, we see that development policy is bound up with one or more racial projects.[2] We outline two distinct formulations of ethnodevelopment discourse: one based on rigid concepts of culture and bounded notions of space, and another based on more flexible understandings of culture and dynamic notions of space. These have distinct implications for indigenous development policies and the kind of racial projects that such policies entail.

Although race has no essential or biological meaning, "it is a social fact of great salience nonetheless. Race naturalizes economic inequality and establishes a social hierarchy that spans the continent [Latin America]" (Weismantel 2001, xxx). Historicizing indigenous development policy in the context of the region's racial formations, the chapter situates indigenous development thinking within a framework that critically evaluates the representations and expected development roles of indigenous people (Warren and Jackson 2002). These roles and representations, in turn, affect the flow of resources and treatment of indigenous populations in development projects. In what follows, we discuss the content and legacy of Andeanism, and then we examine how social capital has become a key concept in recent development thinking in general and in ethnodevelopment policy in particular. Based on a "hyperreal" representation of indigenous people (Ramos 1998), one ethnodevelopment paradigm interprets culture and indigenous identity in ways that reconcile them with neoliberal social policy but may also restrict indigenous movements' agendas. More enabling conceptualizations of culture and space are possible, woven into a second approach to ethnodevelopment that is open to struggles against racism, diverse economic alternatives, and flexible notions of culture.

Andeanism and Its Critics

Culture has always informed how development practitioners and beneficiaries look at the world (Schech and Haggis 2000). This point has particular salience in the Andes, where commentators have historically described a pristine, unchanging, and distinctive regional culture. Termed *Andeanism*, this picture of the region is a "representation that portrays contemporary highland peasants as outside the flow of modern history [and] has tended to ignore the intensifying interlinkage of . . . countryside and cities, villages and shantytowns" (Starn 1991, 64).

Andeanism creates a problematic lexicon for the introduction of international development concepts because they risk becoming complicit in oversimplified representations of Andean indigenous actors. Ecuador and Bolivia are traversed by the Andean mountain chain, stretching from southern Chile to Colombia, passing through western Bolivia and central Ecuador. While the Andes have a preconquest history of political integration across ecological diversity (Murra 1956), the region's continued social and cultural coherence is debatable. In this context, the framework of Andeanism has been questioned by means of analytical deconstruction and denaturalization, which owe much to Edward Said's postcolonial analysis of Orientalism. In his pathbreaking work, Said identified a discourse about Middle Eastern populations and geographies based on East-West dualisms, in which people in the Orient appeared in Western narratives as cultural stereotypes in value-laden imaginative geographies (Said 1978). As an alternative to Andeanism, rural highland dwellers might be seen as "modern, . . . dynamic, syncretic and [with] . . . sometimes ambiguous [identities]" (Starn 1991, 64; also Salman and Zoomers 2003).

Andeanism constituted well-established ideologies and racial projects in Peru, Bolivia, and Ecuador, often traced to the early twentieth-century discussion of

indigenismo (indigenous populations' role in national life). Indigenismo celebrated preconquest achievements and the potential contribution of assimilated
Indians (de la Cadena 2000). Despite an impulse to bridge the socioeconomic
gap between Indian groups and wealthier mestizos, indigenismo and Andeanism fed into polarizing separations of racial groups that entrenched their
perceived differences (Mayer 1991). In spatial terms, Andeanist racial dualisms
were mapped onto a rural/highland and urban/modern grid, denying fluid connections between groups or regions and underpinning a sociopolitical divide. In
temporal terms, Andeanism represented racial/cultural groups in dichotomous
frameworks that positioned Indians outside of history and Western modernity,
often with negative connotations (Fabian 1983). *Serrano* (highland) indigenous
populations, for instance, have often been pictured in landscapes associated with
isolation and barriers to development (Orlove 1993; Radcliffe 1996; Weismantel
2001). Ignoring the close articulation between Indian labor and regional political economies, such representations have also stereotyped Andean populations
as "archaic and primitive," with distinctive, backward cultures (see critiques
in Mayer 1991; Starn 1991). For example, Mario Vargas Llosa—novelist and
chair of a Peruvian government commission investigating an Andean village
massacre—described the region's Indians as rooted in an archaic culture that
is divided socioeconomically and geographically from urban mestizos and national culture (as cited in Berg, Montero, and Montgomery 1983).[3] The report
represented the population of Ucchuraccay, where the massacre occurred, as
backward, illiterate, impoverished, and unable to conceive of progress (Mayer
1991). In turn, Andeanist racial projects often explained and justified Indians'
exclusion from modernity and full nationhood. They also influenced development policy, as when Ecuadorian and Bolivian social and agrarian development
funds did not cover indigenous populations widely, as the latter were considered
insufficiently modern to spark national development.[4]

Others have embraced "the Andean" as a distinctive socio-spatial pattern
while celebrating its contribution to well-being. One example is what we term
eco-Andeanism, in which environmental and social features associated with
the Andean mountains are posed as a solution to poverty and marginalization. The Peruvian-based development organization PRATEC, for example, has
advocated Andean decolonization and autochthonous solutions to environmental destruction and social dislocation while rejecting Western science and
development (Apffel-Marglin and PRATEC 1998). PRATEC was funded initially
by Oxfam America, Terre des Hommes, and the European Union (Apffel-
Marglin 1998, 45), but it later spurned Oxfam America funding for being "too

Western."[5] PRATEC has retained a spatial and cultural imagery of Andean peoples' distinctiveness, yet it broke with the logic of Western progress. Accordingly, it frames development as a discredited endeavor that should be replaced by a regionally specific vision of livelihoods based on the "profound values" of Andean social organization, technology, and philosophy.[6] Eco-Andeanism pictures the region—accurately—as a multiracial space, yet it subordinates this to general, supposedly preconquest, principles. Eco-Andeanism's racial project thus constructs the region as a self-sufficient socio-environmental area, discarding modernity in favor of preconquest norms and practices.

Indigenous social movements have also drawn on Andeanist regional narratives to contest politics as usual. Ecuadorian and Bolivian indigenous movements have criticized colonialist power structures and glorified preconquest societies, thus echoing some elements of indigenismo (Andolina 1999). Statements such as the Bolivian Tiawanaku Manifesto and CONAIE's Proyecto Político (Political Project) read history as an unfulfilled revolutionary and anticolonial promise in which true development is to be based on Andean culture (Andolina 1999, 109–11). Although indigenous movements often differ internally over issues of race and political strategy, the Spanish conquest of the Americas is juxtaposed to visions of primordial purity (ethnic, racial, political, cultural, and economic) in certain narratives and in shorthand explanations for contemporary ills (Harris 2002).

One recent example is from the Bolivian *ayllu* movement.[7] It lays the ayllu as a cornerstone of highland indigeneity and suggests a positive continuation of pre-Hispanic traditions. These include "territorial defense" through politics and spiritual communion through ritual, viewed as pan-Andean practices: "Thanks to this [territorial and ritualistic] system of administration the Andean civilizations controlled the socioeconomic situation of their inhabitants. There were and still are ayllus in Ecuador, Peru, and Chile [as well as Bolivia]" (Cussi, Calle, and Mamani 2000, 61). In a similar vein, ayllu-movement activists have described their territory as located at high altitudes near snow-capped mountaintops; they have also maintained that indigenous Aymaras who migrate to cities will return to the countryside, to "the foundations of [their] soul[s] . . . where someone is always waiting for us" (Cussi, Calle, and Mamani 2000, 60–61).[8] An analogous movement in Ecuador seeks to reconstruct indigenous identities around "pueblo" identity categories that draw on names of pre-Incaic highland cultures. Ecuadorian workshops discussing this process referred to such groups as *pueblos originarios* (original peoples) who "were here first"; they also referred regularly to the notion of cultural loss or decline from an original stasis. The "reconstitution of Quichua pueblos" is thus proposed as a kind of stopgap measure that would not only prevent further cultural erosion but also allow a recovery of some of these losses. In short, these indigenous-movement representations continue the long-term Andeanist practice of fixing race to place, albeit in ways somewhat distinct from those of the past.

In this respect, Andeanism informs particular racial projects that comprise part of wider racial formations in Ecuador and Bolivia, where resources have historically been diverted away from indigenous groups and areas. A racial project comprises "an interpretation, representation or explanation of racial dynamics, and an effort to reorganize and redistribute resources along particular racial lines" (Omi and Winant 1994, 56). A racial formation is a composite of the racial projects in a society during a particular time period (Omi and Winant 1994, 60). Because of the rigid dualisms and claims to radically distinctive values they entail, racial projects influenced by Andeanism exhibit features of essentialism. As Diana Fuss reminds us, essentializing discourses provide meanings that are only partially defined in relation to the historical specificity of a particular cultural formation (Fuss 1990). Whether defined as a lack of modern development or a lack of autochthonous development, Andeanism returns to essentialist notions about the region's places and populations in ways that attribute a bounded, core distinctiveness to them.[9]

Andeanism is also reproduced in the diverse fields of development, social science, and anthropology. It provides a template for ethnodevelopment policy and a meaningful, if restricted, conceptualization of reality. An official from Bolivia's indigenous secretariat, for example, discussed "what happens in this millenarian Andean tradition of space management and productive technology." An INGO staffer talks about reconnecting Andean indigenous peoples "as before colonialism."[10] Personnel from a European bilateral agency spoke of how, in the rural regions of Bolivia's department of Potosí, "nearly all the population has more or less indigenous characteristics."[11] The revised World Bank directive on indigenous peoples largely excludes urban indigenous peoples from their remit (Bank Information Center 2004). Not all development agencies use Andeanist imagery, however. Personnel of the Dutch bilateral agency, for example, have spoken in detail about middle-level organizations, named specific provinces where they work, and considered the multiethnic makeup of their populations in ways that avoid Andeanist stereotypes.[12] This latter discourse may open up more possibilities for context-sensitive, flexible, and multiscalar indigenous development; on the other hand, it may put such agencies at odds with indigenous leaders whose projects seek ethnic autonomy framed in Andeanist imagery.

In the following sections, we draw on interviews, as well as development-agency publications, web sites, and gray literature to examine how social capital–based policy frameworks have drawn on Andeanism in formulating one influential paradigm of indigenous development policy. Later, we outline a field of indigenous development thinking less steeped in Andeanist discourses that underpins a second ethnodevelopment paradigm. In each case, we critically explore how—and the extent to which—diverse strands of current development thinking view ethnic difference "as the result of distance and separation [or] within a history of continuous and multi-layered connections" where Indians live *within* modernity, not outside of it (Starn 1991, 85).

Ethnodevelopment and Andean Indians I:
Tales of Poverty and Isolation

Although indigenous people are no longer represented exactly as they were under indigenismo (Muratorio 1994), some ethnodevelopment policies represent Indians as inherently different from the rest of the national population. Based on relatively rigid notions of culture and space, and influenced by neoliberal concepts, policy statements illustrating this line of thinking portray Indians as homogeneous, poor, spatially circumscribed, and vulnerable. They make such generalizations despite the acknowledged scarcity of detailed information about the complexity of indigenous society and an unacknowledged reliance on a limited number of studies.[13] These representations mark indigenous people as racially distinct and materially poor but also portray them as being rich in social capital and therefore possessing an endogenous form of development potential.

There are two key threads in this essentializing version of indigenous development policy. One of these is the unmarked infusion of Andeanist elements of indigenous poverty, vulnerability, and geographical isolation. Economic poverty is a feature consistently associated with Andean indigenous people in policy documents and interviews. Rather than relate Indian poverty to multilayered connections with colonization, state policies, or racially segregated labor markets, this impoverishment is described in ways that draw on the readily available discourses of Andeanism. The second thread is the re-marking of culture as a form of social capital capable of providing an indigenous route to development. In the words of a report from the Inter-American Development Bank, "[indigenous] culture becomes an asset, rather than an impediment" to progress and development (Deruyttere 1997, 9). In this light, the Fondo Indígena, which has received considerable IADB aid, is envisaged as an opportunity to identify and design a "genuinely indigenous project," in which cultural identity and development make a "virtuous circle" (Deruyttere 1997, 10, 14). Tradition is seen as positive when it can be molded to particular interpretations of modernity (e.g., those defined by free-market capitalism) and when it moves away from the anti-Western, anticapitalist assumptions of certain variants of Andeanism.

In the first thread, indigenous people are represented generically as poorer than nonindigenous populations. One widely cited report made an argument for a high correlation between poverty and (indigenous) ethnicity. Written by two World Bank economists, this 1994 study was based on household survey data in four Latin American countries (Pscharaopoulos and Patrinos 1994). According to this research, "one-fourth of poor Latin Americans are indigenous, but this percentage is higher where there is a large indigenous population" (Deruyttere 1997).[14] Indicators such as infant mortality and food insecurity, as well as inadequate schooling, services, and infrastructure, are also mentioned. In Bolivia, "73 percent of the monolingual indigenous population is poor, as is 64 percent of the bilingual indigenous population" (COWI 1999, 8). Bolivia is compared to sub-Saharan Africa, with both having 95 percent poverty in rural areas (World Bank 1999c). For Ecuador, "in general, it can be stated that all indigenous and blacks . . . are extremely poor," with over 77 percent of Indians in poverty and 42.2 percent in extreme poverty (Encalada, García, and Ivarsdotter 1999, 8ff). The indigenous poverty report was highly significant in shaping World Bank policy, persuading the bank's vice-president to focus on indigenous issues.[15] It is also quoted extensively to argue for targeted programs throughout the Latin American region, even though the report was country specific, based on detailed research in Bolivia, Guatemala, Mexico, and Perú (Davis 2002).[16] Significantly, this representation of poverty emphasized indigenous peoples' lack of the elements of modern development in a way that deflects attention away from structural disadvantages.[17] Moreover, such poverty was perceived as Andean in character. Oxfam America, for instance, has argued that there is more poverty in the Andes than in the Amazon region, while the Danish Bilateral Development Cooperation Agency's (DANIDA) reason for working in Andean Bolivia was its "degree of poverty" and low levels of "public attention" and "institutional presence."[18]

Like early versions of Andeanism, this ethnodevelopment model is concerned about indigenous vulnerability in modern development processes. Development agencies with neoliberal commitments view indigenous peoples' vulnerability in relation to their position in the labor market (World Bank, as cited in Plant 1998, 10, 32; Encalada, García, and Ivarsdotter 1999, 60). One consultant's report, for instance, discussed the Bolivian state's "opportunities to liberate [indigenous people] from repression, neglect and misery" (COWI 1999, 18). Contesting such views, indigenous organizations and their advocates often lobby to remove mention of vulnerability from international statements on indigenous rights, stressing instead their self-reliance and agency, for which they receive support from international advocacy organizations.[19]

Lastly, this image of indigenous development reflects a "spatial incarceration of the native" (Appadurai 1988, 36–49), by enclosing indigenous people conceptually in isolated, rural, community-based geographies. Active indigenous participation in urban and international economies is downplayed, while migration is seen as a forced removal from indigenous people's "natural" location, a point also found in certain documents produced by indigenous organizations. Driven by overpopulation, the growth of commercial agriculture, and declining terms of trade to the "poverty belts" around cities, indigenous people are presented as culturally inclined to remain in rural areas (Encalada, García, and Ivarsdotter 1999, 46). This suggests that involvement with modernity and markets is what permits indigenous people to have a larger political and social role, as if otherwise they would operate solely at a local scale. These imaginative geographies of policy are thereby primed to bypass geographies of nation-state and citizenship (N. Smith 1990; Sieder 2002).

In summary, Andeanism retains influence through ties to an ethnodevelopment policy that pictures Indians as hampered by poverty, segregated in labor markets, and rooted in rural agrarian areas. This construction of ethnodevelopment makes a "hyperreal Indian"—an "ideal type" Indian for purposes befitting certain neoliberal precepts and bureaucratic procedures (Ramos 1998). It is thus that neoliberal social development begins to form a racial project, representing a polarized economy, society, and geography in which Indians can take a modern role, albeit premised on their vulnerability and poverty.

The concept of social capital constitutes a second discursive thread in this approach to indigenous development. In meshing with neoliberal development precepts, it provides further rationale for specific programs and for new applications of indices and measures.[20] Although the concept of social capital has diverse definitions (Hyden 1997), since the mid-1990s development debates have engaged primarily with the notion—associated with the political scientist Robert Putnam—that social norms and networks facilitate collective action, foster good governance, and support economic growth.[21] In the development field, social capital has been defined broadly as "norms and social relations embedded in the social structures of society that enable people to coordinate action and achieve desired goals" (Narayan 1999). The concept's polyvalence permits development economists to talk to other social scientists (Bebbington et al. 2004), but its insertion into global policy and state restructuring raises questions about its status in a wider field of operation (Fine 1999; De Filippis 2002). According to certain advocates of the concept, social capital is found primarily in community and household interactions and comprises relations of trust, networks, associational activity, and solidarity, all of which have beneficial outcomes for income and social development (Narayan 1999). Amid neoliberal state cutbacks, however, social capital risks becoming a development "Band-Aid," substituting unpaid citizen action for state institutions and resources (for critiques, see Fine 2001; Harriss 2002; Molyneux 2002). Against Putnam's interpretation of trust networks as good for community development, critics have questioned the concept's vagueness, its inability to distinguish between different scales of social life, its implicit optimism, and its antistate policy implications (Fine 1999; De Filippis 2002; Mayer and Rankin 2002). In a similar vein, J. Fox (1996) has critiqued Putnam's model of social capital for ruling out power inequalities and ignoring the political and economic contexts of social networking, development, and empowerment.

Debates along these lines also played out in the World Bank's networks of advisors, policymakers, and social scientists during the 1990s (Bebbington et al. 2004). As noneconomist staff in various multilateral and bilateral agencies struggled to challenge the hegemony of orthodox, "no society" neoliberalism, the concept of social capital appeared serviceable, especially when combined with the support of the World Bank president and with NGO advocacy on behalf of civil-society participation (Fox 1997; Bebbington 2002). Out of these complex internal debates, multilateral agencies quickly engaged with the social-capital approach but drew primarily on Putnam's work on Italy, rather than on approaches that combined political economies and social networks (e.g., Fox 1997). It extended Putnam's framework by measuring household participation in community associations and establishing correlations between membership in local organizations and household wealth (Narayan and Pritchett 1999; Grootaert and Narayan 2001; compare Harriss and De Renzio 1997). On these grounds, development policy changed to make more use of community and household participation and to incorporate culturally distinctive institutions and social relations more formally than before.

This definition of social capital has been applied to ethnic and racial differences in development, following the argument that ethnic groups share "common values and culture [and] can band together for mutual benefit."[22] These values include reciprocity, bounded solidarity, and enforceable trust, comprising a moral economy that guarantees access to resources for group members. Here cultural identities are defined as a core set of features, and culture is essentialized in terms of its orientation to a market economy and donor-funded development projects. Reiterating the centrality of social capital to indigenous development, in 2004 the World Bank argued, "The relative scarcity of bridging social capital in indigenous communities suggests that interventions aimed at increasing social capital and agency in indigenous communities deserve serious consideration" (Patrinos and Skoufias 2007, viii).

These conceptualizations had an immediate effect on World Bank policy concerning indigenous peoples, leading to a switch from crisis management (after resettlement and environmental destruction) to a more programmatic attention to planning (Bebbington et al. 2004). Rather than treat indigenous people merely as victims of dam building, for example, policy began to recognize the singularity of indigenous societies in terms of their networks and dense interaction between local groups of households. When applying this to indigenous Ecuadorians and Bolivians, social capital is found in shared values, diverse community ritual cycles, and "moral concepts of reciprocity [and] *compadrazgo* [godparenthood]" (COWI and Consulting Engineers and Planners 1999, 18).[23] It is argued frequently that social capital is something that indigenous people have in large supply: "Social exclusion, economic deprivation, and political marginalization are sometimes perceived as the predominant characteristics of Ecuador's indigenous peoples. But as they often remind others, indigenous peoples also have strong positive attributes, particularly their high level of social capital" (Van Nieuwkoop and Uquillas 2000, 18).

In contrast to Andeanist narratives of untouched archaic cultures, the wedding of social capital and culture in this approach to indigenous development has redefined tradition as a feature relevant to contemporary social life and future progress. Nonmonetary exchange and reciprocity between members of Indian communities exemplify social capital, as do "ancestral and traditional knowledge," identity, close attachment to territories, and a capacity to mobilize labor (Van Nieuwkoop and Uquillas 2000, 3).[24] In discussing the relative cultural authenticity of Bolivian communal structures and peasant unions, an Oxfam America spokesperson argued that Andean Indians "really maintain their culture, their own identity. There's really a lot of vigor in their culture, their technologies, their wisdom."[25]

This view of indigenous culture implies a development strategy of strengthening social capital, permitting both economic growth and the retention of Indian culture, thereby achieving (a particular understanding of) culturally appropriate development. Rather than being extraneous to development's logic, culture is reconceived as an engine driving it (Davis 2002; Van Nieuwkoop and Uquillas 2000, 4). In the words of an IADB report, "strengthening cultural identity and promoting sustainable socioeconomic development are mutually reinforcing" (Deruyttere 1997, 9), an idea that would reverse the vicious circle of poverty identified in modernization theory. As argued by SWISSAID staff members, "Power is when a social group is capable of solving its basic problems within its own parameters, in other words, culture."[26]

One application of this social capital framework is found in the Ecuadorian project of PRODEPINE: project beneficiaries in rural areas were identified through a targeting mechanism that combined variables of social capital, ethnic population (identified via the census measure of indigenous language use), and unmet basic needs (Van Niewkoop and Uquillas 2000). Using numbers of local indigenous associations as a marker of social capital, the combined index identified 288 parishes across the country in which participatory planning was used to devise local development projects.[27] PRODEPINE relied upon "traditional" work parties, mobilized by existing village authorities, to complete local projects. In addition, the project funded the "rescue and strengthening of a rich cultural patrimony," such as ritual sites, festivals, audiovisuals products, and crafts. Despite efforts to "insert culture into income-generating activities and productive investment" (Uquillas 2002, 15), however, World Bank–led project evaluations found this component to be unsatisfactory, as it generated little wealth. PRODEPINE as a whole had regionally variable success, attributed by staff members to the regional differences in social capital, with central Andean highland indigenous organizations seen as having the most (Larreamendy 2003, 124). The Andean-centered vision of this project was also thrown into the spotlight by criticisms from Amazonian indigenous peoples like the Shuar, who claimed that PRODEPINE was inappropriate for their social and environmental settings (Núñez del Prado and Pacheco 2001; Larreamendy 2003).

Another application of this ethnodevelopment model was the Bolivian indigenous development plan (2000–2002) financed by the World Bank. It promoted Indian crafts and music; national and international market penetration;

intellectual property rights over genes, biodiversity, and folklore; and a nutrition policy.[28] The project built up from indigenous social capital embedded in
"cultural knowledge" to generate marketable projects in ethnotourism, ethno-
biology, and agriculture. Following PRODEPINE in Ecuador, the same senior
personnel developed the Bolivian project, which involved "more experimental
types of things. . . . But it's focused on strengthening indigenous capacity, you
know, capacity building, but that's everything, from legal and technical skills
and business entrepreneurial workshops and things like that, to strengthening
small community organizations and then larger indigenous networks."[29]

The incorporation of concepts of social capital into this line of ethnodevelopment policy has attenuated but not eliminated Andeanist legacies. Advocates of
social capital who work on indigenous development policy generally see such
policy as building up from the social capital perceived to exist in local indigenous
organizations and household networks. While this avoids pessimistic overgeneralizations about the limited development potential of cultural or racial groups, it
tends to suggest that indigenous identities are clear-cut, historically consistent,
and separate from mestizo identities. In this context, we turn to examine how
social-capital approaches construct a racial project for indigenous Andeans in
three respects: vis-à-vis the modern economy, in relations with other racial and
cultural groups, and with regard to indigenous cultural distinctiveness. We show
that this project addresses but does not resolve Orin Starn's concern that Andean
rural populations are pictured in relation to nonmarket economies as lacking
ties across racial/cultural groups and through essentialist notions of Andean
culture. In this analysis, we draw on research interviews with multilateral and
other development agency staff, indigenous leaders and professionals, as well
as numerous agency documents and project outlines.

Indigenous People in the Market

As the "capital of the poor" (Woolcock 2000), social capital is viewed as a basis
for internally generated development. To varying degrees in the policy literature, indigenous social capital is perceived as potentially transferable into other
forms of capital, rather than specific and nonconvertible. By emphasizing Indian
social capital as a productive resource, development thinking has placed indigenous populations along an imaginary continuum measuring entrepreneurial
potential. One World Bank web site suggested an evolutionary pattern from a
short-term ability to formulate development strategies to a long-term ability to
access investment resources.[30] Combining social and other capitals is also viewed
as synergistic: social capital represents "the start-up capital for sustainable social

and economic development, because it builds on peoples' values, aspirations and potential rather than imposing a development model from the top down" (Deruyttere 1997, 10). In contrast to classic Andeanism's indigenous "closed universe" and modernization theory's treatment of indigenous culture as a development problem, here indigenous culture becomes part of a development solution, underpinning potential entrepreneurship in global niche markets.[31] Neoliberal thinking underlies this message of investment in different forms of capital: so long as the overall stock of capital is increased, so too the wealth of society grows. Multilateral agencies, for example, have asserted that indigenous and Afro–Latin American human capital development "is no longer a moral preoccupation [but] an economic imperative" (Encalada, García, and Ivarsdotter 1999, 33). According to an influential World Bank policymaker, uneducated indigenous people have "unused human capital," hindering countries' economic growth (Davis 2000).

Such a perspective overlaps with those of indigenous movements to some extent, since they have regularly argued for the potential and accomplishments of indigenous cultures, acknowledged national and global production contexts, and noted the growing diversity of income-generating activities outside agricultural production, such as commerce, crafts, and urban labor.[32] In this vision of ethnodevelopment, Indians appear as potential entrepreneurs entering markets as groups that are already culturally distinctive.[33] This is implied in the words of a senior World Bank staff member, who made an analogy between Latin American indigenous peoples and other ethnic groups: "We think now that there may be a significant role for culturally based—if you like—business initiatives. . . . The market may actually revive a culture and identity. Look at the Jews in New York—that is proof that you can be totally immersed in the world market and maintain your identity and your culture."[34] Advocates of this model of ethnodevelopment have also referred to successful Latin American indigenous entrepreneurs. In Guatemala, "far from all the urban indigenous dwellers are poor . . . [I]ndigenous peoples are progressively breaking into new commercial and professional activities" (Plant 1998, 23). Ecuador's *Otavaleño* traders and Canada's First Nations are mentioned frequently. Similarly, a World Bank representative stated, "If you look at the urban Aymara thing in Bolivia, I really think that there is an astounding integration into the market and capitalism among the Aymara in La Paz. [They're] highly successful business people."[35] Based on these viewpoints, the IADB provided a grant of US$1 million to create and augment the business capacities of Ecuadorian Indians.

The emphasis on entrepreneurial potential distinguishes this paradigm from early Andeanism, which perceived indigenous relations with markets as inherently problematic.[36] Yet indigenous entrepreneurial qualities are not viewed as evenly distributed. One report on Bolivia claimed that indigenous people have not exploited international and national markets, despite the "economic advantages of the live indigenous culture, whether native or vernacular" (World Bank 1999c); another bluntly stated, "Many [Bolivian indigenous people] do not show capitalist characteristics" (COWI and Consulting Engineers and Planners 1999, 18). A policy document on Ecuador suggests that indigenous integration into the market is "quite variable" (Encalada, García, and Ivarsdotter 1999, 59) and ranks the "competitiveness" of different Ecuadorian indigenous groups, in which the lowland Quichua peoples come out on top.

All of this sits awkwardly alongside recurrent portrayals of Indians as characteristically peasant in this variant of ethnodevelopment policy. According to the IADB, "over 90 percent of indigenous are sedentary subsistence farmers . . . grouped together with [mestizo] campesinos" (Deruyttere 1997, 3). Policy documents attribute indigenous problems with the market to questions of geographical isolation, lack of communication, and transportation infrastructures, themes that indigenous people themselves are not slow to point out (Almeida 1991; FENOCIN 1999).[37]

A summary of these studies suggests a development vision of Indians as potential entrepreneurs who nevertheless lack sufficient competitiveness, strategic vision, and human resources to realize this potential on their own (COWI and Consulting Engineers and Planners 1999, 18). From a previous Andeanist dichotomy of modern (entrepreneurial, white) versus traditional (Indian, nonentrepreneurial), the articulation of social capital and culture described thus far has moved to a sliding scale of entrepreneurial potential. This type of market-led development is often viewed skeptically by indigenous leaders, however, who stress the costs of neoliberal economic restructuring and point out that indigenous—and many mestizo—populations have five centuries of experience with the market, often resulting in poverty rather than growth (Tauli-Corpuz 2005, 6).[38]

In these images of ethnodevelopment, indigenous subjects are projected as future contributors to markets in terms of a "warm, fuzzy geopolitics," where northern consumer demand for "simpler" ethnic lifestyles provokes an act of solidarity linked to consumption of indigenous products and services (Kaplan 1995). Such markets include nontraditional exports of organic cocoa, quinoa (an Andean grain), clothing, and wood products (Healy 2001b). As these goods increasingly resonate with global fair-trade and organic markets, this ethno-development approach prioritizes the removal of "bureaucratic blocks to the market" and encouragement of indigenous entrepreneurship around nontraditional exports, albeit in the broader context of private-sector development and the creation of international trade zones (COWI and Consulting Engineers and Planners 1999, 38–41, 45). In the NGO-dominated "alternative" circuits around culture and development, similar niches are listed, including ethnoagriculture, organic agriculture, indigenous crafts, education, and communication for indigenous and popular groups (Mato 1997). Services such as ethnotourism offer culturally distinctive experiences attractive to relatively wealthy global consumers. As noted by Bolivia's former indigenous affairs minister, ethnotourism packages itself to offer "values lost in the West, [such as] generosity, goodness, communalism, participatory democracy, and strong values."[39] Over the longer term, possible avenues for ethnodevelopment are seen to include biotechnology, bioprospecting, intellectual property rights, and medicinal plants; however, such activities are currently embedded within marked power inequalities, in which indigenous people have yet to gain access to control over scientific activity and knowledge valuation (Parry 2002).

To summarize, under this vision of indigenous peoples' relation to markets, Andean Indians are seen as holding a resource—their "ancestral cultures," in the words of an Oxfam America policymaker—with which to develop and generate income. In contrast to early Andeanism, Ecuadorian and Bolivian Indians are represented as well endowed with social capital, which offers the possibility of diversifying livelihoods away from small-scale agriculture. Their culturally distinctive products and services are envisioned as linking them positively with a global, post-Fordist market. Despite these departures from early Andeanism, however, the particular linkage between social capital and indigenous culture described here risks retrenching Andeanism's divide between Indians and mestizos and reinforcing inequalities, by exaggerating the distinctiveness of indigenous culture and making market competitiveness a prime evaluative benchmark.

Indigenous Civil Society and Social Difference

This version of ethnodevelopment policy is also based on an understanding of civil society in terms of local associations, household networks, and traditional organizations. It therefore focuses attention on indigenous institutions and social networks organized according to "traditional" values of reciprocity and rotating leadership. Social stability and networks are pictured in the context of traditional leadership structures characterized by community-based authority combined with spiritual and social roles, such as "democratic [village] assemblies, rule by consensus, rotating leadership, and an egalitarian ethos" (Healy 2000). Despite their embedding in political systems and electoral politics, Indian communities are pictured as detached from modern nation-states, and traditional authorities are attributed to indigenous cultures only. Indeed, for some members of transnational indigenous-affairs networks, Indian communal structures provide an ideal basis for a form of development free from party politics and corrupting interference from the state.[40] According to one multilateral report, communal territory is a "mechanism of cultural resistance" and therefore worthy of support for its contribution to social capital (Encalada, García, and Ivarsdotter 1999, 55).[41] Consequently, this kind of ethnodevelopment promotes "traditional forms of self-management [*auto-gestión*] and government" (World Bank 1998b; World Bank 1999b), exemplified by Andean communal authorities, in whom "you can see a [clear and strong] structure that really acts, has power; it's linked to production and planning."[42] Community-level development is therefore seen to strengthen social networks, as well as provide grounds for economic growth (e.g., Plant 1998, 31).

The focus on isolated rural locations, predominantly social definitions of indigenous communities, and participation as a solution tends to highlight community-level development as the route out of poverty. Such imaginative geographies of policy do mesh well with some indigenous-movement agendas promoting autochthonous and community-based indigenous development. Local and culturally defined development provides a powerful mobilizing idea across transnational indigenous affairs networks, which structure tense and entangled relationships between multilateral and bilateral agencies and indigenous organizations in their struggles to reconfigure development policy.

While this paradigm of ethnodevelopment provides a template for relations between indigenous communities and groups, it does not do so for relations between indigenous and nonindigenous groups. Likewise, this approach to ethnodevelopment elides consideration of the kinds of people who maintain these interactions and the power relations between them (Harriss 2002). In general, it tends to treat civil society as a "black box" rather than as a multifaceted set of social relations (Nederveen Pieterse 2001; Radcliffe 2004). As a result, this ethnodevelopment paradigm can limit possibilities for multiethnic coalitions, in part by representing indigenous knowledge as local and thereby limiting its contributions to specific places. Given the lack of coordination (and at times, hostility) between indigenous and black social movements in Ecuador (Halpern

and Winddance Twine 2000), and emphases on "precolonial" authority structures, this approach can miss opportunities to build up creative intercultural
forms of organization and coordination.[43]

Indigenous Culture and Authenticity
The reconfiguration of the relationship between culture, authority, and racial
groups in the Andes entailed in this version of ethnodevelopment affects resource allocation and the identification of beneficiaries in specific development
programs and projects. Lists of cultural and social features distinguish Afro–
Latin Americans and various indigenous groups, in turn structuring patterns
of resource distribution. This paradigm of ethnodevelopment thereby defines
and polices the dividing lines between racial and cultural groups (Comaroff and
Comaroff 2001; Hale 2002). In Bolivia, the Danish bilateral development agency
granted funds to the vice-ministry of indigenous affairs so that it could change
its working practices, "which should be developed under a totally distinct logic
just for the indigenous people."[44]

Premised upon notions of indigenous cultural distinctiveness and the need to
generate development from the resources inherent in indigenous populations,
programs emerging from this model of ethnodevelopment work constantly to
decide who is indigenous. With this in mind, development practitioners often
identify indigenous beneficiaries by their dress, material possessions, and location. Such visions and criteria are historically and geographically grounded and
emerge from long histories of interethnic interaction, as well as nationalist patterns of ethnic integration and racism. For example, the Otavalans' reputation
as entrepreneurs accrued historically, becoming the basis for their "commercial
reputation" in earlier development programs and their recent celebration in
ethnodevelopment thinking (Kyle 1999; Muratorio 1994). However, a World
Bank report on indigenous development acknowledged the difficulty, even
among professional anthropologists, of identifying indigenous people (OED
Evaluations 2003). Still, the German bilateral agency works with local consultants
to gain this cultural knowledge, and various development agencies use cultural
distinctiveness as a criterion in program design.[45] For example, following its view
that indigenous development occurs where cultural identity has been preserved,
the World Bank funded the strengthening of Ecuadorian indigenous crafts,
festivals, and other "cultural patrimony" in its PRODEPINE project (World
Bank 1997, 2, 3). The UK's bilateral agency representative in Bolivia believed that
lowland groups better fit the category of "indigenous" and in turn saw them as

obvious interlocutors in their programs on indigenous knowledge. In contrast, DFID programs in the highlands did not distinguish between indigenous and nonindigenous beneficiaries in a water project.[46]

Another effect of this "hyperreal" identification of indigenous people is that potential beneficiary groups may adapt to such images and allocation procedures, even when project administrators perceive these groups as inauthentic (compare Rogers 1996; J. Warren 1998). In one ethnodevelopment project, a Bolivian technical consultant suggested, "It would be good to see how many [project beneficiaries] saw themselves as indigenous ten years ago. I know from the places I have worked, for example, that there are communities that say, almost explicitly, 'if we don't call ourselves indigenous, obviously no program or project will come in.'"[47] The implicit racial project of this approach to indigenous development rests upon the notion that Indians are discrete and easily identifiable, marked by their appearance and visible behavior. In the transnational circuits that support local ethnodevelopment projects, criteria of authenticity and distinctiveness continue to be significant. When dealing with international advocacy networks, for example, northern Ecuadorian Indians had to demonstrate personality, representativeness, marketability, and fashionability (all judged by northern criteria) in order to be taken seriously (Lloyd 1998). The outcomes of funding decisions depended on whether advocacy groups felt Indian leaders were "culturally authentic," with lifestyles attractive to northern audiences.[48] Such criteria of cultural authenticity often differ from those of grassroots populations.

The PRODEPINE development project in Ecuador illustrates further consequences of this approach to social capital and culture. For project implementation, the World Bank devised an "objective beneficiary targeting mechanism," which combined information on ethnic populations, poverty, and social capital to generate a map of high-priority areas for intervention. The index used census data on indigenous groups, at a point when the Ecuadorian census did not include questions on ethnic self-identification. National surveys on unmet needs were used to indicate levels of poverty. Social capital was measured according to managerial capacity and the financial, human, and organizational assets found in local indigenous peoples' organizations. In other words, social capital was measured through a proxy indicator of local civil mobilization. As a result of this identification mechanism, 288 Ecuadorian parishes (subdivisions of a municipality) were given high priority for project resources.

In sum, this approach to indigenous development transcends Andeanist understandings of the market, interethnic ties, and Andean culture to some extent. However, due to black-box understandings of social networks, both Andeanism and social neoliberalism naturalize reciprocity and collectivity, which are seen as inherently (and to some extent exclusively) indigenous. Such readings ignore the at times fraught pathways and power struggles that underpin decision making and community governance systems. Assumptions about cultural distinctiveness imply the homogeneity of ethnic and culturally defined groups; development programs emerging from this paradigm tend to reinforce a racial project in which specific indigenous actors and groups are distinct and separate from others. Orin Starn's call to rethink market relations, race relations, and culture has been answered partially, because this ethnodevelopment approach treats indigenous identity as an attractive one. Yet it continues to downplay dynamic, modern, and syncretic indigenous identities. Aspects of Andeanism reappear when Indians' "insertion" into the market is portrayed as if the market were somehow novel to them. Because indigenous people are still treated as distinct from other citizens and separate from wider social relations, ethnic groups are expected to perform cultural distinctiveness to gain access to resources (compare Hale 2002). Neither Andeanism nor this essentializing version of ethnodevelopment foregrounds indigenous negotiation of power relations associated with diverse economies in postcolonial contexts. While promising indigenous populations a transformed role in Andean racial formations and global socioeconomic development, such policies actually represent a further reworking of what White (2002) calls the racial projects of development.

Ethnodevelopment and Andean Indians II:
Tales of Empowerment and Connectivity

Compared with the essentialized form of ethnodevelopment policy outlined above, the one we describe here is predicated on more flexible notions of culture and spatiality and tends to downplay, if not ignore, the concept of social capital as a guiding principle in development planning and practice. Established in a number of Andean locations, this flexible approach to ethnodevelopment has resulted from intersecting efforts by state functionaries, social movements, and NGOs to rework indigenous livelihoods and income security. It articulates concerns with indigenous rights, structural constraints, the fight against racism, beneficiary self-identification, trans- and multiscalar connections, and interethnic and cross-class relations.

This latter model is also more in tune with many explanations that activists in indigenous organizations offer for their socioeconomic situation, and their visions of the way indigenous cultures and communities are embedded in wider networks and interactions. In workshops in Ecuador, for example, indigenous and Afro-Ecuadorian participants have stressed the need for legalization of access to land and water, projects for social and technical infrastructure, and credit to boost local financial systems.[49] Low-income Indian villagers are concerned about limited access to land, small livestock herds, unmet basic needs, and lack of attention from development projects (Hentschel and Waters 2002). Moreover, indigenous confederations have explained these problems in terms of economic exclusion and colonial legacies within a political economy that systematically bars them from economic security and social recognition (land tenure, access to adequate health care and education, and so on).

Likewise, indigenous leaders usually blame racism rather than vulnerability for their disadvantage in modern Andean societies.[50] Although national and international human rights legislation has been passed banning racism against indigenous people (Stamatopoulou 1994; Tennant 1994), Indians continue to face everyday forms of discrimination. In Bolivia and Ecuador, middle-class and low-income Indians are often fearful when circulating in white-mestizo spaces or dealing with white-mestizo people (de la Torre 1999). Racial discrimination pervades Andean indigenous people's experiences in urban and rural areas, shaping choices of job, location, and marriage partner (de la Torre 1999, 107; also Weismantel 2001; Weismantel and Eisenman 1998).[51]

Finally, many indigenous movements highlight the multiscalar and multisited character of livelihoods and political imaginations. For instance, the Confederation of Indigenous Nationalities of Ecuador recently described its actions within a regional context of struggle: "We indigenous peoples are one of the main forces for change in Latin America. From the Chiapas plains to the South American Andes, we have organized and struggled for respect of our basic ancestral rights. And we have provided examples of bravery and commitment . . . to all the peoples of the world."[52]

Indigenous-movement leaders that picture livelihoods at multiple scales share a geographical imagination with a range of multilateral staff, INGOs, and bilateral agencies. Cultural Survival, for instance, abandoned local, community-scale development in the 1980s, criticizing its limited capacity for change (Fox 1998, 132–33). Other INGOs, such as the Inter-American Foundation, put community development firmly within a wider political-economic map (Healy 2000), as did World Bank staffers who advocated broader notions of social capital (see Bebbington et al. 2004). Likewise, indigenous leaders of major movements have highlighted the vital contribution of Indian small farmers to national food supplies, welcoming the opportunity to improve markets while guaranteeing income. Other indigenous leaders have spoken of opportunities for exploring export markets. According to CONAIE's external affairs spokesperson, Indians propose to "open [up] spaces in which [they] can also make [an] offer to an external market that helps the country directly."[53] Although ethnodevelopment has addressed issues of professional skill building, questions of land titling and productivity remain central and integrally related to indigenous development possibilities. Accordingly, indigenous well-being involves university training, events to promote cultural identity, and the production of new ranges of craft goods that can be marketed in new ways (Stephen 1991; Rappaport and Gow 1997; Carrasco, Iturralde, and Uquillas 1999). This development aims to generate a surplus by engaging with the market while avoiding dependencies (Patiño 1996).

This more flexible approach to ethnodevelopment seeks to identify project beneficiaries from the bottom up—by defining Indian identity in relation to personal commitment to a specific agenda or by an institution's position in the transnational indigenous-affairs circuit. For example, in choosing indigenous beneficiaries for scholarships, funding organizations identified potential students variously by language, community origin, political involvement, and aspirations (Laurie, Andolina, and Radcliffe 2003). Also, SWISSAID has worked in the Andes on sustainable agriculture for decades, in effect helping thousands of poor mestizo and Indian farmers, without targeting indigenous peoples specifically.[54] In a recent policy, the UK bilateral agency DfID stressed indigenous people's economic, social, and cultural rights, as well as their multifaceted livelihoods in contexts where they are relatively disempowered and likely to be disadvantaged (Bourne 2001).

Increasing indigenous people's decision-making power, especially through formal and representative politics, is another element of this second approach to ethnodevelopment. Project strategies have included strengthening Indian organizations and consolidating social networks. The Dutch Organization for International Development Cooperation's (NOVIB) rights-based development, mentioned above, exemplifies this approach, also found in Bolivia's former secretariat for ethnic affairs, which hoped to "strengthen [indigenous] capacity . . . through the knowledge of rights, planning, development questions. The basic notion was to strengthen indigenous citizenship [and] participation."[55] Over the past fifteen years, Andean indigenous leaders have become more likely to be elected democratically, possess a university education, and have a national-global vision. Projects grounded in this version of indigenous development policy have supported a wide spectrum of indigenous organizations, ranging from those based in unions to "culturalist" ones. The Latin American regional Fondo Indígena offers development assistance directly to these diverse groups, bypassing the state and NGOs.[56]

This version of ethnodevelopment also strives to break down racial and class stereotypes and to challenge the racism embedded in many Andean areas. In providing a rationale for indigenous development in Ecuador, a Quichua development professional noted, "You know that here in Quito there is a lot of racism, a lot of domination [of Indians], a lot of exploitation. And we aren't considered to be human beings, but animals. They treat us like beasts of burden."[57] In Andean countries, ethnodevelopment initiatives have faced persistent racism in everyday interactions and broader societal discourses. One example was the uproar after the press defined PRODEPINE's indigenous development experts on professional salaries as "*ponchos dorados*" (golden ponchos), illustrating Ecuadorian society's hesitance to recognize indigenous people's skills.[58] Projects that generate awareness and practical applications of indigenous peoples' long-established practices of agricultural experimentation and sustainable development are one antiracist solution (Calvo et al. 1994; Healy 1996; FENOCIN 2000). Another strategy is establishing a feeling of pride and self-worth among Indians marginalized by centuries of racism. In Bolivia, Aymara leaders emphasize this component: "We're in [a] process toward Indian pride, because the blacks [in the United States] did it at one stage. [They said] 'Black is beautiful.'"[59] In sum, different approaches to tackling discrimination coexist in the Andes, including interculturalism and the fight against racism, although the latter is not as prevalent as it could be (Laurie and Bonnett 2002).

Finally, more-flexible approaches to ethnodevelopment treat indigenous culture as a basis for creative thinking outside of standard development solutions, moving beyond simplicities of authentic culture versus assimilation. This overlaps with indigenous-movement views of archaeological sites as part of ongoing traditions, not as museum pieces to be left untouched. In southern Ecuador, indigenous representatives criticized heritage officials for halting indigenous use of archaeological sites in cultural rituals.[60] In Bolivia, the raised-field system was successfully adapted as modern peasant organizations rehabilitated ancient farm beds (Kleymeyer 1993). Based on this approach, the Inter-American Foundation has worked to release the "cultural energy" in grassroots popular culture, and a former Bolivian ethnic secretariat representative asserted, "This tradition is alive; that's to say the knowledge of how to manage diversity [and] climatic irregularities."[61] Rather than focusing on unchanging indigenous culture, this approach to development-with-identity has highlighted the expressive, flexible, and constructed nature of cultural identity and subjectivity in the Andes (Healy 1996).

Based on indigenous participation in decision making and culturally innovative change, this paradigm of indigenous development has set a broad agenda. It has assumed that successful indigenous economic activities depend upon structural measures to open markets for indigenous products and services, whether in food production or export markets (Núñez del Prado and Pacheco 2001). It has raised questions about the place of indigenous groups in racist, exclusionary societies, where Indians have to make empowering connections with each other and strategic alliances with multiethnic and varied class groups. It entails a racial project that challenges racist exclusion, builds on multiethnic ties, and establishes a rights-based framework. By examining the development process from a historical perspective sensitive to race and class hierarchies, this perspective offers a distinctive challenge to development planners and Andean societies. The appointment of anthropologists and INGO advocates to multilateral and bilateral agencies has undoubtedly contributed to a more pliable understanding of indigenous cultures, as well as permitted greater dialogue across institutional spaces.[62] Actors' recognition of their personal displacement from the center of social hierarchies (whether racial, national, or professional) appears to contribute further to this paradigm. Many European advocates for indigenous peoples, for example, come from nondominant populations in their own countries (including Catalans, Scots, and Flemish) (Brysk 1996, 47).

Beyond Social Capital and Poverty

Said former Bolivian vice-president Víctor Hugo Cárdenas, "This conception of prioritizing economic growth to solve the problem of rural poverty, indigenous poverty—this just won't work. [Rather], there's a revaluation of the social; there's a new vision of poverty."[63] This revaluation has articulated concepts of culture and social capital within distinct policy paradigms of indigenous development; instead of floating free in an undifferentiated global field, these two concepts are reworked as they encounter grounded and historically powerful cultural meanings and racial categories in the Andes. Situating our discussion of culture and social capital firmly within an approach that attempts to unravel the "color blindness of development" (White 2002), we have interpreted transnational ethnodevelopment paradigms as racial projects that engage with and coproduce Ecuadorian and Bolivian racial formations. Our consideration of race in Andean ethnodevelopment differs from Charles Hale's (2002) discussion of neoliberal multiculturalism in that it underscores the active roles played by indigenous peoples and others in shaping contemporary development and wider racial projects.

Culturally appropriate development policy appears, in the Andes, to present solutions to problems by filling a "gap"; but as Shore and Wright point out, gaps are "already filled with moral values and preconceptions" (1997, 21). The first ethnodevelopment approach described in this chapter has aimed to fill (perceived or actual) gulfs between indigenous social capital, on the one hand, and economic markets, on the other. Although it opens conceptual doorways for incorporating indigenous groups into modern development, it also masks multiple axes of difference such as gender, age, generation, sexuality, and nationality (de Lauretis 1987; Shohat 1998). For example, in the Andes, communal patriarchies continue to subsume indigenous women into class and ethnic politics, disregarding gender concerns (Mallon 1995; Radcliffe 2002). Similarly, it elides questions about the negative aspects of ethnocultural networks and communities, in which entrenched identities may justify ethnoracial violence, or when economic niches occupied by ethnically identified merchants result in fierce competition between group members (Kyle 1999).[64] More diffuse, but arguably more widespread, are racially discriminatory practices against black or indigenous Latin Americans, whose social networks are often blocked by mestizo and urban actors (Wade 1997; J. Fox 1996). Actors marginalized by racial hierarchies (as well as by gender, culture, and location) are excluded from facilitative social networks and political empowerment, thus raising questions about the downside of social capital (Portes and Landolt 2000).

The second ethnodevelopment approach discussed in this chapter relies more on cross-cultural and multiethnic networks to foment political and economic empowerment. From local government offices in rural Mexico to NGO workers in highland Bolivia and multistranded links in Ecuador's Amazonian lowlands, connections that stretch beyond the local level permit development efforts to move across scales, assisting indigenous access to income and empowerment (J. Fox 1996; Bebbington and Perreault 1999; Perreault 2003). The small town of Guamote, Ecuador, exemplifies how development processes were consolidated through the mutual assistance of indigenous, NGO, municipal, and donor actors across ethnic and cultural lines (Bebbington and Perreault 1999, 415), which is discussed in chapter 3. Crucially, coalitions of actors within indigenous policy networks transcend racial discrimination and segregation to some extent.[65] This more flexible model of ethnodevelopment also notes the intercultural character of indigenous economic activity, based on what Nederveen Pieterse calls "rainbow social and cultural capital" (Nederveen Pieterse 2000). The famous Otavaleño textile traders in Ecuador, for example, skillfully use Indian identity to generate wealth by crossing ethnic and national boundaries in searching for customers and points of sale (Kyle 1999). Certainly, cultural and ethnic groups—especially in the context of racism and marginalization—have created rich networks and forms of identification that transcend local areas (Healy 1996; Egan 1996; L. Smith 2002; Perreault 2003).

As with the notion of ethnic culture, the concept of social capital—despite its current and highly contested ubiquity in the development field—takes on concrete meaning when articulated by specific actors and narratives at regional and other scales. In terms of development, "the Andes" represent a node for transnational connections among ideas and organizations. Networks involved in indigenous development, especially those associated with grassroots efforts and INGOs, are highly mobile, moving between national development agencies, international workshops, local activists and organizations, and multilateral agency meetings. Regardless of their institutional base and professional position, transnational actors have chosen to work *across* expectations of ethnic difference or institutional hierarchies in ways that have often been favorable to indigenous needs at local and national levels. Diverse social actors have also been willing to position themselves—politically, individually, and collectively—to link across national, class, institutional, and ethnic and racial boundaries. Transnational indigenous affairs circuits thus operate with frequent crossings of institutional, professional, and national borders (see map 5).

Such development practices challenge the stereotype of indigenous populations as rooted in remote rural villages or uninterested in pursuing education. They show that the complex politics of representation in transnational circuits is not merely a question of how indigenous people or advocacy organizations might rectify stereotyped images of Indians in the global media, tipping into crisis over who can or should speak about and for Indians (Brysk 1996, 52; Warren and Jackson 2002). Development thinking that expects or encourages cross-cultural coordination and flexible group boundaries challenges Andean

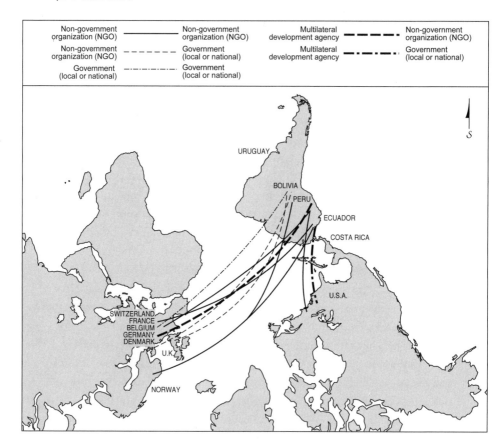

Non-government organization (NGO)	————————	Non-government organization (NGO)		Multilateral development agency	━ ━ ━ ━ ━ ━	Non-government organization (NGO)
Non-government organization (NGO)	– – – – – –	Government (local or national)		Multilateral development agency	━ ·— ━ ·— ━ ·	Government (local or national)
Government (local or national)	—·—··—··—·.	Government (local or national)				

MAP 5. Transnational connections around indigenous development discussed in chapter 2.

The linkages shown here are "South–North," as the chapter focuses on the inter-institutional connections that have facilitated the recent discursive integration of the concepts of social capital and Andeanism. Social capital has been conceptualized largely in the global North, entering the Andes with current ethnodevelopment policy paradigms. While not a wholly indigenous construct, Andeanism has an established resonance within the region that predates social capital's conceptual introduction into Andean countries like Ecuador and Bolivia.

racism more profoundly than thinking that is more rigid or static. But how do these competing visions of indigenous development engage with new territorialities, natural resource access and control, higher education, and gender relations? In the remaining chapters we explore these issues in turn, illustrating in depth the complex and sometimes contradictory ways in which these paradigms of ethnodevelopment, and their representations of indigenous people, are enacted and deployed.

CHAPTER 3

ROBERT ANDOLINA, SARAH A. RADCLIFFE, AND NINA LAURIE

Development in Place: Ethnic Culture
in the Transnational Local

The changes in discourses and networks outlined in previous chapters illustrate how globalization alters imaginative and material geographies.[1] One crucial shift in this regard is articulation around *local* places and scales. While actors have differed in how they value localness, consensus emerged around the local as a "normative place" (Murray 2006, 49–50) that is good or appropriate for development and cultural reproduction. Localness thus gained a transnational hegemonic status at the nexus of state formation, social movement activity, and international development practice. Specific spatial practices define, construct, and maintain the local. By *spatial practices* we refer to the production and reproduction of social relations that make particular locations characteristic and enduring (Lefebvre 1991). In the Andes, local space making has resulted from complex interactions between indigenous peoples and others; it also entailed representation of the local in relation to nonlocal scales. Due to variegated access to resources, decision-making powers, and political legitimacy, ongoing tensions inevitably arise in these multiethnic and multiscalar relations. Some of these tensions stem from indigenous-movement struggles for "counter-spaces" (Lefebvre 1991, 63), where subaltern groups attempt to produce their own distinctive places and livelihoods.

In the 1990s, as the failure of orthodox neoliberal economics to reduce poverty was acknowledged, development policy increasingly promoted social inclusion and good governance around what we term *social neoliberalism*. Social neoliberalism assumes that concerns such as cultural pluralism, environmental protection, gender equity, and popular participation are compatible with market economics and self-help agency. It also posits market-based managerial and technical skills are compatible with, and perhaps even optimal for, nonprofit organizations and institutions. Development of these skills is often cited as key to strengthening institutions and building capacity. Thus, development policy becomes increasingly social, while social and public organizations are expected to become increasingly efficient and entrepreneurial.

As transnationalized governmentalities unfolded in the Andes, they stressed the local as optimal for achieving development objectives. Multilateral and bilateral agencies came to see the devolution of state administration as instrumental in executing social neoliberalism; this move would improve public services, make governance more accountable, and increase equity in the distribution of resources, especially for neglected or remote peoples (Leftwich 1996; Davis 2002, 20; Radcliffe, Laurie, and Andolina 2002a, 292–93; Keese and Freire 2006, 114). National and international NGOs rooted in grassroots development traditions had previously seen local communities as proper sites for development, but they turned to official decentralization as a potentially democratizing process that would give local communities greater political influence.[2] National governments increasingly viewed successful decentralization as a way to decrease their burdens in a context of austerity while at the same time increasing their legitimacy with their citizens and with international agencies (Van Cott 2000a)—even if they risked losing some control over resources, functions, and policy agendas.[3]

Indigenous movements have often conceived of the local as significant for cultural reproduction and effective political participation, leading campaigns for local self-determination and land security (CONAIE 1994b; CSUTCB 1992; CIDOB 1993b; see also Lucero 2003). Along with these efforts, changes in national and international laws facilitated the articulation of indigenous-movement agendas with decentralized political frameworks. ILO Convention 169, for instance, granted rights to "indigenous peoples," a subject it identifies according to specific localized territories. Other actors have reinforced indigenous-local articulations: multilateral agencies like the World Bank and IADB saw local expressions of indigenous culture as a form of social capital with the potential to build other kinds of capital (Portes and Landolt 2000, as cited in Fine 2001). State actors expected indigenous territories to be small in scale and believed that indigenous rights and multicultural principles are best implemented locally.

Two adjustments underpinned this governmentality. First, nonstate actors steadily took on governing roles, as states and civil-society actors were conceptualized as partners in governance and individuals were perceived as subjects with rights and autonomy. The incorporation of civil-society actors would provide a way of governing *through* such autonomous subjects (see Sending and

Neumann 2006, 661) while enhancing administrative efficiency, social inclusion, and policy effectiveness. Second, states reconfigured their geographic control over resources and populations, with localization perceived as best for this kind of governance. Redeployment of state power to local scales played a key part in this, as did a "graduated sovereignty," in which national governance adapted to international pressures through new geographical arrangements that treated citizens differently by population group (Ong 2000).

In an ethnographically informed account, the remainder of this chapter outlines the spatial imaginaries and practices circulating among diverse actors and institutions involved in the production of the local, through linkages between development policies and indigenous movement agendas. First, we examine connections between state reforms and transnational policy agendas, interpreting official decentralization in light of a flexible governmentality that incorporated some participatory and multicultural principles. Next, we turn to illustrating how Andean indigenous leaders have negotiated and appropriated state and donor-led decentralization policies. We follow this with an examination of indigenous leaders' pursuit of counterspaces that contest the geographies and powers of such decentralization. The final section discusses the implications and effects of these processes. "Local" places are multiscalar, by virtue of spatial differentiations within local places and by way of their coproduction by regional, national, and international actors.

Decentralization and Local State Formations in the Andes

Local spaces are often seen as bounded enclosures devoid of outside influences. In contrast, our concept of the local is based on intersections of diverse flows (also see Massey and Jess 1995). In this "extroverted" sense of place, a location's uniqueness derives from the specific combination of social and power relations brought together contingently, as well as the (changing) cultures of the people who occupy spaces in and around that locale. In Ecuador and Bolivia, dominant social geographies have concealed and naturalized racial ideologies: for example, in the association of indigenous populations with mountains, the "wild" jungle, or remote rural areas (Orlove 1993; Radcliffe and Westwood 1996; Wade 1997).[4] Concrete power relations built on and reinforced such divisions through exclusion from urban spaces and services and through the exploitation of indigenous labor and consumption. These patterns generally reproduced inequities and dependencies (see Radcliffe and Westwood 1996; Korovkin 2001; Weismantel 2001).

Both countries also have a long history of state centralization, creating a rigid administrative hierarchy from national to local. The central government appointed officials for each lower scale of government, and these usually wielded more power than their elected counterparts. From 1950 to 1980, Ecuador and Bolivia operated through governmentalities based on nationalist modernization. This privileged the national scale as a space of governance and production: economic policy focused on the domestic market, while political power was concentrated in national governments who were responsible for social integration, pursued through vertical, corporatist structures. This approach also privileged the state and a narrow range of experts as agents, who largely acted on society as a set of objects (see Healy 2001a, chaps. 2 and 3).[5]

Changes underway since 1980 have increased the array and altered the roles of actors involved in producing the local. These changes were both cause and consequence of political democratization and neoliberal adjustments. Predicated on assumptions that state intervention in the economy inhibited economic growth and caused the debt crisis in Latin America, neoliberal policies aimed to instill fiscal discipline while reducing trade barriers, government subsidies, state-generated employment, and public-sector ownership of the means of production (see Conaghan and Malloy 1994). When linked to democratization, a shift in governmentality began with the recognition of new subjects as part of a growing civil society of increasingly autonomous actors, premised in part on the notion that nonstate actors were more responsive and nimble than a top-heavy state. The spatial dimension of this shift, in the form of state decentralization, came after such redefinition of subjects was underway. Decentralization thus entailed a remapping of dichotomous neoliberal assumptions about the relative quality of state (bad) and nonstate (good) actors, on to a scalar divide *within* the state: "A national level, characterized as inefficient, prone to corruption, stagnant and a barrier to modern change ... and a local level ... accorded the attributes of being more dynamic—in which an emerging assemblage of ... civic organizations, linked into the benefits of decentralization, could further democratic change and development" (Slater 2003, 617).

In Bolivia, rural development practice relied increasingly on NGOs, as neoliberal policies enacted in 1985 "led to a significant reduction in government spending but an increase in international development agency funding" (Kohl 2003, 321). These international agencies, moreover, linked up with NGOs "perceived to be more honest, efficient, and responsive to funders' agendas than was government" (321).[6] As a result, the number of Bolivian NGOs rose from 100 to 530 between 1980 and 1993 (Sandoval 1993, as cited in Kohl 2003, 320).

Although dependence on NGOs in Ecuador grew less dramatically, the results were similar. As shown by Arcos and Palomeque (1997), economic crises and reduced government spending combined with international agencies' preferences to generate a marked growth in NGOs: 80 percent of NGOs ever created in Ecuador were born between 1980 and 1995 (25–28). In both countries, some of these NGOs were rooted in more or less radical political traditions and supported a new cadre of indigenous and peasant leaders under incipient democracies (Ramón 1992; Torzano and Exeni 1994; Bebbington 2000). Drawing on this support in the 1990s, indigenous movements compelled national governments to recognize indigenous rights to land, territory, and participation, including the right to self-representation through autonomous organizations.

Political and administrative decentralization in Bolivia and Ecuador followed and built on these shifts. Legislation and policy formulation depended on extensive bilateral and multilateral support (or pressure) within a broad exchange of information about best practices. Bolivia's policy took account of previous decentralization experiences in Colombia, Peru, Argentina, Chile, and Mexico, while Ecuador's also accounted for reforms in Spain, Eastern Europe, and the United States. Both countries relied on advice and financing from the World Bank, the Inter-American Development Bank, the UN Development Program, and various bilateral agencies.[7] In addition, international conventions and norms conceptualized indigenous rights and provided a discursive template for national legislation and ratification (Van Cott 2000a, 2002). In this globalized field, actors adapted decentralized territoriality in the Andes to prevailing transnational ideas of citizen participation, multiculturalism, and effective government.[8]

Bolivia's decentralization, enacted primarily in 1994 and 1995 through the Law of Popular Participation (LPP) and the Law of Administrative Decentralization, was deliberately crafted to center on a municipal scale rather than a departmental scale. This was in spite of—or because of—the fact that most social mobilization for decentralization prior to these laws came from departmental-scale "civic committees." Many Bolivian reformers viewed the civic committees as elitist, or even corrupt, and feared that department-scale decentralization would undercut goals of social equity, participation, and transparency. In addition, a history of regionalist discontent—in a country that borders five others and had lost considerable territory to its neighbors—generated fears that territorial disunity or even secession might ensue should significant power be scaled to the departments (Slater 2003, 624–26; also see Van Cott 2000a, 138).[9] Thus, a municipally centered decentralization allowed the Bolivian state, in principle, to be sovereign, flexible, and inclusive all at once.

This rationale is borne out in specific elements of the LPP. It extended the municipality as a governing unit throughout Bolivian territory on a scale smaller than the province but larger than the canton. Going from the smallest to largest subnational administrative units, Bolivia consists of parishes, cantons, municipalities, provinces, and departments. The LPP also transferred 20 percent of the national budget to municipalities (on a per capita basis), with a mayor and council to be elected directly by all eligible voters. To generate more-accountable governance and foster equitable resource allocation, the LPP recognized and incorporated previously established community organizations as Organizaciones Territoriales de Base (OTBs, Grassroots Territorial Organizations). Their members would coordinate municipal development planning, and their representatives would serve on legally authorized oversight committees (Comités de Vigilancia) to control municipal spending. OTBs were also expected to tap their constituencies for labor on public works projects, now the responsibility of municipal governments (Kohl 2003, 317–20).[10]

Lastly, many, if not most, of the OTBs were indigenous or peasant communities who were officially allowed to retain and draw on their own structures and practices as one way to operationalize indigenous rights and cultural diversity. Another way of locally institutionalizing cultural difference was framed by the 1996 provision for original community lands (Tierras Comunitarias de Orígen—TCOs). This provision was part of a wider agrarian reform law also meant to "stimulate capitalist agricultural productivity" (Albó 2002, 80). The TCO provided collective property title for indigenous peoples, which, in principle, is indivisible, inalienable, and tax exempt. Such collective space is typically viewed by indigenous-movement organizations as indispensable for indigenous self-determination (Albó 2002, 80; Benton 1999, 88), but in the broader Bolivian governing scheme, it was perceived to lie within municipal jurisdictions, which can limit indigenous political reach and effective autonomy (Van Cott 2002, 55–56).

Although Ecuadorian decentralization was more gradual and less coherent than Bolivia's, it echoed the latter's embrace of governmentalities informed by social neoliberalism and a revaluation of the local. Going from the smallest to largest subnational administrative unit, Ecuador has parishes, municipalities, and provinces. In contrast to Bolivia, where municipalities encompass various cantons, in Ecuador the two are largely equivalent. Concrete legislation on decentralization began in 1990, when the Law of Sectional Development mandated that 10 percent of the national budget flow to a local development fund.[11] The municipalities received 80 percent of this fund, while the provinces received

20 percent; international agencies provided one-quarter of the municipal disbursement only, totaling $208 million in 1990 (Moncayo 2004, 92–93).[12] A 1993 law asserted decentralization's general importance in "state modernization" and established the possibility that "community sectors" could have a "self-managing" role in providing services and other economic activity formerly reserved for the state (see Segarra 1997; Torres 1999a, 30–31).[13]

Following major political crises and popular mobilization in 1997, further decentralization was fashioned in a more comprehensive (if still relatively ambiguous) manner. The 1997 Law of Administrative Decentralization and Social Participation and Title XI of the 1998 constitution allowed for the transfer of most state functions to local governments, earmarked 15 percent of the national budget for them, and granted municipal governments the powers to draft ordinances and collect fees. They also adopted citizen participation and responsibility as core principles: the 1997 law recognized neighborhood committees, parish boards, and indigenous and Afro-Ecuadorian organizations as interlocutors between municipal governments and the population, while the 1998 constitution called for the popular election of parish boards and permitted indigenous and Afro-Ecuadorian territories to be created as a new form of local government. In addition, municipal governments were required by law to form advisory commissions and development plans that guarantee a voice in decision making for representatives of social (including indigenous) organizations. Such participation is often extended to development NGOs, who in turn rely on international funding (Keese and Freire 2006, 117–18). In practice, civil-society organizations and municipalities frequently pushed beyond Ecuadorian law, increasing skills through transnational networking while coordinating with each other to design local development policies and participatory institutions (Ortiz 1999, 68–69).

Decentralization in Ecuador entailed a flexible rescaling of state authority. The central government maintained the prerogative to transfer functions to the local level but avoided approving legislation that would grant provincial or indigenous territorial autonomy. In part, this is because of disagreement among political elites (Van Cott 2002), but it may also be due to fears of losing tax revenues should such governments become too autonomous or powerful over their territories.[14] Concretely, the central government retained the authority to decide the extent and pace of devolution to local scales based on the degree to which each local government demonstrated the ability to handle new functions, as part of a formal request of transfer (Keese and Freire 2006).[15] Likewise, the Ecuadorian congress did not approve follow-up legislation to enable constitutionally recognized indigenous territorial circumscriptions to become local governments. In contrast, Bolivia had "original community" land legislation in place since 1996.

Although it was more deliberate in Bolivia than in Ecuador, decentralization in both countries was designed to use relatively autonomous civil-society organizations as a counterweight to municipal corruption and elite co-option and as a means to mobilize voluntary human resources to complement funds transferred to municipalities. Another assumption of this legislation was that professional NGOs, who had been working on community development extensively for ten years in the wake of neoliberal economic reforms (see above), would offer assistance to municipal governments and indigenous organizations in their areas of expertise and seek additional funding from international sources (see Kohl 2003; Keese and Freire 2006).

Decentralization in Ecuador and Bolivia also embedded local places in multiscalar, multiethnic, and inter-institutional relations. Within municipalities, for example, most local indigenous organizations are submunicipal in scale and must come together to co-govern the municipality as a whole, along with other nongovernmental agencies, municipal government functionaries, and elected parish authorities. Furthermore, Bolivian municipalities coordinate with national and departmental Popular Participation secretariats/ministries, while Ecuadorian ones must negotiate the transfer of funds and responsibilities with the central government. In addition, all players involved in decentralization may receive funding or other kinds of assistance from international agencies. Finally, as indigenous and nonindigenous people interacted more intensely with each other, new local relations were expected to be multiethnic. This interaction would potentially erode racialized urban-rural geographies, especially as Bolivia's 311 and Ecuador's 218 municipalities now extended through the entire national territory and the accompanying notion of "rural municipality" unraveled the conventional association of municipal with urban (see Radcliffe, Laurie, and Andolina 2002a, 289).

Indigenous Movements and Official Municipalities

Implementation of this legislation reconfigured local governmental formations in Ecuador and Bolivia through a complex mix of adaptation and appropriation. Indigenous leaders sought to democratize and diversify sociopolitical relations, intensify the coherence of indigenous cultures, and increase access to resources that might improve livelihoods.[16] Nongovernmental and international agencies deepened their involvement in municipal processes with a combination of financial and technical assistance. They shared the objectives of indigenous organizations to some degree but emphasized efficient and transparent administration. In line with the governmentality described above, such administrative concerns were consciously directed at local governments *and* local civil-society actors—like indigenous organizations—who might co-govern local political spaces and represent otherwise marginalized constituents.

The German agency GTZ, for example, made "Democracy, Civil Society, and Public Administration" a "priority area," which it sees as involving "cooperation between state and civil society . . . in government decision-making processes [and] building capacity of civil society organizations to plan and implement development projects and self-help activities" (GTZ 2004a, 6, 7). DANIDA, the Danish bilateral agency, adopted a similar approach in Bolivia. "Our program . . . is rooted in a double strategy. On the one hand, we strengthen the new entities [municipalities] created by the Popular Participation Law; and then, by way of NGOs, we strengthen grassroots organizations to fill the spaces created by the municipalities."[17]

This model of local governance presupposed new forms of agency and novel fields of interaction. Municipal governments would become conduits to enable the myriad of involved players to act in concert and become nimble promoters of local economic development, through innovative ideas and selective interventions that facilitate investment and competitiveness. A Swiss-sponsored program in Bolivia framed this ideal as "the productive municipality" (Rivero 2001; Ayo 2003), while the Netherlands Development Organization (SNV) created a local development planning guide for Ecuador because "municipalities have not regarded themselves as coordinators and facilitators of local development" (SNV 2004, 2). On the nongovernmental side, development organizations that previously operated at a community scale in rural areas would extend their participatory planning knowledge to the municipal scale, increasing urban and rural linkages as they did so. Indigenous organizations would move away from making demands and toward adept policymaking and resource administration, while retaining practices of mobilizing their institutional and cultural networks for development projects. This vision of the local was accompanied by a tacit consensus around the racial project that it entailed. Interculturalism was widely embraced but largely interpreted as including all cultural and social groups in a common, nondiscriminatory political space. Specific participants were free to advocate on ethnic grounds, and preexisting indigenous organizations were officially recognized if not legally registered as agents. But this understanding of multiculturalism implied some degree of integration, if not uniformity, via municipal identities, as well as both national and transnational norms of election and administration. Indigenous movement objectives and racialized local spaces sometimes challenged or undermined this project, however.

In Ecuador, the formation of local governments was patterned by the vague and patchy character of decentralizing legislation, which established possibilities for local "good governance" but "lacked . . . clear requirements or incentives for municipal governments to operate more transparently or to foster citizen participation" (J. Cameron 2005, 372).[18] Moreover, the central government retained the authority to decide, on a case-by-case basis, whether the municipality in question held the capacity to carry out functions proposed in any requests.[19] Although this regime offered few guarantees to indigenous or other organizations seeking to appropriate local government in Ecuador, in practice its very lack of rigidity left room to maneuver and negotiate.

Indigenous organizations associated with CONAIE did just that, remaining a step ahead of national legislation in local innovation. This created what many Ecuadorian social movements called "alternative" forms of local governance. These were permissible under the legal framework but exceeded its requirements for participation and inclusion. After a few key victories in the 1996 elections, councilors and mayors representing the Pachakutik Party gained a majority in twenty-seven municipalities in mid-2000.[20] They institutionalized goals of active participation, interculturalism, and sustainable development through participatory assemblies and committees. The municipality of Guamote (Chimborazo province), for example, formed a cantonal parliament that carried out an eighteen-month participatory workshop involving multiple local associations and over four thousand individuals. It defined development goals and means, then aggregated these into a local plan that provided a picture of communities' self-identified needs.[21]

These participatory bodies went beyond formal legislation, which only called for a civil-society advisory body to municipal authorities.[22] They also concretized the indigenous movement's search for representation outside of formal political parties and drew together a series of its prior concepts and experiences. At local scales, indigenous assemblies have governed and planned development projects in relatively marginal rural areas while challenging racism and exploitation by local elites (Korovkin 2001; Pallares 2002). At wider scales, indigenous movements have called internal assemblies or broader "people's parliaments" to discuss strategies, hold leaders accountable, and address urgent matters (Andolina 2003; Lucero 2001; Van Cott 2002). In this sense, Pachakutik's creation of participatory, intercultural local governments is an infusion of previous social-movement struggles and practices into municipal space. Two-time CONAIE president Luis Macas affirmed as much when strategizing CONAIE's entry into electoral politics in 1996: "[As] our proposal is elaborated from below . . . we need to prioritize something that is important for us: local governments" (Muñoz 1999, 43).

The juxtaposition of slippery legislation and alternative municipalities in Ecuador made the municipalities a site of attraction and opportunity for various development organizations. Several internationally funded Ecuadorian NGOs networked to form the Local Democracy and Development Group, specifically to support alternative municipalities led by Pachakutik mayors following the 1996 elections.[23] These internationally funded NGOs, along with other NGOs that had worked with indigenous organizations on grassroots development in rural communities, sought to accompany indigenous leaders in scaling their activities over wider areas, with the aspiration of increasing their effectiveness and legitimacy by working through municipalities: "After 1996, when Pachakutik participated in elections, indigenous and social organizations were directly assuming candidacies and running municipal administrations. For us these are important experiences that we are granting priority to. . . . This marked a point of transition for NGOs, who shifted from very specific, short-term projects to something broader in terms of empowerment and democracy."[24]

The Dutch agency SNV was drawn to these alternative locales, too, as sites for realizing its principles of participation and inclusion, which it felt would be facilitated by indigenous cultural norms: "One nice thing is they have three principles in Quichua culture: amaquilla, amallulla y amashua,"—don't lie, don't be lazy, and don't steal. "These are development principles we should work with, and are really what we are talking about in other contexts, such as fighting corruption or increasing transparency. They also have practices such as collective labor, reciprocity, and social equity that . . . can be foundations of an alternative development model."[25] The World Bank showed its support for this alternative model by authorizing redirection of PRODEPINE funds to fourteen Pachakutik municipalities by the year 2000. Initially, PRODEPINE had only allocated funding to second-tier indigenous organizations, which mainly operated in rural locations.[26]

Convergence around alternative municipalities in Ecuador was also indicated by the widespread support for the Coordinator of Alternative Local Governments (CGLA), created in 2001. CGLA has facilitated exchanges and communication between Pachakutik-led municipalities, held training workshops in local governance practices, and encouraged implementation of Pachakutik's local governance principles (CGLA n.d.). It received considerable bilateral assistance from Norway, Spain, the Netherlands, Germany, Canada, and Sweden. The World Bank provided technical assistance to CGLA, too, as did the Ecuadorian Ministry of Social Welfare. CGLA has also executed projects financed by the national indigenous development council and by the Ecuadorian Local Democracy and Development Group of NGOs; in other instances it has allied with the Ecuadorian NGO Ecological Action (CGLA n.d., 11). The Dutch agency SNV channeled funds to CGLA on the grounds that it was a more democratic entity than the conventional Association of Ecuadorian Municipalities, while a former GTZ functionary suggested that German development actors viewed indigenous movement–run municipalities in Ecuador as advanced, in bringing government "closer to the people" through decentralization.[27]

This kind of support involved complex connectivity between local and global organizations; it sometimes bypassed national-level governmental institutions and sometimes worked through them. Such circuitry also ran through specific municipalities. Guamote's Local Development Committee included indigenous leaders, municipal functionaries, Ecuadorian NGO workers, and local agents of international donors and supporters (Torres 1999b). After serving his mayoral term in Guamote, the indigenous leader Mariano Curicama coordinated a technical team in CODENPE to improve national-municipal government relations through an information-exchange network. This was part of a broader program managed by CODENPE to support "indigenous alternative municipalities," financed with US$400,000 from Spanish bilateral aid and the Ecuadorian government (*El Comercio*, June 21, 2001).[28]

Unlike Ecuadorian decentralization, Bolivian legislation specified the mechanisms, resources, and responsibilities allocated to municipalities and their submunicipal constituents.[29] In exchange for a fixed transfer of funds, each municipality was required to submit annual and five-year development plans; failure to do so would risk having the national government freeze the municipal allocation, an outcome that was especially dire, as municipalities were also expected to take on new responsibilities in social services and infrastructure.[30] Indigenous, peasant, and neighborhood organizations who wished to participate in this regime had to petition for registration as an OTB (grassroots territorial organization) and select OTB representatives to head municipal oversight committees. Also in contrast with Ecuador, where indigenous movements were often a step ahead of the state in reform of local governance, in Bolivia the Law of Popular Participation caught many indigenous leaders by surprise (Ticona and Albó 1997, 282–88).

Indigenous organizations in the Bolivian highlands initially lacked a platform for governance at that scale, in part because many rural areas were not part of municipal territories prior to the law. This situation compelled local actors like indigenous organizations to play catch-up in order to access resources and institutional space promised by the Law of Popular Participation.[31]

At first, many highland indigenous organizations did not want to play at all. The highland indigenous-peasant confederation, CSUTCB, categorically rejected the law. Among other things, it feared homogenization under the status of OTB, which seemingly threatened possibilities for self-identification or for state recognition of preexisting indigenous and peasant organizations. However, it gradually changed its position, and indigenous organizations throughout Bolivia appropriated the law through mobilization, negotiation, and elections.[32] A series of national marches, for example, compelled the Bolivian government to emit a decree recognizing indigenous organizations according to the names they gave themselves, and not just as a generic "OTB." By 1999, over sixteen thousand OTB petitions had been submitted to the offices of the popular participation and indigenous ministries.[33]

Indigenous organizations also pressured the government into devising a category of "Indigenous Municipal District" (DMI), which guaranteed local indigenous organizations a territorial representative on the municipal oversight committee and appointment of an indigenous district *sub-alcalde* (submayor). It also facilitated implementation of bilingual education and participatory development planning through indigenous organizations and community assemblies (Van Cott 2000, 196–97; Medina 2003, 25–26). By 2002, 136 DMIs had been created in Bolivia, and 36 of them completed their own indigenous development plans (Ayo 2003, 141). The DMI of Uru Iruito, in Viacha municipality, was able to revitalize cultural practices and pride through its district development plan (Albó 2004, 62), while DMI Calcha in Vitichi municipality was able to incorporate traditional authorities into the municipal oversight committee and structure indigenous district institutions around participatory assemblies and authority councils rooted in the local ayllu system (Sub-Alcaldia del DMI Calcha 1998, 8–9, 16). The creation and recognition of DMIs explicitly institutionalized a multiscalar local place that marked certain submunicipal zones as ethnically distinct, a segmentation of governance that deviated somewhat from the model of integrative multicultural municipalities described earlier.[34]

In a few cases, such DMIs were able to transform themselves into full municipalities by employing the Ley UPAs (Law of Administrative Political Units), which allows for groups of five thousand or more to form their own municipality if the group is "socioculturally homogenous" (Ayo 2003, 142). Jesús de Mach-aqa, a highland area often noted for its distinctive indigenous culture, moved from being a DMI within Viacha to being its own municipality in 2004. Local indigenous leaders secured national authorization for this after a long process of negotiation with central government authorities, in which they "regularly displayed their cultural richness to get outside support" and visibly met the criteria of the Ley UPAs (Colque 2005, 8). Finally, indigenous people increased their influence through election to municipal councils and mayorships. By 2002, 62 percent of municipalities had an indigenous mayor and an indigenous ma-jority on the municipal council (Albó and Quispe 2004, 140–41, 147). In 2004, eighteen mayoral elections were won by politically "autonomous" indigenous representatives, who for the first time were allowed to run as candidates in elections outside the framework of political parties. These representatives have begun to redefine their municipalities according to local indigenous norms and institutions (*La Razón*, June 20, 2007).[35]

Development agencies responded to Bolivia's mix of tighter legislation and perceived deficits among grassroots organizations by helping indigenous or-ganizations catch up to decentralization's opportunities and challenges, or by filling in the remaining gaps between official requirements and actors' skills or desires. Although these development strategies responded to the Bolivian context, they also emanated from transnational paradigms of good governance, informed by social neoliberalism and faith in the local scale as a stimulant of democracy and development.

One example is the Municipal Democracy Support Program (PADEM) of the Swiss bilateral agency COSUDE. It promoted "democratic values and devel-opment equity" and aimed to "strengthen municipal governability" through "administrative capacity" and "responsible participation of social organiza-tions."[36] In implementing this program, COSUDE directly assisted a select group of municipalities, while the Swiss NGO Ayuda Obrera Suiza (AOS) played a complementary role, mainly in the largely indigenous Oruro department. AOS not only educated indigenous and campesino organizations on the new legisla-tion but actively encouraged them to take advantage of it, in what appears to be a conscious reshaping of indigenous-movement practice. An AOS functionary told us that his organization persuaded indigenous-peasant counterparts of the "need for new responses . . . to go beyond criticizing and be able to launch proposals and influence public opinion." According to this same informant, AOS assistance successfully facilitated indigenous-peasant influence in municipalities through electoral and participatory channels.[37]

A second example is DANIDA's "Indigenous People, Decentralization and Popular Participation Sector Programme," which operated in the departments of Potosí, Chuquisaca, and La Paz. On the one hand, the program aspired to improve municipal governments' skills in financial administration and public investment and deepen their promotion of participation and indigenous rights. On the other hand, it sought to further the ability of Indians and women "to exercise their . . . rights within the Law of Popular Participation, Law of Municipalities, and related legal provisions" (DANIDA 2001, ii; also see DANIDA 2004a). Its aid facilitated the completion and recognition of indigenous communities' petitions for OTB status and the creation of DMIs (Ayo 2003, 74–75). DANIDA first provided such assistance through the national Subsecretariat of Ethnic Affairs and later through the Bolivian NGOs Fundación Diálogo and Potosí Social and Legal Research (ISALP).[38]

In a similar vein, the World Bank–Bolivia officer in charge of decentralization described the LPP as an empowering, radical change and explained the bank's role and agenda in it as follows: "Devolution to local government, strengthening local government, and the empowerment of society to take control of public expenditure. . . . Implementation of this vision requires strengthening institutions, not only of governments, but society."[39] The bank's Rural Community Development Project (PDCR) enacted this view by contracting NGOs and otherwise financing the completion of required municipal development plans, as well as indigenous district development plans. For the first five years after the introduction of Popular Participation, NGOs and consultants wrote most municipal development plans, often with international financing from the World Bank and the U.S. Agency for International Development (USAID), (Kohl 2003, 319, 323).[40] In sum, transnational connections operated across different scales and worked through both governmental and nongovernmental organizations; policies and practices sought to remake civil-society associations into autonomous agents of governance, but according to preconceived standards.

On the one hand, these examples suggest that support from development agencies may allow local indigenous organizations in Bolivia and Ecuador to extend their development actions and knowledge (Radcliffe, Laurie, and Andolina 2002a, 297). This is especially important in the context of neoliberal-driven state budget cutting, as well as the aforementioned limits on transfers from national to municipal governments. According to Kohl (2003), NGOs and official donors had empowering effects when they focused on educating the population on their new rights and powers and transferring administrative skills to municipal employees and leaders of civil-society organizations. In some cases, NGOs also obtained outside grants to complement the municipal budget (324–26). On the other hand, narrow emphases on administrative efficiency and related technical skills had exclusionary effects, by reproducing urban biases and crowding out community participation.

Due to its frequent portrayal as an exemplar of local development, the Ecuadorian municipality of Cotacachi is a good case for exploring these tensions in greater depth. Located in the highland province of Imbabura, Cotacachi has been governed by an indigenous Pachakutik mayor, Auki Tituaña, since 1996.[41] The reforms enacted there have built on a long-term struggle by the local, second-tier indigenous organization, the Unión de Organizaciones Campesinas e Indígenas de Cotacachi (UNORCAC), to influence municipal politics (J. Cameron 2005, 372), as well as Pachakutik's vision of participatory, intercultural democracies embodied in people's assemblies.[42] Cotacachi has also built on considerable external support, through a combination of Ecuadorian NGOs, national government programs, and international development agencies.

One of Mayor Tituaña's first acts in 1996 was to convene an "Assembly of Cantonal Unity." It meets in full once per year and generates a local development plan, with an average attendance of six hundred delegates from local civil-society organizations. The adoption of a participatory budget model in 2001 afforded Cotacachi civil society an even greater opportunity to scrutinize municipal revenues and expenditures and thereby assess whether community priorities and government promises have been fulfilled.[43] In between these annual plenary meetings, cantonal development committees meet regularly to execute the development plan and mediate between and consult with various interest groups. These committees are examples of what we call hybrid development institutions, composed of representatives of local civil-society organizations, the municipal government, Ecuadorian and foreign NGOs, bilateral donors, and agents of the national state (Ortiz 2004).

This form of participatory, intercultural local politics has generated a number of notable achievements. Municipal services and infrastructure have improved markedly. Medical coverage of births in Cotacachi was 100 percent by 2001, and infant mortality was nine deaths per thousand births, compared to twenty-five per thousand nationwide. Housing and service indices, meanwhile, increased 10 percent more than the national average (Ortiz 2004, 172–76).[44] As a result, Cotacachi was the first Ecuadorian municipality to earn full decentralization of jurisdiction in health from the national government, in 2003. This put the municipality in charge of the canton's hospital and rural health centers and made it responsible for the payroll of personnel previously salaried by the national health ministry (Torres 2004, 83). Finally, by relying on *mingas* (collective labor) and other resources mobilized by local communities and civil-society organizations, the municipal government reduced the financial costs of its operations by an estimated 13 percent (Ortiz 2004, 183).

Political culture and practice in Cotacachi have also changed. Indigenous leaders won city council positions and have participated regularly in the cantonal assembly. Over 70 percent of local indigenous residents agreed in a recent survey that "everyone participates more in decision making" (Ospina 2006, 298), while societal groups have accepted responsibilities for planning and administering cantonal policies and projects.[45] Likewise, 70 percent of locals believe that racism has declined in Cotacachi, based on increased pride among indigenous people and greater mutual respect between indigenous, mestizo, and black people in the canton (Ospina 2006, 298–99).

These accomplishments have facilitated—and been facilitated by—relationships across space and scale, many of which transgress previous boundaries. Mayor Tituaña has nurtured a rural-urban coalition to buttress his participatory agenda, which has faced majority opposition in the municipal council.[46] This multiethnic, inclusive approach has also aided Cotacachi's attraction of outside support. By 2001, it had garnered US$3.6 million in external financing through agreements with twenty-one organizations (Radcliffe, Laurie, and Andolina 2002a, 300). In 2002, external monies constituted 46 percent of Cotacachi's municipal budget (Ortiz 2004, 183), greatly facilitating the gains in social development described above.

Other kinds of assistance have also been provided. The internationally funded Ecuadorian NGO Tierra Nueva supported a team of bilingual Quichua-Spanish promoters for workshops of up to two hundred local people, which enhanced indigenous participation in devising cantonal development plans.[47] The bilateral agency, German Development Service (DED), provided technical support through a *cooperante*, who served as co-coordinator of Cotacachi's participatory budget process.[48] External support was also directed toward "South-South" exchanges of experiences between Cotacachi and various alternative municipalities in Latin America. One exchange between Cotacachi and Colombia's Pasto town council provided both with contacts for additional funding and assistance (Muñoz 1999, 50).[49]

The sum of these reforms and networks has redefined the imaginative geography of Cotacachi, converting a largely invisible local space into a transnationally visible place. This is illustrated strikingly by two UN-supported awards to Cotacachi, as a "best practices" municipality (2000) and as a "City of Peace" (2002).

The latter designation is now painted on a road sign at the entrance into the municipality, notifying ordinary travelers and external supporters alike. "Donor and development organizations that previously entered Cotacachi as if it were a *no-man's land*, now must operate under the umbrella of local development plans. They cannot set up in the canton to execute projects designed elsewhere, but need to see if what they offer responds to local problems and priorities, as well as negotiate their entry within the local institutional framework" (Ortiz 2004, 131; emphasis in original). Such negotiation and socialization is, however, a two-way street. Parallel to the processes of popular participation, resource mobilization, social integration, and cultural pride are more subtle dynamics of exclusion, dependency, and segregation. Racialized subjects and geographies are reproduced in Cotacachi even as they undergo transformations.

Although popular representation and social-development administration in Cotacachi is more inclusive, it takes place through a tripartite division into racially marked geo-zones, namely the more mestizo "urban," an indigenous "Andean," and a mestizo-black "subtropical" zone.[50] These zones are *not* equivalent to parishes, an official scale of administration smaller than the municipality, but rather overlap a number of parishes. Cantonal committee representation and municipal expenditure are divided equally among delegates from the three zones, yet the Andean and subtropical zones have a larger share of the municipality's population (42 percent and 38 percent, respectively) than the urban zone (20 percent) *and* have higher poverty rates (Ortiz 2004, 136). By defining equity (a key principle of social development) in these zonal terms, the municipality and cantonal assembly have exacerbated inequities in terms of demographics and livelihood and have reproduced urban bias.[51]

In response, leaders of the local indigenous organization, UNORCAC, have occupied the municipal building to protest revenue distribution. They have also complained, "We don't feel [fairly] represented, since we have three delegates on the Development Management Committee but have nearly 50 percent of the population."[52] Such biases mirror other exclusionary features of the cantonal participatory assembly. The annual plenary meeting is always held in the city center, facilitating the participation of urbanites over those in other parts of Cotacachi canton. Assembly meeting dates, rhetorical styles, and Spanish language use are more amenable to middle-class, urban mestizos than grassroots members of rural indigenous communities (Ortiz 2004, 152; Ospina 2006, 107). Default use of Spanish implies that the bilingual promoter teams formed with NGO support (discussed earlier) were needed to increase indigenous participation, which was deficient vis-à-vis nonindigenous groups.[53]

Assumptions about the nature of development and the possession of technical skills have also led to exclusion in Cotacachi. For example, UNORCAC's plan to center sustainable local development on community tourism was trumped by an alliance between the indigenous mayor and urban townsfolk around an ecotourism "mixed firm," which would "generate revenues for local [public] self-administration and individual investors." Some people within this alliance "believe[d] that UNORCAC lack[ed] management capacity . . . and might therefore jeopardize the tourism project, seen as a central element of cantonal development" (J. Flora et al. 2006, 443–44). While Mayor Tituaña might not share this view of UNORCAC's abilities, he may have sided with urbanites because he felt they had to "say yes to local development, to social development . . . and above all yes to economic development. Previously, municipalities were charged with public works projects but . . . put aside the role of fomenting economic development" (Tituaña, as cited in Muñoz 1999, 49).

This marginalization of UNORCAC and its member communities may be reinforced by a new governance technology that Cotacachi municipality is adopting: a cantonal atlas based on GIS. The atlas was financed by USAID and supported through a transnational agreement between the municipality, the Universidad Católica in Quito, and the University of Georgia in the United States.[54] Whatever utility it may have, the atlas was produced largely outside of Cotacachi (in Quito and the United States), and its primary audience consisted of "*técnicos*, planners, and politicians . . . to support decision making on socioeconomic and environmental issues in Cotacachi" (Mejia and Hidalgo 2006, 453). Moreover, the "Cultural Space" part of the atlas effectively reduced local indigenous culture to land use and archeological ruins (see Mejia and Hidalgo 2006, 455). For some, like UNORCAC leader Nicolás Gómez, use of the atlas might add to simmering frustration about decision making in the cantonal assembly: "One goes to the assembly and speaks a lot, but what the delegates say is not taken into account; the experts decide. In the committees, there is little [effective] community participation; the experts speak about technical matters with technical language."[55] Note that it is "in the committees," more than any other part of the Cotacachi assembly framework, where functionaries of NGOs, the national state, and external donor organizations participate as technical assistants (Ortiz 2004, 163). UNORCAC, in turn, has maintained a certain distance from the cantonal assembly, which it regards anew as a primarily mestizo space, albeit one that indigenous delegates are welcome to enter (Ospina 2006, 73–77).[56]

Tensions between inclusion and exclusion are present in other Andean municipalities. In Bolivia, for instance, the World Bank facilitated inclusion by pressuring the municipal government of Mizque to recognize the Raqaypampa zone as an indigenous municipal district and by "assuring" the mayor that an indigenous development plan for Raqaypampa would be financed by the World Bank.[57] This development plan included active community participation but also elicited participant complaints about "technical language in planning sessions, which made the grassroots feel stupid while the experts used planning terminology."[58] Before creating their own municipality in 2004, Jesús de Machaqa constituents created a DMI and elected an indigenous leader to the Viacha city council. The council member pursued personal, rather than constituent, interests, however, and arrived in a suit to an annual, poncho-filled inauguration of indigenous authorities, while handing out free bottles of Coca-Cola to attendees (Albó 2004, 41–42). Indigenous leaders tried to overcome this deficiency in representation by making costly journeys to Viacha city, but their requests to the municipal government there often went unheeded, in part because the mayor prioritized "well-elaborated" development plans (Blanes 2000, 79). Back in Ecuador, the indigenous mayor of Saquisilí proved able to create participatory development plans with the help of bilingual promoter teams financed by the NGO Tierra Nueva. Yet, mestizo townsfolk assumed that the indigenous mayor lacked "technical skills," which initially undermined his credibility with them and the efficacy of his administration (Larrea and Larrea 1999).

In sum, actual practice matched expectations about the local to some extent. Internetwork spaces emerged as different kinds of actors set joint agendas and negotiated differences; in some cases, such circuitry formed hybrid institutions, like planning or oversight committees for local development. This interaction created multiscalar locales enveloped in complex distributions of sovereignty: lines of authority between nongovernmental and governmental agencies blurred and bent, and organizations with spatial extensions, ranging from submunicipal to global, converged on local spaces delimited officially by a national state.

The examples above also illustrate how municipal-based development has provided both points of articulation with indigenous movement agendas *and* new kinds of marginalization and pressures for cultural integration. In many cases, indigenous leaders and organizations increased their presence in municipal politics and development planning. The mayor of Cotacachi, moreover, adapted the model of a municipality that actively promotes economic development in concert with agents from civil society and the private sector.

Concrete social-development gains and infrastructure improvements sometimes resulted. Yet even in these exemplary scenarios of remarkable change,
forms of exclusion and discipline reproduced urban biases, racialized geographies, and other social hierarchies. Recent studies of decentralization's effects
on Andean indigenous people point to the relative strength of local indigenous
organizations and their allies, or to class relations and resource and asset distribution, as relevant factors (Albó 1999; J. Cameron 2005; Van Cott 2006). We
have shown that political cultures and expectations also matter. These include
assumptions about geographical identities, images of capability and authority,
and conceptions of development success.

Indigenous Movement Counterspaces
in Transnationalized Contexts

Parallel to partaking in official decentralization, indigenous activists also proposed distinct geographies and subjects of development, through ayllus in Bolivia and Quichua-speaking pueblos in Ecuador. Hereafter referred to as the
"ayllu movement" and "pueblo movement," these represent efforts to produce
counterspaces based on valuations of the local that challenge overtly those of
official decentralization. Dissatisfaction with local politics described in the previous section is one motive for these efforts. Bolivian scholars who are sympathetic
to indigenous movements have argued that municipal structures and practices
are not adequately responsive to indigenous cultural characteristics or political
demands.[59] Similar concerns were expressed in Ecuador by indigenous leader
and former CODENPE director Luis Maldonado: "In a municipality, you're not
going to develop our [indigenous] way of life, our institutions, and our contribution to the democratic system. Who will guarantee that with a municipal
government, our rights are going to endure?" (*El Comercio*, June 19, 2001).

The pursuit of local counterspaces also reflected a racial project that sought
multiethnic participation through what indigenous leaders call *complementaridad* (complementarity, a balanced but differentiated pairing) rather than synthesis (see also Medina 2003, 30). Concretely, proponents of ayllus and pueblos
believed that equitable diversity is best pursued through some degree of explicit
segmentation between ethnic and racial groups. This demarcation does not
entail full enclosure or local autarky, however. Bolivian indigenous leaders, for
example, transcended rural and highland senses of indigenous place in their
willingness to engage with urban-based indigenous intellectuals and lowland
indigenous leaders. In Ecuador, pueblo-movement partisans understand it as

part of antiracist struggle, in part through informing white and mestizo society of the diverse, self-defined names and markers of indigenous groups. In breaking down overgeneralizations about "indigenous" culture, such activists see the pueblo movement as a precursor to a more profound and respectful intercultural practice.[60] One example of this was the engagement of Cayambe city residents with Cayambi pueblo activists in 1999. They held public debates on Cayambi indigenous culture and compelled the municipality to eliminate references to the Inti Raymi (Sun Festival) celebrations as "folklore," on the grounds that Cayambi Indians have a living culture and that they must not be represented by others as mere objects of the past.[61]

The ayllu and pueblo movements aspire to create more-autonomous spaces for indigenous development, which take shape as a new kind of "ethnic administration." This administrative model differs from prevailing norms by institutionalizing and territorializing cultural difference as a point of departure, and it contrasts with past forms of ethnic administration in the Andes by incorporating internationally recognized indigenous rights. As such, ayllus and pueblos can be interpreted as both introverted and extroverted places: as ethnically homogenous sites of cultural sustainability they are introverted, and as platforms for direct relations with other cultural groups they are extroverted.[62] In principle, enacting this administrative framework goes beyond the graduated sovereignty that marks official decentralization by increasing indigenous spatial autonomy and requiring a greater sharing of authority between indigenous counterspaces and government units. In practice, however, such autonomy is subject to technologies of government that seek to make such counterspaces "disciplined and responsible" (Dean 1999, 153, 168), according to social-neoliberal policy frameworks.[63]

Ayllus and the TCO in Bolivia

The Federation of Ayllus and Communities of Ingavi Province defines *ayllu* as "a group of families circumscribed by a territory, united by ties of kinship . . . a common language . . . collective labor, and their own rituals." These ayllus are governed by "the original authorities: *mallku, jilakata, kamana,* arising from the heart of the ayllu with ability to lead for a predetermined period" (Federation of Ayllus and Communities of Ingavi Province, quoted in Choque 1999b, 15). In strengthening and reconstructing local ayllu territories and federating them into wider-scale *markas* and *suyus,* an increasing number of Bolivian indigenous leaders believed that indigenous people could administer resources through customary practices as a means to improve livelihoods and consolidate rights to determine their future. A marka is a local space that comprises several ayllus; in precolonial times, markas were incorporated into broader cultural regions called suyus. Suyus were themselves multiscalar: Qollasuyu refers roughly to the highland region of Bolivia, once a key region of the Inca state, called Tawantinsuyu ("land of the four regions").[64]

Institutionally, this ayllu movement led to the creation of the National Council of Ayllus and Markas of Qollasuyu (CONAMAQ) in 1997, which is now recognized nationally and internationally as a legitimate indigenous representative. Well before decentralizing state initiatives, small groups of Bolivian indigenous activists and intellectuals debated the declining class-based political system, the rise of neoliberalism, and the potential of ayllu structures. Following a series of small workshops involving national NGOs and indigenous authorities, ayllu federations emerged in northern Potosí and the department of Oruro in the late 1980s; by the mid-1990s, several ayllu federations sprang up in La Paz department. In contrast to the preexisting highland indigenous federation, CSUTCB, which was subdivided strictly along lines of state administrative units, the ayllu federation of northern Oruro comprises a suyu of "Karankas" people, at a level in between that of province and department. This suyu includes thirteen markas (see map 6), each containing a number of ayllus. Some of these ayllus match canton boundaries, while others do not (see map 7). The Federation of Ayllus of Southern Oruro considers ayllu strengthening to be intimately related to "reconstituting the Quillacas-Azanaques nation," which at one time comprised a space including present-day territory of Argentina, Bolivia, Paraguay, and Chile (Choqueticlla, Maraza, and Vázquez 2000).

Maps 6 and 7 thus represent a significant diversification in the labeling of highland indigenous groups in Bolivia, relating culture to territory and scale, as well as language use. As noted in chapter 1 (map 3), highland indigenous people were identified politically as either Aymara or Quechua almost exclusively until the mid-1990s. While these names are still prevalent, they have since been joined by more localized labels such as the Karankas and Quillacas peoples (noted above), and by others like Pacaje and Machaqa. Map 6 was provided by the Jacha Karankas ayllu federation in 1999; it is meant to represent the Karankas suyu in northern Oruro department. This suyu is subdivided into thirteen constituent markas, which are in turn assumed to have cultural differences between them. The centermost marka on map 6, Qhurqui (shaded dark gray), is shown in more detail in map 7, further disaggregated into eighteen component ayllus. Map 7 was produced by Ayllu Sartañani and the Andean Oral History Workshop, two pro-indigenous NGOs that took a lead role in actively promoting this more

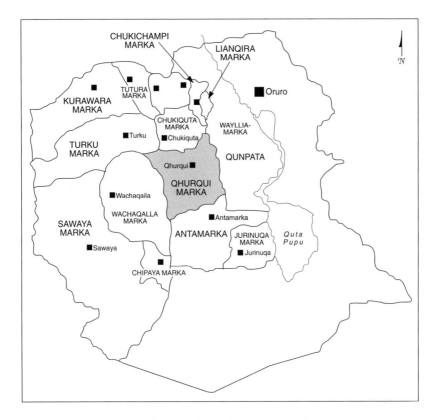

MAP 6. Markas comprising the Karankas indigenous group, Oruro Department, Bolivia.

Each marka identified here contains a number of ayllus. The ayllus of Qhurqui Marka (shaded grey) are represented in map 7.

territorial, "mosaic" view of highland indigenous cultures and identities. Such a view did not, however, widely inform public discourse or policymaking in Bolivia until the mid- to late 1990s.

Public recognition of these alternative indigenous identities resulted from a combination of local indigenous activism and international support, as well as the state-led decentralization schemes discussed in the first half of this chapter. Early moves toward this distinctive political conception of highland Indians in Bolivia occurred through local-global connections that largely bypassed the state (between 1987 and 1994, roughly). International assistance included financing, along with research and technical help in organizing development projects, provided by Oxfam America, the Inter-American Foundation, and the European

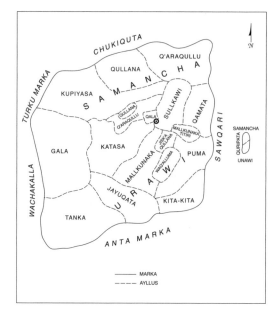

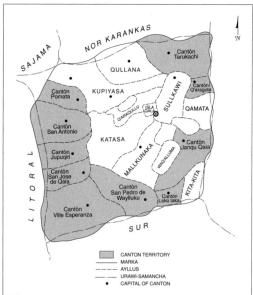

MAP 7. Ayllus and municipal boundaries in Marka Qhurqui, Oruro Department, Bolivia.

Traditional ayllu boundaries overlap with those of official cantons in some but not all cases. Note also that traditional ayllu names in this marka generally differ from the canton names.

Union (Izko 1992; Healy 2001a, 195–96). After the Bolivian government passed indigenous-rights and participatory legislation in the mid-1990s, official development agencies, like DANIDA and the World Bank, channeled monies to ayllu organizations through the Bolivian ministries of land, popular participation, and indigenous affairs. These donors also supported Bolivian NGOs like the Andean Oral History Workshop and ISALP, which offered professional assistance to ayllu movement leaders (Andolina, Radcliffe, and Laurie 2005, 687).

Leaders of the ayllu movement have striven to build a culturally appropriate development framework based on the ayllu, marka, and suyu. As stated by the Ingavi ayllu federation, "[The] ayllu is a system of social organization that allows us an adequate 'control' over diverse ecological levels and the management of natural resources in our territory . . . and obligates all members of the ayllu to cultivate communal lands by rationalizing seeding [and] rotating crops" (Cussi, Calle, and Mamani 2000, 61–62). These practices are, in turn, supported by reciprocity and collective labor among community members; they are also regulated by ayllu authorities politically and spiritually.[65] Such authorities (usually called mallkus or *mayores*) are chosen in communal assemblies and hold office for one year only, which, at least in theory, facilitates accountability, dialogue, and consensus-based decision making (Ticona 2003). Mallkus also conduct personal visits to all households and lands within the ayllu, conversing with families and making note of agricultural land and landscapes, in a kind of informal census.[66] If this system is functioning well, movement leaders argue, ayllus can revive the days when they produced not only for subsistence but for markets throughout Bolivia (Choqueticlla, Maraza, and Vázquez 2000, 87).

Although ayllu-movement leaders and sympathizers have emphasized localisms and eschewed neo-Inca imperial designs, they have viewed the ayllu in relation to other scales. The national ayllu council, CONAMAQ, for example, frames its agenda according "to rights and recognition granted by the state and attendant legislation."[67] Local ayllu federations have done likewise. Lorenzo Inza of Ingavi (La Paz department) evoked ILO Convention 169 in making claims to territory, arguing, "We have rights to territory [which] incorporates everything on the surface, subsurface, natural resources, water, trees, mountains, etc." (Cussi, Calle, and Mamani 2000, 61). Some ayllu-movement leaders have also participated in exchanges with counterparts in Ecuador to share views and experiences concerning customary law, indigenous-rights legislation, and land and territorial issues.[68] Together with assistance provided by various Bolivian and international agencies, the multiscalar framing and organizing of indigenous activists has transformed ayllus from largely informal, local places to transnationally legitimate political subjects.[69] By making this particular cultural form of indigeneity visible within a broader context, the ayllu movement was able to convene sufficient recognition and support to stabilize a new "traditional" kind of indigenous community within an otherwise rapidly changing world of shifting relations and identities.[70]

Efforts to further consolidate ayllu-based counterspaces operated largely through the "Original Community Lands" (Tierras Comunitarias de Orígen) provision of the 1996 Ley INRA (National Agrarian Reform Institute), which allowed indigenous groups to obtain collective land titles. Vicente Flores of CONAMAQ regarded the TCO as "an instrument to recover the original lands of indigenous peoples; it is reencounter with cultures, uses and customs; it is reparation for 500 years of injustice and oppression; it is synonymous with life and development" (Almaraz 2005). In contrast to Bolivian municipal districts, which were drawn in the first instance without significant indigenous participation, specific TCO claims have originated by demand from indigenous organizations. Also, TCOs can be created out of discontinuous spatialities, useful for indigenous groups who cannot be bounded easily in a single territory.[71] A third contrast to official municipalities is that TCOs explicitly acknowledge indigenous rights: "The denomination of TCO includes the concept of indigenous territory in accordance with the definition established in . . . ILO Convention 169 [such that] the distribution and redistribution of resources for individual and familial use inside of original community lands will be ordered by the rules of the community, according to their uses and customs" (INRA Law, Article 3, as cited in Barragán 2007, 96). Such rights would include consultation on the use or exploitation of natural resources by anyone not belonging to the TCO. The INRA Law also reaffirms community autonomy in regulating internal land use, which might be deployed in a way to mitigate the fragmentation and erosion of family plots (Fundación Tierra 2007; DANIDA 2004c, 20). Collective titles might also provide ayllu authorities with greater leverage over semiurban residents, strengthening the authorities' ability to tighten rules of ayllu belonging to include not just landholding but also community service.[72]

While the TCO titling procedure begins at the request of indigenous communities, the full process involves a group of players that bridges both state/society and national/international divides. The principal Bolivian state agencies involved are the National Agrarian Reform Institute and the indigenous ministry. The former oversees TCO claim submissions, study, dispute resolution, and public information; the latter certifies the "ethnic character" of the indigenous group making the claim and determines its "spatial needs" (INRA 2006).[73] International donors provide the bulk of the financing and some technical assistance, while private cartography and survey firms are contracted to establish the formal boundaries of each claim. Officially, representatives of national indigenous confederations provide oversight and feedback, as do NGOs who work closely with indigenous organizations. To foment dialogue and coordination among these actors, INRA housed an "Inter-institutional Commission on TCOs."[74] According to a former INRA TCO director, this commission allowed "each organization with a TCO [to give] a report on how INRA has carried out its work in their area; in what ways [it had] failed and what [it had] done well."[75]

The wide range of actors involved in producing local Bolivian counterspaces has both enabling and constraining implications for indigenous organizations. Regarding the former, international support is critical: it has contributed nearly 75 percent of financing, covering everything from equipment, vehicles, and payment for private contractors to personnel salaries in the land and indigenous ministries (INRA 2006, 62; DANIDA 2004b, 38–40, annexes E and F). DANIDA sponsored eighty-nine TCO highland claims in the departments of Potosí and Oruro, while the World Bank supported nearly twenty-five highland TCO claims in the departments of La Paz and Cochabamba (DANIDA 2004b, 6; INRA 2006, 26; Arratia 2004, 8). By the end of 2006, over one hundred TCO titles were granted or "assured" in highland areas of Bolivia.[76] A handful of them cross state administrative divides: Raqaypampa TCO includes parts of three provinces (Arratia 2004, 10); eight TCOs in Oruro and Potosí cross provincial (and thus municipal) lines, and one of these TCOs transcends the Oruro-Potosí departmental boundary (DANIDA 2004b, 110–11).[77]

DANIDA's support for TCOs went beyond that of the World Bank in two respects that empowered indigenous organizations. First, it supported training to enhance local indigenous leaders' participation in TCO processing (DANIDA 2004b, 30). While results of the most recent programs are not available, earlier training projects supported by DANIDA helped mallkus in Jesús de Machaqa. In 2001, they successfully challenged state arguments about missing paperwork and thereby unblocked the titling process for their ayllus' TCOs (Barragán 2007, 109–10).[78] Second, DANIDA provided follow-up support for fifteen highland TCOs with a Gestión Territorial Indígena project (GTI—Indigenous Territorial Administration). It sought to improve the ability of indigenous people in newly titled TCOs to create development initiatives, administer natural resources, elaborate policy proposals, and negotiate with governmental and private agencies (DANIDA 2004c). It also hoped to create a normative, legal, and institutional framework for indigenous territorial administration within the Bolivian state.

Indigenous organizations involved in this project viewed it as a step toward establishing greater control over natural resources and instituting a mode of governance over their community spaces (DANIDA 2004c, 8; Almaraz 2005).

As such, the indigenous territorial administration project has pushed beyond Bolivian law, since the INRA Law does not stipulate TCO policy mechanisms and the Bolivian constitution did not directly recognize TCOs as state administrative units. Demonstrating the development viability of TCOs might make up for these limitations, thus eliciting more flexibility from the Bolivian state and more funding from international donors. In fact, other organizations have begun to promote indigenous territorial administration in the Bolivian lowlands: the Bolivian Decentralization Vice-Ministry (with World Bank financing), a German bilateral agency, and a Bolivian grassroots development NGO (Almaraz 2005). If perceived as successful, Bolivian TCOs may become local nodes for new transnational connections around indigenous development.

Denmark's support for TCOs was grounded in a combination of indigenous-rights and social-development criteria. Regarding the former, it regarded TCOs as crucial for fulfilling the promise of ILO Convention 169, including the "right to rule themselves by their own values, authorities, [and] justice systems" as well as "the right to culturally differentiated education and health services" (DANIDA 2004b, 23). Regarding social development, Danish development agents have envisaged TCOs as an antipoverty instrument, assuming that territorial resources and economic solidarity help to meet basic needs; they also perceived them as spaces to foment participation, gender equity, and environmental sustainability.[79] Based in part on DANIDA's view that "the ayllu is social capital," the indigenous territorial administration program aimed to tap indigenous cultures' economic potential going beyond basic needs.[80] Thus, DANIDA supported TCOs at a level that could strengthen indigenous culture and society internally and to improve indigenous peoples' "articulation with public and private entities for a participatory and comprehensive administration" (DANIDA 2004c, 37).[81]

In sum, this multiscalar interaction for TCOs facilitated the aspirations of ayllu advocates, who see "the reconstitution of ayllus [as] an Andean strategy for indigenous self-determination on the world stage" (Choque 2000, 18) and "not isolated from the market" (Cussi, Calle, and Mamani 2000, 73). Denmark-supported TCO projects, totaling over US$20 million, modeled such interaction through inter-institutional connections that engaged and circumvented the Bolivian state: on the one hand, they supported state land and indigenous ministries; on the other hand, they financed Bolivian NGOs—who in turn provided training for indigenous organizations.[82] Denmark's monies were likewise divided between state institutions and NGOs; those channeled to the latter flowed directly from DANIDA's bank account to NGO accounts (DANIDA 2004b, 47; DANIDA 2004c, 73).

Other dimensions of the INRA Law and TCO creation have ambivalent, and even restrictive, implications for highland indigenous peoples in Bolivia. The extent of TCO land titles and resource control, for example, is limited by a set of "socio-spatial fixes" (Radcliffe and Laurie 2006) embedded in the law and its implementation. First, communal control over land and resource use is confined to surface use rights; underground resources are considered the property of the national state. Local TCO titleholders have the right to participate in consultations about how subsurface resources are used and are entitled to payment for any damages, but they cannot unilaterally appropriate such resources or veto their appropriation by outsiders.[83] The ayllu movement's models of ethnic territorial administration (described earlier) go beyond these limits. Second, most titled and "financing assured" TCOs in the highlands are at the scale of ayllu; most marka-scale TCO claims, and the two existing suyu-scale claims, have been delegitimized.[84] In some cases, ayllu-scale TCOs are the preference of indigenous communities, as in Jesús de Machaqa; in other cases, however, communities disagreed on the scale of TCO claims (Barragán 2007, 108–10; Colque 2007, 148–49). In the latter situations, the Bolivian state and international donors played a part in resolving such disagreements. For example, the Suyu Pacajes council submitted a TCO claim for over one million hectares in La Paz department, which, along with other wider-scale claims, was dubbed a "mega-demand" and subjected to censure.[85] A Bolivian land minister declared that highland TCO claims were "out of control," while the World Bank cut off financing for titling of the Pacajes claim and contracted a Spanish consulting agency to take a survey of indigenous locals, effectively displacing the Pacajes indigenous leaders in their roles as local representatives.[86]

Denmark reinforced this disciplining of indigenous counterspaces in 2004 when it chose to support thirty-seven new highland TCOs that were small in area and "able to harmonize objectives with those of Indigenous Municipal Districts in order to improve conditions for governability" (DANIDA 2004b, 32). This tying of indigenous counterspaces back to conventional spaces (especially municipalities) is furthered in DANIDA's indigenous territorial-administration project: fourteen of the fifteen TCOs it selected for this project were ayllus concentrated within municipal boundaries (DANIDA 2004c, 45). Moreover, each TCO was expected to create a development plan that allowed "integration on the municipal level and incorporation . . . into municipal development plans"

(48).[87] Although DANIDA's assistance prioritized indigenous rights and aspired to make TCOs into a recognized administrator, it did so within a vision of the Bolivian local that centers ultimately on the municipality.

The perception of indigenous TCOs as potentially excessive (that is, transgressive of official expectations of what constituted a "local" scale) has also manifested in development policies and practices that orient indigenous subjectivities. These perceptions are, in turn, shaped by the notion that indigenous leaders are incompetent managers of local territories. At one extreme, indigenous leaders are seen as unable to use modern technology. Responding to ayllu demands to accompany state technicians, a former INRA functionary reacted as follows: "The indigenous [believe] they have to accompany all of the steps that INRA does. Now it is going too far, as they are requesting everything up to GPSs [Global Positioning Systems, used for mapping territory]. They don't know how to handle that, nor is there any reason for them to know, nor is it going to benefit anyone if they are using GPS."[88] DANIDA projects are considerably more inclusive and respectful but operate according to similar logic. For example, indigenous organizations have not accessed project funding directly; monies earmarked for civil-society organizations are channeled exclusively to support NGOs, who provide training to indigenous organizations and "careful technical support" (DANIDA 2004b, 34). Additionally, the ayllu titling project's "unassigned" fund may be accessed by indigenous peoples but only "according to the advances in . . . capacities of indigenous organizations" (DANIDA 2004b, 9–10).

The Denmark-sponsored Indigenous Territorial Administration project sought to orient indigenous participation away from making demands and toward making proposals as a general practice. Its training in systems of organizing, administration, accounting, and monitoring was geared toward moving development plans "beyond descriptions . . . to strategic, concrete, and operative proposals" and to avoid "repeating the error of many plans elaborated in rural areas, which appear as vast catalogs of demands that lack realistic prioritizing or investment proposals" (DANIDA 2004c, 31, 47). However, because such training might not be effective over the long term for mallkus and other indigenous leaders who hold office for one year only, DANIDA proposed to create a new indigenous subject: the TCO *gerente* (manager), whose tenure may be more stable and long term than that of traditional authorities (DANIDA 2004c, 47).

Understood in terms of governmentality, these indigenous spaces and subjects have been forged within specific development frameworks and transnational connections. Such subjects and spaces were expected to be autonomous but were seen to require certain skills and orientations in order to exercise that autonomy "properly." In effect, this regulation of indigenous peoples' agency to achieve development would mean *altering*—not just building on—indigenous cultures. Following Dean (1999), this case illustrates how, in the governmentality of development, aid is "presented as a quantitative increase in capacity, [but] acts as a qualitative transformation of forms of subjectivity" (70).

Quichua Pueblos in Ecuador and the CTI

Like their ayllu-movement counterparts in Bolivia, supporters of Ecuador's pueblo movement sought to create counterspaces in a multiscalar fashion; they also did so in a transnationalized context informed by international development frameworks. In Ecuador, the pueblo movement was led by two actors: the predominant highland indigenous organization ECUARUNARI and the state indigenous development institution, CODENPE, whose members are appointed by ECUARUNARI and other regional affiliates of CONAIE. In 1999, ECUARUNARI named ten distinct indigenous groups in the highlands, which disaggregated what it had previously represented as a singular indigenous *nacionalidad* (nationality), into the following pueblos: Cayambi-Caranqui, Otavalo, Quitu, Panzaleo, Salasaca, Chibuleo, Guaranga, Puruhae, Cañari, and Saraguro (see map 8).[89]

The movement's multiscalar scheme conceived of each pueblo as part of the larger Quichua nationality and composed of smaller-scale *comunas*.[90] Although they do not retain as much precolonial structure and practice as the Bolivian ayllus, Ecuadorian indigenous comunas are often governed through communitywide assemblies and leadership councils called *cabildos*. Some cabildo officers carry out functions akin to Bolivia's ayllu authorities, although they occupy offices designated with Spanish terms such as *presidente, tesorero* (treasurer), and *síndico* (comptroller), (Korovkin 2001, 50–53; Kowii 1992).[91] In sum, Quichua pueblos occupy an imagined space between "the unifying poles of community and nationality" in Ecuadorian indigenous movement ideology (Lucero 2003, 24).

Although pueblos became visible during the late 1990s as CONAIE vied with other indigenous federations for control of the Ecuadorian state's indigenous development institution, attention to cultural distinctiveness among Quichuas preceded this period. What are today called Cayambi indigenous leaders, for instance, promoted local cultural events during the "five hundred years of resistance" campaign in the early 1990s. Distinctive Quichua identities became visible in food, dialect, music, and dance, especially in festivals like Inti Raymi: "Around here there is . . . dancing in circles with three characters. But when we

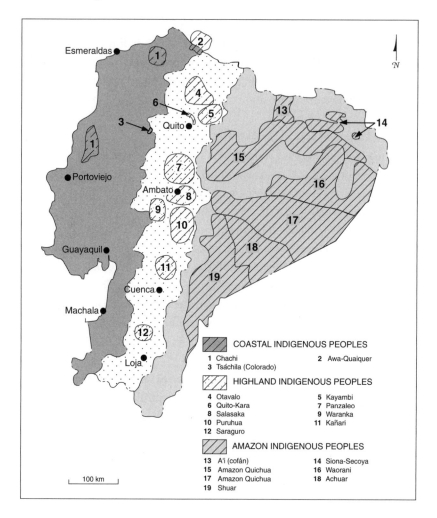

MAP 8: Selected indigenous identity groups in Ecuador, including pueblos.

The highland region of Ecuador is where the constitution of Quichua-speaking pueblos has proceeded the furthest. The numbers 4 through 12 mark some of these pueblos. Maps of indigenous people in Ecuador prior to pueblo reconstitution would not have distinguished among the Quichua-speaking people as this one does.

went to Otavalo or Saraguro, we did not see this dance; it is particular to the Cayambis, which reaffirmed our identity as Cayambi."[92] Other pueblo identity referents were notably gendered, such as the colorful and complex dress of many highland Quichua women. According to a Cañari member of CODENPE, "the women [in the Sierra] are those who most have their identity, most have their vision." He added that, outside of the areas where male indigenous people are identifiable by clothing and hairstyles, "in the other provinces . . . the women possess . . . identity that is palpable and visible."[93]

The pueblo movement's organizing principles match perceived cultural boundaries, and new representative institutions reembody and respatialize the broader indigenous movement. According to participants in pueblo-reconstitution workshops, each pueblo would have a parliament made up of member comunas; in turn, it would be a constituent of a broader Quichua parliament of all highland pueblos. In the long term, some activists expect ECUARUNARI and its member federations to transform into executive councils and secretariats of the Quichua parliament and pueblo parliaments, respectively: "What we want is for all of that [federation] nomenclature to disappear, and [instead] to work as pueblos."[94]

The geography of each pueblo is envisaged as extending beyond the scale of the Ecuadorian municipality and transcending provincial boundaries. Cañari activists, for example, argued that Cañar Indians can be found in Azuay, Cañar, and Riobamba provinces; Cayambi pueblo activists represent their constituents as occupying spaces within the current provinces of Pichincha, Imbabura, and Napo.[95] ECUARUNARI narrated this geo-identity change in terms of restoring a "harmony" between place and people broken by the state's historical fragmentation of indigenous lands, while stressing the possibility of rebuilding pueblos through new constitutional and legal provisions.[96] "The [existing] provincial organizations respond to previous organizational and political identity, still subject to the . . . geographical boundaries imposed by the Ecuadorian state. We insist that we should surpass those limits, to create space for reidentifying as pueblos in the way that we were and are." (ECUARUNARI 1999c, 3)

Like their counterparts in the Bolivian ayllu movement, Quichua activists in Ecuador view pueblos as spaces of development that are more appropriate than conventional ones. That is, they perceive pueblos as counterspaces in which ecologically and socially sustainable development not only fulfills environmental and cost-effectiveness criteria but also reproduces collective ethnic subjects.[97] Such development builds on socially distinctive relations of communal labor, reciprocity, and control over resources—but "without closing ourselves off."[98]

Workshop discussions debated how indigenous pueblos would begin to "value [their] own products" (over those coming from elsewhere), have greater control over prices, draw on indigenous agricultural knowledge, link production holistically and ecologically to other aspects of life, and favor crop diversity. Pueblo counterspaces were also envisioned as exercising new indigenous rights to receive and manage development funds directly. Doing so would try to ensure that indigenous livelihoods are accounted for in private-sector production, and it would also aim to enhance indigenous participation in the distribution of natural resources within a territorial concept that includes water, air, and subsoil, as well as surface land.[99]

As did the ayllu movement in Bolivia, pueblo activists have constructed their counterspaces within a complex interplay of scales. An ECUARUNARI spokesperson stated in a pueblo movement workshop, "We have some of the necessary materials . . . we have the [1998] constitution, advances in international conventions like [ILO] convention 169, and [we have] some pueblos with experiences of change, for example the Cayambi, Quitucara, [and] Chibuleo *compañeros*."[100] For promoters from Cayambi pueblo, the 1998 Ecuadorian constitution and ratification of ILO Convention 169 were significant for their "recognition of collective rights," providing "more strength and . . . legitimacy" for Cayambi identity-based organizing. At a smaller-scale meeting of community presidents (cabildo heads) in Cangaua, a few of the attendees identified themselves spontaneously as Cayambis in discussing local issues and problems.[101]

As mentioned earlier in the chapter, Ecuadorian pueblo activists had no legislation in place to further institutionalize counterspaces, in contrast to Bolivia. However, because the 1998 constitution provided for Indigenous Territorial Circumscriptions (Circunscripciones Territorial Indígena, CTIs), new indigenous territorialities were conceived according to the constitution and national and international indigenous rights, as indicated by CODENPE's legislative proposal. "This proposal . . . is for Indigenous and Afro-Ecuadorian Territorial Circumscriptions [and] their recognition as autonomous local governments, to exercise fully the collective rights in the . . . constitution. The creation of a circumscription . . . is grounded in historical, sociopolitical, cultural, and geographic realities, as noted in . . . Title XI on Decentralization and Territorial Organization of the constitution, and Article 2 of ILO Convention 169, ratified by the Ecuadorian government in April 1998" (Lozano 2000, 3–4, 78). While envisioning that CTIs would vary in size, from the equivalent of a village up to a province, the CODENPE proposal assumed that most Quichua pueblo claims for CTIs would be on a scale equivalent to that of municipalities (Lozano 2000, 88–90).[102]

ECUARUNARI's proposals followed principles similar to those of CODENPE, although they differed in form. On the one hand, some Quichua pueblo advocates considered establishing various circumscriptions to allow for both geographic discontinuity and pueblo unity. A Cayambi pueblo scheme, for instance, envisioned two Cayambi CTIs in Pichincha province, a third in Imbabura province, and a fourth in Napo province. While each CTI would have legally established autonomy and competencies, they would all register officially as Pueblo Cayambi territories and coordinate policies across CTI and provincial lines, possibly as a Cayambi *mancomunidad* or pan-CTI structure.[103] On the other hand, ECUARUNARI produced a draft bill (Ley de Comunidades) to consolidate comuna governance around the cabildo (and over various competitors, such as water boards) and facilitate comuna linkage to wider-scale Quichua pueblos (ECUARUNARI 1999d).[104] The pueblo remains the primary local space in these territorial proposals, but it is conceptually and strategically linked to smaller-scale comunas, as well as wider-scale discourses and actors.

Multiscalar frameworks also shaped proposals for the administration of development programs via indigenous circumscriptions. ECUARUNARI's strategy assumed a nested "participatory planning" framework, where, at the narrowest scale, each comuna would devise a development plan in community assembly. The cabildo presidents would then participate in pueblo-scale development planning as community representatives to their Quichua pueblo. Each pueblo's development plan would then link to wider scales via connection to a Quichua parliament (which would include representatives of all highland Quichua pueblos) and to CODENPE (which would include representatives from all indigenous nationalities and pueblos in Ecuador).[105] CODENPE's CTI proposal stipulated "planning and implementing sustainable development projects and programs with communities." This would entail competencies for CTI governments over environmental protection, natural resources, watersheds and river basins, tourism, health and traditional medicine, community justice, and intercultural bilingual education (Lozano 2000, 83).[106]

Such planning was premised on tapping cultural norms of reciprocity and solidarity, while having indigenous people acquire and deploy outside professional and technical knowledge. One CODENPE functionary, for example, believed that after legislating circumscriptions, a technical methodology of territorial inventory would follow: "An indigenous territorial circumscription is simply the boundary, whereas a territorial ordering allows you to see more profoundly—agricultural zones, population, natural resources, and river basins. Territorial ordering from a geographic point of view . . . is better for . . . distributing what a space has available to foment integral sustainable development."[107] To increase the number of trained indigenous professionals to carry out this and other technical tasks, CODENPE signed agreements with the Latin American Faculty of Social Sciences (FLACSO) and Universidad Católica in Quito to create targeted higher-education programs.[108] ECUARUNARI followed suit by redirecting its women's leadership-training school toward pueblo-based development. Workshop participants who discussed this linkage tended to represent Quichua women dualistically: as culture bearers who wear clothing and prepare food distinctive to their pueblos (a showcase of tradition) and as skilled graduates with the ability to administer and evaluate local development projects (an expression of modernity).[109]

The Danish NGO IBIS provided financing for both the pueblo movement and the women's training school. While it did not use the same criteria as DANIDA in Bolivia, IBIS justified its support of pueblos in light of present, local articulation rather than the recovery of cultural histories: "Even if not all Quichua groups identify with names of the past like Kara or Panzaleo, the process of considering their identity allows them to recognize themselves and intercede in local processes, which is valuable."[110] Likewise, IBIS differed from DANIDA by allowing an Ecuadorian indigenous organization (ECUARUNARI) to directly receive and administer project funds, but it still infused disciplinary elements consistent with social neoliberalism. For instance, IBIS's Pueblos Quichuas project provided training in accounting, evaluation, and financial management for an administrative team who would then participate in project oversight along with ECUARUNARI's governing council and its "national technical team" (ECUARUNARI 1999c, 10, 14). IBIS also maintained oversight over the project through a procedure of semiannual reports. Its director in Ecuador explained to highland indigenous activists that doing so would "build trust" between IBIS and ECUARUNARI, "assist in good management" of the project, and thereby "improve the image of ECUARUNARI and enable it to obtain funding from other agencies." In addition, the project was to be carried out in a way that would enhance "social and political control over leaders," meaning increased accountability and less corruption.[111]

Ecuadorian indigenous leaders were able to lead national debates on territorial legislation but were ultimately unable to see their proposals translated into law. The Ecuadorian congress rejected ECUARUNARI's Ley de Comunidades, which proposed to redefine indigenous comunas and link them to wider-scale pueblos. CODENPE's CTI proposal was never submitted to the legislature. One reason for the latter may have been the oft-cited difficulty of drawing geographical lines between ethnic and racial groups in the Ecuadorian highlands. But discrepancies in Ecuador's National Commission on Decentralization (convened in 2000) may be just as important. Indigenous representatives, from CONAIE and CODENPE, expected CTIs to have powers on par with municipalities, but government and political-party commissioners insisted that any legislation on indigenous circumscriptions should scale them down to submunicipal districts, whose competencies would be negotiated with their overseeing municipalities. Indigenous leaders found this restriction unacceptable, and no agreement was reached, despite facilitation by the German bilateral agency GTZ, which sponsored and participated in the commission.[112]

As a result, Ecuadorian indigenous activists were unable to consolidate Quichua pueblos territorially as CTIs. However, some corresponding institutional changes have occurred. ECUARUNARI renamed itself the Confederation of Kichwa Pueblos of Ecuador, and individual leaders in ECUARUNARI's governing council are identified by both province and pueblo.[113] The Cañar provincial federation produced a "life plan" (akin to a long-term, wide-ranging development project) in which (re)formation of a Cañari pueblo appears as one prominent goal, along with institutional strengthening of local indigenous organizations.[114] Meanwhile, ad hoc Quichua pueblo assemblies have met across provincial lines to discuss broad development goals and choose pueblo representatives to the national indigenous development council, CODENPE (personal communication with ECUARUNARI adviser, August 30 2007).

To summarize, indigenous organizations in Bolivia and Ecuador have made strategic use of official provisions to institutionalize counterspaces of ayllus, markas, suyus (Bolivia), and pueblos (Ecuador), with varying degrees of success. The concomitant reorganization of national space worked concretely through transnational, mixed-actor networks, challenging conventional state sovereignty and administrative boundaries. At the same time, the state attempted to contain subaltern efforts to reappropriate spaces and places by treating them as bounded units. International development agencies sometimes reinforced this containment, while standardizing emergent administrative practices in ethnic spaces where "fresh actions" are being attempted (see Lefebvre 1991). In contrast to the Bolivian case, Ecuadorian pueblo activists faced limitations primarily in legislative approval rather than legislative implementation. However, government officials and international donors in both countries adopted criteria of local governance or development that steered the ayllu and pueblo movements toward limited scales of territory and toward autonomous but guided forms of agency.[115]

Indigenous promoters of ayllus and pueblos often view them as extroverted places in wider spatial and temporal horizons, but sometimes envision them in ways that may reinforce the exogenous disciplining of indigenous territoriality. This may reproduce longstanding racialized geographies associated with Andeanist imageries. Ayllu-movement leaders, for example, have distinguished between indigenous *comunidades* (communities or ayllus) and town centers, re-marking the former as rural or remote. They also envisaged urban sites as problematic for ayllus: as launching pads for union or political-party penetration, seen as bearers of Western norms that devalue ayllu traditions; and as sites responsible for weakness in productivity and governance, for drawing too many people away from comunidades (Choqueticlla, Maraza, and Vázquez 2000; Plata, Colque, and Calle 2003, 56–62). In a similar vein, ECUARUNARI (1999c) justified its pueblo project as a means to address *rural* poverty and to reduce migration to hostile cities: "A high percentage of the indigenous population has suffered a migration process to urban centers, but in practice this has not solved their problems. In some cases these problems have worsened to the point that they [migrant Indians] have formed marginalized belts of urban poverty with consequent social problems" (ECUARUNARI 1999c, 4). Likewise, Cayambi pueblo activists in Ecuador suggested that indigenous territorial circumscriptions would exclude the cities of Cayambe and Pedro Moncayo, and that the municipality of Cayambe would have to "be reduced to the urban zone as such," thus reserving rural spaces as indigenous territories.[116]

Between Empowerment and Dependency

Recent production of local spaces in highland Bolivia and Ecuador reveals the complex dynamics of "reloaded boomerangs" and multiscalar power relations. Current Ecuadorian and Bolivian ethnic geographies are the outcome of reforms within national territorial administrations and international policy circuits, where indigenous leaders and representatives constitute just one set of voices. Simultaneously, Andean spatial practices reflect international policy agendas that convene around decentralization and recognition of indigenous rights. As Keck and Sikkink's boomerang model suggests, international support provided crucial leverage, resources, and legitimacy that facilitated the inclusion of indigenous actors within—and sometimes indigenous appropriation of—emergent local polities and development practices. On the other hand, the financial and normative leverage that international agencies hold over national states and local elites can also be wielded over the very beneficiaries of their actions, such as indigenous peoples and organizations. This "reloading" of transnational connectivity engages with indigenous organizations through and around states, and it is part of what generates the dual effects of empowerment and dependency illustrated in this chapter. These consequences, however, go beyond allowing or disallowing otherwise free-floating indigenous agents to pursue pregiven interests and needs; transnational interaction and connectivity may alter indigenous peoples' self-images, agendas, and practices, although such changes are usually partial rather than wholesale.

In this way, the effects of reloaded boomerangs result not only from complex transnational networking but also from tensions and disciplinary practices within social neoliberal governmentality. Considerable overlap exists between indigenous-movement agendas and social-neoliberal emphases on participation, accountability, sustainability, equity, and intercultural inclusion. Yet significant differences remain in establishing their precise meaning and the proper methods for realizing these principles. Social neoliberalism assumes that social criteria are compatible with efficiency, competitiveness, and accumulation in capitalist market economics; however, in Ecuador and Bolivia this assumption fed into tensions and tradeoffs between effective participation and technical knowhow, between designs for multicultural inclusion and indigenous desires for autonomy, and between different understandings of sustainable development. Although many indigenous leaders value acquisition of Western professional and administrative skills, this does not fully resolve these issues. Indeed, this chapter shows how inequity, ethnocentrism, and nontransparent governance may result.

These tensions go unaddressed or unmarked in part because, within social neoliberalism and official decentralization, markets and market access are viewed primarily as a solution for indigenous development, while considerations such as distributions of wealth and property are elided. In Bolivia, DANIDA gave municipalities support based on poverty measures and indigenous population density but made no connection between Bolivia's neoliberal economic policies, poverty, and low indigenous incomes.[117] Yet the revival of ayllu-based organizing in Oruro and Potosí began in the mid- to late 1980s, precisely in the midst of Bolivian "shock therapy," as budget cuts and tariff reductions meant that highland indigenous people, like other Bolivians, experienced massive layoffs (from the mining sector in particular) and increased competition from a flood of agricultural imports. A local indigenous federation claimed that ayllus in southern Oruro sought an alternative to that situation but were inadequately represented by peasant unions and received no effective state help (Choqueti-clla, Maraza, and Vázquez 2000, 85, 88–89, 100). In Cotacachi, Ecuador, Mayor Tituaña addressed negative neoliberal economic outcomes through a massive increase in social spending and public services for locals. But Cotocachi's alternative government did little to overcome the impacts of financial stabilization policy (via dollarization) on the already-limited profitability of smallholding agriculture (Ortiz 2004, 185–86). Moreover, indigenous people generally have the smallest and least-fertile holdings (J. Cameron 2005). Finally, Cotacachi's reliance on external financing was exacerbated by its inability to tax local export-oriented agribusinesses, who contribute taxes only to national coffers (Ortiz 2004, 144–45; J. Cameron 2005).[118] Although they are physically close to such nodes of capital investment, indigenous people (and others) in Cotacachi are geo-economically distant from its actual revenues because of specific intersections of local property rights, national taxation policy, and international trade networks.

We should not conclude, however, that the global simply overpowers the local. Local places can channel global flows through the power of appeal and attraction. Exemplary places like Cotacachi may even give local actors leverage over outsiders. Mayor Tituaña has argued that Cotacachi compelled development agencies to "adjust their actions," but he also acknowledged that external support flows to municipalities "to the extent that there is [local] seriousness, organization, and proposals."[119] In other cases, the simple presence of indigenous people and organizations in a local place can motivate and (for some) justify international assistance and intervention. This is particularly the case where outside agencies perceive the potential for successfully fulfilling their mandate. In this chapter, examples include Spanish bilateral aid flowing to Ecuadorian indigenous alternative municipalities, IBIS's support for Quichua pueblos, and DANIDA's ongoing support of Bolivian indigenous organizations and TCOs (see table 2). By way of these examples, the chapter has explored how and with what effects the local operates as a hegemonic focus in transnational development circuits and democratization processes. The hegemony of a specific conception of the local, and the multiscalar relations that constitute the local, demonstrate Bruno Latour's (1993, 122) argument that networks "are by nature neither local nor global but are more or less long and more or less connected" (see map 9).

TABLE 2. Selected funding lines for indigenized local spaces in Bolivia and Ecuador

Source Organization	Amount (USD)	Purpose	Period
DANIDA (Danish bilateral)	$20,000,000	Bolivia: claims and administration for indigenous community lands (TCOs)	1997–2009
DANIDA (Danish bilateral)	$701,769	Bolivia: technical and juridical assistance for indigenous ayllus: OTB and TCO registration	Pilot in 1997, 5 years' funding
AECI (Spanish bilateral)	$2,885,600	Ecuador: strengthen indigenous movement-led municipalities	2001–2008
IBIS (Danish NGO)	$376,000	Ecuador: support reconstitution of Quichua pueblos	1999–2003
COSUDE (Swiss bilateral)	$8,405,757	Bolivia: support municipal democratization, indigenous rights, and empowerment	2004–2009

Sources: INRA (2006); *El Comercio*, June 21, 2001; http://aeciecuador.org/site/file/content/14/; ECUARUNARI (1999c); COSUDE (2006); authors' interviews, field notes, and primary documents.

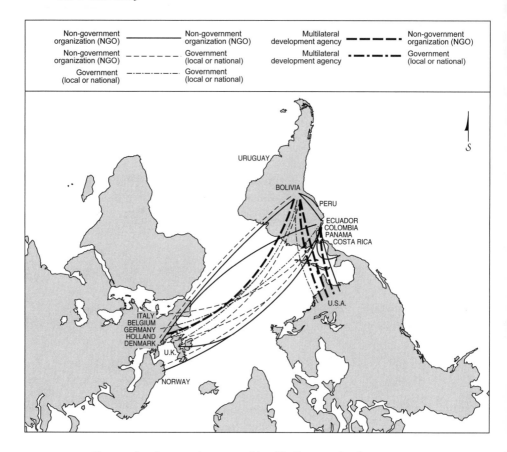

MAP 9. Transnational connections around local indigenous development.

These connections around local development and identity are both South-South and South-North. The South-South links are trans-Andean and primarily between NGOs, while the South-North linkages also include bilateral and multilateral governmental agencies.

The emergent form of "graduated sovereignty" in highland Ecuador and Bolivia is also telling in this respect. Globalization does not necessarily evacuate state sovereignty but rather entails territorial reproduction through the spatial reorganization of state practices (see also Ong 1999). Both Bolivia and Ecuador had central governments that wanted to maintain authority over redefined local spaces, but each used different methods to rescale state power. The former relied on nationwide legal requirements for submission of written municipal development plans to allocate locally entitled resources; the latter insisted on municipalities taking the initiative by submitting individual requests for transfer of faculties and resources, which the central government could approve or reject as it saw fit. Still, both central governments retained only so much control; appropriations and disruptions by local elites or subalterns were commonplace, and development agencies, if not indigenous organizations, became decision-making or regulatory bodies in ways not fully directed or monitored by central state institutions.

In addition, indigenous development policy in the Andes situated the re-deployment of sovereignty in ways distinct from those in other parts of the world. While Ong (2000) focused on Southeast Asian states' adjustments to the globalizing economy's profit and investment imperatives, we have stressed state responses to a wider set of concerns. Here, economic calculations were informed and attenuated by social development priorities, democratic principles, and social-movement agendas. Governance connections were formed more between the state and development agencies or social-movement organizations than between the state and private corporations. Indeed, graduated sovereignty in Ecuador and Bolivia arose as much from indigenous-movement demand (e.g., indigenous districts and collective lands) or from taken-for-granted local geographies (e.g., Cotacachi, Raqaypampa) as it did from imposition by the national government.

Underlying the spatial demand of some Andean indigenous movements is a distinct racial project that would segment governance on ethnic and racial grounds. Indigenous protagonists of the ayllu and pueblo movements intended these as grounds for relating with others. But those others, whether sympathetic or antagonistic, sometimes hold a different understanding of interculturalism and feel alienated or threatened. [120] Heated debates in both countries continue over how best to further indigenous rights and local development, oscillating between discursive poles of integration and partition.[121] Addressing this last issue may require greater specification of the indigenous movement concept of *complementaridad* between indigenous and nonindigenous locales.[122] This might take place through an equitable, intercultural dialogue, where indigenous activists take the lead but include others, development agencies among them.

Doing so might reduce tensions between indigenous and nonindigenous Andeans and develop innovative possibilities for interaction. It may also open discussion about the incorporation of indigenous knowledge into local development projects and processes, as a counterweight to the infusion of Western managerial practices into otherwise distinctive local spaces. This is especially important for ayllus and pueblos, which are envisioned by their proponents as highly distinct from existing socio-spatial forms. As explained by leaders of the Potosí Ayllu Council, "The ayllu . . . has its own economic structure, its social and political structure. We think that for this reason we need to recover all that exists, in order to present it to the country as an alternative."[123]

CHAPTER 4

NINA LAURIE, ROBERT ANDOLINA, AND SARAH A. RADCLIFFE

Neoliberalisms, Transnational Water Politics, and Indigenous People

Similar to the reconfiguration of local scales discussed in chapter 3, indigenous people's engagement with ethnodevelopment paradigms has shaped the transnational arenas where water policies are designed and debated. As water has become one of the major resources for contests over neoliberalism, Andean indigenous movements have gained recognition among diverse sets of development actors operating at various scales, ranging from anticapitalist campaigners and NGOs to donor organizations and states. Lauded by some for their ability to turn the global tide of water privatization by mobilizing cultural rights and customs, and heralded by others for bringing collective management and communitarian control into neoliberal governance models, the role of indigenous identities and movements in contemporary water politics is far from straightforward. Conceiving of Andean water policies as a site for contestation and negotiation over development, this chapter examines the ways in which neoliberal projects attempt to enroll indigenous people as water users, and how, in turn, indigenous movements shape the context for the formation of water policy. Representations of indigenous people influence mobilizations of cultural identity by those seeking to resist or appropriate neoliberal forms of governance.

Neoliberal policies have shown uneven implementation in the water sector. During the 1990s, a largely orthodox approach to development underpinned government water legislation in the Andes. Based on a narrowly economic neoliberalism and a restricted sense of modernity, this approach largely excluded indigenous viewpoints and participation on the grounds that indigenous people lack "modern" knowledge. Doing so led indigenous organizations to reject neoliberal criteria, contentiously disrupting the legislative process through mass protest and alternative water-law agendas in both Ecuador and Bolivia. In Bolivia, such protests culminated in the now internationally renowned Cochabamba Water War, a formative event for global debates on water policy. Struggles over orthodox neoliberal water laws in the Andes centered indigenous identities and agendas on cultural difference, intercultural participation, and state obligation.

In contrast to the approach to water seen in national legislatures, indigenous irrigation has a long history of participative involvement in development networks at a range of scales. In these networks, indigenous people have often been construed as active users of irrigation projects—participating in project oversight, negotiating project terms, and cooperatively undertaking institutional reforms. On the surface, therefore, indigenous engagement in recent irrigation projects would exemplify culturally sensitive forms of social neoliberalism. Yet the outcomes of social neoliberalism in irrigation remain ambiguous, as languages of efficiency, inclusion, and management styles have become key discursive sites of negotiation over development.

Below we indicate how these languages and paradigms have specific effects on subject construction and resource valuation. We do not suggest that only indigenous people are affected by water issues; access to water differentiates people socially and economically, regardless of where they live (rural or urban) or how they self-identify (indigenous, mestizo, and/or campesino). Rather, we are interested in the relation between indigenous movements and cultures on the one hand, and transnational debates and practices over neoliberal policies on the other. Is it the case that "local peoples and cultures try to [represent] themselves according to a 'modernizing' model . . . copied from abroad" (Boelens and Zwarteveen 2002, 21), or is the popularity of ethnodevelopment creating an opportunity for legitimating alternative modernities or postmodernities with regard to water?

International principled-issue networks (Sikkink 1993) and transnational circuits have been important in shaping and challenging translationalized neoliberal water policies, especially with regard to indigenous people. Certain specific networks have influenced indigenous involvement with water policies in Ecuador and Bolivia, and indigenous movements have engaged with orthodox neoliberal water reforms in ways that promote the commodification and privatization of water in diverse ways, including resisting international donor community-supported top-down reforms designed to meet the needs of the private sector. Indigenous movements adopted a proactive stance in claiming rights to more culturally distinctive water laws that recognize collective ownership and indigenous expertise under pluricultural constitutions. Their engagement with other social movements and NGOs occupied different positions vis-à-vis neoliberal water policies. Social neoliberalism is constituted and enacted through irrigation projects that are viewed by donor organizations and indigenous movements alike as successful examples of ethnodevelopment. The two regional irrigation projects we analyze illustrate the type of transnational networks and relations involved and highlight the importance of struggles over language and representation in determining their effects and consequences.

Indigenous People and the Transnationalization of Water

"The next set of great wars will be over water."[1] When Jorge Loor—the campesino leader of an Ecuadorian small farmer's political organization—made this comment about the probability of future water wars, he was reflecting upon his participation in the Second World Water Forum, held in the Netherlands in 2000, and the effect that his use of cultural symbols had on the transnational audience gathered at the forum. "Entering the event with a machete [and a *wiphala*, a rainbow colored indigenous flag], well, of course everyone gave us weird looks . . . but after 40 minutes or so we were approached by a famous Dutch radio program . . . that interviewed me precisely because of the symbols I was carrying. So the machete served as a node for making connections, and it helped me make contacts with the other participants from the [American] continent . . . from Colombia, Peru, Venezuela, and Chile."[2] This event illustrates the increasing presence and visibility of cultural symbolism in transnational water-policy arenas. Although Jorge Loor does not identify as indigenous, nor would indigenous activists in Ecuador see him in that way, the cultural symbols he carried did resonate in a transnational setting outside of the Andes. Signaling his cultural difference, Jorge was able to build alliances with international NGOs and other Latin American delegates. He managed to overcome language barriers and make critical contributions at NGO meetings against water commodification that took place outside the official forum. Jorge and other third-world activist accounts of local opposition to water privatization provided NGOs with concrete material for their action, while also forging new transnational contacts.[3] It is unclear how durable or dense these new contacts were, but Andean water issues are evidently less localized as actors and concepts move across scales and make new connections. The mobilization of indigenous cultural identities under ethnodevelopment paradigms and the emergence of transnational networks around water politics have played central roles in these shifts.

Water politics have only recently become global. Although the UN held a water conference in 1977 in Argentina, a far greater number of international water events took place after 1990, culminating in world water forums in Morocco (1997), the Netherlands (2000), Japan (2003), and Mexico (2006). Other international events have included the "Water, Environment and Sustainable Development" conference in Dublin (1992), the "Water and Sustainable Development" conference in Paris in 1998 (Bustamante 2000, 131), and extensive coverage of water at the 2002 World Summit on Sustainable Development in Johannesburg (Goldman 2005). The growth of international meetings on water has coincided with the most aggressive period of neoliberal water policies promoted by the international development donor community. On the one hand, donor institutions have organized international forums as a means of spreading the privatization message (Goldman 2007). For example, one Ecuadorian NGO member referred to the 2000 World Water Forum in the Netherlands as "basically a space to legitimate the privatization of water on a global scale."[4] On the other hand, antiprivatization coalitions have used these spaces to garner support by extending their networks and lobbying.

Indigenous issues have also gained transnational visibility in relation to water through these interactions. High-profile reports discussed at international events have illustrated global awareness of the importance of water management within indigenous livelihoods. For example, the International Commission on Dams report, published in 2000 and coinciding with a world water forum, highlighted the negative impact of mega-dams on indigenous people worldwide. In Latin America, the UN-affiliated Economic Commission for Latin America and the Caribbean has also issued statements and organized workshops on water use and legal reform. Inter-American meetings on water issued declarations in San José and Buenos Aires (1996), while Bolivian developmental NGOs arranged a transnational electronic forum to debate water policy, which highlighted threats to indigenous uses and customs inherent in proposed or new legislation (CGIAC 2000b). Building on established Latin American alliances concerning indigenous land rights, indigenous groups have engaged in transnational networking over water issues. "The theme of water is rather local, and [transnationalization] is more recent. Where we have had rich experiences and relations of mutual support internationally is in the theme of land; we have relations with Brazil ... with Peru, with Ecuador, including with Argentina and the Mapuche compañeros of Chile."[5] These networks and meetings have served as nodes for building connections around water issues, linking these to other issues like land and accumulating criteria and vocabulary for future encounters.

Andean Water Policy and Politics

Water policy in the Andes reflects broader international trends of state reform and commercialization in the water sector. Heavily supported by multilateral and bilateral aid agencies, these policies have focused largely on promoting greater private-sector involvement in water management in countries of the South as a way to generate new sources of investment (World Bank 1995; Nickson 2001). The World Bank has been a key actor in designing and promoting frameworks that move away from the region's previous focus on a state-run water supply. The bank has articulated new approaches to water use within neoliberal development models by emphasizing development through market incentives, competition, and free trade by private actors. Through new legislation and selective funding, the bank has actively encouraged Andean governments to reduce their public expenditures by selling or transferring water rights and water systems to private hands.

Accusations that state-run systems are inefficient and costly have underpinned much of the push for private-sector involvement in delivering water services (Nickson 2001; Nickson and Vargas 2002). As a result, a "demand-based" paradigm constructing water as a commodity emerged in the Andes and elsewhere. In this model, water users were represented as customers and consumers of commodities, rather than rights-bearing users of resources and services (Marvin and Laurie 1999). The Inter-American Development Bank (1998) modified this paradigm through an "integrated water resources management" approach that centers conceptually on water basins and considers all sources and uses of water within them; it also calls for participation by water users, as well as experts in geology, engineering, and physical geography. As a result of such initiatives, donors working in the Andean region increasingly labeled private-sector investment as pro-poor, particularly when it supported user participation in water provision and extended water networks to poor communities (Laurie and Crespo 2003; Laurie and Crespo 2007; Komvives 1999).

Indigenous organizations and grassroots development NGOs have traditionally adopted agendas contrary to these kinds of private sector–led approaches. Their position on water policy has been influenced by more than three decades of grassroots agricultural development, during which they have collaborated with other NGOs, governments, and donors and experienced varying degrees of success in improving water management and irrigation. As a result, indigenous water politics have been shaped by concepts and criteria shared with regional Andean grassroots development traditions, such as the "Andean irrigation" and "small-farmer irrigation" approaches, influential in Bolivia and Ecuador since the 1970s (CESA 1991; COSUDE 1998; Boelens and Dávila 1998). Drawing inspiration from the rich heritage of community water management in arid and semiarid highland environments, sometimes dating back to pre-Colombian periods, the Andean irrigation and small-farmer irrigation models have focused on supporting the indigenous and campesino sociocultural networks involved in water management, recognizing the crucial role that community decision making and Andean uses and customs (*usos y costumbres*) play in water management.[6] Uses and customs comprise a system of social organization and rules for water management tied to Andean reciprocity and mutual-support networks. Decisions are made in assemblies, and conflicts are resolved by judges appointed by indigenous water organizations. Some organizations retain rituals that thank Mother Earth, and a strong body of knowledge on water conservation and climate change underpins water-management strategies (Crespo 2003).

Concepts and criteria shared among these actors emphasize equitable resource access, improving productive and management capacities of indigenous and small farmers, environmental protection, community-based farming and irrigation systems, and attention to Andean culture.[7] As a result, involved individuals and organizations have become both principled actors and experts in grassroots development and water issues, working with campesino and indigenous organizations through what they call "technical support" and "discussion spaces." Most of these organizations obtain funds from government and NGO sources, and sometimes they work directly with foreign or international organizations on agricultural projects. For example, GTZ has been very influential in funding development projects and research on Andean irrigation in Bolivia, while also supporting privatization (see Gandarillas et al. 1994; Sánchez et al. 1994; Fernández and Crespo 2004).

While criteria concerning the importance of community participation are shared between different actors interested in promoting culturally sensitive irrigation projects, degrees of actor engagement vary. Some proponents of Andean irrigation negotiate elements of neoliberal models that stress productivity and management skills; they see indigenous cultural traditions as secondary to more socioeconomic concerns. NGOs such as IEDECA and the Center for Ecuadorian Agricultural Services (CESA) in Ecuador, for example, work with both indigenous and nonindigenous small farmers and see little difference between them.[8] In contrast, organizations such as PRATEC (Peru) and the Center for Communication and Andean Development (CENDA), in Bolivia, promote development only through cultural recovery, lest it become colonialist and ineffective (Healy 1994).[9]

Positioned in relation to various aspects of neoliberalism, experiences of water policies in neighboring countries have also contributed to a more transnationalized context for indigenous organizations and NGOs to draw upon, as one member of IEDECA explained. "There are abundant [policy] currents like the Chilean and Bolivian [models], where water is a tradable good like any resource. This means, that in the Ecuadorian context, a proposal could be passed that in a short time would mean that the [indigenous and campesino] communities would no longer have access to water. That is a huge concern of the users themselves, and . . . we are trying to support [them] through debates and analyses."[10] In this way, transnational development-with-identity networks have provided spaces for discussion and negotiation over neoliberal water policies. They generated shared criteria and vocabulary for designing, negotiating, and contesting policies and projects, which allowed for a range of positions on neoliberal agendas to emerge. Some indigenous leaders accept a need to improve productive, marketing, and management capacities of indigenous peoples where water management is concerned. However, many make this conditional on direct indigenous participation in the full range of interventions, as we shall see in more detail later in the chapter.

While neoliberal discourses of self-management, regulation, and governance were adopted in some cases, other elements of neoliberal approaches to water management proved more controversial. Indigenous movements in Bolivia and Ecuador called for a continued state role in controlling water resources, regulating water use, and providing water infrastructure, rather than relying on free-market forces—especially in the face of the growing power of private water companies (see CONAIE 1996a; CIDOB, CSUTCB, and CSCB 1999). Even NGOs that have engaged overtly with the efficiency and productionist logic of neoliberal approaches have maintained a critical distance from orthodox neoliberal water legislation focused on privatization. This is especially true when they believe it underemphasizes full participation, local collective organizing, and concerns over food security.

For many indigenous activists, free trade and private water management are also antithetical to indigenous conceptualizations of water. In their view, water is not individually owned under Andean cosmovisions and cultural practices. Instead, they see it as part of a holistic ecological conception and collective property regime based on use rights rather than ownership rights, as Nina Pacari, a leading indigenous figure in Ecuador, explained. "In the indigenous world, water, like rocks, mountains, and trees, is conceived as a living being that feels, converses, watches, and protects. This concept is rooted in the har- . monious relation between humans and nature" (Pacari 1998, 299).[11] Although some indigenous actors accept certain aspects of neoliberal water agendas, other elements are soundly rejected because they impinge on closely held understandings of indigenous uses, customs, and rights. These points of convergence and divergence form the basis of the transnational networks that have developed around water issues in the region.

Hybrid Development Institutions and Water Networks in the Andes
Development networks focused on water and irrigation operate in the Andes within and across scales. These networks have helped to create situations where NGOs and indigenous organizations may negotiate neoliberal paradigms as experts in water and irrigation. In some cases, these networks engage with hybrid development institutions like CODENPE in Ecuador. Taking on the hybrid appearance of those same organizations, water networks receive funding from a variety of sources, rely on alliances between interest groups, and provide a space that embraces those who support *and* contest state-sponsored neoliberal agendas.

The Consortium for the Sustainable Development of the Andean Eco-region (CONDESAN) illustrates well these hybrid characteristics of water and irrigation networks. CONDESAN draws in a range of actors who may not be natural allies, but who do facilitate the formation of issue-based networks. Based in Peru, CONDESAN was created in 1993 to increase equity and sustainable resource management. Its membership is pan-Andean but dominated by Bolivian organizations. It makes use of an electronic information system and receives bilateral aid from the Netherlands, Switzerland, and Canada (CGIAC 2000a).[12] In Bolivia, CONDESAN assisted in the formation of the Cochabamba Integral Water Management Commission, which in 2000 expanded to become the Bolivian Integral Water Management Commission (CGIAB). This commission includes CONDESAN as an associate member, as well as a number of Bolivian NGOs, research centers, development agencies, and the transnationally funded National Irrigation Program of Bolivia (CGIAB 2000).

Dialoguing with actors taking many different positions, CGIAB became a respected forum for discussing water policies. It continues to serve as an important issue-based network in which members do not necessarily share the same principles. Despite receiving funding from proprivatization donors such as USAID, the commission has been able to create an "inter-institutional" coordinator to promote discussion on water-law proposals and their implementation. With public access to research materials and frequent transnational electronic forums, CGIAB has contributed to water debates beyond Bolivia while maintaining dialogue between opposing factions and supporting its members in their own spin-off networking. Since 1998, the Center for Campesino Promotion and Research (CIPCA), an important Bolivian NGO involved in grassroots irrigation and a core member of the commission, was instrumental in arranging discussion forums for indigenous and campesino organizations to develop a comprehensive water-law proposal as an alternative to neoliberal state laws. Illustrative of the hybrid nature of these network spaces is the fact that the World Bank sponsored this alternative water-law discussion, despite the bank's open support for the Bolivian government's neoliberal water-law proposals.[13] In creating this forum, CIPCA worked with the Solón Foundation, which, like CIPCA, opposed privatization. Their networking facilitated dialogue with those who favor privatization, including key members of the Bolivian congress, while also creating a "technical group" that aimed to harmonize indigenous-campesino alternative water-law proposals.

In Ecuador, too, interactions that blur conventional political roles and relationships have emerged. The networking activities of the NGO IEDECA, which supports smallholder agriculture production and irrigation in the Ecuadorian highlands, illustrate the ways in which spaces of dialogue are created while respecting different positions on neoliberal interventions.[14] Although hailing from a tradition of radically alternative grassroots development and holding many views counter to those of the World Bank, IEDECA agreed to run the Ecuadorian branch of the bank's Structural Adjustment Participatory Review Initiative.[15] This was an independent popular consultation exercise reviewing the impacts of adjustment. In entering into such a relationship with the World Bank, IEDECA positioned itself as an organization able to monitor the way in which consultative exercises are followed up in policy implementation. Within such relationships forged over indigenous development, traditional institutional roles in consultancy, participation, and monitoring may undergo change: organizations like IEDECA that support highland indigenous and peasant communities have critiqued donor organizations while engaging directly with them through monitoring partnerships. Map 10 illustrates the complex of North-South and South-South transnational linkages around water issues noted here.

In this section we have argued that transnational development-with-identity networks embraced both actors who were opposed to neoliberal intervention in the water sector *and* those who were open to adopting certain neoliberal

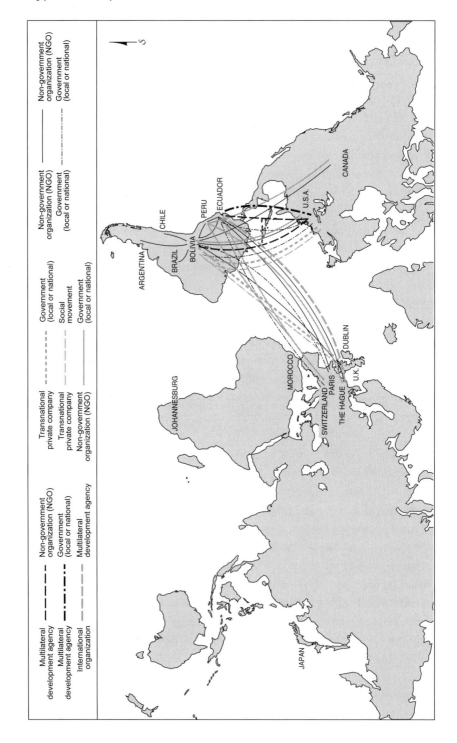

criteria they feel would strengthen participation and decentralization. Therefore, these diverse networks have become important sites for negotiating development policies, projects, and legislation. The overlap among different networks provided a shared set of criteria and vocabulary through which a diversity of actors could interact and negotiate. Emphasis on different neoliberal priorities and contrasting understandings of terminology, however, sometimes led to disagreement and conflict in particular contexts.

In contrasting the politics of national water legislation and the politics of local irrigation development projects, we can see that, on the one hand, irrigation development projects and water-law debates are transnationally situated in terms of policy paradigms and action circuits. On the other hand, they represented two distinct forms of neoliberal development, thereby illustrating multiple constructions and configurations of subjects, objectives, and forms of participation. In the first section we trace processes of comprehensive and sector-specific water-law reform in Ecuador and Bolivia during the 1990s. In the second section, we analyze two irrigation projects that diverse actors saw as examples of best practice during the same time period. Although economic and social-development criteria were present in both settings, as were indigenous-movement agendas, the two contexts revealed different emphases and distinct consequences.

Contesting Development Orthodoxies: Protecting Culture, Challenging Institutions, and Rejecting Privatization

Indigenous and campesino organizations have disputed the design and implementation of water laws by drawing on already-established transnational alliances (for example, around land issues) and by developing new connections around water policies. Concerned that tradable water rights and private water systems could reduce or eliminate their access to water, indigenous people in both Ecuador and Bolivia protested neoliberal water legislation as creating

◄ MAP 10. Transnational linkages around water and natural resource issues.

The complexity of this map represents the circuitous and entangled character of multiple, intersecting issue networks coming together around water. The networks explored in this chapter involve transnational corporations in addition to NGOs, social movements, and official agencies and have numerous connections with European sites as most early global water forums were held there.

the potential for economic and cultural harm. In Ecuador, the main protests were over the design of a new comprehensive water law. In Bolivia, contests erupted over the design of a comprehensive water law and the passage and implementation of a law specific (in theory) to potable water and sewage. In both countries, this activism concentrated on questioning how approved or proposed legislation defined the following: water ownership rights; diverse use rights (domestic, energy, irrigation, etc.); concessions of use rights; user fees, prices, and fines; responsibility for water works systems; and representation on water consultation and governing boards.

Government water-law proposals in Ecuador and Bolivia have largely followed neoliberal economic lines, adopting the aforementioned demand-based paradigm to water promoted by international agencies. This, along with tying aid and debt relief to privatization agreements, led to the formulation of water policies from the top down. Development funding has been channeled through institutional-strengthening programs intended to improve state companies prior to going to market (Castro 2007). Constructions of knowledge about the national water sector shifted to the international arena, as influential foreign consultancy firms directed and monitored these programs, much to the chagrin of local and national water experts (Laurie 2007).[16] Multilateral agencies that advised and funded draft water legislation left the processes of public debate, decision, and implementation to government officials. But these officials usually turned to internationally trained professional experts for additional guidance on water-law provisions. These actions tended to marginalize indigenous people and campesinos from participation in debate, as the knowledge relied upon (and reproduced) in these contexts did not take indigenous knowledge and understandings about water into consideration.

These top-down processes limited possibilities for overlap and agreement among the actors involved, creating a highly politicized interaction that influenced the formation of networks and the positioning of indigenous movements. Grassroots development NGOs and other social organizations generally took the side of indigenous organizations, while multilaterals usually supported government officials. Opposition movements and NGOs formed *coordinadoras* (coordinating bodies) that mobilized protests championing alternative platforms. Indigenous and campesino organizations led or participated in these protests on the streets and in discussion forums with government officials, asserting water and participation rights based on cultural and political distinctiveness while demanding state guarantee of such rights.

Water-Law Politics in Ecuador

Ecuador's 1972 Ley de Aguas nationalized water rights and established the National Institute for Hydro Resources (INERHI) in Ecuador (Corporación de Estudios y Publicaciones 1994, 22). However, the growing scarcity of uncontaminated water, a rising number of court cases over water rights, and increased use of irrigation water by nontraditional export industries started to raise new concerns.[17] These were further politicized in 1994 when the state attempted to follow World Bank, IADB, and USAID policies by liberalizing water rights and reforming water institutions to enhance efficiency and self-help in water management. INERHI was abolished and replaced with the National Water Council (CNRH). Water management was decentralized to regional development councils, and state water infrastructure was transferred to nonpublic hands through a World Bank–sponsored Technical Assistance Program for the "Irrigation Subsector." That same year, congress passed an agrarian law proposal—drafted by a USAID-sponsored think tank—that proposed privatization of water rights. CONAIE led a successful nationwide protest against that law, resulting in indigenous participation in the law's revision, which assured that water rights stayed in public hands (Acción Ecológica 2000, 5; Selverston-Scher 2001). In short, the Ecuadorian government signaled its interest in liberalizing the water industry with transnational donor support, while indigenous organizations signaled their determination to stop or limit that move.

Following this, various actors drafted new water-law proposals. One from the National Water Council was submitted to congress in 1997, reflecting the World Bank's focus on efficiency, private-sector participation, institutional reform, and personnel training. The proposal recommended consultant boards to oversee reform and, following the IADB's model, proposed a dialogue with all actors involved in water to establish the "integral management" of "vital resources like water" (MAG 2000). The National Water Council's proposal contained the following features:

- It broke with the format of the 1972 water law that tied water to agrarian development
- It included clauses on environmental protection, integral management, and "sacred waters" but restricted their definition. Environmental criteria were linked to protection of basins, but not to mountaintops with water sources, which are spaces often occupied by indigenous peoples

- It recognized formal state control of water but contained articles on private participation, investment (including concessions), and the transfer of systems (infrastructure) to private hands
- It promoted efficiency and productivity criteria
- It proposed a water superintendent with links to the Ministry of Agriculture and with representation largely from ministries and chambers of agriculture

During 1995 and 1996, indigenous leaders drafted an alternative water-law proposal in workshops with provincial and local organizations, sponsored by grassroots development NGOS. CONAIE submitted its proposal to congress in January 1996. This proposal contained specific indigenous understandings of "integral management," where water is seen as lifeblood linked with other natural elements. It also retained a strong role for the state in water administration:

- It adopted parameters of the 1972 law and retained state control and ownership of water
- It emphasized equity in access to resources, use of water for ritual purposes, environmental protection, and integral water management by local communities
- It focused on irrigation and proposed an irrigation investment fund
- It discussed co-management and co-responsibility for water systems by users and the state, not the transfer of water systems to private hands
- It kept the National Water Council as the state overseer, but its representation would include delegates from indigenous organizations and environmentalists

While national actors submitted these proposals, they grew out of and constituted transnational platforms. The National Water Council proposal was a product of ideas and interactions among state agencies, international development organizations, and national and international consultants. Similarly, the CONAIE proposal shared criteria with environmental organizations and with grassroots development organizations working in Andean irrigation and small-farmer irrigation (IEDECA, CICDA, and Ostrom 1995). An emphasis on water's use for indigenous cultural and ritual purposes in these alliances indicated attempts to scale indigenous knowledge beyond the local in order to construct and legitimate national indigenous water expertise.[18]

Although the Ecuadorian congress received CONAIE's draft water law through proper channels, it never seriously considered this proposal, nor did it involve

CONAIE actively in discussion. Instead, it debated the National Water Council's proposal and others submitted by successive presidents in 1998 and 1999.[19] Although representing distinct groups and working on different issues, common discontent led indigenous, campesino, irrigator, environmental, and grassroots development organizations to form the National Coordinator of Water Users (Coordinadora Nacional de Usuarios de Agua, CONAUA) in January 1998. This coordinator organized meetings to raise consciousness about the water-law proposals while also mobilizing marches to Quito in July 1998 and June 1999 to protest the content of congressional water-law proposals and the exclusion of most user groups from consultation processes (Acción Ecológica 2000, 5–6): "They [the Congress] were going to impose a water law that had not been consulted on . . . so we said no, wait a minute: here we are indigenous people and campesinos who use water. Water cannot simply be exploited [economically], but has to be used for everyone's benefit, with rights guaranteed for the entire citizenry. . . . Water is used as part of our culture . . . and we have rituals involving waterfalls. So that's why we carried out various mobilizations in Quito."[20]

Similar dynamics unfolded in a 2000 congressional forum on the water law, which was supported by transnational donors. To further its aims for water reform and good governance in Ecuador, the IADB offered funds for the Ecuadorian congress, through its Economic Committee, to run a series of consultative workshops on the water law in the spring of 2000. Following its exclusionary practices of 1998 and 1999, congressional organizers selected the National Water Council proposal as the basis for discussion and ignored CONAIE's proposal. In addition, representatives of indigenous organizations, other social movements, and the Water Users Coordinator failed to receive invitations until the day before the workshop and did not receive copies of the discussion proposal prior to attending.[21] Delegates from CONAIE and other social movements challenged the legitimacy of the forum, as well as the content of the discussion proposal. In so doing, they asserted rights to both political autonomy and cultural difference, as well as equal rights to active national participation. As CONAIE's director of land and water stated: "It is not right that we have to discuss a proposal that we have not participated in. Three years ago we presented a water-law proposal [and there should be time to discuss it] . . . if these concerns are taken into account, fine, we will participate. If not, we as CONAIE will unfortunately not be able to continue."[22] These criticisms were countered by the director of the congressional commission, who tried to reestablish legislative authority and revealed distinct understandings of good governance and knowledge, emphasizing (nonindigenous) professional expertise: "I . . . speak to you as an anthropologist who has worked for twenty years in indigenous communities. . . . I know perfectly well that indigenous peoples have the biggest problems with water in the highlands. . . . It will be very interesting for you [indigenous leaders] to listen to people who have been following the process of this law . . . people who know about the topic of water."[23] It was never suggested by legislative officials or professional invitees that indigenous people or campesinos might be experts on water issues.[24] However, CONAIE and CONAUA members questioned these representations and reasserted their rights and knowledge. As one member argued, "The users have never been taken into account . . . especially indigenous people and campesinos . . . we work [the land]; together with the water we are strong. Maybe you do not think we have brains; that we are incapable, but we are Ecuadorians too: we have the right to be represented."[25] As the workshop ended in April 2000 with little agreement, the debates were drafted into a series of recommendations for future workshops and consideration by congress. Although this was ostensibly a national political contest, the criteria and proposals drawn on—and the circuits that participants in the meeting belonged to—were transnational. For example, indigenous leaders, water users, and environmentalists threatened to stage protests like those that had recently occurred over the introduction of new water laws in Bolivia if full participation and user needs were not incorporated. Such tactics illustrate the importance of transnational examples in informing policy negotiation in national contexts. Also, follow-up sessions obeyed lines of polarized transnational networks: the World Bank and IADB called a session with the Congressional Economic Commission to discuss the progress of the water workshops. To counteract this alliance, French and Ecuadorian grassroots development NGOs called meetings to oppose privatization and support indigenous awareness of, and opposition to, the proposed legislation.[26]

Water Law Politics in Bolivia

Water legislation in Bolivia, as in Ecuador, has been located within efforts by the Bolivian government to harmonize the economy and state with broader neoliberal and globalizing tendencies. During the 1990s indigenous, campesino, and urban neighborhood organizations were largely excluded from the official design and debate of proposed water legislation. In turn, indigenous organizations contested this set of policies by rejecting water privatization and insisting on wide participation in water affairs. They also claimed rights to cultural difference and tradition through the defense of uses and customs. Polarization, similarly to those in Ecuador, emerged as opposition movements and NGOs formed coordinators that mobilized protests around alternative platforms, while government officials and international development agencies allied to varying degrees with transnational water companies like Aguas del Tunari, which took over the concession for the city of Cochabamba in November 1999.

Unlike the 1972 Ecuadorian water law, Bolivia never passed a law establishing full public dominion over water. Its only previous water law was passed in 1906, which effectively granted property rights over water based on where waters lay.[27] Reforms since 1990 created contradictory and confusing situations with respect to the Bolivian water regime. On the one hand, constitutional reforms in 1994 established original state dominion over natural resources like water and recognized indigenous rights to their own customs and use of resources on their lands. Meanwhile, laws passed in the 1990s (including the mining code, the electricity law, the forestry law, and the natural resource regulation law) followed a different logic, allowing companies with resource concessions to use and manipulate water sources according to their needs, without requiring consultation with affected populations even if the concession was on indigenous or campesino lands (Solón 2001). These other laws created the basis for government water-law proposals, of which there were over thirty. A 1988 Bolivian senate proposal set out principles for what it claimed was "modern water legislation," informed by the global demand-based paradigm for water use and provision (Bustamante 2000, 121–22). Drafted with help from the French government and the Konrad-Adenauer-Stiftung Institute, a 1997 government proposal followed similar principles and logics:[28]

- It formally acknowledged the 1994 constitution's assertion of state dominion over water but was based more on laws facilitating concessions and private participation
- It emphasized the economic values of water and sought to establish "a water concessions market," allowing those winning concessions from the state to sell or redistribute that concession to third parties
- It granted use to all actors through a single concession regime. Concessions would have a maximum length of forty years and could be renewed. Concessions for farmers in the countryside required demonstration of prior property rights
- Mining, oil drilling, and hydroelectric activities were considered public utilities and had priority over other uses. However, enterprises would be legally responsible for environmental protection

- It proposed a water superintendent as the highest regulatory agency.
  This agency would grant and revoke concessions, charge for patents,
  and establish user fees. Representation was to include delegates of the
  Planning and Sustainable Development Ministry, other government
  officials, and business organizations, but indigenous or campesino
  representatives were excluded

Indigenous and campesino organizations, together with NGOs working in grassroots development and legal affairs (such as CIPCA, the Center for Legal Studies and Social Research (CEJIS), and the Solón Foundation) developed an alternative proposal in April 1999.[29] These organizations believed that indigenous customs and uses of water had to be respected and that the state should maintain ownership over water resources, in part to guarantee protection of those cultural and historical rights. They also argued that the state needed to guarantee access to water resources, which would include state payment of costs to supply water. Finally, these organizations insisted on direct participation in the oversight of any new water regime. This alternative proposal worked within the framework of the 1994 constitutional reform designating state control over water and indigenous rights to natural resource use and the 1906 water law's recognition of property rights granted automatically through long-term use. It asserted that access to water is a human right guaranteeing familial and collective well-being. As such, no market for water or water concessions would be allowed. It granted rights to users through a dual regime of authorizations and community water rights. Private companies would be required to submit a water resource management plan and an agreement with affected populations in order to gain authorization, which would be valid for twenty years and would be renewable. They would also have to pay an annual patent charge and fines for any contamination. Indigenous and campesino communities, neighborhood water cooperatives, and irrigation organizations would collectively register community water rights, which were defined as free of charges and not subject to trade or transfer, by concession or otherwise. Finally, it proposed a national water council as the top national agency for water. This council would have equal representation between state representatives and water users, including indigenous, campesino, and urban neighborhood confederations.

While these two water-policy platforms shared some criteria, they are more notable in their differences, particularly in their emphases on the economic, modern, and institutional aspects of reform, versus social, customary, and participatory elements. A twenty-two-day march of indigenous campesinos from

Cochabamba to La Paz in September and October 1998 was the first mobilization to challenge the content of government water-law proposals and raise objections to the procedures of debate on them. Organizers specifically opposed the creation of a water superintendent and the failure to recognize indigenous uses and customs in water management. Although divisions among leaders weakened the march, indigenous and campesino organizations were able to agree to the common water-law proposal and compel the government to commit to developing a consensual law with civil-society participation, prior to submitting it to congress.[30] Lowland indigenous leaders also affirmed these goals, as suggested by CIDOB adviser Alberto Rodríguez:

> All of the laws since 1985 have been passed . . . without us being consulted, and many of them violate indigenous and campesino rights. . . . In reference to the water law, we have a big problem because the government had signed agreements with the World Bank to accelerate the privatization of water . . . because of the $50 million that it will give [the government] to implement the law. [The indigenous and campesino confederations] have disagreed with the creation of superintendents . . . because . . . they are above any law, and offer concessions to their friends and transnational companies.[31]

As it happens, it was the granting of a concession to a transnational company (Aguas del Tunari) in the Cochabamba region that spurred quick congressional passage of a Water and Sewer System Law (Law 2029) in the fall of 1999. These events, in turn, sparked major popular protests throughout 2000. Following a shift away from big dam-development projects and toward water privatization, the Bolivian government and the World Bank believed Cochabamba's water scarcity problem could be solved by privatizing the system and securing international investment.[32] However, privatization faced widespread public opposition, and the rushed approval of Aguas del Tunari's concession confused the population about the rules on water. These events also angered indigenous and campesino organizations that had mobilized against the proposed new comprehensive water legislation and were actively involved in attempts to negotiate with the government when Law 2029 was passed (Crespo 2003; Laurie 2005). Law 2029 created a national water superintendent with the power to grant concessions over *all* water resources under a common license regime. Together with the contract signed between the state and Aguas del Tunari, this situation not only allowed the company to raise tariffs (by 200 percent in some cases) but also permitted it to place water meters on alternative systems that were not connected to Cochabamba's formal city water network.[33] In effect, the company had the power to monitor private and cooperative wells, charge *cochabambinos* for the monitoring equipment, and tie water user fees to the dollar via the U.S. consumer price index (Crespo 2003; Laurie, Andolina, and Radcliffe 2002).

When these legal and contractual policies were announced, sporadic road-blocks and demonstrations transformed into more-organized and intense protest events. A committee for the defense of water, established in the fall of 1999, transformed into the Coordinadora para la Defensa del Agua y Vida (Coordinator for the Defense of Water and Life), which included a broad range of water users across differences of class and ethnicity. It brought together middle- and working-class neighborhood groups, professionals, labor unions, university students, women's organizations, and water cooperatives from low-income neighborhoods in Cochabamba. Campesino organizations and indigenous peasant irrigators who had led previous opposition to water legislation joined these protests, forging an unprecedented rural-urban alliance. Following the logic and symbolism of the draft indigenous-campesino confederation water-law proposal, the coordinadora bound its objections to price increases and well privatization to the protection of cultural uses and customs. It invoked Andean indigenous cultural imagery to construct an untouchable, sacred set of social and cultural water rights, such that one campaign poster read, "Pachamama, Wiracocha, and Tata Dios gave [water] to us to live, not do business with." In street protests, urban mestizos echoed the cultural politics of indigenous campesino and irrigator organizations by interpreting price increases under foreign ownership as a new form of colonial pillage. Claiming water as "life blood" and an inheritance from her ancestors, one protestor called upon all Bolivian women to protect their cultural heritage and fight with their lives if they had to (Laurie, Andolina, and Radcliffe 2002, 231–32).

This articulation of diverse interests and identities also proved powerful internationally. Successfully networking with transnational anticapitalist movements focused on rejecting privatization, coordinadora leaders were invited to speak at rallies in the United States during the struggle. In this way, certain actors jumped scales and established important links with transnational anti-privatization movements elsewhere, which in turn supported Bolivian demands for the annulment of Agua del Tunari's contract and the revision of the national Potable Water and Sewage Law. Indigenous symbolism played an important role in these transnational encounters, opening up space for indigenous platforms to embrace nonindigenous actors. For example, Óscar Olivera, a coordinadora leader who traveled to the United States, was seen as an indigenous hero by North American members of the transnational antiglobalization network (including indigenous members), even though in Bolivia he is recognized as a mestizo union activist (see also Laurie 2005; Laurie forthcoming). Such events suggest that the racial marking of issue networks around water can generate opportunities for alliances such as the coordinadora to gain political legitimacy by working and identifying with indigenous movements and agendas; they also place indigenous movements in positions to decide on the content and purposes of alliances.

Transnational representations of the Cochabamba Water War as an indigenous struggle contributed to the success of the popular protest nationally and allowed indigenous and nonindigenous actors to change and overturn neoliberal water legislation. After presidential efforts to suppress the protests by force failed in April 2000, the coordinadora was able to compel the government to meet its demands (Crespo 2003). Together with canceling Aguas del Tunari's contract, cutting back price increases, and guaranteeing control over private wells to individuals and cooperatives, the coordinadora succeeded in participating in a revision of the Potable Water and Sewage Law, so that it recognized alternative water systems such as indigenous uses and customs. This revised legislation was named Law 2066.

The Cochabamba coordinadora framework—which protest leaders called the "first global opposition to the neoliberal water model"—became famous worldwide and reinforced polarized transnational networking in antiprivatization and proprivatization lobbies. Indigenous leaders from other parts of the world visited Cochabamba (Laurie 2005), and Bolivian indigenous leaders were invited to Ecuador to speak on water privatization and protest. Subsequently, the Bolivian government was forced to shelve its comprehensive nationwide water-law proposals in September 2000 (Solón 2000).

The state's introduction of new water legislation, supported by bilateral and multilateral agencies, was driven by orthodox understandings of neoliberalism and exclusive modernization that subordinated social and participatory concerns to economic and efficiency criteria in both Ecuador and Bolivia. In turn, indigenous organizations, campesino organizations, and other movements openly contested this articulation of neoliberalism. They designed and promoted alternative proposals, carried out mass mobilizations, formed alliances with nonindigenous actors, and networked transnationally. In doing so, they projected cultural subjects and national identities that differed from narrow images of modernity focused on property rights, asserting the possibility for alternative forms of modernity and for inclusive notions of Andean cultural heritage. Indigenous and other social organizations rejected a rigidly market-based logic for water distribution and demanded rights to participation and accountability while challenging national and transnational institutions that excluded their contributions, views, and interests.

Given the contentious character of water-law politics, open dialogue with development players like the state and international donors was restricted, in contrast to the irrigation projects described below. However, a diversity of opposition groups drew in middle-class urban consumers, mestizo campesinos, irrigator organizations, rural and urban unions, indigenous organizations, women's groups, and professional organizations. These operated at a range of scales to share experiences and coordinate strategies. So while the context of neoliberalism in water legislation differs from the context of irrigation discussed below, the networks and alliances established to negotiate these trajectories embrace many of the same actors working in strategic alliances through transnational linkages.

Constructing Best Practice?
Ethnodevelopment in Andean Irrigation

The configuration of neoliberal policies in the irrigation sector has been influenced by a longer history of development interventions and networks than those linked to the recent initiatives on Andean water legislation. Improving irrigation, greening arid lands, and providing abundant water supplies for commercial crop production have been central to modernization policies since their heyday in the 1950s. Originally inspired by the promise of technical solutions, Andean irrigation projects have increasingly come to concentrate on sustainable forms of development and small- to medium-scale irrigation projects (Laurie 2004). Environmental problems, and the failure to generate a sense of ownership among local communities, have contributed to the demise of the mega-project and the rise of Andean and small-farmer irrigation models in donor-sponsored development. This is not to say, however, that donor interest in improving irrigation is now confined to community-based initiatives. Neoliberal-driven investment in wide-scale irrigation for commercially viable nontraditional exports, like the flower industry in Ecuador, indicates the continued role played by donors in supporting agroindustrial commercial production. Nevertheless, research on Andean irrigation is increasingly influencing donors, NGOs, and the state by highlighting the sustainability of projects that engage with community forms of knowledge and decision making. These findings are likewise shaping community relationships with outside agencies and setting new contexts for neoliberal articulation with irrigation.

The longstanding engagement of diverse development actors in Andean irrigation and small-farmer irrigation has the hallmarks of "good" development-with-identity. These approaches are characterized by close attention to cultural practices, respect for indigenous knowledge, uses, and customs, and collective forms of decision making and resource management. For many development actors (including some indigenous organizations), these characteristics increasingly resonate with the principles and objectives of social neoliberalism. Irrigation projects in the Andes accommodate concerns about equity, participation, environmental protection, and interculturalism, while at the same time maintaining criteria of efficiency, productivity, and marketing as major priorities. At the same time that social criteria are applied to economic development, efficiency criteria are also applied to social organizations. As a result, discourses of social capital have increasingly found a home in irrigation research and practice (see also Kähkönen 1999).

NGOs and indigenous organizations have given mixed responses to neoliberal interventions in irrigation and have drawn on networks operating through multiple scales to support their positions. Proponents of neoliberal approaches expect institutional decentralization, flexible partnerships, and proper management techniques to generate successful irrigation projects. However, this new institutionality is actively contested by some NGOs. For example, the influential Bolivian NGO CENDA focuses on how local-scale community experimentation with crops and irrigation produces sustainable change, and questions Green Revolution practices supporting the introduction of high-yield varieties of grain, which often require higher levels of irrigation and chemical inputs and perpetuate the need for new projects (Calvo et al. 1994). Although CENDA is a national NGO that has worked closely with indigenous groups in Raqaypampa for well over a decade, it is also linked into transnational development networks. For instance, it receives funding from a range of donors and INGOs, including the Catholic Agency for Overseas Development, the Inter-American Foundation, the Kellogg Foundation, and most recently DANIDA.

Whether opposed to or ambivalent about neoliberal agendas, the forms of institutionality involved in irrigation have framed policy elite's notions of success and have shaped the context in which indigenous organizations operate. Providing both limitations and possibilities for indigenous peoples, neoliberal approaches to irrigation have influenced how indigenous groups represent themselves and their goals, as well as how others represent them. The follow-ing analysis of the Patacocha-Tucayta irrigation project in the Cañar region of south-central Ecuador, and the Ch'aky Irrigation Project in the Raqaypampa region of Bolivia (see maps 1 and 2 in the introduction), illuminates the positive overlap and negative tension involved in designing and executing irrigation projects that follow ethnodevelopment principles.

These two irrigation projects are widely held to be best-practice examples of ethnodevelopment in irrigation based on four criteria:

- The potential for the project to enhance productivity in the medium term
- The participation of beneficiaries (indigenous campesinos) in key aspects of the project
- The innovative coordination between governmental and nongovern-mental actors on multiple levels
- The relative cost effectiveness of the projects

For leaders of indigenous organizations, both irrigation projects fulfilled long-term demands for self-managed development that improves their access to resources and decision-making power. The projects also enabled them to main-tain and deploy certain cultural practices, especially collective property rights and management of irrigation systems. Key to this policy formation was the willingness of financiers and project executors to facilitate indigenous participa-tion, which permitted development agendas to overlap and encouraged flexible interaction between the different kinds of organizations that financed, designed, and implemented these projects.

The Patacocha Canal in Ecuador

The Patacocha Canal began as a community-led initiative in the early 1970s that sought to provide more water for the semiarid lands of Cañar Province, and particularly for the indigenous campesino communities affiliated with the local Tucayta association (Federation of Indigenous Communities of Cañar), whose landholdings experienced droughtlike conditions for the majority of the year.[34] The difficult terrain and mountainous conditions prove daunting for these communities, who relied on their own inputs through community labor systems based on *faenas* and *minga* to construct the canal. Turning to the state for support, the canal was converted into a large-scale, integrated, modernization mega-project comprising a main irrigation line and an exten-sive system of secondary networks and channels. The communities continued to provide labor to cover cosponsorship obligations required by the state. How-ever, by the 1980s, when the project was under full state control, little progress had been made because—according to former Tucayta president Francisco Quinde—community ownership of the project had become limited. "There was little community participation, and the state continued to be the owner of the project, while the executing institutions and people of Tucayta were simple users [instead of] feeling like participants in development. There were many problems and failures."[35]

In the mid-1990s new ideas and actors were introduced, and the project was transformed from a perceived failure to a seeming success through a com-bination of reflective learning by the organizations involved, economic and institutional reforms, and the adoption of a social-neoliberal approach by the Swiss bilateral donor agency, COSUDE, which assumed financing of the project in 1995.[36] What resulted was a cooperative, negotiated process in which Tucayta limited its protest against neoliberal policy and its assertion of cultural differ-ence—despite its being a member of CONAIE, which was actively involved in contesting neoliberal water legislation during this period, as discussed above.

A series of transnationally supported legislative changes set the context for the emergence of an ethnodevelopment circuit around the Patacocha Canal. In 1993, a "state modernization" law worked in tandem with the World Bank–funded "Transfer Assistance for Irrigation Infrastructure Project," allowing the state to contract out or otherwise transfer services and infrastructure to private companies, NGOs, and civil-society organizations (such as Tucayta). This law also contained decentralization provisions, allowing regional and provincial development parastatal organizations to construct water systems. The Economic Reconstruction Center of Cañar, Azuay, and Morona Santiago provinces (CREA) became the new regional development organization responsible for works in the area where the Patacocha irrigation system was being built and restored. To fill out the partnership between the Tucayta communities, COSUDE invited CESA to carry out the project and find a partner agency to work with in order to accommodate economic, decentralization, and participatory concerns. CESA then chose CREA, the new regional development council, due to its efficiency and responsiveness to local needs. A CESA functionary commented, "We ana-lyzed other actors [besides CREA] ... and under the criteria of efficiency, agility, experience, operational autonomy, and noninterference of a political (party) nature, we eliminated [the other actors].... [Unlike a private contractor] who would disappear once the work was finished, CREA obeys regional develop-ment needs, and therefore should respond to the interests of local populations.

That was an advantage" (CESA and CREA 1998, 26). This hybrid partnership was meant to cement and enact the Swiss donor's social-neoliberal view: that the project should conform to the government-led privatization and decentralization process, as well as support indigenous community concerns over participation and equitable access to water resources.[37] It therefore revealed the strong influence that transnational donors' understandings of both neoliberal best practices and Andean models of irrigation had on the revitalization of the Patacocha project.

However, by choosing CESA to spearhead the local partnership, COSUDE selected an NGO that it was already funding. Therefore, the hybrid partnership seemed to support local participation and avoid onerous donor involvement, but it also increased indirect donor control over the execution of the project. This control at a distance is illustrated by the fact that, when the indigenous organization Tucayta asked to retain a collective management system over the canal once it was complete, its demands for greater autonomy were agreed to under the proviso that Tucayta demonstrate its capacity to efficiently manage the system collectively after project funding was complete. Proof of efficiency involved submitting a yearly plan with a public works schedule (collective labor), a documented system of user-fee collection and sanctions against theft of water, proof of sufficient personnel budget, and a computer to monitor water users (CESA and CREA 1998).

By complying with such requests, local actors completed what Mawdsley, Townsend, Porter, and Oakley (2002, 833) have called development "information loops" required by the managerialism and audit cultures of development NGOs operating in transnational communities (see also Townsend, Porter, and Mawdsley 2002). By linking neoliberal and grassroots development logic, both the Swiss donor *and* the Tucayta communities asserted that the management skills acquired represented an advance for indigenous peoples and constituted a form of empowerment. Said one COSUDE technical adviser, "The project is interesting because the [indigenous] organization has passed through the typical stages of Ecuadorian rural development. Fifteen years ago they were about vindication and were always in opposition, and they have passed through a very interesting transformation to be responsible managers . . . and there is an indicator of their self-esteem as indigenous people, reinforced by economic empowerment."[38] The coordinator of the Tucayta technical team, meanwhile, observed, "We have transcended the vindication [opposition] phase to . . . autonomous management, and we are even thinking about small-business development for our communities. With this, Tucayta wants to demonstrate that indigenous people can take up positions to spaces but with capabilities to be competitive."[39]

What is noteworthy here is the fact that the indigenous leader constructed indigenous subjects as efficient managers and competitive entrepreneurs, thus worthy of participation, rather than culturally distinct users of a resource with specific rights.[40] This understanding contrasts sharply with the water legislation process, where indigenous leaders asserted their cultural rights but were seen by other actors as having little to contribute and as obstacles to progress. Where the enactment of transnational agendas positioned indigenous peoples as inferior subjects in water-law debates, the transnational irrigation projects situated them as potential equals. On the other hand, this equality rested not on a rights-based discourse but on being capable and responsible under a neoliberal development model.

To summarize, in the Patacocha irrigation project, donor emphases on actor participation, indigenous farmers' access to water, and the protection of fragile ecological zones overlapped with indigenous organizations' platforms calling for active participation and self-managed grassroots development. Although it was not one of the project's express goals, it did result in a system of indigenous collective management of irrigation water, so long as the local organization met expectations of efficiency, institutional reform, and project management. Tucayta negotiated the terms of the project and provided regular oversight, rather than contesting and disrupting the process. Likewise, it framed its rights and obligations more in terms of productivity and efficiency than in terms of cultural difference or communitarianism, although it combined such terms in a way that resonated with neoliberal definitions of indigenous social capital. This social-neoliberal framework enabled consensus building and cooperative interaction among key actors (indigenous communities, local NGOs, and donors) even though, as in the case of water legislation, those actors operated on different scales (local, national, international) and had different connections to government institutions such as regional development agencies and national ministries.

The Ch'aky Irrigation Project

Much like the Patacocha project in Ecuador, the Ch'aky project in Bolivia was situated within state legislation and international development policy based on a social-neoliberal framework.[41] This approach sought to combine economic liberalization and decentralization with social criteria such as participation, equity, and multiculturalism by placing more resources and development responsibilities in the hands of local authorities, especially at the municipal level, and permitting representative civil-society organizations (OTBs) to acquire legal recognition and oversee municipal planning and expenditure. Bolivia's agrarian reform law also allowed for indigenous collective land titles, called original community lands (TCOs). Bilateral and multilateral agency initiatives sought to strengthen the principles and criteria expressed in these Bolivian state reforms (Van Cott 2000).

The Ch'aky project involved the construction of a series of irrigation lagoons, proposed by the indigenous Quechua communities in Raqaypampa (Cochabamba department) as part of a broader Indigenous Development Plan (Plan Indígena), the first such plan produced under the Law of Popular Participation. With the help of the NGO CENDA, the Raqaypampa communities forged their development plan through participation in research and assembly-based decision making. Its main elements included the need for education and teacher training rooted in indigenous culture, the establishment of the Raqaypampa region as an indigenous TCO, and greater access to irrigation water. As in the case of Patacocha, the Ch'aky project was seen as worthy of funding *because* of the participatory character of the development plan, which fit into new partnership-style management and financing mechanisms. One official in the state's PDCR asserted that the strength of Raqaypampa indigenous organizations and their NGO partnership allowed for solid planning skills and irrigation capacities: "Thanks to the great organizing capacity of the *comunarios* in Raqaypampa [they were able to] elaborate a plan that is practically their own. By way of the executing agency, in this case CENDA, we as the financial entity simply support the development financially and technically . . . but in the execution we do have to see how the people administer resources and manage [the project]."[42] Launched at an indigenous music and cultural event, the Raqaypampa Indigenous Development Plan embodied development-with-identity approaches that give value and priority to indigenous culture. Because of its extensive indigenous participation, the plan was quickly interpreted as an example of best practice in ethnodevelopment by various donors and state agencies. The World Bank played an important role in supporting and disseminating such models by providing specific funding and grants through Bolivian government agencies. The PDCR received World Bank funds slated for strengthening local organizations so that they could elaborate development plans as part of Popular Participation; the Bolivian state's Small Farmer Development Fund (Fondo de Desarrollo Campesino, FDC) received monies for a participatory grants scheme designed to encourage indigenous participation in decentralized development planning. Indicating the high level of institutional connectivity in ethnodevelopment circuits, the PDCR brought the Raqaypampa Indigenous Development Plan to the attention of the World Bank and recommended that its infrastructural aspects (the irrigation lagoons) receive funding from the FDC's participatory grants. These inter-institutional arrangements enabled the local plan to be funded by national and transnational sources. While these relationships mirror those developed between Tucayta and the Swiss development agency in Ecuador, the Raqaypampa plan was inspired by wider cultural-identity goals which, as we shall see below, clashed to some extent with the neoliberal standards in ethnodevelopment funding.

As the Indigenous Development Plan greatly increased the profile of the Raqaypampa communities in ethnodevelopment circuits, community leaders were able to call a face-to-face meeting with high-ranking government and World Bank officials in order to debate project criteria. At this meeting, indigenous leaders and CENDA representatives expressed concerns that the project should not divide the community and should follow Andean experimentation in agricultural practices. Although the government wanted all the lagoons to be built quickly and called for indigenous organizations to co-finance the project, the World Bank representative backed the community position. As a result, the Raqaypampa leaders negotiated a smaller project to commence in one area that they had selected as a trial project. Depending on the success of the trial, it was agreed that the communities could apply for funding for the remaining lagoons and that the contribution of local labor would be sufficient in this case, foregoing the usual FDC requirement for financial sponsorship by project beneficiaries. This was an important assertion of autonomy by the Raqaypampa communities. However, complying with FDC requirements meant relating to its modernizing and liberalizing agenda for agriculture. The indigenous demands for the lagoons had to be articulated in terms of their contribution to market-oriented agricultural productivity. In the Indigenous Development Plan, it was clear that the lagoons would only indirectly contribute to production in that way. This highlighted contradictions in the implementation of ethnodevelopment and required further negotiation, which resulted in a compromise in which all actors agreed to a fiction. At the meeting, all parties acknowledged that the lagoon water was intended to secure farmers' livelihoods by ensuring the availability of drinking water for livestock in times of scarcity, rather than to increase crop yields. It was the latter goal, however, that was emphasized publicly in order to secure funding.

Further tensions in the compatibility of neoliberal approaches and indigenous development occurred when the World Bank representative claimed that the bank could not guarantee collective indigenous land titling (TCO status), despite the fact that the Raqaypampa Indigenous Development Plan was premised on obtaining it. Moreover, he contradicted the collective land titling principle of TCO claims by insisting that individual landownership certificates be produced for each land parcel where the lagoons would be built. These certificates were needed, it was said, to prove that each piece of land had been transferred to the project. Community representatives, however, were adamant that these stipulations undermined their focus on gaining collective territorial status (TCO) for the whole community through the Indigenous Development Plan. Despite the heated discussion, the individual certificates were, in the end, required for the project to go ahead, and the community representatives acquiesced to the terms.

In both the Patacocha and Ch'aky irrigation projects, development policy with commitment to social principles was practiced by international donors (COSUDE and the World Bank) and grassroots development NGOs (CESA and CENDA), which opened internetwork spaces and created provisional hybrid institutions that enabled indigenous communities to participate and shape decisions. Despite clashes in the Bolivian case over the implementation requirements for ethnodevelopment, the overlap between indigenous and revised neoliberal agendas in both countries created enough points of agreement to gain indigenous support and allow flexible—and at times innovative—interactions. Although a Tucayta member pointed out, "we didn't have a network as such" and a CENDA delegate declared, "historically water is owned by God," indigenous organizations in both Cañar and Raqaypampa interpreted water as a resource that could be used to increase economic productivity, strengthen institutions, and hone management skills.[43] In contrast to the debates over national water legislation, these indigenous organizations did not deploy cultural rights in a paradigmatic contest with neoliberal agendas for water; instead, they entered into negotiation over these agendas, with differing degrees of success.

Indigenous Water Politics and Social Neoliberalism

In this chapter we have argued that transnational ethnodevelopment networks and circuits derive not only from money flows but also from agenda and discourse overlay. This was evidenced in the differential manifestation of neoliberal agendas in the water sector. While distinct circuits operated for protagonists of neoliberal water policies and those who opposed them, some meetings and connections provided discussion spaces that brought different factions together.

The diversity of network linkages means that a wide range of positions on neo-liberal interventions in the water sector emerged in the Andean region, as well as globally, often generating principle-issue networks intended to unite like-minded groups at and across different scales. For example, the antiprivatization movement linked local water conflicts in Cochabamba to national water-law debates and transnational antiglobalization networks. In some cases networks followed a common issue but did not hold to the same principles. Yet even these networks may provide spaces for dialogue that can facilitate connections with other groups. The complex relationship between the international consortium CODESAN, the Bolivian national water commission CGIAB, and the spin-off network that promoted alternative water-law proposals nationally and rejected privatization locally illustrated the variety and multiscalar nature of these internetwork spaces.

Representing some of the most vibrant sites for debating neoliberal development trajectories, indigenous issues gained notoriety in water networks. Indigenous symbolism conferred a powerful identity to nonindigenous actors internationally and united protestors across local rural-urban, indigenous-mestizo, and class divides. In policy circles, a focus on cultural identity provided platforms for indigenous law proposals and indigenous development plans. These, in turn, legitimated indigenous-movement complaints about the lack of consultation over new laws, such as those that CONAIE and CONAUA expressed to Economic Affairs Committee of the Ecuadorian national congress.

While the defense of cultural rights was a cornerstone of indigenous resistance against national water legislation in the Andes, the role of cultural identity was less definitive in irrigation project debates. To differing degrees, both Tucayta and Raqaypampa leaders were able to control irrigation projects in their regions, retaining collective management of irrigation systems even within dominant donor models of water and land commodification. Our analysis suggests that this control has been achieved, in part, because indigenous actors engaged overtly with the accountability, efficiency, and monitoring criteria at the forefront of neoliberal managerialism. A more serious commitment to multiculturalism on the part of donors, NGOs, and the state might have allowed more room for alternative cultural framings of indigenous interests and identities. This, however, would have required additional money and time for studies of indigenous conceptualizations of water use and of customary legal frameworks for allocating and exercising water rights. While CENDA's approach allowed for this in Bolivia, our analysis has shown that even in this exemplary case, efforts were still constrained by the parameters of donor agendas.

Neoliberal water legislation has been vehemently challenged by indigenous people at a national scale, but indigenous communities conformed to modernizing representations of their identities and agendas in local irrigation projects. While this appeared a pragmatic maneuver in the Bolivian Ch'aky project, Tucayta in Ecuador seemed to go further, internalizing the "efficient managerial" representations found in modernization models imported from outside (Boelens and Zwarteveen 2002). Nevertheless, constructions of indigenous subjects as enterprising managers who do not want active state intervention do not necessarily support Bretón's (2001a) conclusion that current neoliberal development turns local indigenous leaders into technocrats and budding business managers instead of political activists and representatives. As the Raqaypampa case showed, development languages and power relations are contested, and role identities proliferate. However, the compromise and consensus-building processes associated with neoliberal irrigation projects do suggest that the depoliticizing effects (if not intent) of social-neoliberal development may go beyond keeping party politics on project sidelines.

Social neoliberalism extends the logic of the market economy to new spheres and practices, as organizations undertake institutional reforms and define themselves in ways that are compatible with neoliberal understandings of water management. As a result, the transformative power of neoliberalism might confirm critics' fears of generating the subjects and citizens that development "wants." Through ethnodevelopment networks, diverse actors have been equipped to deploy examples of best practice and neoliberal terminology in a political fashion, often for different ends. Nevertheless, the ways of thinking about development in relation to water remained colonized by visions of productivity and modernization that were increasingly influenced by neoliberal notions of freedom and good governance. A seemingly strategic, yet incremental, use of neoliberal language and logic occurred in the Andes. Whether alternative modernities or postmodernities can be forged in the longer term by the indigenous actors negotiating these languages remains to be seen.

CHAPTER 5

NINA LAURIE, SARAH A. RADCLIFFE, AND ROBERT ANDOLINA

Transnational Professionalization
of Indigenous Actors and Knowledge

The exclusion of Indians from access to education has a long history in the Andes. In recent years, however, important changes have occurred in the relationship between indigenous populations and educational provision, especially with regard to higher education and adult training. Multicultural state reforms in the Andes, together with ethnodevelopment approaches, have transformed the nature of indigenous higher education and professionalization. Whether in state agencies, donor organizations, national and international NGOs, or indigenous organizations, professionals are in great demand. The rise of ethnodevelopment and its legislative and institutional counterparts has created an urgent need for more trained professionals and qualified personnel. In this context, professionalization in indigenous affairs has become a highly significant aspect of contemporary state and social transformation in Andean countries, smoothing the passage of national-identity projects that follow from new pluricultural constitutions. These reconfigurations of indigenous peoples and education—for so long considered incompatible terms under the tenets of modernization—are also crucially transnational: they engage state and nonstate actors in relationships at local, national, regional, and international scales. As a result, teachers, curricula, notions of good development, and funding flows move across diverse boundaries.

Indigenous politics and social neoliberalism have created new contexts for the professionalization of indigenous people.[1] Funded by a range of donors, Andean professionalization is producing a transnational curriculum on indigenous development that informs popular training programs and university courses and sets parameters for practices and understandings of good ethnodevelopment. The curricula, courses, and programs shape and transmit development-policy agendas as they engage transnational networks and a multiethnic set of actors. International funding regimes currently address social inclusion at the two ends of the formal-education system—primary and higher education—whereas Latin American states are largely investing in primary education.[2] Although much research has been done on primary and secondary education, few scholars have concentrated on higher education.

Particularly lacking is research on the role that transnational practices play in intercultural/multicultural education and how such processes intersect with those of state formation. While the Ecuadorian and Bolivian states have set the legislative context for proindigenous educational reform in the Andes (with the support of international donors), indigenous professionalization is forged through transnational practices that, in turn, circumscribe state–indigenous movement relationships while shaping national and regional identity projects.

The emergence of this paradoxical space—a sign of how indigenous professionalization directly engages with the state while at the same time creating and mobilizing networks that are able to bypass it—represents a crucial and dynamic element in Andean professionalization. On the one hand, many transnational relationships around indigenous professionalization are South-South, based on exchanges within the Andes, and give rise to a transnational political indigeneity in the region. On the other hand, these relationships are often mediated by funding agencies, which target a range of state agencies and indigenous organizations involved in professionalization in Bolivia and Ecuador. As a result, recent indigenous professionalization and interculturalism programs differentially empowered diverse actors in indigenous-affairs networks, generated critical engagements with state reforms, and shaped the relationship between development and governmentality. While some indigenous actors are better placed than others to take advantage of professionalization, the challenge for social movements, states, and donor communities alike is to ensure that professionalization processes maintain dynamism by allowing increasing numbers of Indians to define and enact culturally appropriate development.

Educating indigenous people so that they can participate more fully in development and nation building has historically been important in Andean state formation (K. Clark 1998). While the teaching profession has provided one of the main sources of indigenous professionals (Oliart 2001a; Oliart 2001b; Rival 1996), in recent years new "Indian careers" have also been forged in political and development administration. To some extent, this scenario represents an outsourcing of national identity-making projects, where Indian professionalization is transferred to donor organizations or key indigenous leaders. But the complex relationships and multistranded power flows involved in these development circuits suggest another, equally important, result of transnational professionalization networks: they engage ethnically-defined actors within the Andes more directly in governmental identity projects by enabling them to enter political debates and policymaking as critical and proactive agents.

Access to education for indigenous people, for instance, has often been at the cost of denying or downplaying their cultural roots (Gelles 2000; Weismantel 2001). Yet for Andeans, higher education has also helped challenge phenotypic definitions of race by promoting understandings of identity that deemphasize "innate intelligence and morality" (de la Cadena 1998, 147). As a result, demands for higher education and training that validate indigenous heritage have played an important role in indigenous political engagements with the state and have come to influence donors under development-with-identity agendas. While subject to the conceptual baggage that social-neoliberal notions of the "professional" may carry, Andean indigenous actors have negotiated these positions by appropriating the resources (especially expertise and solidarity) of transnational professional communities. They also illustrate the institutionalization of ethnodevelopment in a variety of arenas through the growth of hybrid development institutions and networks that include indigenous people. As such, the state and indigenous organizations are also "in-sourcing" international development to further their own identity projects.

In the Andes, the convergence of indigenous and donor interests in development-with-identity has been negotiated in new higher education and adult training programs. These programs often draw on established experiences in popular education and indigenous politics, but they are new in their scales of operation, institutional forms, and mobilization networks. They are also new by virtue of curricula content and personnel deployment, including the proactive, transnational indigenous subject they project and their engagement with neoliberal development discourses. Following the framework described in the introduction, these new forms of indigenous professionalization serve as "reloaded boomerangs", which create spaces where multiple understandings of development with identity are produced, with empowering and disempowering effects on indigenous groups.

Transnational spaces of professionalization range from indigenous training schools that promote leadership skills through to higher education programs in public and private universities that concentrate on master's-level training in ethnodevelopment (Laurie, Andolina, and Radcliffe 2003; Laurie, Andolina, and Radcliffe 2005). For indigenous organizations, these programs are a way of strengthening their leadership, as they comprise means of equipping leaders with the latest development thinking. This enables them to be on a more equal playing field with donor and state organizations. Likewise, proindigenous NGOs view such programs favorably. Official development agencies value professionalization programs additionally as a means to create a new generation of professionals capable of delivering decentralized antipoverty programs. While donors and ethnic movements agree on the need for professionalization, they differ in their understandings of the relationship between identity issues and neoliberal development strategies. Indigenous movements often mobilize a language of opposition to racism and neoliberalism, whereas donors and states tend to focus on social inclusion and market viability. Struggles over representations of indigeneity and notions of culturally appropriate development in these professionalization spaces therefore attempt to accommodate different—and in some cases incompatible—political traditions of education within a social-neoliberal development framework. As a result, professionalization spaces constitute sites where transnational definitions of good development are produced and contested.

It is important to clarify the relationship between neoliberal development paradigms and the increasing focus on the human and social capital of indigenous groups. In so doing we analyze the indigenous subject represented in donor funding rationales and in indigenous-movement demands for culturally appropriate education. We examine the emergence of an intercultural education paradigm, investigating the relationship between interculturalism and popular education. The analysis then turns to indigenous knowledge, illustrating the role played by the transnationalization and professionalization of indigenous knowledge in donor and indigenous development discourses. The specific transnational practices underpinning the promotion of indigenous professionalization demonstrate the importance of a regional demand for culturally appropriate professional training, as well as the creation of transnational classrooms and curricula. The institutionalization of indigenous professionalization challenges state forms of governmentality in relation to education.

Neoliberalism and Indigenous Education as Capital

The literature on human capital argues that those who have been socially and economically excluded can be brought into development through education, full citizenship rights, and the promotion of good governance. Transnational funding targeted at indigenous people reflects donor interest in enhancing human capital as part of a wider social-development agenda. This agenda rests on understandings of participation that require community members and leaders to be empowered to become agents in their own development. Such representations of higher education and training for indigenous groups coincide with indigenous-movement concerns but convert community promotion into discourses of participation and democratization. "I don't want to work with one political party" in the promotion of indigenous education, says Armin Schlegl from the Hanns Seidel Foundation. "What interests me is civic training and democracy. The underdevelopment of this sector occurs mostly through the lack of education of poor people. So it is necessary to work from that base here."[3]

Indigenous movements' call for culturally appropriate education illustrates Merilee Grindle's (2000) argument that the source of good governance is "the demand for good governance rather than its supply" (32). On the other hand, the explicit agenda of many bilateral organizations to support the formation of human capital reflects donor-country initiatives on democratization and professionalization. For example, in keeping with Danish government interests in supporting multicultural legislation, DANIDA seeks to strengthen local municipalities, and IBIS works with indigenous social organizations in both Ecuador and Bolivia.[4] From the viewpoint of such international donors, indigenous professionalization programs help train the personnel necessary to occupy key roles in the new, "inclusive" legislative context that frames current national development plans. As alternative forms of education gain recognition, the monopoly that the church and state have historically had over national projects of identity is challenged.

The constitutional recognition of Ecuador and Bolivia as pluricultural states in the mid-1990s framed an acknowledgement of the diverse educational needs and realities of the national population, yet embedded this in transnational circuits running through the Andes. The perceived needs of Latin America's "pluricultural states" have played an important role in the growth of new university and training courses. The recent introduction of proindigenous and socially inclusive laws throughout the region has produced a legislative implementation gap, as governments have been slow to act upon new laws (Van Cott 2002).

While new legislation has, in theory, created opportunities for the recognition of indigenous self-determination through changing landownership, natural-resource legislation, and decentralization, the state seldom has sufficient personnel capable of effectively putting the new laws into practice and fulfilling public—and especially indigenous—expectations. The limited number of indigenous professionals has forced agencies to rely on personnel from "other cultural groups who may be unaware of indigenous reality" (Encalada, García, and Ivarsdotter 1999, 70). Despite multicultural discourse and legislation, indigenous movements and agency directors feel that the shortage of indigenous professionals in the field of development hampers successful project implementation, especially in large-scale decentralized projects where international agencies increasingly emphasize the self-management capacity of local communities.[5] The political and economic context of reconfigured states and hybrid development institutions greatly affects the increased demand for transnationally savvy policy consultants.

Development agencies and indigenous leaders have expressed an urgent need for training and investment in leadership at local scales in order to ensure that legislative changes are implemented in favor of poor and indigenous communities. According to Isidoro Quinde of CODENPE, "The parish [village] committees are obviously going to need the [human] capital to hand to plan and carry out their development and for project implementation. That's why I think it is necessary to train the human resources, so that they become generators of local development."[6]

As the leader in education reform and the largest financial contributor, the state remains the most important educational actor in Latin America, implementing decentralization and privatization measures in a context of an overall reduction in education spending (Laurie and Bonnett 2002). Prior to the 1994 constitutional and education reforms in Bolivia, the state promoted popular education for indigenous people and engaged with pluriculturalism in policy formation through the National Service for Literacy and Popular Education (Servicio Nacional de Alfabetización y Educación Popular, SENALEP). In 1983, SENALEP developed a national education plan based on intercultural and bilingual education. This plan was important because it was the first education program to formally recognize Bolivia as a multicultural and pluricultural nation (Chambilla 1994). Subsequent education reforms in the Andes in the late 1980s and early 1990s followed this trend by promoting new education laws. In 1989, Ecuador was first to approve a program of bilingual intercultural education (run by DINEIB—Bilingual, Intercultural Education Program Directorate); Bolivia passed an education reform law in 1994.

Both reforms built on earlier experiences of state-led initiatives, as well as NGO programs working with indigenous communities.[7] Prior to receiving state funding, many early initiatives were financed by international donors. Before the government assumed a more direct role, for example, the German development agency GTZ financed a state-endorsed program for Ecuador, MACAC ("war cry" in Quichua).[8] Bolivia's Education Reform Law also drew on transnationally funded experiences of highland indigenous education and was especially influenced by the success of Quechua literacy classes and curricula reform in Raqaypampa, Cochabamba (Healy 2001). Directed by local communities in partnership with the national NGO CENDA, this program was sponsored by a diverse range of INGOs, including the Catholic Agency for Overseas Development and the Inter-American Foundation. Transnational donors therefore played an important role in legitimating local experience as it was scaled into national multicultural legislation.

Transnational involvement in Bolivian indigenous education also included the World Bank, which took a leading role in the 1994 education reform. The bank financed foreign consultants to develop a proposal through the Technical Support Team for Education Reform. Subsequently, the implementation of the law itself was underwritten by loans from the World Bank and the IADB; UNICEF sponsored the design and production of teaching materials.[9] Bolivia's educational reform placed bilingual and intercultural education at the center of its changes, prioritizing and producing material in Bolivia's four main languages (Aymara, Guaraní, Quechua, and Spanish) and promoting a more participative learning style (Albó 1999; Alem Rojo 2000).

While most pro-indigenous education reforms in Latin America represent intercultural education mainly in terms of primary-school education (Aikman 2000), donors have also been interested in higher education for indigenous people and have helped to mainstream these interests into state laws.[10] Traditionally, there has been little international investment in higher education, but donor concerns about social exclusion have changed that (Cortina 2000).[11] This funding, in turn, is the primary source of support for indigenous professionalization programs (table 3).

Development professionals in bilateral and multilateral organizations, national and international NGOs, and academic institutions draw on a wide range of experiences and forms of training to validate their positions in their fields. With an NGO sector of fused grassroots and academic interests helping to set agendas, new courses are designed to meet the training needs of career consultants, academics, and indigenous activists.[12] As a result, NGOs, states, donors, and indigenous movements are major contributors to the demand for indigenous professionalization.

In the context of development-with-identity, generators of local development seek a more holistic approach toward themes such as culture, society, and environment. As a result, donors following neoliberal approaches have

TABLE 3. Higher education programs in development-with-identity in Ecuador and Bolivia

Place	Origins	Courses and Aims	Funding	Student body	Neoliberal and Good-Governance Discourse	Transnational Classroom and Curriculum
Universidad Andina Simón Bolívar (Ecuador)	1987 Inter-culturalism program started	Masters in Interculturalism Open short course in local development Train consultants Train University lecturers	PRODEPINE	Indigenous and mestizo Some international students from the Andean region, including Bolivians	Human resources Aimed at the periphery Pioneering social compensation Generate ability Teaching transversal themes	One full-time lecturer (American) One lecturer has taught in Canada One lecturer teaches in CEIDIS (Bolivia) Teaches Bolivian local development
FLACSO Ecuador	One of several FLACSO institutions in Latin America	Diploma in indigenous affairs, about to become a masters' Train people for them to return to their community	PRODEPINE Hanns Siedel Foundation Belgian embassy	Indigenous and mestizo Andean regional international students, including Bolivians	The new (pluricultural) institutionality New frameworks Ethnodevelopment Positive discrimination (akin to affirmative action) Strengthen local capacity Citizenship	Director has taught in Spain Uses Bolivian materials and case studies to deliver a comparative course

	History	Programs	Funders	Students	Themes	International links
The Indigenous University Ecuador	CONAIE's idea in 1988 Revitalised in 1998 In operation since 2004	Indigenous law Bilingual intercultural education Agroecology Take university to the community Validate indigenous knowledge	CODENPE Northern universities	Indigenous students	Ethnodevelopment Intercultural development Indigenous framework Human Resources	Northern lecturers teach Northern universities validate degrees A series of universities to be developed across the region
La Universidad Salesiana Ecuador	Initiated in 1994 Built on a bilingual education program for teachers in place as of 1991	Applied anthropology Local development Social communication Train people for them to return to their community Link students to local contexts	PRODEPINE Catholic funds Hanns Siedel Foundation GTZ CODENPE	Indigenous and mestizo	Sustainable development Pioneering Equality Excluded sectors Human resources Institutional strengthening	GTZ has linked this program to Bolivian ones Sees itself as an exemplar in Latin America
CEIDIS Universidad Mayor de San Simón, Cochabamba, Bolivia	New relationship between CENDA and CESU postgraduate school Regional consortium with Peru, Chile, and Argentina	Diploma in indigenous affairs since 1999 Converted to masters in 2001 Critical engagement with interculturalism and Bolivian reforms as a political project To reflect on interculturalism globally	Kellogg Foundation DfID/British Council	Mestizo and some indigenous Some international students from Latin America and Europe	Develop critical tools Generate analytical ability	International lecturers including Ecuadorians Historical links with Ecuador via CENDA and Bartolomé de Las Casa in Peru Lecturers doing postgraduate studies in the U.K., Spain, Mexico, and Ecuador

TABLE 3. *Continued*

Place	Origins	Courses and Aims	Funding	Student body	Neoliberal and Good-Governance Discourse	Transnational Classroom and Curriculum
PROEIBANDES San Simón Bolivia	First began in 1995, built on staff experiences in Puno in bilingual education	Masters in intercultural bilingual education Share Bolivia's reform experience Train professionals (mainly teachers) working in communities with indigenous languages	GTZ	Mainly indigenous, some mestizo Many indigenous international students	Human resources Interdisciplinary gaze Academic exchange Collaboration between indigenous peoples	Lecturers from the Andean region, Latin America, Europe, and North America Satellites in other countries Latin American countries to recruit Very high international profile

Sources: Authors interviews, student questionnaires, program web sites, and promotional material (1999–2002). In the questionnaires, students were asked to identify their ethnicity.

clear ideas about the type of versatile professionals they want their investments in human resources to produce. Indigenous movements, hybrid development institutions, and academic organizations alike are cognizant of these funding drivers, as suggested by an Ecuadorian academic responsible for negotiating funds for a program where donors pushed for an integrated theoretical training, including managerial and financial skills:

> We interviewed 80 development organizations to ascertain which types of new careers they were looking for. . . . What came out of this study was that they were looking for [a specific] profile of a development actor who has an integrated vision of development. [Someone] who would know what development meant in its different facets: how to link the local, the national, and the global, what the new trends in local development would be, what they are [now]. The person would work the sociocultural and the intercultural axes; the environment would be another axis. This new profile of a professional would know about finance and project administration, that is to say . . . they would know how to read tables, charts, percentages, [and] they would know participative methodologies.[13]

While the need for the professionalization of indigenous personnel is articulated at local, national, and international scales by various interested actors, professionalization has also been perceived as an important trans-Andean issue. "What can be recognized is that there is a real demand for postgraduate training for indigenous professionals in the whole region," said Fernando Garcia of FLACSO. "I say this because in a conference that we had in Chile, the Chilean Aymaras and the Mapuches were really interested in the theme. In Bolivia, it's the same and it's the same in Peru. . . . It's also the same with the group of Colombian indigenous people. The indigenous topic is beginning to be debated as a regional theme."[14]

The majority of training and higher education programs on ethnodevelopment policy aim to attract indigenous students, but they define indigeneity in various ways. Funding agencies shape selection criteria and sometimes influence the definitions of indigeneity adopted in specific programs. For example, in Ecuador, PRODEPINE's indigenous student fellowship program insisted that a local community organization's recommendation is crucial in student selection and may count more than the candidate's academic experience. Other donors have relied on language-based definitions, accepting students because they speak one or more indigenous languages. These and other definitions are contested, however, because of the assumptions they make about markers of indigeneity. A lecturer on a Bolivian intercultural master's degree program, well known for its excellence in linguistics, argued that language-based definitions are particularly controversial. "If I speak Spanish, that doesn't mean I'm Spanish. If I'm the son of a plantation owner and I speak Quechua, that doesn't mean I'm Quechua. So this thing about looking for people who speak indigenous languages is forcing things too much."[15] Whatever the specific selection criteria for training and higher education programs, in general, donor conceptualizations of indigenous people reflect the strong links made between indigeneity and poverty as outlined in chapter 2.

However, as Armin Schlegl, the director of the Hanns Seidel Foundation in Ecuador, indicated, this priority can be difficult for donors when indigenous demands are mobilized in ways they view as undemocratic. "I have good relationships with the three biggest [Ecuadorian indigenous] organizations, CONAIE, FENOCIN, and FEINE. I provide them with monitoring services; people who receive scholarships assess projects there. So we have an open family now. For example, Salvador Quishpe, involved in the coup of January 21 [2000], had a scholarship from the Foundation; he's one of our former scholars. Several of our former scholars participated in the coup. Other people weren't that happy [with our financing of indigenous activists' studies] but yes, I respect that [their right to participate in the coup]."

Indigenous movements and education donors have converged around the representation of Andean indigenous peoples as excluded from a racialized education system. They also agree on the need for targeted programs to further indigenous educational achievement, which is couched in a multicultural emphasis on combining indigenous-language retention with Spanish acquisition. Yet neoliberal good-governance policies rarely corral indigenous agency, as indigenous movements continue to emphasize issues of social and economic inequality. Despite the contradictions between human- and social-capital investments in indigenous professionalization, and resistance from some Indian individuals to seemingly proindigenous agendas, the demand from ethnic social movements for culturally appropriate higher education and training found an audience in transnational circuits and in neoliberal multicultural states.

Juggling Multiple Roles: Expectations of Indigenous Professionals

Transnational donor expectations concerning professionalization have drawn indigenous actors into new political and work spaces that cross institutional and political party boundaries. While these spaces encourage Indian people to undertake culturally appropriate professional roles, sometimes on a full-time basis, these roles may be incompatible with the demands of indigenous-movement leadership, which require ample personal time dedicated to maintaining community legitimacy and cohesion.

Indigenous movements have long demanded culturally appropriate higher education and training that reflects indigenous realities and practical needs. This demand also projects a subject that faces severe discrimination in terms of access to education (on both financial and cultural grounds) and devaluation of indigenous knowledge.

For example, Vicenta Chuma, head of Ecuador's ECUARUNARI women's section, stated that a key principle underlying these demands is the freedom to attend educational institutions without having to sacrifice cultural identity, as was the case in the past: "Indians could not go to school because they had to have money. They had to change their surnames, and if boys had ponytails in their hair they had to cut them off, and if we [girls] wore *polleras* [indigenous skirts] we had to take off the polleras and put on other kinds of skirts."[16] For leaders like Vicenta, culturally appropriate education recognizes indigenous values and knowledge and seeks to strengthen indigenous political structures, organizations, and leadership. They also believe that such forms of professionalization equip indigenous communities to generate their own development projects based on knowledge of their reality, without relying on outside experts and technicians.[17] For indigenous women specifically, realizing these goals involves working on self-esteem and confidence in order to equip them to have a greater role in community leadership and tackle opposition to female participation from male partners and leaders (Pachamama 2000).

The divergent demands on community leaders have produced difficulties in implementing Bolivia's pluricultural legislation. The need for knowledge about the Law of Popular Participation, as well as bureaucracy around the registration of communities as OTBs and TCOs, has placed rotational models of community leadership under considerable strain (Blanes 2000; McNeish 2001). The conflicts that result have reflected contradictions inherent in development models that seek to invest in both the human capital of individuals and the social capital of collectives. In this way, indigenous professionals are often expected to play a dual role as both leaders and development workers, while remaining collaborative community members (Rival 1996; Blanes 2000).

Financial costs, including user fees for university and schooling introduced under neoliberal policies, also present constraints for indigenous students. Social movements have asserted that this constitutes a form of educational privatization and further limits indigenous people's access to higher education. This view is illustrated by Vicenta Chuma: "The new constitution is favorable to us as, for example, collective rights are recognized; on the other hand, the privatization of education means that we can't go to university because everything has to be paid for over and over."[18] As this quote illustrates, the relationship between neoliberal reform and multiculturalism in education and professionalization is complicated, and its results are ambivalent. Moreover, as argued by CONAIE's ex-president, university systems have to change because indigenous students cannot afford to live in the city: "We are trying to establish a university that can go to the community rather than the other way round. The community and the students always have to go to the university. This is absolutely impossible, first because the students can't pay their costs in the city. Second, I believe that the university must engage with [students'] reality."[19] This demand has, in turn, led to a variety of alternative education initiatives, many of which have found an intellectual and political home within interculturalism.

Interculturalism: Making Indigenous Professionalization Culturally Appropriate and Transnational

The promotion of multicultural education in the Andes is framed by a paradigm of interculturalism, which concentrates on understanding the relationship between Western and indigenous practices, spaces, and knowledges.[20] Critiques of limited academic and disciplinary understandings of indigenous issues have contributed to the emergence of interculturalism as an important and contested arena, forged through democratizing struggles over pluricultural constitutions. In a transnational context of political and policy convergence, donors, indigenous activists, and educators have generated a common language in discussions about professionalization, indigenous curricula, and education policy. By providing a platform that brings together diverse actors, interculturalism has become a crucial pillar of indigenous professionalization, joining with neoliberal influences in a multiscalar fashion (see also Laurie, Andolina, and Radcliffe 2003).

In Latin America, interculturalism goes beyond what is conventionally understood as multiculturalism. Whereas the latter promotes "unrelated juxtapositions of knowledge about particular groups without any apparent interconnections between them," interculturalism implies "comparisons, exchanges, cooperation, and confrontation between groups" (Cushner 1998, 4). Increasingly, interculturalism is framing specific types of professionalization, not only through the development of teacher-training programs seeking to cater to the needs of indigenous teachers but also by introducing interculturalism into more-general courses on community, rural, and local development.

Supported by international donors, intercultural programs are playing a role in shaping national and regional identity projects in the Andes. Interculturalism has come to represent multiculturalism in practice, providing a framework for both indigenous movements and state political practice. In the context of the Andes, interculturalism not only requires that respect be afforded in equal part to indigenous, Hispanic, and Afro–Latin American cultures, but also to a variety of distinct indigenous cultures. In this way, interculturalism views indigenous subjects as involved in the construction of a dialogue through discrete cultural spaces of mutual respect among all ethnic and cultural groups. Interculturalism's position as a dominant paradigm, however, is not fully consolidated; concrete intercultural spaces remain fragile and contingent on maintaining open lines of communication and alliances across different interests and ideologies. Consequently, interculturalism as a policy framework is still evolving, and donors continue their attempts to define its relevance more clearly across a growing range of topics, stepping into the gap between state pluricultural reform and its effective implementation.[21] Moreover, the term *intercultural education* often means different things to different actors. With respect to indigenous professionalization, diverse interest groups focusing on culturally appropriate education have appropriated interculturalism. Its influence on education policy, and specifically on indigenous professionalization, has been established through periodic conflicts and negotiations over the politics of human-capital development and identity formation, while drawing on previous political and educational experiences.

The politics of Latin American interculturalism was initiated in the 1980s when the emergence of intercultural bilingual education coincided with processes of democratization and the growing awareness of indigenous groups as social and political actors (L. López 2000). For many years, Indian issues were studied as part of anthropology or linguistics, but the paradigm of interculturalism has developed a more interdisciplinary and politicized approach to indigeneity and development, moving the focus of indigenous issues away from its discipline-specific origins. One landmark program in this respect operated in Puno, Peru, during the 1980s, with GTZ and UNICEF funding.[22] Another influential program on indigenous issues flourished in this period at the Instituto Bartolomé de Las Casas in Cuzco, Peru, drawing students from NGOs and academic institutions across the region.[23] Despite the importance of these initiatives, however, many early courses were criticized for overemphasizing linguistics and adopting outmoded notions of culture. While the Puno program had an important international influence on the development of intercultural bilingual education, its focus on linguistics was increasingly viewed as limited, and some argued that the program failed to grapple with the complexity of culture and cultural issues.[24] In a similar way, while linguistics has a narrow focus on language, anthropology has been critiqued for its inability to detach its cultural analyses from colonial gazes, and anthropologists increasingly believe that interculturalism provides an important way to move beyond the exoticizing tendencies in their discipline.[25]

Building on such academic origins, interculturalism has developed into both a strategy and a process in the context of the "pluriform of reality" in Latin American nations (Godenzzi 1996, 569), becoming part of broader calls for democratization. Such a political perspective on interculturalism has wide support from transnational donors, which further infuses the intercultural paradigm into development planning. Interculturalism has also become an important concept in indigenous-movement discourse, as illustrated by a keynote speech from the Ecuadorian indigenous leader Luis Macas at an interculturalism conference in Bolivia.

> The challenge in these times of modernity and the era of globalization . . . is precisely to transform history. . . . I believe this is everyone's task; it isn't only that of the indigenous people for the indigenous people, of the students for the students, or academics for academics. . . . Mutual learning must carry on taking place in this epoch. . . . *In Indianizing this America* [*en indianizar esta América,* emphasis in original], I am not speaking in the sense that everyone has to put on a hat, a poncho, and let his or her hair grow and make a little *wanquito* [ponytail] and the problem is solved. I think that when I say Indianize America we are saying that necessarily we have to overcome in the political, the economic, cultural, and in the social.[26]

The conference at which Luis Macas spoke was organized by a transnational consortium of institutions and drew together indigenous leaders from a range of nationalities, as well as academics and donors from across the Andes, Europe, and North America. It provided an unusual space for discussion among leaders from Guaraní, Quichua, Quechua, and Aymara groups, and for shared political and academic platforms for speakers and participants across differences of ethnic and cultural identity. Luis Macas's words indicate how, when linked to indigenous calls for proindigenous change, the practice of interculturalism is firmly located within a dynamic understanding of the relationship between globalization, culture, and identity politics. The production of this transnational space may serve as a rallying cry for political, economic, cultural, and societal change.

To summarize, transnational interculturalism offers a malleable understanding of culture and identity that embraces change and focuses on political alliances and networks at a range of scales, from local and regional to national and global. It allows actors from across these scales to come together in spaces that accommodate both critics and supporters of neoliberalism. Rather than simply representing the international outsourcing of national identity projects, therefore, donor support for interculturalism has generated new social relations of knowledge production that engage with space and scale in diverse ways, aiming to produce new possibilities in identity making. The politics and expectations of many of the actors involved have been shaped by their personal socialization in diverse popular-education training spaces.

From Popular Education to Intercultural Social Development

Historically, popular education played an important role in Andean rural development, producing diverse experiments in alternative education for a wide range of communities with different needs and formal-educational backgrounds. More recently, diverse experiences have been drawn together in a more focused emphasis on intercultural approaches to social development, as indigenous political demands on the state have insisted that education and professionalization should relate more specifically to indigenous concerns.

Linked to NGO support for empowering pedagogies, popular education was promoted throughout the 1970s and 1980s in agricultural extension work (Urioste 1987; Revesz and Blondet 1985; Gianotten and De Wit 1985). It influenced a number of emerging special areas, including Andean and small-farmer irrigation models.[27] With policy shifts toward social neoliberalism, examples of successful decentralized grassroots experiences of popular education have "scaled out" in recent years to inform national policy. While there are many cases of empowering popular-education programs, community initiatives in the highland area of Raqaypampa have been particularly influential in debates about education reform and have been disseminated as best practice in intercultural bilingual education by UNICEF (Healy 2001a). Nevertheless, this transition from a local experience of popular education to status as a transnational exemplar has not been seamless.

While pro-indigenous popular education has been integral to supporting indigenous livelihoods and political autonomy in Raqaypampa for many years, more recently it became a formal demand on the state when it was named in an indigenous development plan designed to engage directly with decentralization legislation.[28] By working with a national NGO (CENDA), Raqaypampa achieved considerable success in grassroots programs in Quechua-based bilingual adult literacy throughout the 1980s and 1990s.[29] During a debate over a World Bank–supported irrigation project for Raqaypampa, indigenous community leaders of diverse ages and from many communities attended with exercise books and pencils, ready to take notes to report to their constituents. As this display was not in keeping with the negative image implied by statistics on indigenous poverty and illiteracy, one NGO representative explained it as the result of numerous popular-education programs carried out in short-term workshops (*capacitaciones*) on a range of topics over many years. Yet controversy arose around this program when the Raqaypampa communities themselves hired teachers to operate outside of the official school system and arranged a curricular calendar around labor needs at harvest time. As a key actor in indigenous education policy in the Andes, UNICEF stepped in to support the Raqaypampa schools against state attempts to close them (Regalsky 2001). Subsequently, UNICEF's support for this experience influenced the importance that Bolivia's Education Reform Law placed on decentralized community control over education. Transnational-donor intervention therefore scaled out local experience in popular education, enabling it to inform NGO, INGO, and government policy (Healy 2000; Regalsky and Laurie 2007). The Raqaypampa struggles over indigenous popular education reflect an increased convergence between popular education and intercultural agendas, as indigenous movements and NGOs see the possibilities for indigenous development and autonomy under pluricultural constitutions.

Interculturalism has increasingly framed both popular adult training and university professionalization spaces as a result of this convergence. The curricula of these programs cover old and new topics while deploying Freire-type teaching methods.[30] Whereas NGO-led grassroots popular education in the 1970s largely concentrated on technical training in agriculture and production, the remit of contemporary intercultural courses is often broader. They reflect social-development interests in strengthening civil society and promoting strong citizenship and leadership training, as well as fortifying the role of poor and indigenous communities in decentralized development planning. For example, the first seminar in an ECUARUNARI program for indigenous women and young people in Ecuador covered familiar topics such as local sustainable development; yet the project management and evaluation modules contained "a focus on participation, gender, culture and ecology," thereby linking with the gender-mainstreaming focus of social-development agendas.[31] Other modules covering established topics like political and organizational leadership and involving consciousness raising for leaders were followed by a new element consisting of in-depth analyses of local, national, and international contexts.

The teaching methods of the ECUARUNARI women's training school were interactive and based on problem solving, maintaining a clear Freire-type structure for sessions. One of these sessions, on the international context for women's leadership, provides a chronology (1980–1998) of key international activities and events that created political opportunities for indigenous movements (table 4). Indicating an extroverted sense of place, the seminar method was explained as follows: "This workshop seminar should bring indigenous women closer to a knowledge and understanding of politics. [It does this] through a methodology that stimulates debate from the different positions and political tendencies that the different social actors maintain in the national and international situation with regard to the political project of indigenous people and the state. In this way this module uses life histories of the great historical leaders of the aboriginal peoples in order to recoup the oral tradition and the role played by women in indigenous uprisings" (Consejo Coordinación de Mujeres del ECUARUNARI 1998, 15).

Postgraduate university courses have also stressed the need to move between international and local realities. Converted from an graduate diploma to a master's degree program, the CEIDIS course in Cochabamba had a series of modules on globalization, cross-border learning, and the changing international context for indigenous politics. Yet it also involved fieldwork modules in a single Bolivian province, Morochata. Here the students worked closely with local communities in mapping the socio-spatial relations of production in order to generate an indigenous development plan (IDP) that emphasized the importance of indigenous knowledge. Drawing on the Raqaypampa experience with indigenous development plans, student involvement in the production of an IDP in Morochata was intended to help support the community's claims for autonomy under proindigenous land reform and decentralization. Fieldwork methods emphasized community participation using interactive workshops, group mapping exercises, and questionnaires. Reflective community workshops, in turn, discussed these methods' limitations in terms of empowerment. Engaging with the work of Henri Lefebvre (1991) and others in the classroom, the students were encouraged to critique static and frozen conceptualizations of space as they reflected upon the constraints on mapping Andean indigenous practices and knowledge.[32]

TABLE 4. Outline provided for an ECUARUNARI women's training school session on the international context for women's leadership

Opportunities	Why important
Nobel Peace Prize Winner Rigoberta Menchú	She is indigenous
Indigenous uprising in Chiapas, Mexico	They rebelled for indigenous voice
Discussion of the UN Declaration on Indigenous Rights	It is being debated on the national level [in Ecuador]
Indigenous Vice-President of Bolivia	He is indigenous
Pope John Paul II visit to Cuba	Creates further opportunities for peoples [in Latin America]
Advances in science and technology	Can be used for our well-being
Occupation of [Japanese] embassy in Peru by Tupac Amaru Revolutionary Movement	To make sure our rights are heard
Relations among social movements	Creates more popular unity
The body of Ché Guevara is found	Helps to unify peoples [of Latin America]
The prize that Luis Macas received [Goldman Environmental Foundation prize]	He is indigenous
Participation of women in China [at UN Women's Conference in Beijing]	Ensured treatment of women's rights [at the conference]
Fall of the Berlin Wall	Decline of socialism

Source: Consejo de Coordinación de Mujeres del ECUARUNARI (1998).

The multiscalar deployment of interculturalism in such professionalization programs is indicative of its success in generating spaces where a range of diverse actors with different politics and positions can come together to discuss, debate, strategize, and plan. Below we suggest that the combination of academic study and hands-on engagement in community development also reflects the increasing professionalization and transnationalization of indigenous knowledge, which opened up opportunities for indigenous leaders to gain a voice in current development paradigms and circuits.

Indigenous Knowledge:
Becoming Professional and Transnational

Over the last two decades there has been a transformation in how indigenous knowledge is circulated and valued (Sillitoe 1998). On the one hand, advances in international human rights, the recognition of indigenous peoples in international law, and greater interest from international development agencies, NGOs, and the corporate world have contributed to the higher profile of indigenous knowledge. On the other hand, the emergence of indigenous knowledge as a key element in social-movement discourse has facilitated the creation and strengthening of certain transnational linkages and networks. Donors, indigenous movements, NGOs, and states alike agree that respect for indigenous knowledge is central to fulfilling an intercultural agenda. However, they do not share representations of this knowledge in relation to space and scale, nor in relation to nonindigenous knowledge.

In the emerging academic literature, most definitions of indigenous knowledge are linked to natural resource management, attributes of a specific territory, or information held by a particular group that is assumed to live in bounded geographical spaces (e.g., M. Warren 1991; Grenier 1998). Even though pro-indigenous NGOs emphasize that indigenous knowledge involves innovation, experimentation, and adaptation (see Calvo et al. 1994), most definitions reveal fixed-space understandings of indigenous subjects. In such definitions, the emphasis is on survival mechanisms and the role of information—about a limited territory and its environment—in community reproduction, rather than on more fluid, multiscalar definitions consistent with social constructionist approaches to indigeneity.

By contrast, the influence of indigenous movements on legislative reform during the last two decades has meant that policy understandings of indigenous knowledge have been informed by these movements' emphasis on modes of thinking. Such approaches focus on diverse ways of knowing and processes of learning, rather than on the acquisition of specific kinds of information. Indigenous knowledge is thus defined in sociocultural, relational terms instead of space-bound understandings that fix knowledge to particular local areas. Indigenous activism around such interpretations has successfully influenced state education policies in the Andes to the extent that reform laws have engaged with the logic, frameworks, and epistemologies of different ethnic groups. For example, Ecuador's bilingual intercultural education program, DINEIB, is characterized by a critique of the Spanish model of education through the promotion of Andean notions and ancestral forms of thinking and learning—"*moradas incáicas del saber*," or Inca ways of knowing (Rival 1996, 409; also see Medina 2001, 5).

Another result of these struggles over policy reform and new expertise is the professionalization of indigenous knowledge. Uma Kothari (2005) discusses how the construction and validation of experts through the knowledge they possess shifts in relation to scale as development paradigms change. She argues that colonial administrations prized colonial officers' in-depth knowledge of a local space, territory, and sociocultural and economic context. In contrast, contemporary development workers operating in a range of paradigms are generalists and are valued by the development industry for the generic tools they can apply anywhere. Therefore, in contemporary universalizing development, she argues, possessing local specialist expertise is not much valued but rather is viewed as a distraction for professional development professionals.

In the case of ethnodevelopment, however, the relationship between expertise and the scaling of knowledge is more complex. In particular, having local *and* transnational expertise is increasingly valued. Indigenous knowledge is often scaled at the local level because the success of antipoverty programs is seen to depend on engaging with local realities, thereby creating a demand for proficiency in local, contextualized, and indigenous knowledge(s). At the same time, the drive for universalism is apparent in a preoccupation with applicability beyond a particular locale or region. Donor-led development organizations promoting ethnodevelopment often view indigenous knowledge as locally scaled but transferable between local contexts. In contrast, some Indian activists and intercultural state discourses (such as DINEIB) laud local knowledge while asserting the universal relevance of indigenous ways of knowing.

Recognizing indigenous knowledge as key to the enhancement of local social capital, donor organizations involved in ethnodevelopment have launched various large-scale programs to transnationalize local knowledge. The World

Bank's "Indigenous Knowledge for Development" program, UNESCO's "Best Practice of Indigenous Knowledge," and UNDP's "Indigenous Knowledge Program" all seek to transfer local indigenous knowledge to other contexts.[33] In this way, indigenous knowledge is only seen to have more general importance when experiences or best practices move from one local place to another. Central to such donor initiatives is the idea that indigenous knowledge must first be professional (that is, ordered and systematized) in order to be circulated and shared. Representations of indigenous knowledge as inherently oral and local provide the motivation for developing systematization mechanisms, reflecting donor concerns that the full commercial potential of indigenous knowledge could remain untapped or, with the rise of genetic patenting, be taken out of the hands of indigenous communities (Lander 2001). The production of local indigenous knowledge is thus bound up in transnational discourses and networks, even though the definitions of indigenous knowledge and power positions held by network actors may be diverse and contested.

Greater systematization and institutionalization of information flows usually implies increased monitoring, through report-writing procedures that often constrain Latin American actors in their attempts to insert ideas into donor agendas (Townsend, Porter, and Mawdsley 2003). In the case of NGOs with politicized, explicitly proindigenous agendas, monitoring and evaluation processes can become conduits for the introduction of new knowledge; this, in turn, can become a new tool of social neoliberalism. For instance, an evaluation of CENDA by a consultant working for an international funder caused resentment in the NGO because of its emphasis on social capital.[34] Such incidences reflect the explicit ways in which indigenous knowledge and social capital are currently being linked in donor discourse and increasingly institutionalized in transnational ethnodevelopment networks.

While donor support aims to circulate and transfer indigenous knowledge from local experiences, indigenous knowledge remains a contested policy and political field. In some cases, indigenous movements question policy formulation by using techniques based on strategic essentialism. In calling for support for an Ecuadorian indigenous university, for example, Luis Macas said, "I believe that our knowledge has unfortunately been left out of scientific recognition. For all the results that it has achieved over thousands of years, in many aspects our knowledge definitely does not have the same scientific value. I think that's precisely why we should revalue it; give it its own value, its own authenticity, the scientific value it should have. [Indigenous knowledge] should not be cast strictly as empirical knowledge."[35] Although the binary process of othering that seeks to distinguish between Western and indigenous knowledge has been widely critiqued, ethnocultural movements themselves often draw on this distinction as part of a political platform. Leaders emphasize how indigenous knowledge has been downgraded by colonization and the practices of "scientific" knowledge.

Macas's position on indigenous knowledge questions its local scaling, thus challenging established geographies of knowledge production that draw a sharp distinction between local indigenous knowledge and the construction of an international knowledge system (see also M. Warren 1991). Curricula of indigenous-led professionalization programs further illustrate multiscalar understandings of indigenous knowledge held by indigenous-movement leaders. FENOCIN's women's training program makes visible the potential global benefits of widening particular areas of indigenous knowledge. In their training module on nutrition and traditional medicine, FENOCIN aimed to ensure that indigenous medical knowledge was seen as having the potential to influence medical techniques globally, rather than only as a traditional, local competitor to Western medicine. "We have a lot of knowledge about traditional medicine among our *compañeras* and from our ancestors. . . . Combined with Western medicine, we could change not just Ecuador but also the world, as we have seen with the plant *uña del gato*, which is a medicinal plant."[36] Thus, the FENOCIN agenda for intercultural indigenous knowledge is based on respecting and combining different perspectives for global answers, rather than merely sharing local knowledge. The desire of indigenous organizations and leaders to break out of the representation of indigenous knowledge as empirical and local can be seen as part of a strategy to become generalist experts and development initiators rather than passive objects and recipients of change.

Transnational Networks: Programs, Actors, and Classrooms

Indigenous professionalization has mainstreamed interculturalism in a range of development courses that attempt to scale out knowledge from local experience and give academic space to indigenous thought. These aims are pursued through transnational networks and contested processes involving various teachers and specific classroom attributes. In Bolivia, the main postgraduate programs are located in the state Universidad Mayor de San Simón in Cochabamba (CEIDIS and the Training Program for Intercultural Bilingual Education for Andean Countries, PROEIBANDES) and in the Universidad de la Cordillera, a private university in La Paz. Additionally, intercultural modules and courses are appearing in other interdisciplinary centers and programs throughout the country.[37] In Ecuador, graduate programs currently operate in the Universidad Andina and FLACSO, while an undergraduate course is offered at the Universidad Salesiana. University courses and training programs alike attract students and teachers who have been socialized in popular-education paradigms with an emphasis on participative learning, individual and collective empowerment, and education as a process rather than outcome. Many teachers thus move seamlessly between delivering popular training and university graduate courses (see table 3).[38]

Most graduate and popular-training courses providing indigenous professionalization operate in spaces that are transnational in terms of program structure and funding, as well as in the nationalities of students and teachers.[39] In some cases, classrooms are transnationalized through donor support for regional Andean alliances, as exemplified by the structure for the two Bolivian programs based in Universidad Mayor de San Simón. PROEIBANDES operated out of a number of Andean countries by means of satellite nodes that helped in the selection of students. German (GTZ) core funding established and maintained the program, which was selected from a number of options once Cochabamba's vision of a transnational program was conceived. National governments and indigenous organizations helped fund student scholarships, with approximately forty students split between two master's degree programs.[40] The program students are mainly indigenous schoolteachers with future careers in policymaking for NGOs and government bodies.

The CEIDIS program also has transnational origins. It was founded as part of a consortium bringing together NGOs and universities in Chile, Argentina, Peru, and Bolivia to deliver a range of activities including graduate training on interculturalism. In Bolivia, the members comprised the NGO CENDA, with extensive popular-education experience, and CESU (Centro de Estudios Superiores Universitarios), the social science graduate college of the Universidad Mayor de San Simón, which has extensive experience in delivering specialist short courses and graduate degrees. The student body at CESU was smaller than at PROEIBANDES, with seventeen students registered for the diploma program in the first year, subsequently converted to a master's program with transnational funding. From the beginning, teaching in the consortium was concentrated in Cochabamba. While some students were from the other member-country institutions, the majority of them were Bolivians, drawn from NGOs and local government agencies—the traditional market for CESU courses. Although the program was not targeted exclusively at indigenous students, applicants for consortium scholarships needed a letter of recommendation from their community, ethnic organization, or NGO to indicate their commitment to ethnodevelopment.[41]

Donors have supported transnational programs in order to promote exchanges of knowledge and experience as part of fulfilling an intercultural agenda, as a GTZ representative indicated:

> I think this process [interculturalism] could be really interesting in a masters course where there are other countries too. . . . Just last week we had a regional seminar in Peru where the Shuar from Ecuador realized they had a lot in common with the Aguarunas in Peru. . . . [I think] that if an invited specialist comes to give a course on Quechua culture, Quechua history, or the Shuar language, that it shouldn't just be for the Shuar alone or the Quechuas alone. It should be for everyone. In the beginning the students didn't want this, but little by little they are also becoming interested. Isn't this the first step to interculturalism?[42]

In this way, transnational classrooms mix students from a variety of countries and indigenous nationalities to generate exchanges of experience. In turn, these intercultural experiences help reshape senses of identification and belonging as different ethnic groups find commonalities. Such re-formations of identity are also evidenced in popular-training programs where students are usually from just one country. As a leader from FENOCIN's women's section explained, mixing students from different indigenous nationalities or from distinct ethnic and geographical backgrounds is part of her organization's intercultural practice: "We have done mixed workshops at the national level where black compañeros, indigenous compañeros, and campesino compañeros have participated . . . from the sierra, from the coast and the Amazon. . . . Interculturalism in many aspects is difficult to understand. But with the national federation's women section we have seen it; we have practiced it. . . . We have exchanged our languages, our customs, the indigenous customs, and the black customs. This combination of shared experiences of customs and of culture has enriched us."[43]

Programs may also be structured around wider transnational learning spaces. Both the FENOCIN and ECUARUNARI training programs are involved in exchanges, conferences, and other activities with institutions in Latin American countries like Bolivia and Brazil, while students and teachers alike take part in Latin America–wide forums.[44]

Core funding for program management and scholarships has been available from a range of international donors, including GTZ (German), COSUDE (Swiss), the Kellogg Foundation (United States), the Hanns Seidel Foundation

(Germany), and the World Bank. Some of this money was channeled through nationally based hybrid institutions such as PRODEPINE (table 3, above; and map 11, below). Providing more than seven hundred scholarships to indigenous Ecuadorians for university education, PRODEPINE was one of the most important sources of funding for indigenous professionalization in the region. Originally intending to train ninety indigenous Ecuadorian students to the *licenciatura* level in local development planning at the Universidad Salesiana, high demand and low student dropout rates placed PRODEPINE in a powerful position to negotiate extra funding from the World Bank and to expand the program to other courses and universities.[45] In 1999–2000, it sponsored 120 students in the planning, anthropology, and communications departments at the Universidad Salesiana. The Universidad Andina and FLACSO programs also received students on PRODEPINE scholarships, which covered tuition and materials, as well as a US$300 monthly stipend. An additional budget was also available for student motivational activities and short courses in transferable skills, such as computing and Internet use.[46]

Although the World Bank has an open attitude toward PRODEPINE's management of the scholarship program, PRODEPINE's officers kept close control over the awards.[47] It acts "just like any other client, paying for the students who enroll in university."[48] This close control reflected PRODEPINE's vision for indigenous professionalization, which focuses on delivering academic results while also fulfilling a political agenda of promoting diversity:

> They [The World Bank] have accepted all the suggestions we have raised because we have achieved things with their support that have focused attention at the level of communities' needs. More than anything else what is being consolidated is the future trajectory of the communities. Imagine if all we did was to train people in development questions . . . before you knew it we would be producing a very developmentalist generation, with a narrow vision. So the fact that we have diversified the career [options] will mean that the level and criteria of future opinions will be more diverse. This will allow us to make the process richer.[49]

Focused on supporting local community structures as a form of good governance, PRODEPINE scholarships required that recipients carry out 130 hours of volunteer work per semester in a local institution.[50]

In addition to these long courses with well-established regional institutions, indigenous professionalization has drawn on a preexisting model of short-term training. Funding structures for professionalization are sometimes designed to respond quickly to demands from local communities. For example, in addition to support for master's-level courses, the hybrid development institution CODENPE has sponsored short courses for indigenous communities that have a specific, immediate need or personnel gap.[51] Indeed, some donors believe that the only way to produce culturally appropriate education and development is to focus on the specific needs of local communities.

Despite the academic credentials of university education, it is not necessarily the case that popular education is more informal than university courses (see details in Laurie, Andolina, and Radcliffe 2005). The professionalization and institutionalization of transnational indigenous development networks has generated training programs that have become more academically formal. For example, the ECUARUNARI training school for women comprised a three-year diploma-awarding program, with exams, coursework, and graded class participation. In addition, such training courses often run curricula that are more flexible than university programs, including distance learning, workshops, seminars, and short in-residence courses. Given the gendered nature of the double or triple burden that community, domestic, and paid work represents, these flexible training programs are often more appealing to women. For example, in Ecuador, many indigenous women opted for the ECUARUNARI women's training program after finding that their needs and objectives were not met by standard university education (Pachamama 2000). As a result, the ECUARUNARI program, which has received some funding from the Danish NGO IBIS, decentralized with the hope of facilitating greater access for women with domestic responsibilities.[52] As an alternative to governmental decentralization processes, the work of ECUARUNARI and IBIS built on local governmental formations and civil-society organizations at the provincial and municipal scales, using an innovative combination of gender and cultural criteria.

However, successful investment in human capital through scholarship systems such as these may be difficult to achieve alongside the promotion of social capital. For example, the PRODEPINE scholarship application required letters of recommendation from local organizations; but there is no guarantee that individual recipients have a sense of collective cultural identity or community solidarity. As a result, PRODEPINE also found it necessary to introduce formal consciousness-raising activities as part of their program. "Consciousness-raising with the students [is] an ideological task because, despite the fact that they are selected by their organizations, they do not have a social consciousness. They don't have a commitment to the organization. The idea is to get them to do voluntary work with the organization . . . to promote a cultural identity because we have noted some weaknesses there."[53]

Conceptualizations of national, cultural, urban, and rural geographies therefore shape the way in which programs are developed, such as the significant emphasis of donor funding on a perceived need to link professional indigenous people closely to their communities of origin. The leaders of undergraduate courses at the Universidad Salesiana have aimed to train only those people who intend to return to work in their own areas. Permanent residence in Quito after studies are completed is perceived as a failure, draining human resources from their home communities and contributing to out-migration of future leaders.[54]

Transnational Teaching Staff

While learning spaces for professionalization are transnational by virtue of their program structure, student diversity, and funding mechanisms, their early formation owes much to the small but transnational cadre of professionals who teach modules and courses. Many programs draw on a pool of international scholars and policymakers. Most members of this group of scholars, practitioners, and activists are mutual acquaintances, and they move between programs, universities, and countries for brief periods of time. Hence, teachers based in La Paz may teach short modules in Cochabamba, while others move regularly between Ecuador, Peru, and Bolivia. In other cases, however, staff members make more permanent moves across borders. For instance, one Bolivian institution recruited an individual based at an Ecuadorian program that was linked to a different Bolivian institution, because he had an intimate knowledge of both countries.[55]

The teaching biographies of these lecturers indicate that many have studied abroad (often in the global North). For example, of the fifty-eight contract teaching staff involved in delivering the social sciences master's degree and the diploma program in indigenous peoples' rights at the Universidad de la Cordillera, in La Paz (2000–2001), thirty-six had graduate degrees from northern universities. While some northern scholars enter this circuit, Latin American (often Andean) teachers constitute its majority (see table 3 above). Even in programs with higher than the usual numbers of northern teachers, such as at the Universidad de la Cordillera, Latin American academics greatly outnumber those from North America or Europe.[56] In this sense, these transnational classrooms are based largely on South-South personnel connections.

Understandings of development-with-identity are therefore created within the Andean region as much as through North-South flows of ideas.

Generally, these teachers have charted out interdisciplinary careers as both scholars and practitioners, as they have carried out in-depth work in specific communities and developed strong collaborations with local organizations. Their individual careers often reveal mobility between disciplines, thereby building up multidisciplinary perspectives. For example, the teaching cadre includes individuals that have moved from linguistics to environmentalism and rural development, from gender studies to ethnicity, and from anthropology to linguistics and gender studies. What program directors, donors, and potential employers prize about these teachers is their ability to transfer real-life experience and policy knowledge across borders. "I taught the conflicts class in a way that meant I could bring in lots of outside people," said Catherine Walsh from UASB, "Those people ranged from folks that worked with COICA [a pan-Amazonian indigenous organization], folks involved in Afro-American and Afro-Ecuadorian movements, involved in a more legal perspective, on collective rights or legislative projects that impact indigenous peoples, environmental concerns, and confrontation with oil companies. . . . The intention of inviting most of the speakers was to have people that are immersed in day-to-day struggles, conflicts [and] concerns pertaining to interculturality."[57]

Moreover, university administrators have emphasized the training of career consultants and a new generation of academics with an applied focus in ethnodevelopment: "Our study plans [are] to train . . . studious people who can become teachers in the university. In fact, former students from here are teachers in various universities in Quito and the interior of the country. . . . Then there's a group of people who can live from what they know under the name of consultancies and specific pieces of work and applied research."[58] In this way, a small group of highly mobile Latin American scholars, moving within Andean development circuits, have come to shape how development is taught, while (re)producing a larger mass of policy-engaged activist-academics. (See appendix 3 for summary biographies of selected teachers and administrators.)

Transnational Curricula Define "Good" Andean Development
The mobility of teaching staff generated consensus around what the transnational classroom should provide and legitimated an accepted understanding of what constituted successful ethnodevelopment policy in the region. Professionalization courses were characterized by what we term *transnational*

curricula, coalescing around ideas of interculturalism and shaped by learning across borders. The use of international comparisons in both popular training and university courses has served to disseminate best practices, as illustrated with curricular use of specific female role models, examples of particular pieces of state legislation, and sharing of knowledge about forms of protest.

First, in popular leadership training, internationally renowned indigenous leaders are represented as role models to inspire students. Given the increasing emphasis on female leadership in indigenous transnational circuits, the reclaiming and highlighting of indigenous women's roles in indigenous movements is notable. Nobel Peace Prize winner Rigoberta Menchú represents a transnational icon in contemporary leadership training programs (table 4, above). Additionally, historical figures such as the Ecuadorian Dolores Caguano, who fought to obtain education for Andean peoples in the early twentieth century, are being celebrated as role models. Indeed, Caguano's activism inspired the formation of the ECUARUNARI training school for women, which bears her name (Pachamama 2000).[59]

Second, state legislation is discussed in transnational classrooms in order to contextualize the nature of indigenous engagement with the state. From the mid-1990s until at least 2003, the Bolivian legislative experience was well regarded throughout the Andes. For example, the 1994 Bolivian education reform was disseminated widely in Ecuadorian courses as an example of innovative legislation that strengthens indigenous identity. An Ecuadorian lecturer suggested that the suite of reforms introduced by the government of Bolivian president Gonzalo Sánchez de Lozada was important enough to be taught in professionalization degrees elsewhere in the Andean region. "Principally, we have taken international experiences for discussion topics. . . . From Bolivia we have taken the topic of participation, of participative planning, [and] the Law of Popular Participation in Bolivia, which is the innovative effort that characterizes the Bolivians with respect to the topic of the indigenous population."[60] Although devised in nonstate spaces with nonstate actors, curricula engaged in a continuous assessment of the changing legislative and political contexts that development-with-identity is forged in.

Third, curricula drew on examples of nonstate organizing and the strategies deployed by social movements. For indigenous movements, this entailed sharing tactics and strategies of engagement with a range of (often nonstate) actors. Thematic issues were treated within a comparative framework, and specific political strategies were analyzed with a view to learning lessons across borders.[61] For example, CONAIE's organizational structure was analyzed and discussed in Bolivian curricula as an exemplary intercultural alliance playing a protagonist role in lawmaking and development-with-identity. One module on indigenous politics taught by Ecuadorian university staff in Bolivia included a session on the success of indigenous and campesino protest tactics, such as marches and roadblocks, in the two countries. A CONAIE video was also shown in Bolivia to promote discussion among representatives from proindigenous NGOs, indigenous social movements, and functionaries of relevant government departments.[62] These discussions, held in 1999, occurred during the Bolivian municipal elections and the first mobilizations against water privatization in Cochabamba, and they thus fed into wider discussions about tactics and alliances for the Committee for the Defense of Water, in which several students were involved. This committee was subsequently reconstituted as part of the Coordinator for the Defense of Water and Life that successfully challenged the state's neoliberal water policies. Transnational practices associated with indigenous professionalization have thus framed the way that indigenous agendas engage with state development approaches. In particular, they involve the validation and contestation of exemplary models that figure in transnational Andean higher education curricula.

The State as Referent
in Transnational Development Circuits

Although state roles in education and other aspects of development became more complex and contradictory as ethnodevelopment networks increasingly drove Andean professionalization, these roles have been far from marginal. Debates over Bolivian best-practice models, as well as CONAIE's attempts to launch an indigenous university in Ecuador, illustrate how the state remained a key mediating institution in transnational development circuits and practice, whether as a target for protest and criticism, a stumbling block to be worked around, a facilitator of hybrid development institutions, or as a point of access for resources.

Transnational curricula validated the Bolivian national experience of education reform outside the country, while its best-practice status was actively debated within the country. Bolivian professionalization programs have provided channels of debate to the extent that the two main programs on interculturalism in Cochabamba (CEIDIS and PROEIBANDES)—both of which were funded by transnational donors—took distinct positions on national education reform. One engaged directly with training people to implement and copy this reform, while the other sought to foster a critique of prevalent interpretations of intercultural education. Using Bolivia's educational reform as a point of reference, PROIEBANDES aimed to deliver specialist training for a regional indigenous movement (Laurie, Andolina, and Radcliffe 2003). CEIDIS felt, however, that PROIEBANDES's approach was allied too closely with the government's agenda: "We would rather work the topic of interculturalism as the political aspect of intercultural education. So from the start we [CENDA and CESU staff] were in agreement that while PROEIBANDES was a more functional thing, more operative . . . , ours needed to be more analytical [and] critical. Overall, [the program needed] to train [students] to investigate the full reality—not to generate technicians who would incorporate themselves into the Education Reform Law."[63] Whether drawing on transnational circuits to support or question Bolivian national education reform, professionalization programs have been highly engaged in the implementation of state legislation and constructions of best-practice models in Bolivia. In this way, professionalization programs have refined and shaped national projects of identity by producing graduates capable of stimulating and maintaining wide-ranging debate, while drawing on transnational networks and resources.

In contrast to these programs within established university systems, CONAIE's proposal for an indigenous university in Ecuador aimed to "go to the community rather than the other way round."[64] CONAIE launched such a university to offer professional training in education, law, and agro-ecology, establishing regional nodes in Chimborazo, Guayas, Pastaza, and Quito. CONAIE's Universidad Indígena proposal was first launched in 1988 as part of the indigenous movement's demand for intercultural, bilingual education, the thrust of which subsequently focused on primary and secondary education. The proposal was resurrected in 1994, however, after data from a CONAIE study indicated that less than 1 percent of Ecuador's indigenous people attended university.[65] For almost a decade, however, congress refused to grant the proposal legal status or recognize it as a state university. Subsequently, CONAIE moved to establish the Universidad Indígena parallel to the national state system.[66]

These efforts to establish an indigenous university illustrate how indigenous networks may engage the state directly *and* mobilize transnational connections to bypass it. Originally intending to work through the state system, attention shifted to founding an independent university with the support of transnational linkages: "We are dedicated to creating the Universidad Indígena because the state will never give Indians a chance," said Isidoro Quinde from CODENPE. "You know that [the government] might approve it out of fear, but really, it is difficult for it to get approval. [So] what we have done is create a chance with the other universities, for example with Arizona University and two Swiss universities. They are going to sponsor us. The university is going to select [from] three degrees, three academic areas: one is indigenous law, the other is bilingual intercultural education, and the other is agro-ecology."[67]

The alliances around the Universidad Indígena proposal in Ecuador indicate how transnational connections create opportunities for indigenous social movements to work around official state opposition while also remaining allied to certain nation-state governing bodies. The role of CODENPE as an Ecuadorian hybrid development institution has been central to this kind of politics. CODENPE receives funding from the Ecuadorian government and is heavily involved in supporting indigenous development through local government. Nevertheless, its position as a hybrid institution, with personnel appointed by indigenous organizations, allowed it to adopt a critical stance toward state practices that impinge on indigenous development. Its direct links with transnational funders has also created strong networks that provide a certain degree of autonomy. In the longer term, it is feasible that CODENPE's dual position will yield positive results for the Universidad Indígena. In 2004, for example, the Ecuadorian legislature finally granted it public status; since then it has commenced operations.

By locating this university in various parts of the country, CONAIE also sought to prioritize cultural roots and secure the continued backing of its indigenous support base. The Universidad Indígena aims not merely to train technicians capable of implementing reform but also to provide a space to systematize indigenous understandings and knowledge, including political knowledge about struggles over legislation (Laurie, Andolina, and Radcliffe 2005). Alongside existing programs in established universities, the Universidad Indígena therefore provides an example of the strength of transnational indigenous-affairs networks where such diversity in training options exists.[68]

While there is clear evidence that Andean states have responded to pressure for greater sensitivity to indigenous issues and agendas in education and professionalization, it is necessary to consider the wider governmentality issues raised by such proposals in order to understand why the Ecuadorian state has been ambivalent about granting public status to the Universidad Indígena. CONAIE's university might threaten state jurisdiction over higher education, for example, by departing from the usual practice of full-time university attendance and course delivery by professional teaching staff nominated by university rectors representing state authorities. The Universidad Indígena's overt focus on strengthening indigenous struggles against state reform poses further challenges to state control. "The experiences that the indigenous movement had during the struggles [against state reforms] have not necessarily been systematized," notes Luis Macas. "So everything that went on has not been organized. It has not been systematized. So one of the things that the Universidad Indígena has to do is to provide follow-up [*seguimiento*]. These studies will serve to nourish the indigenous movement."[69] Given this agenda, it is therefore perhaps unsurprising that the state was reluctant to grant approval. In Michael Watts's terms, the state was being asked to approve a "governable space of indigeneity" (2002, 24) that, in effect, would lead to it relinquish a governing role in order to take up a legitimating one.

Examining governing processes in this way casts an interesting light on the role that CODENPE, as a hybrid development institution, eventually played in garnering support from international sources to implement the Universidad Indígena proposal. Illustrating the contradictory ways in which transnational boomerang politics may work, CODENPE's part in the state's institutionalization of transnational ethnodevelopment networks helped to generate counterspaces that set up alternative pathways of governmentality (in this case in relation to education). CODENPE provided the means to support and maintain open communication with the indigenous movement while cultivating channels that could facilitate state monitoring of the university project as it develops. The outcomes of governmentality under ethnodevelopment therefore remain open to negotiation.

Without doubt, neoliberalism has provided an impetus to indigenous professionalization not witnessed previously in postcolonial times. It has changed views about who can be professionals and what being a professional means. Traditional understandings of professionalization, based in processes of *mestizaje* and the disowning of indigenous origins, have been challenged as indigenous men and women have swelled the ranks of professionals in recent years. In a global climate that emphasizes self-regulating citizenship while ratifying collective indigenous rights, new forms of professionalization have been forged in a variety of network settings, as social-neoliberal policies on inclusion and poverty have interacted with the political strategies developed by indigenous social movements. The sometimes accommodating and sometimes conflicting ways in which these forces have struggled to achieve acceptable forms of governance has generated debate and produced diversity in the delivery of professional training and the value placed upon it. As a result, the types of knowledge and expertise that are valued in development have shifted.

Neoliberal policies have set the stage for indigenous professionalization, but they did not determine which outcomes emerged through ethnodevelopment. The curricula of professionalization courses have been influenced by neoliberal notions of "good development," but the languages that support these may also serve as tools to generate critique or replicate alternative experiences. Despite the financial power of international donors, it is not possible to ensure that professionalized actors will behave like socially inclusive neoliberal subjects, as chapters 3 and 4 illustrate in relation to specific struggles over land, water, and decentralization policies. Negotiating the tensions around investing in individual human capital, supporting collective identity, and expanding decision making have altered how universalism is interpreted in knowledge production. Whether by emphasizing what neoliberals would call "best-practice transferability" or by focusing on indigenous ways of knowing across different ethnic groups, local expertise has come to be valued in new ways by people holding different political and institutional positions.

Transnational definitions of good development have a complex relationship with local, national, and regional constructions of ethnic alliances, indigenous expertise, and development. The export and contestation of national exemplars of indigenous development through professionalization influence what becomes accepted as good development. These processes occurred in a multiscalar fashion evidenced by the flow of transnational, state, NGO, and indigenous-movement funds to professionalization programs and the mediating role played by hybrid development institutions in development-with-identity networks (map 11).

However, overlap between donor, state, and indigenous-movement interests in professionalization is accompanied by key differences and divergences. The indigenous movement continues to highlight issues of exclusion, in part by emphasizing the need to recognize their knowledge as something more than informal, unscientific, empirical, and local. On the other hand, donors are most interested in leadership training and investment in human and social capital in order to fulfill a good-governance agenda less dependent on, but still connected with, the state. For them, interculturalism represents a way to contain the contradictions of neoliberal social inclusion; for ethnic organizations it is often a rallying call to "Indianize this America." Questions about the extent to which those agendas are ultimately compatible remain central to indigenous professionalization debates.

In unpacking the relationship between governmentality and development, Michael Watts has argued that the "governable spaces of indigeneity" become

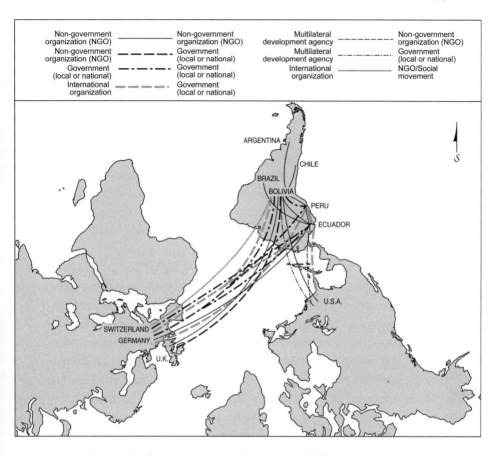

MAP 11. Transnational connections around intercultural higher education and professionalization programs.

Networks shaping flows of funding and placement of education programs run largely South-North, while South-South links are important in exchanges of ideas and personnel regarding the content and purposes of education programs and curricula.

vehicles for political claims focused on local government and customary rights.[70] While our research concurs with his findings, it also suggests that the governable spaces produced are *multiscalar*. Demands for local autonomy *are* reflected in the emphasis that Andean indigenous social movements place on training indigenous leaders capable of engaging in decentralization processes and producing their own development plans. However, the governable spaces they produce are not confined to local and national scales. They also operate through transnational networks, institutionalized in a range of hybrid development institutions and educational consortia that converge around intercultural understandings of knowledge production and development practice. What is considered governable in indigenous professionalization is thus redefined to include territories, curricula, student and teacher recruitment practices, and institutional infrastructure.

Our work also indicates that indigenous professionalization is highly transnationalized and influenced by donor interests, but that the nation-state retains a crucial role as a player and a referent. Many students enrolled in these programs aspire to future careers as experts in ethnodevelopment, in local and national government as well as in international organizations, official and nongovernmental.[71] The state therefore remains an important target for professionalization aspirations and shapes the trajectories that emerging professional communities forge. Intercultural paradigms and practices open up professionalization spaces where greater numbers and more diverse architects of national projects are produced and development plans are debated. One way that current professionalization programs will be measured over the coming years is through the ability of new professionals to rework the power relations and hierarchies found in current transnational development approaches and imaginaries.

CHAPTER 6

SARAH A. RADCLIFFE, NINA LAURIE, AND ROBERT ANDOLINA

Gender, Transnationalism, and Cultures
of Development

In previous chapters we have argued that indigenous development networks are multiscalar and based on contingent transnational linkages among diverse actors that are sometimes conflict ridden. The current chapter advances this argument by showing how these transnational relations are profoundly gendered. Following feminist accounts of globalization, we start from the premise that the "subjects of globalization are always embedded in gender relations" (Nagar et al. 2002, 12) and that transnational processes are "mutually constitutive of and bound up with gender at all levels" (Freeman 2001, 1012). Notions of masculinity and femininity, and their differential valuation, are part and parcel of transnationalism. Yet theorization of transnationalism has often been implicitly masculine, founded on global-scale views and other seemingly male-dominated arenas (finance, formal politics, formal-sector work) instead of built on the interaction between public and private spheres or between women and men across a number of scales (see critiques in Brah et al. 2002; Freeman 2001; Katz 2001; Marchand and Runyan 2000; Nagar et al. 2002).

Extending a feminist analysis of transnationalism to the field of development leads us to address two primary questions: In which gendered ways—and with which gendered consequences—have transnational networks around indigenous development operated? And how have neoliberal development assumptions reinscribed previous, problematic ways of conceptualizing gender and representing Andean indigenous women in policy? The transnational boomerang that facilitated indigenous development policy also reloaded it by gendering indigenous development in ways that were both empowering and disempowering. As a result, indigenous and nonindigenous women reinitiated transnational action when they found that on-the-ground implementation of indigenous rights or development failed to deal with gender issues sufficiently or appropriately.

After providing an overview of Andean gender relations, this chapter explores the gendered assumptions and consequences of social-capital concepts applied to indigenous development in Bolivia and Ecuador. Development actors have attempted to address gender inequality through the framework of Gender and Development (GAD). Indigenous development networks came together initially around social-capital concepts rather than a GAD approach (perceived as potentially divisive for indigenous populations). One result has been the construction of implicitly restrictive roles for indigenous women and the elision of gender inequality. This pattern is illustrated in the case of an Ecuadorian development project for indigenous and Afro-Ecuadorian peoples, PRODEPINE. Ethnodevelopment policy constructed gender issues in specific ways, and these in turn shaped project priorities and components. Renewed transnational activism, however, pressured PRODEPINE to introduce GAD measures halfway through the project.

Indigenous women's transnational networking also provides a context for the analysis of the gendered power relations at play within indigenous movements and in the predominantly white-mestizo Latin American women's movements. In Bolivia and Ecuador, women's voices have frequently been muted in village and regional political arenas, which indigenous women's transnational networks have tried to rectify by supporting women's leadership programs and establishing better spaces for women within indigenous organizations. We question the treatment of gender differences as an incidental and local component of a largely global story. Moving beyond conceptual frameworks that "implicitly construe . . . global as masculine and local as feminine" (Nagar et al. 2002, 1009), our multiscalar approach examines the mutual influence of scales, from the body to the regional, national, and global. In doing so, we highlight the complex interplay of international gender and development policy, national-level political and institutional settings, and local development projects.

This complex interweaving of transnational activism has differentiated between indigenous women and indigenous men, just as it has reconfigured relationships between indigenous women and nonindigenous people (also see Weismantel 2001). As a consequence, indigenous women's interests and views remain poorly expressed in gender policy and claims for indigenous rights, and they are thinly represented in development institutions and networks. This does not mean that indigenous women are passive observers of global or Andean restructuring; they have appropriated international meetings and communication networks to voice their demands in ever-widening spheres. The implementation of development-with-identity in the Andes confirms the postcolonial feminist argument that global restructuring cannot be reduced to "generic bodies or invisible practitioners" (Freeman 2001, 1010).

Likewise, the fact that the transnational field of indigenous development is multiethnic and embedded within complex racial formations requires us to further examine how gender, race, and ethnicity intersect to shape the relative visibility and authority of different actors across scales (Alexander and Mohanty 2001). This pattern of racialized gender relations has an array of effects, influenced by the contingent and complex intersection of Andean social relations with global policy. First, the existence of gendered hierarchies and gendered public-private relations *within* diverse ethnic groups informs the interventions made by indigenous women and men in a number of transnational arenas, while also shaping their political authority within indigenous movements for development and social change. Second, female and male actors express and constitute gender interactively—for example, in development projects that offer credit programs for women yet are staffed largely by indigenous men. Third, gender proves to be embedded in values and attributes associated with certain patterns of behavior, knowledge, and roles within wealth generation and policymaking.

Andean Gender Relations and Livelihoods

Andean indigenous women—like other women of color—are situated at the intersection of several oppressions that inform their politics (Bronstein 1982; hooks 1984; Nash and Safa 1980). As subjects, they are "en-gendered in the experiencing of race and class, as well as sexual relations, [and are] therefore not unified but rather multiple" (de Lauretis 1987, 2). This multiplicity lies at the heart of their movements against class, race, and gender inequality (Shohat 1998).[1] Across these ethnic, class, and location diversities, Andean indigenous women experience highly variable gender ideologies and practices due to "scattered hegemonies of global economic structures, patriarchal nationalism . . . , local structures of domination and legal-juridical oppression" (Grewal and Kaplan 1994, 17).[2] Such differentiation multiplies their experiences and produces a variety of interests and identities regarding development and transnational relations. Drawing upon ethnographic literature, this section provides a preliminary overview of Indian women's responses to the issues raised by Andean development. Later in the chapter we revisit these responses in light of specific projects and initiatives.

In the cosmovision of many Andean indigenous peoples, male and female roles are viewed as complementary. Yet uneven capitalist development and the marginalization of peasant and indigenous livelihoods challenge this vision, as households have relied upon a strategic combination of subsistence and market agriculture, migration, local labor, and product markets to guarantee a minimum income (Bourque and Warren 1981; Phillips 1987). Poverty has reorganized gender and household divisions of labor, as well as the development priorities of indigenous women. In the words of one female indigenous leader from Ecuador, "Women's most specific problem is poverty. [Development experts] talk about our right to health, to mental well-being, but how are we to have this if we're worried about sending our kids to school with lunch? What will I put in the pot to cook? Another problem is the lack of understanding in the home [between spouses], because there is no shared work . . . How can we overcome this?. . . . There is [also] violence."[3]

Urban and rural labor markets remain highly segregated by race and gender, which intersect to exclude indigenous women from many work opportunities (Weismantel 2001). The division of labor in rural villages tends to allocate tasks to women that are undervalued by other villagers or by census categories. Communal patriarchies inform these gendered valuations and reinforce them indirectly by representing women as relatively peripheral to indigenous economies and household survival.[4] Although feminist research documents rural women's agricultural work (Deere et al. 1999; Phillips 1987; CESA 1993), for example, it often remains unacknowledged by village leaders, policymakers, and national governments. In paid labor, too, indigenous men and women earn different wages (Oaxaca Declaration 2002). Recent figures suggest that only 10 percent of Ecuadorian indigenous women engage in paid work, although nine out of ten work in some form. Over two-thirds of Ecuador's indigenous women receive no payment for their labor on family farms or in small-scale informal-sector activities and marketing (PRODEPINE 2001). Such family-based and low-status jobs, moreover, deny women social security coverage, the right to unionize, and access to training.

As national economies undergo restructuring, gender divisions of labor have shifted. Men migrating to cities and other countries in pursuit of paid work has increased inequalities and differentiated roles between women and men (Nagar et al. 2002). One Ecuadorian activist noted, "We women have the most contact with the village; sometimes men migrate. . . . But this money doesn't always help the household. Sometimes it's [used] to build a house, [or] for men's vices. But women have to have an income, and then the family is better off."[5] By disrupting women's social networks, rapid impoverishment and widespread migration have further isolated many indigenous women, especially those who cannot read or write. Many rural women *are* in regular contact with farms, animals, and lands. But this is because men have migrated away and women have taken on new tasks; it is not a simple expression of cultural traditions. Indeed, female indigenous leaders point out the rapidly changing rural division of labor under the pressures of (often male) out-migration and rising levels of poverty. "As we know," notes an indigenous leader, "all cultures are changing, and these relations between men and women are going to change. It's not a question of imposing [change], but that the culture itself is going to see the need for changes" (Tibán 2001, 6).

Although a few indigenous women manage to pursue education, the majority of them lack access to literacy training, and they have few life-course options as a result. Despite the extension of state rural education in the 1970s and 1980s, a combination of parental disapproval and household poverty has prevented many girls from continuing education beyond primary levels.[6] In addition, state budget cuts in education, filtered through communal patriarchies, tend to keep more indigenous girls out of school than boys. In Ecuador, over one-third of Indian women are illiterate as a result of low levels of school attendance. In the highlands, indigenous women received just 1.4 years of schooling on average, compared with 2.4 years for indigenous men and 7 years for Ecuadorian women on average. And only 2 percent of indigenous women have received work-related training (PRODEPINE 2001). Parallel to indigenous women's low level of access to formal education is a widespread view that women maintain ethnic group values, languages, and cultural identities through their roles in social reproduction and household spaces (raising children, teaching them indigenous languages, transmitting ancestral knowledge). Criticizing cutbacks that further threaten female education, one Ecuadorian activist explained, "We're fighting to keep the state working in education, health. We women follow [state restructuring] anxiously—if these things go private, we're going to be seriously screwed up."[7] In fact, Andean indigenous women are less likely than men to be fluent in Spanish, the predominant language. In the Ecuadorian Andes, 16 percent of indigenous women are monolingual Quichua speakers, compared with 3 percent of indigenous men (PRODEPINE 2001).

Political and development arenas also remain off-limits to many indigenous women, who—unlike the handful of women who have gained top leadership positions, such as Nina Pacari in Ecuador and Alicia Cañaviri in Bolivia—have insufficient education, self-esteem, and social support networks. Many Andean women are silenced in decision-making venues by machismo and the muting of their concerns (Bourque and Warren 1981). Women attend village-level meetings but often feel unable or unqualified to voice their concerns publicly. "Our problem was that we couldn't talk in the general meetings of men and women," according to one Ecuadorian activist. "First, it made us afraid, apprehensive, like . . . 'what would [men] say?' So whatever problem we had, we didn't complain, we stayed quiet." Such silence by women has, in turn, hampered efforts to raise gender concerns and place them on the agenda. Many women also face considerable resistance from husbands when they do attempt to make careers in peasant confederations, indigenous social movements, or party politics (Choque 2000, 29; Pacari 2002; Radcliffe 2002). These patterns vary over the Andean region, however, as does the insertion of a gendered or feminist perspective: in some areas of Bolivia, men and women organize separate federations; in Chimborazo, Ecuador, male migration has permitted women to transform their identity and organize numerous local associations; in Cotocachi, Ecuador, one-third of the members of the Committee for Local Development are women, yet the organization remains resistant to adopting explicit gender themes.[8]

Within disadvantaged ethnic populations, gender remains a significant axis of difference with regard to livelihoods and opportunities for transforming access to resources, education, employment security, land tenure, and decision-making power. Nine out of ten indigenous women have unmet basic needs (Chuma and Palacios 2000), and many face obstacles to their organization and leadership. These include meager family support, insufficient education, poor health, domestic violence, relative immobility, and excess work burdens (Cervone 1998).

Gender and Indigenous Development Policy:
Social Capital and GAD

Faced with the social costs of neoliberal economic restructuring, development policy in the 1990s extended into issues of "gender, participation, human rights, governance and the diversity of civil society" (Siddarth 1995, 31) in efforts to understand the social relations underpinning capacities for self-development in a free-market context. Gender's appearance in this list acknowledges its long history of politicization in development-policy circles, but the ways it has been interpreted and applied remain highly contested. Understanding gender as a factor informing indigenous development requires us to examine policy concepts at the intersection of two core debates: first, gender's perceived relation to social capital, which underpins thinking around Andean development-with-identity and social-neoliberal policy; second, development thinking around gender inequalities. These two global development debates' relation to the Andean context can be connected by tracing the complex interactions between the multilaterals, indigenous social movements, and national governments in the production of concrete ethnodevelopment policies and projects.

In her careful analysis of Latin American development, political scientist Maxine Molyneux argued that social-capital concepts "encode normative assumptions about women" (Molyneux 2002, 177), even though they do not explicitly discuss gender differences or inequalities in development. In reviewing multilateral and government policies, Molyneux showed how social-capital conceptual approaches idealize communities, as well as assume that women's productive and reproductive work is "traditionally" available. Women thereby gain a key, but gendered, role in such representations of an abstract "community" and its resources. Examining this policy framework critically, we suggest that Latin American women's relations with families, economies, and social organizations are downplayed and simplified and that longstanding analytical blindness to *men's* role in communal reproduction is perpetuated in socio-capital models.

This has occurred in spite of decades of activism among feminists, development practitioners, and leaders in addressing women and men's distinct development experiences and seeking to redress gender inequality, which resulted in a gender and development paradigm. GAD offers a framework that challenges masculine privilege and builds on notions of female empowerment but remains an unwieldy policy instrument burdened by its largely unexamined cultural values and its claims of universal applicability, based on notions of modernization's triumph over tradition (Jolly 2002). Gender activists have established transnational policy frameworks and institutional spaces to promote empowerment by means of gender "mainstreaming."[9] Emerging originally from GAD and adopted as official United Nations policy after the 1995 Beijing international women's conference, gender mainstreaming has been enacted primarily through national bureaucracies for women's affairs, affirmative action in electoral politics, and policy guidelines for development interventions (Rai 2003;

Cornwall, Harrison, and Whitehead 2004; Walby 2005). Mainstreaming requires that all areas of policy, programs, administration, financial activities, and procedures take gender concerns into account. It galvanized the UN Development Program and other international organizations to promote gender-sensitive forms of development (Razavi and Miller 1995). Under neoliberal pressures, however, development policymakers "remainstreamed" GAD by emphasizing women's incorporation into the market and self-regulating citizenship, while downplaying more politicized dimensions connected to goals of empowerment (Schild 1998). Critics of mainstreaming have pointed out that its aim of ensuring equity is problematic, because it also equates gender with *women*; consequently, women's ethnic, racial, and national differences remain largely unacknowledged, and men's roles stay unexamined.[10]

During the past twenty years, over one hundred countries have established state-level bureaucracies to mainstream gender issues in public policy—a potentially significant restructuring of the state (True and Mintrom 2001). Compared with other Latin American countries, Ecuador and Bolivia have experienced low levels of gender mainstreaming, as gender issues have not acquired the political and administrative focus or resources found elsewhere (True and Mintrom 2001, 32; on Ecuador, see Lind 2005). Internationally, mainstreaming was widely endorsed by Swedish, Dutch, and Norwegian bilateral agencies, along with multilateral agencies, whose funds promoted gender-based development activities in World Bank programs and within various Latin American countries, including Ecuador and Bolivia (Siddarth 1995; Razavi and Miller 1995). The Norwegian, Danish, and Dutch bilateral agencies have long advocated gender frameworks based upon notions of empowerment.[11] In the Dutch case, all staff attend training on gender mainstreaming and empowerment; similar programs operate in their Latin American offices and programs. Western nation-states have also influenced gender policy at local and regional scales in developing countries by funding southern NGOs and civil-society organizations, although these latter organizations vary considerably in their engagement with gender mainstreaming.

Global guidelines suggest that gender mainstreaming is compatible with other policy priorities, such as poverty alleviation or indigenous development.[12] In practice, the institutional and political environment has militated against the fulfillment of gender equity agendas. Andean ethnodevelopment policy, informed by certain social-capital concepts, is a significant illustration of such limitations. As indigenous women are seen to contribute to social capital through the transmission of language and culture and their loyalty to community life and family labor, normalized gender divisions feature strongly. Reviews of thirteen grassroots ethnodevelopment experiments across Latin America (Atkins and Rey-Maqueira 1996; Carrasco, Iturralde, and Uquillas 1999) rarely mentioned women as producers or as leaders but made frequent mention of their illiteracy and distinctive dress. While men are largely invisible with regard to reproductive tasks, indigenous women are associated strongly with domestic and reproductive activities. For example, a multilateral report on indigenous development suggested that "like women in the rest of the world, indigenous women tend to give more attention and priority . . . to the daily needs of the family" (Encalada, García, and Ivarsdotter 1999, 8). And a private German foundation presented Indian women as mothers who nurture Andean and indigenous cultural and social distinctiveness (Hanns Seidel Foundation 1997). Echoing Molyneux's argument that social-capital models represent Latin American women as central to cultural continuity, a report on indigenous women's credit organizations asserted, "Women are key reproducers of ideas, knowledge, values, and social procedures" (Tene, Tobar, and Bolaños 2004, 4; see also Mayer and Rankin 2002). In discussing ethnodevelopment, a senior World Bank anthropologist went so far as to claim, "Women, in effect, are the culture; where the culture is made," through female work with young children and traditional medicine.[13]

These representations of indigenous gender relations within a dualism between tradition and modernity reproduce the notion that indigenous people are rural.[14] Indian women are associated with rural agricultural work and the traditional heart of indigenous "communities," while extensive female work in urban labor and product markets is rendered invisible.[15] By viewing what is termed "women's traditional work" as secondary to men's work and subsumed in sociocultural reproduction, such social-capital frameworks can segue into policy suggestions that reinforce circumscribed development roles for women. Microcredit schemes, for example, are designed to extend income security in women's productive activities while enhancing community social capital and historic identity (Mayer and Rankin 2002). Microcredit projects in Bolivia, Ecuador, and Peru have been interpreted as particularly successful within this way of thinking, as if they overcame any contradictions by involving women (Tene, Tobar, and Bolaños 2004).

During the 1990s and early 2000s, the increased prominence of social-development policy and indigenous development programs created further demand for gender components. According to one development professional, "one of the issues that has changed is, as social-development issues grow, there has been a demand for the indigenous project. And in that context there has been a demand for gender input."[16] The Inter-American Development Bank has designated indigenous women as one of the groups to include in participation mechanisms (along with youth and elders), as they are considered most likely to be otherwise marginalized from decision-making processes. Its rationale cited indigenous women's disadvantages with respect to resources, education, and income (Deruyttere 1997, 15). IADB's gender mainstreaming plan (2003–2005) called for cross-linking gender and ethnicity by prioritizing indigenous and Afro–Latin American women's needs and bringing gender into the Strategic Framework for Indigenous People (Inter-American Development Bank 2004). In making this crucial connection, such frameworks associated participation with sensitivity to gender, as if the two were equivalent. As one development staffer said, "If you have a participatory approach, it's not that hard actually to do a 'gender job.'"[17]

Indigenous organizations and their leaders have constructed a gender politics that inadvertently facilitated the predominance of social-capital approaches within indigenous development policy. In so doing, they resignified the body as a basis for engagement with international development policy on gender, in turn altering meanings of indigenous gender relations and national development projects. Ecuadorian and Bolivian indigenous intellectuals have often highlighted Indian women's distinctive characteristics as the symbolic and material embodiment of ethnic communities, focusing on women's clothing, use and transmission of Indian languages, and continued residence in rural indigenous communities. Unprompted, one male indigenous policymaker told us that "women are the reserves, really, the possessors of their [groups'] identities; this is palpable and visible."[18] Alongside such ethnic-identity claims grounded in women's bodies—arguably the smallest scale of a multiscalar politics—is a rejection of what is perceived to be an overseas and imposed politics of feminism. When discussing participation issues with Mayan representatives, for instance, Bolivian leaders rejected the idea of separate male and female meetings, arguing, "Bolivia cannot follow the Mayan example, as feminism is not an ayllu view of gender."[19]

In transnational interactions with indigenous leaders over development, some multilateral staff suggest that gender politics is remote from, or irrelevant to, indigenous populations. According to one male ethnodevelopment expert working at the World Bank, "It's not easy to incorporate gender into indigenous organizations, since it's outside their area of concern; it's more important in the Western world."[20] Development specialists working in the Andes have even argued that international gender policy is meaningless to regional cultures; it is thereby dismissed more easily as extraneous to local needs.[21] However, other development actors have worked around perceived or actual resistance to gen-der concerns. "There was a gender review of the World Bank project portfolio, and [gender specialists] went to see counterpart organizations. The relativism question was the first thing to come up. The [specialists] didn't challenge this but asked staff about gender roles; [indigenous project staff] didn't know much except anecdotally."[22]

The defensive position of gender policy is compounded institutionally and politically by the lack of a clear approach in dealing with the cross-cutting development implications of ethnicity and gender. Only recently has ECLAC called for the "visible and equitable participation of women and men from all ethnic groups" (Peredo 2004, 56), while global discourses on democratization and human rights have often been blind to gender and ethnicity as interlocking axes of disadvantage (Molyneux and Craske 2002, 9). Consequently, develop-ment thinking and practice in this arena has moved into relatively uncharted terrain that entails institutional, political, and resource reverberations at mul-tiple scales. Theoretical discussions around what is termed "intersectionality" in Latin America and elsewhere remain preliminary, offering few immediate policy lessons (Paulson 2002; McCall 2005; Valentine 2007). By putting its efforts into separate ethnic and gender programs, development policy further compounds the lack of meaningful policy and practical linkages *between* gender and ethnicity. Despite existing institutional guidelines for mainstreaming that theoretically would have required attention to gender issues at the initial planning stage, the World Bank began its policy and project forays into indigenous develop-ment without a consistent gender policy. In Central America and Mexico, too, indigenous development projects were designed without the bank's current policy on gender relations and inequalities in development.[23]

National authorities charged with implementing joint ethnic and gender policies face an uphill struggle to articulate these axes of difference in the face of seemingly incompatible agendas. A comparative study of gendered rights under neoliberal land reform argued that, in Bolivia and Ecuador, where indigenous movements had the greatest impact on legislation, women's individual rights have been the least secure (Deere and León 2001). In Bolivia, the then national Sub-secretariat for Ethnic, Gender, and Generational Affairs was charged with fulfilling the multicultural and gender-sensitive programs for new forms of citizenship by transversal programs in gender and ethnicity (Paulson and Calla 2000). Yet the separation of gender and indigenous rights offices, combined with the resistance of leftist civil servants to gender equity, forced women's concerns into an administrative "ghetto" (Paulson 2002). For instance, a senior government representative suggested that having gender and ethnicity "together . . . took political force away from the indigenous theme; it lowered its ranking in the structure of the state"[24] (compare to Laurie with Calla 2004). At the international scale, similar difficulties have appeared. In early 2000, the World Bank appointed a gender and ethnicity specialist to its Gender Unit, which led to coordination and communication difficulties with indigenous programs located in the Latin American and Caribbean Social Development Unit. The half-time "gender and indigenous issues" position was expected to liaise between the gender and indigenous peoples' offices in order to help prepare gender-aware participatory methods for indigenous development. With this appointment, ethnodevelopment projects would begin to insert gender concerns at the planning stage. Starting with Central America in an effort to reverse previous shortcomings, participatory planning sought to account for indigenous women's concerns in establishing a clear gender policy.[25]

At the same time, World Bank indigenous development projects for Bolivia and Peru started to create more prominent places for gender issues. "You'll see in the Peru [project] there is a very strong component that everyone believes in: raising everything in a gender-sensitive way. [This means] really trying to promote female participation in the consultation workshops, female representatives of indigenous communities, equality in the beneficiaries of the [project] training program . . . to make sure that there is equal attention to gender issues in every aspect of the project."[26] What this can mean in practice, however, is that gender becomes another "component" of a project, added into an already crowded set of agendas. "With the execution of projects, it's the same problem—gender is added to twenty other issues."[27]

An alternative means of working with the intersections of ethnicity and gender is to begin from initiatives *internal* to indigenous movements. For instance, the Danish NGO IBIS articulated a policy to support an Ecuadorian federation's "construction of its own gender discourse" as a key component of the pueblo reconstruction process. By working with the federation's female members, the NGO more readily supported agendas for gender equality in ethnic representation without being critiqued for imposing an external feminist agenda (IBIS 2004). Such practices represent an outcome for transnational networks that is different from the ones described in relation to PRODEPINE and other World Bank ethnodevelopment projects.

Different strands of gendered thinking go into making Andean indigenous development. Approaches based on certain conceptualizations of social capital entail a symbolic positioning of women at the heart of communities but effectively rank them as secondary with regard to livelihood and productive questions and reinforce associations between women and cultural tradition. Social-neoliberal policy frameworks for indigenous development already contain within them a focus on ethnic difference, which entails—given the lack of a fully integrated "gender and ethnicity" approach—the demotion of gender issues, making it less likely to adopt a gender and development approach. GAD policy, on the other hand, is informed by women's empowerment goals but retains an association with a race-blind and implicitly Western and feminist agenda that is unpalatable to ethnic anticolonial activism or difficult for many development institutions to endorse, in light of their focus on indigenous cultural distinctiveness. Gender concerns are sidelined in other neoliberal projects, as well (Kabeer 1994; Parpart 1995; Lind 2005), but indigenous development networks show how frameworks rooted in traditional community-based notions of social capital combine with the indigenous movement's emphasis on women's symbolic and material role in cultural reproduction to reinscribe gender policy at the juncture of neoliberal social policy and weak national institutions charged with gender mainstreaming.

Gendered Social Capital on the Ground: The case of PRODEPINE

Ecuador's Indigenous and Afro-Ecuadorian Peoples' Development Project (PRODEPINE) provides an example of how normative and institutional dimensions of transnational policy thinking on gender played out on the ground. Funded by the Ecuadorian government, the International Fund for Agricultural Development (IFAD), and the World Bank and underwritten with unpaid labor of local communities, PRODEPINE operated from 1998 to 2002. Discussions about this project were underway by 1997, when an initial project appraisal for a US$25 million loan was drawn up by World Bank staff using international NGO expertise.[28]

Although explicit gender policy was largely absent from the overall project appraisal document, women did benefit in some respects. For example, local development projects funded by PRODEPINE were required to avoid "marginalization or excessive workloads for women or any family or community member" (as cited in M. Larrea 2002, 16). Also, PRODEPINE's technical director argued that what he called the project's "transversal" gender policy infused gender issues into all aspects of the project. Women made gains in the allocation of study grants, with female indigenous students receiving over 40 percent of the scholarships.[29] Microcredit schemes operated through over 540 credit unions and benefited around fourteen thousand indigenous and Afro-Ecuadorian women (Uquillas 2002). At the same time, unacknowledged notions of gender underpinned certain project components. The project's rural investments included microcredit programs intended as "a mechanism to develop human and social capital by creating awareness among the target population about the benefits of using credit" (World Bank 1997, 7). Reflecting the gendered notions of social capital discussed above, the document directly mentions women alongside microcredit *cajas solidarias* (savings schemes), whose "main mandate is to reach out to women groups [*sic*] or to establish seed experiences in isolated locations where there are no financial institutions" (World Bank 1997, 44). Such cajas were, in fact, established for groups of women and not men.[30] As with microcredit schemes in Bolivia and Peru, PRODEPINE's cajas solidarias were widely interpreted as successful because they generated small amounts to alleviate household poverty while continuing women's perceived role as cultural symbols and reproducers of ethnic communities.

Furthermore, gender was positioned secondarily to the project's primary objective of alleviating indigenous poverty. "At first, we gave a lot of attention to the topic of ethnicity, as it was obviously connected to the topic of poverty, social exclusion, which was the most acute and urgent theme. The topic of gender was rather marginal, although from the beginning there was a concern to incorporate the issue."[31] A detailed analysis of PRODEPINE produced for internal circulation by a gender consultant (M. Escobar 2002) revealed that gender was not strongly incorporated in all project subprograms or a major concern of office personnel. Women made up less than a quarter of PRODEPINE staff between 1998 and 2000, and 21 of the female employees (out of 182 total employees) were limited to the lower administrative levels as secretaries, concierges, administrators, and accountants. Likewise, the cajas discussed above were allocated only one-tenth of the financing for "general" local development projects. These microcredit programs, moreover, built upon and arguably reinforced preexisting bonds of communal control. One evaluation emphasized how the women's credit groups regulated individual women's behavior, while traditional (male) community authorities gave the projects extra viability (Tene, Tobar, and Bolaños 2004, 4, 10).

At the national scale, it might be expected that gender mainstreaming in administration would act to reinforce GAD agendas. However, the Ecuadorian National Women's Council (CONAMU) was constrained by a number of interlocking factors. Although CONAMU played a key role in defining GAD policy and projects, it had no specific programs for indigenous women.[32] CONAMU has faced a masculinist state and society that rely upon women's unpaid labor, reinforce public-private divides, and treat women's issues as unworthy of support (Craske 1998; Lind 2005). Staffed largely with urban, mostly feminist, and predominantly white-mestiza women, CONAMU agendas reflected this political and institutional context and held little leverage with regard to PRODEPINE. As two of the most influential social movements during recent Ecuadorian history (and occasional allies), the indigenous movement and women's movement have a precedent of noninterference in each others' interests.[33]

These obstacles and limitations were overcome to some extent through additional transnational networking, as members of Ecuadorian women's organizations, in conjunction with multilateral and NGO staff, reoriented some of PRODEPINE's gender policies and practices. In 1999, under increasing pressure from gender specialists, the indigenous council CODENPE, which held formal responsibility for overseeing PRODEPINE, admitted that it lacked a clear definition of gender and its importance for indigenous development.[34] By PRODEPINE's midterm review in 2000, the dynamics around gender politics in the project had changed at a number of scales. Transnational networks informed by GAD were able to insert a new gender concern that addressed—however problematically and incompletely—some earlier inequalities. During the late 1990s, local activists in Ecuador, international development agencies, monitoring organizations, and feminist staff (male and female) networked to demand a different agenda in indigenous development. By way of channels in Washington and Quito, the World Bank began to change expectations of indigenous institutions such as CODENPE, implying that it was hypocritical to exclude gender disparities from its human rights agenda.[35] Affected by the change of direction, PRODEPINE acknowledged the marginalization of gender concerns within the project, leading to what its staff termed a "reflexive response" to the issue.[36] Although from the start women and men had participated in local development activities, PRODEPINE managers and staff came to see gender policy as weakly embedded. According to one such staff member, "The great weakness of gender in PRODEPINE is that from the initial phase the [gender] program hadn't begun" (quoted in M. Escobar 2002, 47).

A transnationalized review process was implemented to alter this pattern. Two consultancies were dispatched; one was carried out with World Bank funding and another by an Ecuadorian team of gender specialists who assessed PRODEPINE together with eighteen other projects underway in Ecuador.[37] They found that PRODEPINE had achieved little with respect to gender equity and, concretely, that female beneficiaries had received the smallest share of funds. As explained by a consultant close to the process, "PRODEPINE has come some of the way, because it understands that they have had two evaluations and in [these] the topic of gender has been appearing as if they had done nothing about it. So practically every time, they were given deadlines to work on it."[38] Infusing GAD norms into PRODEPINE, the reviewers recommended "mainstreaming" gender into all project components, particularly to provide support for female farmers in land titling, getting men to share domestic chores, and promoting the nonfarm rural sector (PRODEPINE 2001). The review also highlighted how little was known about international gender norms within Indian nationalities and pueblos: "Gender issues vary greatly by ethnic group, but little has been documented. Gender issues include differences in access to land, credit, and leadership positions."[39] PRODEPINE signed an agreement with a gender-specialist team in order to "enhance the existing knowledge, capacities, and skills in PRODEPINE to improve the gender focus in all the components and programs of the project" (CODENPE 2001, 25).

An array of changes in development personnel, priorities, and procedures occurred as a result of the gender review. At the most general level, CODENPE was encouraged to improve its institutional gender balance, while the World Bank provided technical support, training, and assistance in gender planning and the measurement of indicators to both the CODENPE and PRODEPINE staff. Within PRODEPINE, a female indigenous specialist in gender was appointed to oversee the mainstreaming agenda, and one female technician was placed in charge of information systems. Gender analysis was to be carried out on 127 participatory assessments, as all local development projects were to be systematically reviewed. Administratively, the gender component was incorporated into the project in the section on cultural heritage, whose original role was to promote ethnic festivals, music, and other cultural productions. In practical terms, the cultural heritage program began to consult with grassroots female and male leaders, take life histories from women and men, and involve both genders in creating inventories of cultural items.

While gender issues increased in visibility and prominence as a result of these changes, they were framed as an additional element and awarded a lower priority. In an annual evaluation, the cultural heritage program within PRODEPINE mentioned that a specialist was appointed to the national office to incorporate gender but ranked that achievement last, after others such as producing four videos, carrying out three workshops and forty-four festivals or cultural events, and supporting thirteen cultural groups (CODENPE 2001, 6). Moreover, cultural components in the project received small budgets; according to one regional staff member, "other" programs received around US$1 million annually, compared with US$10,000 for culture and gender (M. Escobar 2002, 47). In the PRODEPINE national office, the total number of female employees actually dropped, although a few women had been promoted to more-senior positions. Other technicians—the seven regional coordinators and the national directorate—remained exclusively male (M. Escobar 2002).

Another administrative and practical aspect of PRODEPINE intersected with gender in ways ambivalent for the latter. Participatory development methods were perceived by multilaterals, NGOs, and development practitioners as the cornerstone of the project's exemplary and innovative character, but these were also assumed to include women and men equally. As such, specific gender initiatives were often perceived as unnecessary due to the supposedly intrinsic equality of "participation." Said one national technician working on participation, "Beyond the good or bad methodology that might include a gender perspective or not, we have to be persuaded of the need for a gender perspective in development. I find it only marginally useful that in a workshop for devising development plans women can sit separately or not" (M. Escobar 2002, 45). PRODEPINE's gender specialist was more critical of existing practice. "The local development projects are not as participatory as one thinks. Women who were involved in the projects . . . did not have a voice when defining the project's implementation."[40] There were attempts to reconcile opposition to GAD with an approach that was supportive of women: "a participatory method appropriate to the characteristics of the indigenous peoples . . . avoiding the external interference and stereotypes" (M. Escobar 2002, 37). On this basis, PRODEPINE's gender specialist argued, "in the future, the local projects [would] have to define spaces for women to have effective participation in decision making." Nevertheless, a detailed assessment of one community development "self-diagnostic" (in Tungurahua province) found that women's participation was limited to assistance and basic needs rather than a full exercise of citizenship (Aulestia 2002).[41]

Resistance to internationally derived gender politics remained embedded among project staff who viewed gender as an imposed and inappropriate concern. In the words of one environment professional, "PRODEPINE programs [are forced] to find gender equity or inequality" (M. Escobar 2002, 40). Similarly, a national coordinator of rural investments said, "The Gender Program, through the [World Bank] consultancy, began to sensitize all personnel [about gender]

aggressively . . . it hasn't been proven whether we are or are not accentuat-
ing the gender inequalities, as we don't have instruments and methodologies"
(as quoted in M. Escobar 2002, 46). Echoing the experience of Bolivia's gender
and ethnic ministry, the gender review of the Ecuadorian project found that it
was difficult to resolve problems of inadequate political will and the association
between gender equity and "external," rather than endogenous, concerns.

Like the practices of other Ecuadorian development organizations (Martínez
Flores 2000), PRODEPINE exemplified how a technical and rational project
may resonate with underlying gendered associations and norms (Elson 1991).
Northern "masculine" values such as technical rationality and disembodied
competence are often established in local development interventions that are
staffed and funded by national and international NGOs or by the Catholic Church
(Hooper 2000a; Hooper 2000b).[42] At its inception, PRODEPINE managers represented the project in masculine terms: "PRODEPINE has development funds
to give to [grassroots organizations], it has an efficient team."[43] As in World
Bank projects generally (Bessis 2001), PRODEPINE's operational procedures
followed what might be seen as masculinist management norms that stress
technical expertise and sophisticated new data-management techniques as the
primary tools for alleviating poverty (see also Kondo 1999).[44] Multiscalar activism around gender equity elicited policy changes in PRODEPINE, although
the technical nature of the project reinscribed a particular gendered politics
that went beyond attention to women: the outcome in regard to gender equity
was less an empowerment agenda than an efficiency and productivity agenda.
Inserting a gender component was interpreted as an added value (PRODEPINE
2001), a masculinist criterion of measuring progress in which gender policy
was perceived as an additional issue to be taken into what was already framed
as a technically efficient project. Gender inclusion and equity became questions of administration, as we see in these words from a national PRODEPINE
employee, who noted that once gender policy was introduced, "there was a
need for formats, internal norms, matrices, forms, regulations, and operative
manuals to be reformulated" (M. Escobar 2002, 46). Although gender issues
undoubtedly gained more prominence from transnational activism around
women's empowerment, the wider context of gender relations (including communal patriarchies, development agencies' expectations of gender divisions
of labor, and coordination with the national women's council) compounded
the difficulties of putting this empowerment agenda into practice, leaving the
project open to ongoing criticism.[45]

Although limited in its impact on indigenous women, the reconfiguration of the project's gender politics illustrates how transnational activism across a number of scales and sites can rework indigenous development's gender politics in a nondeterminist and contingent way. Policy transformations around gender engaged racialized and gendered actors in transnational fields without clear North-South lines of power and involved questions that cut across multiple public and private spaces (Hyndman 2001). At the same time, PRODEPINE exemplified what some commentators condemn as the subordination of gender equity to ethnocultural agendas (Deere and León 2001). What we have shown here, however, is that such ethnocultural agendas, and the obstacles they have created for gender equity, may be *transnational* constructs that are not reducible to traditional or local patriarchies.

Indigenous Women's Transnational Activism

At the local, regional, and global scales, indigenous women's networks have provided new venues for indigenous women to work toward relevant and politically feasible discussions regarding their development rights. Indigenous women's networking transcends particular scales, cutting between local federations, international NGO meetings, and exchanges of experiences throughout Latin America. By "weaving in and between local, national and transnational scales of power, [Indian women] create new spaces of participation . . . consciousness, identities and discourse" (Blackwell 2006, 115). Indigenous women have created transnational networks while actively entangling with gender and development frameworks. Extending a postcolonial feminist and critical analysis, this section examines indigenous women's transnational networks and how they act to reconfigure the gender politics of indigenous development.

Indigenous women's relationship with Latin American feminism and women's movements are characterized by a range of positions, from extreme skepticism to critiques of their frequent elision of racial issues. As distinctively racialized and gendered subjects, indigenous women have been marginal to the largely mestiza-white women's movements. The relatively few indigenous women who do participate in these meetings have often come away believing that analysis of their specific demands and concerns was inadequate, and they thus decided to create networks more fitting for debate and discussion on their specific gender and ethnic challenges (Alvarez 2002, 566–67). One reason for indigenous women's disengagement from the women's movement can be seen in critiques—from a number of perspectives—of the broadly feminist agenda that prioritizes strategic over practical interests and divorces gender from other axes of social difference such as class and race or ethnicity. While indigenous women activists recognize gender discrimination, they situate it within hierarchies of race, class, and nationality. One Andean woman at a provincial meeting said, "If there is a greater difficulty for a woman, how much more so for an indigenous or peasant woman? [Noting] this doesn't mean that there has been the choice of a feminist perspective."[46]

From the viewpoints of many third-world feminists and women of color, GAD approaches are severely limited by their uncritical deployment of the category "woman" without accounting for culture, nationality, and race (Chua, Bhavnani, and Foran 2000). In this vein, some Andeans are skeptical of international efforts on behalf of indigenous women. "We haven't got a specific plan for indigenous women . . . Beijing + 5, [government] reports for 1995–2000, the Latin American and Caribbean regional meeting . . . equality, blah, blah. . . . For indigenous women, we have nothing."[47] Indigenous women's awareness of the intersecting axes of gender and race/ethnicity raises observations of processes by which only certain (largely mestiza) women gained authority within national women's institutions and thereby perpetuate, however inadvertently, indigenous women's exclusion from development policymaking. For example, a number of Ecuadorian indigenous women have called for direct indigenous representation in the National Women's Council, CONAMU (Chuma 1999). One senior Ecuadorian leader noted, "What appears to me to be important [is that the women's movement] incorporates a vision of [indigenous] peoples, so the ethnocultural line is included, just as inside the indigenous movement there must be a gender perspective."[48] However, the experiences of indigenous women in continentwide *encuentros* were largely negative, prompting them to create their own umbrella organizations and networks. For example, Ecuadorian indigenous women convened the first Continental Encuentro of Indigenous Women of First Nations, held in Quito in August 1995, which nominated a specific delegation to speak to the representative of Latin American NGOs in Beijing (Blackwell 2006). In other words, a newly established national network for diverse women of color from different political organizations extended and reconfigured connections to a continental scale, jumping into a role at the forefront of transnational networking.

Indigenous women have tended to be strategic and selective in their deployment of, and engagement with, the rights language of the international women's movement. For instance, the women's team from a national federation of indigenous, peasant, and Afro-Ecuadorian organizations found the Beijing Platform for Action and the UN Declaration condemning violence against women to be useful in framing and articulating their demands, even though they did not endorse all of the content. In another instance, indigenous women in Cañar province, Ecuador, mobilized over a thousand people in marches for International Women's Day (March 8). One distinctive component of indigenous women's articulation of gender and ethnicity is their emphasis on incorporating indigenous men. Western feminist frameworks were for many decades organized around a male-female binary, a perspective that Andean indigenous women usually find unhelpful, as do many third-world feminists. According to one Ecuadorian indigenous leader, "Gender is . . . something that is imposed [by the West]." [49] Another remarked, "When others speak of gender, they mean women, but what I understand is that . . . gender is a whole, what is male and female." [50]

Indigenous women have often built their political agendas on the outgrowth of colonialism and current global political economies (Vinding 2000). An early seminar of indigenous women of the Americas held in Santa Cruz, Bolivia, in 1992, discussed at length colonialism's cultural impact and women's struggle for land and rights (also see New York Declaration 2005). Following the UN women's conference in Beijing, indigenous women elaborated on this anticolonial politics, condemning combined ethnic and gender discrimination and demanding female participation in development planning (Olowaili Declaration 2000; Beijing Declaration 1998). At the 2002 Indigenous Women's Summit of the Americas, participants discussed the question of empowerment in the context of globalization, focusing on how indigenous women live under conditions of discrimination, racism, and poverty. Indigenous women's agendas thus position their gendered experiences firmly within an account of the historical, political, and economic processes that have countered the realization of their rights. Compared with gender and development approaches that tend to view third-world women as victims of their culture (Chua, Bhavnani, and Foran 2000; Schech and Haggis 2000), Bolivian and Ecuadorian indigenous women located their cultures within a broader frame of globalized power relations, as have their counterparts in Mexico (Speed, Hernández, and Stephen 2006).

As with colonial histories and women's movements, however, there are diverse articulations of these positions. One strand argues that women and men struggle together, but that women's role in ethnic activism must be accorded full recognition by indigenous federations. "Men and women together, we have done a lot, carried out our uprisings," yet "indigenous representatives—our own male companions—forget about indigenous women"[51] (see also Chuma 1999, 184). Other critiques speak to chauvinism that marginalizes women's spaces in decision making with regard to development. Speaking at an international conference, a woman from the lowlands of the department of Beni noted "lots of barriers [to women] from machismo," although she also acknowledged that many indigenous men are supportive of female organizing. In one Bolivian altiplano community, indigenous women were deprived of spaces for organizing, a result that the women strongly resented: "The [organization leaders said], 'Well, here the women's offices will be closed. We are ethnic peoples now; we have to move together unified.'"[52] In short, indigenous women have identified exclusionary patterns of organization and increasingly question them. A CONAIE female leader claimed, "It's true we haven't been able to develop separately as women, or to struggle. Now I'm in a struggle—a debate—with colleagues. They accept [gender issues], but still there's a discriminatory behavior [toward those issues]."[53]

Another strand of indigenous women's thought—often expressed informally and outside the confines of federation meetings—criticizes the sexual and domestic behavior of (some) indigenous men as unjust or unwanted.[54] But many of them still see men as crucial allies in reworking patterns of gendered exclusion (Choque 1999a, 29). In comparison with white-mestizo men, who have long deployed sexual and other violence against indigenous women in Latin America (D. Nelson 1999), indigenous men share experiences of racism, exclusion, and marginalization with indigenous women. While they demand a role in decision making, women recognize that indigenous men's support is crucial, for example, in persuading other men to seek alternative ways of working around gender issues.[55] At a pueblo reconstitution meeting, one male leader spoke at length, remarking, "Women should not be mistreated . . . they have suffered a lot. . . . Men and women have to share things; there can't be this [old] system anymore, as we are changing over time." Married couples promise to help each other, "but frequently there has been machismo. . . . A lot of the time we leave women to do everything, or we don't value women's work."[56]

Indigenous women have increasingly articulated diverse viewpoints about the intersections of gender and ethnicity through various venues on multiple scales. In the 1990s, three continentwide meetings of indigenous women laid the groundwork for 110 women from twenty-six countries to attend the 1995 Beijing international women's meeting. This added voice to their demands for the recognition of cultural values and their critiques of neocolonialism and modern geopolitics (Vinding 1998). One conference statement noted the importance of "the distinct interests and concerns of indigenous women [who] often face barriers both as women and as members of indigenous communities" (Beijing Platform for Action 1995, paragraph 32). With respect to international indigenous rights, one Ecuadorian leader argued, "We have collective rights for indigenous people . . . but we don't have anything within this collective right for indigenous women."[57] These women have also stressed the need to harmonize constitutional rights with indigenous norms and have asserted that laws designed to increase female political participation need to accept indigenous women's representation of ethnic groups *and* gender interests.[58]

Such transnational networking has allowed indigenous women to consolidate broader understandings of how gender and ethnicity vary across contexts and to compare their experiences of mobilization (Anonymous 1998; Cervone 1998; ECUARUNARI 1998; Choque 1999a). While in Bolivia on an exchange, five Ecuadorian indigenous women and men talked constantly about women's roles, to the surprise of their hosts and the transnational donors present. The Bolivian indigenous representatives felt uncertain about this topic, although the donors welcomed such discussions.[59] In a meeting in El Alto supported by Oxfam America and Norway's Saami indigenous group, Bolivian *mama t'allas*—female indigenous authorities married to and complementing male mallkus—debated the difficult process of combining ethnic identity with a weightier political role.[60]

In addition to providing political grammar for debating gender, transnational networks have acted to reconfigure development practice among indigenous populations. One example is the establishment of a training school to empower indigenous and Afro-Ecuadorian women in development projects and community relations. Established via a series of regional and national outlets, ECUARUNARI's Escuela de Formación de Mujeres "Dolores Cacuango" has trained women to "recognize their history, origin, and identity" through recuperation of indigenous knowledge, community identity, and the value of women (Pachamama 2000, 6; also see Laurie, Andolina, and Radcliffe 2005).[61] Initially, the federation training program was dominated by men (women made up only one to two percent of students).[62] As a counterweight, indigenous women mobilized support locally, nationally, and internationally, leading to the foundation of a women-only training academy, which enrolled its first students in 1998.[63] By late 2001, more than three hundred women were certified in development administration, political organization, and identity and culture,

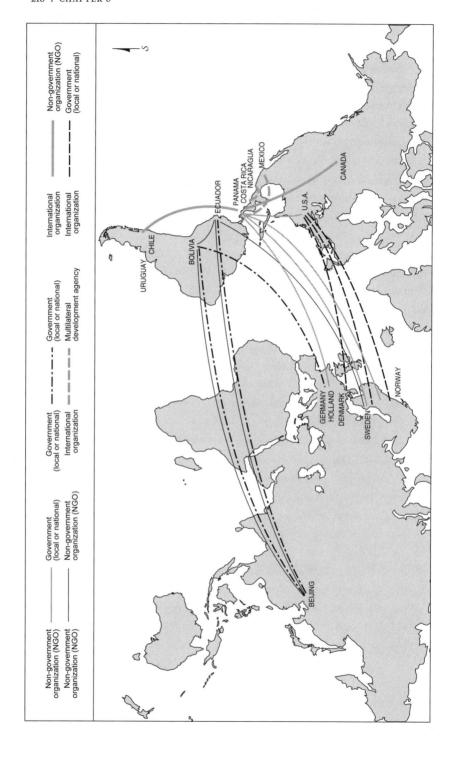

with a collective aim of tackling profound gender, ethnic, cultural, and inter-generational inequalities (ECUARUNARI 2000b, ECUARUNARI 2001). A Norwegian development NGO funded the school until 2000, while the United Nations Fund for Women (UNIFEM) provided additional resources.[64] At a later stage, the Danish nongovernmental agency IBIS stepped in to support female leadership training through this school. The school's female leadership has stressed how community, provincial, national, and even international leaders can be trained there, expanding women's decision-making powers.[65] Indeed, the school has already contributed to the consolidation of women's position in transnational development networks, as one graduate from Bolívar Province devised a successful project that acquired international funding. Map 12 illustrates the multiple connections around gender and indigenous development considered in this chapter.

With increased coordination, identity strengthening, and discursive competence across scales, female indigenous leaders have highlighted the long-term goals of establishing and enacting gendered *and* racial/ethnic rights. As such, indigenous women's perspectives cannot be subsumed under global feminism or local ethnic politics. Indeed, Mercedes Prieto and co-authors (2004) have argued that female indigenous leaders are building bridges between ethnicity and gender (compare Deere and León 2001). Articulating a complex politics of position that shifts constantly between women's and indigenous interests, indigenous women suggest that neither agenda is sufficient on its own. Activism for indigenous women is as much about building networks on and across scales (local, national, global) as it is about debating whether they fit existing, one-dimensional categories.

The Gendered Consequences of Transnationalized Development

The multiethnic and multiscalar relations that constitute transnational Andean indigenous development networks operate in specific gendered ways and have particular gendered consequences. These relate to the grounded interactions

◄ MAP 12. Transnational connections around gender and indigenous development. International organizations are part of many of these linkages around gender and indigenous people due to the significance of the UN, its 1995 Conference on Women in Beijing, and follow-up indigenous women's forums, especially in the Americas.

between multilaterals, national ethnic movements, government agencies, and local societies as they operate in—and with respect to—Ecuador and Bolivia. They also relate to a series of twists on modular transnational "boomerang" processes as outlined by Keck and Sikkink (1998). First, indigenous women have an additional layer of marginalization to circumvent, illustrated by the initial gender invisibility in PRODEPINE and the race/class devaluation in Latin American women's conferences. Second, as this marginalization was (re)produced transnationally, dissatisfied indigenous women networked through alternate transnational and multiethnic connections to create more empowering political spaces, such as indigenous women's conferences, and development projects, such as ECUARUNARI's indigenous women leadership school. As such, the gendered outcomes of transnational networks concerned with indigenous development are diverse, with variable consequences for the empowerment of indigenous women.

Those transnational spaces that we find to be empowering and appropriate for indigenous women are characterized by a number of features: the expression and pursuit of difference and equality issues in a structured and transparent way; the recognition and incorporation of context-specific intersections of gender, race, culture, and nationality; the acknowledgment of indigenous women's mobility across space (and between scales) and the support to facilitate such mobility; and indigenous women's meaningful participation vis-à-vis men (indigenous and not) and nonindigenous women. These features are found unevenly across the Andes. The World Bank–sponsored Ecuadorian ethnodevelopment project PRODEPINE failed to incorporate issues of gender inequality and women's mobility fully within its accounting of cultural and racial differences. On the other hand, the Latin American women's movements, as represented within international encuentros, mirrored the tendency of GAD policy to focus on a generic gender inequality instead of grappling with context-specific and racialized gender interests.

By contrast, the international indigenous women's meetings encouraged and practiced mobility, celebrated cultural and national differences, and grounded discussion firmly in agendas that were largely unmediated by indigenous men or nonindigenous people (compare Blackwell 2006). At the same time, these networks have constructed ties to other actors in order to forge spaces at national and local scales that allow a more systematic gendered approach to development to take shape. The ECUARUNARI women's training school is one crucial example of this. Other female leadership opportunities have emerged as well. In Bolivia, the Aymara women's Center for the Integral Development of Aymara Women

(CDIMA) carried out training of women from the early 1990s. Ecuador's peasant, indigenous, and black federation FENOCIN also opened a training school in 1999 funded by a Dutch development agency. This program offered skills in development project elaboration, administration, basic accounting, parliamentary procedures (law and rights), nutrition, and traditional medicine.[66] In a separate program, the Inter-American Development Bank interpreted its social-inclusion remit to fund Andean female leaders' political and civil participation in a project that was prompted by the 2002 Oaxaca indigenous women's summit and used a US$120,000 Norwegian donation for gender empowerment.[67] Finally, the United Nations has also supported indigenous women's efforts to further their leadership and advocacy skills through follow-up meetings after the 1995 UN women's conference in Beijing.

Still, the combination of features that enable empowering and appropriate forms of indigenous development is often held together only with difficulty. One reason for this is the embedding and framing of indigenous development within social-neoliberal agendas, with their attendant forms of governance and differentiation.[68] Largely advocated by nonindigenous women and men of various ethnic groups and often made a condition of funding by donors, "gender mainstreaming" has endeavored to addresses gender concerns across policy sectors. To some extent its agenda is compatible with indigenous women's attention to the structural factors that systematically disadvantage them. Yet mainstreaming is deployed institutionally, discursively, and interpersonally in ways that obscure the racially and culturally specific nature of gender relations and of indigenous women's disadvantage. On the one hand, key actors have represented GAD as extraneous to core concerns of ethnic beneficiaries and societies, foreclosing discussion about its applicability to Andean indigenous development. On the other hand, neoliberal interpretations of social capital have understood indigenous gender relations as traditional and uncontested, offering a static (and often inaccurate) picture of women's mobility and participation. In the case of PRODEPINE, alternate transnational networking infused international gender concerns through administrative procedures that gave more visibility to women and gender, but also worked within neoliberal masculinist practices and discourses emphasizing efficiency and productivity. In short, this ethnodevelopment project started without a policy framework to tackle gender hierarchies, postponing pro-women policies in favor of pro-indigenous policies. In the end, however, these policy and practical dimensions hindered a coherent and institutionally defendable policy that integrated gender and ethnic issues in a way that can be applied effectively.

With respect to gender in ethnodevelopment, then, neoliberal governance was put into effect through an absence: the lack of a critical gender politics and its default mode of "gender as usual." Neoliberalism's "gender as usual" for indigenous development is not the simple continuity of ethnocultural tradition, however. Microcredit programs, the ongoing reconfiguration of land and resource markets, and the restructuring of labor relations all have an impact on indigenous gender relations. In response, indigenous women have articulated their own understandings of these processes to find purchase on a critique that permits them to engage not only neoliberal development policy but also the gender politics of indigenous movements. Placing gendered and racialized subjects at its center, they account for the reconstitution of male-female inequalities within the multiethnic relations that produce and channel Andean indigenous development arenas.

Transnationalism, Development, and Culture
in Theory and Practice

Indigenous politics and policy in the Andes highlight how development and culture intersect in complex but patterned ways. Weaving together an understanding of discursive, organizational, and social connections, we have provided a poststructural account of the uneven character and effects of these processes. Our study of new encounters between indigenous peoples' movements and networks of development actors has implications for academic study, development policy and practice, and social-movement struggles for collective empowerment. This concluding chapter discusses these ramifications and then contextualizes them with respect to recent political changes in Ecuador and Bolivia, centered on the governments of "post-neoliberal" presidents Rafael Correa (Ecuador) and Evo Morales (Bolivia).

Implications for Academic Inquiry

Our call for nuanced analyses of indigenous politics suggests the need to think across scales and underscores the exigency of joining critical, theoretical insights from various academic disciplines on development, international relations, social movements, globalization, gender, ethnicity, and race. Because of the intricate and expansive character of the relationship between development and culture, we opted for a theoretical composite that affords explanatory amplitude and complexity over a theoretical unity that might furnish explanatory austerity and simplicity.

We approached this theoretical synthesis by refining two prevailing approaches to transnationalism. First, in contrast to the singular ethnic groupings of transnational communities comprised of diaspora migrants or global business expatriates, we interrogated a multiethnic transnational community of policy-making institutions, advocacy organizations, and indigenous social movements.

Second, we took the end point of the transnational-activism literature in political science as a point of departure. In Keck and Sikkink's (1998) "boomerang" model of transnational issue networks, political connections across country borders may discipline national states according to international norms and alter their practices. However, we see this outcome as *initiating a new process* of relations between different kinds of actors around the network's common issue(s)—in our case, indigenous rights and development. Policies and practices therefore undergo continual transnational negotiation through transformed paradigms and new spaces of interaction, which "reload" the boomerangs initially launched by transnational campaigns on behalf of weaker players operating in local and national contexts.

Ongoing relations across scales and boundaries implore us to analyze transnationalism within multiethnic social fields. Intersections of race, class, and gender are at play, contributing to new subject positions and forms of stratification. To some extent, actors and agendas involved in indigenous development have articulated *across* ethnic and national lines, but *around* a muting of class. As a public identity category, class has been downplayed to varying degrees by dominant and weaker actors, including the World Bank, the Swiss bilateral development agency, CONAIE, and CONAMAQ. As part of concrete social processes, however, class is still significant in establishing a global political economy and local social hierarchies (Gibson-Graham 1996). The acquisition of new class status through professionalization, for example, has intensified as education and training programs targeted the indigenous as a category of people and subject of learning. This may stratify positions among those who identify as indigenous, as when newly trained indigenous people qualify for decision-making positions over those who are not professionally certified (e.g., in state indigenous-affairs agencies). Such stratification may be gendered, too. When development agencies or indigenous organizations envisage indigenous women as strategically placed in the (re)production of social capital or culture via family ties, domestic locations, and community bases, women's access to professional training can be devalued or obstructed (also see de la Cadena 2000; Molyneux 2002). On the other hand, professionalization and training can erode conventional barriers between indigenous and nonindigenous people who identify as professional, as with the multiethnic composition of staff in PRODEPINE's national office. Furthermore, indigenous movements have appropriated professionalization and other knowledge-building activities as part of wider transformative projects of interculturalism, as in the ayllu and Quichua pueblos movements examined in chapter 3.

While other scholars would recognize that indigenous development policy and practice occur within a transnational social field (Crang, Dwyer, and Jackson 2004; Vertovec 2001), we have analyzed this transnational field as political as well, since it comprises contested processes of resource allocation, policy endorsement, and identification of key decision makers and beneficiaries. The languages of constituency building and legitimization in development circuits are as finely attuned to political context as those of any political party. Therefore, the extent to which indigenous peoples and organizations can transform development discourses and subjectivities within this field is increasingly significant. The cases we have considered suggest that this resituation of indigenous affairs has complicated the action of indigenous-movement organizations, as they progressively alternate between challenging, negotiating, and affirming development principles and policies. An additional outgrowth of our study, then, is the importance of examining transnational political processes beyond mobilizations and campaigns, and beyond the formal incorporation of new norms and subjects into legislation or legislatures. We need to enter the channels of policy design, implementation, and administration, while being aware that such channels do not necessarily parallel national or other pregiven boundaries. This is particularly challenging for the social-movement literature, which tends to locate social-movement politics largely on the fringes of political and administrative institutions or agencies (see, e.g., Hanagan, Moch, and te Brake 1998; Tilly 1999). One lesson from our work is to approach this through a concept of scattered hegemonies (Grewal and Kaplan 1994) rather than a binary model of domination from above plus local resistance from below. While political science has traditionally reproduced such "above and below" models, attention to the institutional and social connections between multiple scales provides a more grounded and nuanced analysis of transnational politics.[1] Moreover, our approach extends ethnographic studies of policy by examining how novice subjects in the policy world—indigenous peoples in this case—contest and reshape projects and programs in multiethnic networks (see Shore and Wright 1997).

In turn, greater concentration on governing powers and practices is vital. Our book has shown that nongovernmental organizations, social-movement representatives, and international agencies of various kinds have gained increasing influence over indigenous development policy in countries like Ecuador and Bolivia. However, it also demonstrates that these transnational relations are sometimes facilitated by states and that networks and interactions may go through *and* around states simultaneously. State influence over indigenous subjects and national development has therefore shifted but not evaporated.

As a focus on indigenous professionalization illustrates, transnational actors have influenced the climate that welcomes seemingly pro-indigenous education, and they have mobilized at times to pressure or circumvent the state and work directly with indigenous organizations and other NGOs. Yet state institutions implemented and managed the education reforms, which were in turn funded and monitored in association with transnational actors. These mixed-actor circuitries are facilitated by the increasing willingness of NGOs to work with state agencies (Bebbington 1997b; Vellinga 1998) and by international donors requiring that states work with NGOs and civil society (A. M. Clark 1995).

Enmeshed with the issue of governance by transnational networks is the matter of relative power. Networks may be formally horizontal yet stratified in practice. In spite of ethno- and social development's acknowledgment of indigenous uses and customs, for example, indigenous knowledge is often undervalued even while evoked in limited form. This was illustrated by many multicultural higher education programs reviewed in chapter 5, as well as by the irrigation projects discussed in chapter 4 and the local development processes considered in chapter 3. These positions and suppositions are especially important to recognize when dealing with multiethnic and "North-South" transnational relations, which carry baggage of racism, sexism, and imperialism (Alexander and Mohanty 2001).

Some of these features of indigenous development networks are shaped by what Keck and Sikkink (1998) call "issue characteristics" and "actor characteristics" (203–9). In contrast to the human rights and environmental issues examined by Keck and Sikkink, most states—certainly Ecuador and Bolivia—see development as being in their interest and are more flexible in allowing nongovernmental and international development organizations to have influence, in the expectation that doing so will increase policy effectiveness. As we noted in the introduction, development is so malleable a concept that it is effectively a multi-issue issue and often connects networks as it links issues together. This accounts in part for the involvement of many different kinds of actors within development policymaking and implementation, which in turn explains some of the diversity of players governing indigenous development.

The same polyvalence of development induces disagreement around its specific meaning and the optimal ways to attain it. States like Bolivia and Ecuador—and the power holders within them—may want development, but they have been ambivalent about ethnodevelopment. Because of this, indigenous development networks continue to advocate for indigenous people as well as shape policies. In development organizations with indigenous teams or programs, most personnel support indigenous rights and are genuinely concerned for indigenous peoples' well-being. At the same time, these personnel are usually perceived as policy experts, giving them additional clout with governments and multilaterals. As such, indigenous development network members do not necessarily coordinate campaigns, but they can build on each other's actions. For example, in the late 1990s, indigenous organizations in Bolivia were increasingly discontent over the slow and paternalistic implementation of the 1996 INRA Law, specifically the provision allowing the creation of Original Community Lands. Indigenous organizations sent reports abroad that documented and criticized the process as a violation (or insufficient recognition) of indigenous rights, and international supporters flooded the national land institute, INRA, with letters supporting the Indians and condemning INRA.[2] The Bolivian state responded that its budget did not allow more TCO claims to be processed or for any increase in the speed of processing, and therefore development agencies with programs for indigenous people stepped in to increase funding for administrative tasks (INRA 2006). While TCO creation still faces a number of limitations, this combination of civil mobilization and development aid effectively unblocked the process and secured greater cooperation from the Bolivian state.[3]

Such transnational leverage may benefit indigenous peoples, but it also contributes to network hierarchies. In human rights advocacy campaigns, the information and knowledge of otherwise marginalized actors is highly valued, but this input is less significant within indigenous development networks, where financial resources and "expert" knowledge take on great value. In the case of Bolivian TCOs, we saw in chapter 3 that Danish bilateral assistance was crucial in swaying the state to process claims in the highlands; but DANIDA also wielded leverage over indigenous beneficiaries. In TCO project designs, DANIDA allocated project resources according to which actors it saw as most capable, placing indigenous organizations on the bottom of that hierarchy.[4]

Governmentality theory is a fruitful ingredient of an approach that addresses these manifestations of power while regarding transnationalism as a social *and* political field. Regarding the latter, Dean (1999) claimed that governmentality "provides a bridge between the comprehension of our social existence (or 'life conduct') and our political conduct" (199). One of its attractive features in this respect is the treatment of subject formation as a core aspect of governance and policy. This is especially significant when considering the involvement of identity-based movements in the making and implementation of policy, and when contemplating the entanglement of culture and development. In chapter 3, we discussed how indigenous territorial administration projects in

Bolivia posed the creation of a new indigenous subject, the territorial manager. The territorial manager is not an identity that indigenous organizations had previously expressed or mobilized around, and it was a figure counterposed to original authorities (such as mallkus) often cited as a distinctive element of indigenous culture and even a form of social capital in highland communities. In chapter 4, we showed how an irrigation project in Ecuador contributed to a redefinition of indigenous identities that assimilated contemporary managerial norms. In that case, however, a new identity category did not emerge; the meaning of existing ones was altered instead.

The adoption of governmentality theory also increases our analytical purchase on the subtle workings of power in transnational fields. One reason is that governmentality conceives of the enabling and constraining dimensions of policies and processes as two sides of the same coin. Chapter 4 illustrated this tension in its analysis of indigenous participation in externally funded but locally scaled irrigation projects. Local indigenous organizations drew to some degree on their own governance practices to design projects and run irrigation systems, yet they were expected to have or acquire accounting, computer, and personnel-management skills in order to receive funding and exercise autonomy in project execution. As discussed in chapter 1, PRODEPINE in Ecuador provided local indigenous organizations with unprecedented opportunities to design their own development plans, but they had to do so according to a common national formula designed in part by the World Bank and prove that they possessed the infrastructure and training needed to manage funds and projects in developmentally appropriate ways.

Governmentality theory also offers a nuanced approximation to power relations by accounting for their presence in contexts where those involved are veritably supportive of the subjects they work with and strategize for. Those we interviewed in the agencies supporting indigenous projects and programs were motivated to help indigenous people and never expressed any desire or intent to dominate them. All the same, they frequently adopted and deployed matrices of development and government that included elements of control as well as of empowerment.

A governmentality account of indigenous or transnational politics is, however, partial. This is one reason why, as stated in the introduction, we took up Hale's (2002) suggestion to combine Foucauldian theory of governmentality with a Gramscian concern for hegemony and subaltern struggles. Mitchell Dean (1999) has, in fact, acknowledged that governmentality does not encompass "struggle or competition between . . . groups or individuals attempting to influence, appropriate or otherwise control the exercise of authority" (198). As shown in chapter 1, the forms of governmentality that enrolled and affected Andean indigenous peoples were produced in part through political struggles and hegemonic articulation. The latter inflected ongoing transnational advocacy for participation, diversity, equity, and sustainability in development; it did so by incorporating those principles—partially—into other policy paradigms and implementation mechanisms that in turn "bounced back" to engage and affect indigenous movements. This articulation facilitated consensus around local-ness, interculturalism, dialogue, and proficiency building; but the negotiation of differences was pervasive, and contentiousness hardly disappeared.

Taking governmentality and hegemony together allows us to consider how neoliberal paradigms imbricate *and* contradict indigenous-movement agendas and how the latter leave room for alternative visions of culture and development. First, the recognition of indigenous culture as compatible with growth and prog-ress validated indigenous-movement claims that indigenous cultures contain the bases for development and improved livelihoods. Second, representations of discrete indigenous cultures dovetailed with indigenous movements' efforts to recover and organize around more "authentic" ethnic figures of ayllus and pueblos. Third, ethnodevelopment policy's emphases on community participa-tion endorsed indigenous movement claims for (and rights to) inclusion within development in general and self-managed development in particular. Finally, the accentuation of efficiently administered ethnodevelopment overlapped with the desire of some Andean indigenous leaders to increase economic productivity, learn marketing strategies, and enhance managerial and technical skills.

However enabling and harmonious this may appear, it also objectified indige-nous people and clashed with some indigenous movement viewpoints. When collating local cultural distinctiveness into one concept as a form of capital, ethnodevelopment policy framed Andean indigenous cultures as a bundle of factors that can be harnessed to market-led growth. This version of ethno-development policy aspired to overcome exclusion of indigenous peoples from the benefits of national and international markets by investing in social and human capital (Davis 2002). Such conceptualizations resonate with earlier mod-ernization models that sought to remove the barriers to economic "takeoff," but conflict with more communitarian subjectivities of many indigenous lead-ers. Even though indigenous organizations like CONAIE and CONAMAQ have distinguished themselves categorically from class-based associations, they often oppose neoliberal policies such as free trade and privatization. They have also represented features of indigenous identity as embodying an alternative form of development that contests neoliberal individualism and homogeneity through social solidarity, wealth redistribution, and collective citizenship (CIDOB 1993b; CONAIE 1994b; CONAMAQ 2000d; CSUTCB 1992).

In Ecuador, for example, highland activists have sometimes asserted that indigenous communities operate according to a communal economy completely opposed to the logic of the market (Guerrero and Ospina 2003, 140–42); others have claimed that indigenous development is rooted in a holistic and spiritual connection with land, whereas Western cultures understand land as a resource to be exploited and traded.[5] Finally, ECUARUNARI viewed the reconstruction of Quichua pueblos as a way to avoid "inserting ourselves individually—and accepting homogenization—as 'indigenous citizens' in national life." Instead they sought to "organize . . . as collective citizens, as pueblos and nationalities" (ECUARUNARI 1999c, 8). In Bolivia and Ecuador, these communitarian models were not only evoked against neoliberal national water legislation but also expressed in programs that indigenous organizations see (at least to some extent) as beneficial. Indigenous professionalization programs engaged in disputes about the cultural meanings in curricula and the cultural identities of students, while German-supported local-governance training programs were devalued by some Bolivian indigenous mallkus for concentrating on "written formalities, running counter to an oral and customary organizational culture" (GTZ 2004c, 141). In sum, subaltern consent and resistance are principal forces in the scattering of hegemony and prove significant for the content and purview of governmentality.

The final but equally important pieces of our theoretical synthesis are geographical. Attention to space and scale is vital if we wish to understand how governmentality and subaltern struggle function; it is also essential for theorizing the relationship between transnationalism and globalization. Spatial representations and "imaginative geographies" (Said 1978) underpin assumptions about development efficacy, cultural identity, and political authority. As outlined in chapter 3 and discussed in other chapters, the potential of local scales for development and cultural reproduction was largely agreed upon; prevailing governance strategies worked through municipal zones and procedures created to enhance diversity, efficiency, growth, and participation simultaneously. By acting within them, indigenous leaders and organizations were subject to social-neoliberal governmentality. But they also struggled and resisted: in some cases indigenous organizations appropriated municipal governments; in others, they mobilized around local counterspaces like ayllus and pueblos. Also, the indigenous *body* has gained new visibility as a site of development. That is, indigenous peoples are celebrated for contributing social networks and informal governance to civil society and for their production and distribution of ethnic services and goods to a global market. As the indigenous body is represented with particular attributes, skills, and potential, distinctive bodily performance becomes part of exchange and political processes, whether in the villages of the Andes or the meeting rooms of the World Bank.

In a similar vein, while governments and development agencies often define indigenous identity and territoriality as a bounded space, indigenous organizations see their territories as outward-looking places. Water policy and professionalization programs assumed that indigenous knowledge was local in character, while indigenous movements tried to assert that their knowledge of water had national relevance in the area of planning and that their ways of knowing had universal relevance in the area of education. Indigenous proposals around ayllus and pueblos envisaged them in multiscalar fashion; Bolivians conceived of ayllus as belonging to wider markas and suyus, while Ecuadorians pictured indigenous pueblos as agglutinating smaller-scale comunas and composing a larger Quichua nationality. The indigenous movements' territorial proposals, whether scaled at the municipality or wider, were, however, disciplined by the state and some development agencies. As such, these geographies laid out the grounds (literally) for negotiation and contest over control of territory and other forms of political authority. Graduated sovereignty in the Ecuadorian and Bolivian highlands (in the form of TCOS and CTIs) was, in short, affected by governmentalities through the local but was also a product of hegemonic struggles involving a variety of players whose visions and valuations of the local differed.

Just as these examples illustrate how governmentality and hegemony work spatially, they highlight how spatial practices that redraw and resignify boundaries are part and parcel of globalization (also see Hudson 1999). Accounts of transnationalism that focus purely on border crossing will paint a more deterritorialized picture of globalization than is warranted, since imaginative and lived geographies give form to movements and interventions across borders. Consider further the relation between state decentralization and indigenous development programs described in chapter 3. Although reforms in both countries were internationally influenced and informed, decentralization was more extensive and thorough in Bolivia than in Ecuador. It included more precise allocations of funding and responsibilities and provided more legal assurance of civil-society participation and recognition of cultural diversity. These contrasts in official reforms shaped approaches to ethnodevelopment by international agencies.

Functionaries of the World Bank with expertise on indigenous affairs suggested that Bolivia's systematic and participatory decentralization obviated the need for a separate, large-scale indigenous development program, while Ecuador's more patchy decentralization urged one.[6] In Bolivia, networking and funding associated with official aid flowed mainly through national government institutions and local municipalities, even though localized indigenous subjects were the intended beneficiaries. Ecuador's decentralization had more linkages between local and global actors involved in indigenous development, and the presence of the national state was less profound. PRODEPINE is one example. Although co-governed at the national level by a tripartite commission of delegates from the World Bank, national indigenous confederations, and the Ecuadorian state, it identified multicommunity, second-tier indigenous organizations as its main interlocutors and funding recipients. Even as decentralization and indigenous development intensified connections across national borders and multiple scales, these borders and scales were redefined rather than eroded. In turn, the state has acted as a mediating institution in which national interests—reconfigured around social neoliberalism—were aligned simultaneously, albeit contradictorily, with actors from both outside and inside territorial boundaries.

In sum, the relationship between development and culture has played out through discourses and interactions that both cross scales and reshape them, doing so in ways that both open and close possibilities for indigenous politics and development. Analogous processes are occurring in countries other than Bolivia and Ecuador. The World Bank had extended its ethnodevelopment projects to Peru (Oliart 2004), and Hale's (2002) study reveals the complex intersections of neoliberalism and multiculturalism in Guatemala. Likewise, Atkins and Rey-Maquieira (1996) and Ramos (1998) have considered ethnodevelopment and multicultural governance in Colombia and Brazil, respectively. Best-practice models in indigenous development do not only circulate among donors in Latin America. In Africa, for instance, groups like Masaai pastoralists in Tanzania and the Ogoni in Nigeria have claimed indigenous rights due, in part, to the influence of the International Working Group on Indigenous Affairs, foreign donor organizations, and the ILO (G. Cameron 2001; Watts 2003). The World Bank has completed consultations with government officials and ethnic group representatives in Asia, Africa, and Latin America on a new global development framework for indigenous and tribal peoples (Satish 1999), and World Bank programs for Indonesian indigenous peoples reveal dynamics similar to those in the Andes (see Li 2007). This transnationalization of ethnodevelopment will pose new challenges and possibilities for indigenous and other ethnically distinct peoples, as well as for policymakers working in indigenous and ethnic affairs.

Implications for Policy and Practice

Agencies of various stripes have come up with "another round of solutions" (A. Escobar 1995, 217) through social neoliberalism and ethnodevelopment paradigms. Some of these solutions reveal shortcomings that we consider here. We hope to improve policy and practice in doing so, but we also recognize that there are fundamental issues concerning development that will be left untouched. While we favor nonneoliberal (or less neoliberal) approaches to indigenous development, in contrast to those analyzed in this book, our suggestions focus on process more than outcomes: we look to extend indigenous peoples' influence over the definition of development subjects, goals, and technologies; we suggest greater diversity of evaluation and measurement criteria; and we urge greater equity in the transnational fields of actors who design, implement, and evaluate development policies and programs.

Pursuing these aims entails moving beyond indigenous professionalization and training to broader deliberation—which would include nonprofessional indigenous men and woman—about how their norms and practices may or may not contribute to development and how resources might best be allocated. A more serious commitment to multiculturalism in development projects, for instance, might allow more room for indigenous interests, identities, and capabilities to be framed in diverse ways. This would require that cultural and social diversity be valued for the distinct development goals, strategies, and tools it might generate, rather than appreciated for its amenability to premeditated or prevailing ones. It would also necessitate more money and time for studies of indigenous conceptualizations of resource use and customary legal frameworks. Efficiency and replication, in short, cannot always be the priorities to which indigenous development must bend. A series of points follow from this.

One is the policy challenge to move beyond a hyperreal Indian (Ramos 1998) that fits formulaic development frameworks, strategies, and measures to specific bodies. This implies breaking with the assumption that indigenous culture and identity are steeped in timeless traditions—unconnected to class, gender, and location differences—or marked by visible bodily or behavioral distinctiveness. Such assumptions may have exclusionary and divisive consequences for people and organizations unable or unwilling to perform an "authentic" indigenous identity, even though they could viably claim to be indigenous. Examples include small agriculturalists near Misicuni Dam in Bolivia or indigenous activists affiliated with peasant confederations such as CSUTCB or FENOCIN (see Laurie, Andolina, and Radcliffe 2002; Andolina, Radcliffe, and Laurie 2005; Lucero 2006). Likewise, those features of indigenous culture defined as social capital should not be viewed as essential traits but as sets of norms and practices produced historically through multiscalar relations. If development funds are to build on social capital, agencies must pay careful attention to the process involved in constructing this capital in order to avoid tapping into something that is not substantively there. In addition, by representing indigenous communities and cultures as undifferentiated wholes, funds that are assumed to benefit entire communities may favor certain segments over others (see Cooke and Kothari 2001). They may not reach the poorest people, such as those without access to water. Or they may fail to improve the livelihood of indigenous women or enhance their ability to strengthen family well-being. Such failures could then in turn affect communities negatively overall. As such, opportunities for self-definition need to be expanded, and criteria for ascribing indigenousness must be more flexible.

Deficiencies in subject definition can undermine measures of indigenous development. World Bank Indigenous Affairs leader Shelton Davis (2002), for instance, acknowledged that social-capital indices for its programs in Latin America incorporated few criteria normally associated with indigenous cultures. Indeed, these and other measures of indigenous resources and capabilities have included an array of human, technical, and physical-capital standards that are distant from prevailing understandings of indigenous cultural norms and practices. Three related problems derive from this. One is that ethnodevelopment, meant to "build on people's values . . . rather than impos[e] a model from the top down" (Deruyterre 1997, 11), instead becomes top-down as it inscribes externally devised norms that misrepresent or downplay indigenous peoples' development potential. Another dilemma is the exclusion (or assimilation) of those people whose cultural strengths are undetected by existing measures. A third predicament arises when higher assessments of capital and proficiency elicit larger funding allocations, as in PRODEPINE and the Bolivian TCO titling project supported by DANIDA. This dilemma suggests that to become developed you must already be developed (that is, already have measurable human, technical, and physical capital); it also means that funds go to those appraised as most capable, rather than those most in need. Along with revision and reflection among donors, greater public scrutiny of these measures and deeper indigenous participation in their construction would be in order.

Caution should also be exercised when supporting exemplary cases and attempting to duplicate them elsewhere. Poor fit across contexts leads to unintended consequences and unwarranted comparisons. In the case of the Bolivian ayllu movement, CONAIE and CIDOB have been held up by NGO supporters (Bolivian and international) as exemplary organizations based on partial readings of their identity and behavior (e.g., they have class-free identities, strong negotiating capacity, and successful representatives). This modeling contributed to the acknowledgment and reconstruction of indigenous ayllus, previously downplayed in highland Bolivia. Yet it also charted a path for ayllu-movement organizations that led them toward political cooptation. In addition, the rise of the ayllu movement has further divided the Bolivian indigenous movement organizationally, since, for the ayllu movement, being like CONAIE and CIDOB meant being unlike CSUTCB, a Bolivian peasant (and largely indigenous) organization that the ayllu movement now rivals (Andolina, Radcliffe, and Laurie 2005). One respondent involved in support for ayllus acknowledged that his Bolivian NGO was partly—although unintentionally—at fault for these divisions, while an interviewee from an international donor NGO argued that his organization was not responsible for such unintended consequences.[7]

In a different vein, those who promote Otavalan merchants as models of "entrepreneurship-with-identity" project a limited image that excludes poorer Otavalans who lack access to the textile trade entirely or who produce the culturalized textiles that merchants commercialize. Andolina's compadres in Peguche, Ecuador, are an example of the latter. Once the Ecuadorian tourist trade was damaged with dollarization (1999), they were unable to compete in small-scale textile production and resorted to wage labor, working locally and transnationally but remaining worse off in terms of income. In short, we concur with Nina Pacari, the first indigenous woman to be named Ecuadorian foreign secretary: "Indigenous peoples in different countries face different issues, not least the timing of neoliberal reforms [and] the nature of constitutional reform . . . they can learn from each other, though there is not 'one model.'"[8]

The spatiality of indigenous cultures and economies should be reconceived within less-bounded images of the local in order to capture how their practices often link rural and urban spaces or stretch to national and international scales. Extended-family networks, cited by development agencies as a key source of social capital, frequently stretch across scales and give these multiplace con- nections their concrete form. While we support the notion of improving or reactivating rural economies, development funds allotted to discrete rural locales may not take full advantage of the livelihood strategies and social capital forms that indigenous families and communities have created (see Bebbington 2000). Moreover, it may be insufficient to insert culturally distinct, local entrepreneurs into the world market as traders of ethnic products and services (Brysk 2000, 289–90). Competition among Andean indigenous groups and between Andeans and other international producers over cultural product niches, fashionable and fluctuating preferences of first-world consumers "buying ethnic," and new rela- tions of dependency are all possibilities that a more global and multiscalar vision of indigenous cultural and economic space might anticipate more aptly.[9]

A related point is that indigenous development needs to be seen within na- tional and global macroeconomic environments, which may need to be changed in order for indigenous people to prosper. As argued by Jan Nederveen Pieterse (2001), a growing coalition of reformist governments and international institu- tions like the UN could embrace an approach where "participatory development and human development form a strategic combination of . . . perspectives" (166–67). Such an approach would include labor and wage standards, controls on short-term capital movements, taxes to limit currency speculation, and foreign debt reduction for poor countries. It would also entail reducing corruption and cronyism, enhancing accountability of both national and international govern- ing institutions, and a general "review of . . . trade and investment policies" (Nederveen Pieterse 2001, 167).

With or without these macrostructural reforms, indigenous peoples should be allowed to invoke their legal and constitutional rights to challenge or modify national or international development policies—including those related to structural adjustment—that might harm them indirectly. Within Andean countries, this power has not been effectively granted; modification of such policies therefore tends to result from protest movements, which sometimes ally with transnational campaigns against privatization, as in the case of neo- liberal land and water legislation. Internationally, the procedures of the World Bank's Operational Directive 4.20 on indigenous peoples cannot be invoked for macroeconomic policy reforms supported by the World Bank (Treakle 1998). Consultations with indigenous leaders on revisions of OD 4.20 did not change that limitation, despite indigenous representatives' assertions that the World Bank is a subject of international law, which includes indigenous rights.[10]

Indigenous rights might also be invoked as a way for indigenous organizations to appropriate current performance technologies and scrutinize development programs in order to enhance their transparency and responsiveness.
Former and current British Department for International Development staffers
Eyben and Ferguson (2004) have proposed that all recipients of development aid
might be subjects of international human rights and that development agencies
should formulate rights-based approaches and agendas. They also recommend
transnational mechanisms of accountability, such as a "social audit" (168–69).
This might be suitable for indigenous development networks operating in and
through the Andes, as it would give the indigenous peoples involved a chance
to assess the objectives and values of donors and projects, not just results. One
Bolivian indigenous organization proposed another, perhaps more radical,
strategy: phasing out the technology of the development *project* and replacing
it with the development *contract*. According to this organization, indigenous
communities and organizations would—based on their own goals and priorities—decide what kinds of assistance they need and then make purchases and
contract providers using donor monies and advice (Cussi, Calle, and Mamani
2000, 72–73).[11]

As suggested by Eyben and Ferguson's remarks, some of the implications of
our study are being considered by donor-agency personnel. Hinton's (2004)
recap of diverse practitioner reflections on "inclusive aid," for instance, resonates
with some of the points made here. In addition to suggesting reforms to incorporate recipient rights and permit policy risk-taking, she called attention to "a
mounting tension between the pressure to show results of . . . interventions and
the need to allow time for inclusive processes of reflection, analysis and policy
formulation." She added that "the consequence of imposed time frames is a
loss of local ownership" (212–13). Hinton also indicated that donor assessment
efforts have focused on organizational efficiency, which entails financial costs
of hiring consultants and opportunity costs of neglecting "interorganizational
issues and partnerships" (215). Finally, she argued that "organizations' failures
to embrace complexity" and "tendency to creat[e] standard portfolios of aid
projects" can "exclude alternative perspectives and reinforce existing patterns
of dominance" (218).

Although Hinton does not address the relation of these problems to broader
development paradigms, she suggests methods that mirror our emphasis on
the importance of discourse and governmentality, as well as inequities within
indigenous development networks. First, Hinton has called for "personal critical

reflection" among development personnel. One purpose of this is "to situate themselves with respect to . . . institutional values and . . . explore taken-for-granted assumptions" (217). Another is to become more conscious of power relations within and among organizations in development networks, and the ramifications of these. She also recommends changes that build a greater sense of community between development agents and recipients of assistance: establishing longer terms for donor-country office staff, increasing personnel knowledge of local cultures and languages, and fostering their relations of affect and trust with those who receive aid and participate in projects (217).

These issues and recommendations also pose challenges for indigenous organizations and leaders. Ethnodevelopment paradigms may adopt project funding and evaluation criteria that do not necessarily correspond to indigenous-movement platforms. In effect, this creates contradictions between indigenous-movement tactics and goals, as when indigenous organizations collude with neoliberal efficiency and self-help criteria when engaging with certain projects, yet challenge those same criteria on the level of macroeconomic policy. Regarding the latter, Bolivian indigenous organizations have attended anti-FTAA meetings throughout the Andes, while CONAIE has led anti-FTAA protests in Quito and sent its leaders to continental strategy meetings in Havana. It has also contested debt repayment practices and loan conditions at Paris Club discussions.[12] National indigenous organizations may therefore benefit from local, regional, and national discussions about the consistency of their position across scales and situations, as well as the possible pitfalls of being co-opted into development paradigms they may be opposed to politically. Such a debate was, in fact, held in Ecuador among CONAIE affiliates, which eventually led to the decision, in 2005, to reject a second phase of PRODEPINE. Not all indigenous leaders (even within CONAIE) agreed with this decision. Nevertheless, it was ratified in a CONAIE assembly, and a counter-campaign that asked grassroots indigenous organizations to write letters of support for PRODEPINE II generated only a dozen responses.[13] Reasons given for CONAIE's decision to spurn PRODEPINE II include the disproportionate amount of project funds that were spent on administration and consultancies, divisions among CONAIE affiliates as new second-tier associations were created to receive PRODEPINE funds, concern that documentation of indigenous development plans and organizational capabilities gave the state excess powers of surveillance and manipulation, and the failure of development plans that emphasized investments in market-access infrastructure (such as roads and processing plants for agricultural products) over direct financing of agricultural production.[14] In a direct critique of how development alters subjectivities, CONAIE also complained that PRODEPINE created competitive desires among indigenous activists to become "top experts" and led many second-tier indigenous organizations to overvalue economic and technical issues relative to political and social affairs.[15]

Such discussion notwithstanding, a decision like this might be tied to clearer and more-specific indigenous-movement platforms on the character of indigenous economies and their links to broader macroeconomic policies and processes. Research and discussion of alternative development projects outside of prevailing ethnodevelopment models would help to generate firmer standpoints on development within the indigenous movement and clearer bases for negotiating the terms of projects and measuring their success. Although indigenous organizations in Ecuador and Bolivia have generated economic development platforms, these tend to be less specific and less thorough than their political and cultural agendas. As one Ecuadorian indigenous activist told us, "We talk about economic self-determination all the time, but I don't think we always know what we mean by it."[16]

Indigenous leaders may also want to reflect further on the recent emphasis on authentic indigeneity. We support the recuperation of distinct cultural practices and histories; our concern, however, is that identities such as ayllus and pueblos that claim authenticity in opposition to union organizations and class-based ideologies have the unintended consequence of fitting in with neoliberal narratives that position such organizations and ideologies as backwards. Indigenous workers might, then, have little discursive space for recognition and empowerment, while middle- and upper-class whites and mestizos may be able to appropriate indigenous symbolism for their own benefit, as suggested by some of the transnational water coalitions described in chapter 4. Likewise, presupposing that feminist thinking is incompatible with indigenous culture might overburden indigenous women with responsibility for transmitting Indian culture to future generations. This may reinforce their ties to the home, while men monopolize negotiation with the "other" and adaptation of "external" practices and knowledge.

In sum, indigenous development may carve out specific roles that constrain indigenous identities or lead to assimilation, or on the other hand it may prove enabling and supportive of autonomy. If only class-free indigenous organizations are viewed as authentic, if indigenous individuals are professionalized in programs that exclude indigenous knowledge, or if women are cast as social-capital (home)makers, the paths of indigenous futures risk a problematic bifurcation. Some paths may go nowhere, trapping indigenous people in remote locales; others may take indigenous people across scales and cultural boundaries in ways that lead them so far from where and who they were that their current self-images and quotidian practices are uncritically altered. Either outcome would contradict the stated goals of all ethnodevelopment paradigms and would imply reconfiguration rather than resolution of the paradox between indigenous cultural affirmation and economic marginalization.[17]

Indigenous Development and the Post-neoliberal Turn

At the time of this writing, Ecuador and Bolivia appear to be moving away from neoliberalism to some degree under the leadership of the Correa and Morales administrations, respectively. The central government in each country has, for example, taken steps to reclaim national space as a "commons" for its own citizens. They have done so largely through a reassertion of state control over natural resources and revenues. Contracts with and concessions to transnational corporations have been reviewed for consistency with national legislation and international human rights; they have also been scrutinized for equitable profit distribution between the foreign company and host country. Legislation to control transnational capital flows through taxation has been considered in both countries. Revenues captured through these reforms have been targeted primarily at public investment in education, health, pensions, and infrastructure. Bolivia has extended this logic to international development aid as well. On the one hand, international development agencies are expected to coordinate their objectives with those of the Bolivian national development plan; on the other, agencies must register the quantity and destination of all development financing with the Bolivian state and list all NGOs working with such funding (*El Diario*, November 17, 2007).[18] Finally, neither Ecuador nor Bolivia has signed a free trade agreement with the United States, despite heavy pressure from the latter, especially in the Ecuadorian case.

Following Gwynne and Kay (2004), one might argue that these policies are based on an emergent "neostructural" paradigm. The policies are structural insofar as they are grounded in assumptions that the global political economy and national society are complex hierarchies with entrenched privileges and biases, rather than level playing fields of free agents. The state, in turn, is expected to be proactive in defining its country's links to the global system and in stimulating social transformation and economic development. Such policies are "neo" in that they view global trade and investment as opportune and seek to involve disadvantaged social groups in national change and development (262–65).

In the words of one analyst, "The focus placed on the national character of policies and . . . state capacities implies . . . an improved balance between the processes of globalization and domestic politics. This change, however, implies no swing toward economic nationalism or the state takeover of private companies. Nor does it imply the administrative control of prices . . . or government promotion of import substitution, all of which were pillars of the 'classic' . . . national popular regimes" (Vilas 2006, 247–48). In fact, Ecuador and Bolivia have retained the financial stabilization and political decentralization regimes installed by their neoliberal predecessors. Neither of these policies were part of "classic . . . national popular regimes," either.

As with all critical junctures, then, we can expect the post-neoliberal one to bear legacies of its antecedent paradigms and struggles. These are visible in recent proposals for new constitutions in Bolivia and Ecuador drafted by indigenous movements and parties. These proposals have appropriated some elements of what we have called social neoliberalism, while discarding or downplaying others. The draft constitution approved by constitutional-assembly delegates in Bolivia, for instance, retained the decentralized administrative structure of the current state but added indigenous territories as an additional unit, and they allowed regions to be constituted by popular demand through a referendum. The majority that approved this constitution belongs largely to the MAS Party led by President Morales, a long-time leader in the indigenous movement.[19] These indigenous territories and popular regions would have status equal to municipalities, rather than being subordinate entities. Autonomous "indigenous territorial administration," which emerged in the pilot development projects described in chapter 3, is recognized as an indigenous right in this draft constitution. Echoing the water struggles and paradigms discussed in chapter 4, the proposed constitution specifies water as a "strategic resource" that is state owned; it cannot be privatized, and the state cannot create concessions for its administration. Social and environmental criteria dominate stipulations for water use, while indigenous and campesino *usos y costumbres* concerning water are guaranteed. These provisions on water are embedded in the proposal's "plural economy" model; it recognizes public, private, and communal forms of property and livelihood but stipulates that the state must actively promote community economies as a way of prioritizing equity, sustainability, and autonomy.[20] These proposals also had transnational repercussions. At the 2006 World Water Forum in Mexico, the Bolivian government's position generated much solidarity in declaring that access to water should be a human right (Laurie and Crespo 2007).

CONAIE's (2007) proposal for constitutional reform in Ecuador is similar but not identical. Like Bolivia's provisional constitution, it keeps previous decentralization reforms and intensifies them. For example, it would raise the portion of the central budget allocated to local governments from 15 to 25 percent. It has also provided for a *cabildo abierto* at the municipal scale, which would be analogous to the cantonal assemblies and popular parliaments of alternative municipalities described in chapter 3. As in the 1998 constitution, indigenous territories are here proposed as a decentralized unit of the state. However, CONAIE stipulated that the central government and private actors be obligated to recognize indigenous territorial authorities as official interlocutors. This proposal grants ownership of subsurface resources to the central state but provides indigenous territories with effective veto power over extraction and use of such resources by outsiders.[21] CONAIE (2007) has also mirrored MAS in Bolivia by posing water as state property and prohibiting its sale or commercialization. While it does permit concessions of water services, CONAIE's proposal has stipulated that food security, fair distribution, and universal access must be priorities. It supports this with a clause prioritizing human and domestic water first, followed by irrigation for family and community farms and finally agroindustrial irrigation. The broader development model in CONAIE's proposal is also pluralist, recognizing private, public, mixed, cooperative, and communitarian forms of property and economy. Its core development principles have thus drawn on those of social neoliberalism with certain transformations, listing "efficiency" as fifth out of six, while placing "economic democracy" (active participation) and "social justice" (equity) first.

Two other appropriations of social neoliberalism and ethnodevelopment are notable in CONAIE's constitutional template. First, it took up social neoliberalism's emphasis on professionalization by stipulating that academic institutions and training programs must be both subjects and objects of development policy, while obligating the state to foment and foster indigenous ancestral knowledge. The latter can be viewed as a corrective to the social depreciation of such knowledge discussed in this book. Second, CONAIE has projected "participatory planning" toward all levels of the state, as a technology of agency *and* performance. A national planning system running through the central and local governments is meant to reach consensus on policy and serve as a platform for action; fulfillment (or not) of the plan is a measure of performance—for everyone, from indigenous authorities to mayors to the national president. In fact, the president would oversee the national development plan and be required to report on it comprehensively to the legislature and the general public in his or her annual speech in August.

We do not know how much of these draft and provisional constitutions will be included in the final official versions; parts of them will probably appear, while those excluded are likely to shape future agendas.[22] Although CONAIE's constitutional scheme has established indigenous pueblos as a subject of rights (and guarantees each pueblo a seat in the national legislature), Bolivia's provisional constitution does not recognize ayllus, markas, or suyus. These entities can gain status as indigenous territories, but ayllu-movement federations wanted direct recognition of them in the new constitution. The ayllu movement also proposed that indigenous territories should control subsurface resources, but this measure is not included in the provisional constitution (Viceministerio de Tierras, n.d.). In addition, neither constitutional design possesses a chapter on women's rights, even though gender equity is a principle of political representation in both. Nor do their chapters on indigenous rights address indigenous women's issues or position indigenous women in relation to development. Thus, even if both constitutional proposals were to be adopted officially in their original form, indigenous subjectivities and gender issues would remain disputed and be subject to ongoing negotiation.

Participatory approaches to indigenous development focusing on grassroots livelihoods, indigenous rights, and gender equity will also remain important. This is not only because current post-neoliberal governments may be removed from office (or their constitutional reforms revoked) but also because a neostructural, state-activist orientation may crowd out grassroots initiative or autonomy. There is already evidence for this turn of events. In designing representation for the Bolivian constituent assembly, for example, the Morales government did not provide for autonomous indigenous seats, even though it is committed to indigenous representation in principle. Instead, MAS cut deals with indigenous organizations to run assembly candidates on the MAS ticket. In a similar gesture, MAS ran candidates in the 2004 Jesús de Machaqa municipal elections *against* the indigenous marka organization (ayllu federation), which chose candidates according to internal cultural norms and expected the official election process to be a mere formality. Because MAS candidates won two of the five municipal council seats in that official local election, the marka consensus plan to rotate power annually and allow all of its member ayllus to exercise municipal office—and thereby infuse indigenous political norms into municipal institutions—was scuttled (Colque 2005).

Furthermore, indigenous professionalization spaces in Bolivian universities are being reduced. This may narrow the previous proliferation of pathways toward professionalization outlined in chapter 5, which had opened up different constructions of expertise. At the time of writing, however, CEIDIS has not functioned for a year, and the Universidad Mayor de San Simón only just agreed to take on two core PROIEBANDES staff after the program effectively closed in December 2007, when GTZ funding came to an end.

In Ecuador, the Correa administration has sent mixed signals on mining activity and popular resistance to it. Correa and his administration have challenged a Canadian mining company and may revoke its concession; it has also claimed that it would subject all concessions to review in order to insure that national laws are not being violated. But it has not responded to far-reaching demands by protest organizations to declare Ecuador free of large-scale mining and grant indigenous peoples and nonindigenous farmers some rights over subsoil resources (Mychalejko 2007; Rodríguez 2007). Indeed, Correa refused to dialogue with organizations opposed to mining, and he ordered their protests repressed on the grounds that "eliminating mining concessions is inconceivable" due to the costs that the state would have to bear (Moore 2007). A recent government proposal to forgo oil development in Yasuní National Park has sought international "compensation" of US$350 million per year for the opportunity costs (*Diario Hoy*, December 14, 2007). Although hailed internationally as an innovative plan, it is largely a deal between the Ecuadorian state and international donors that effectively commodifies indigenous-occupied land, even if it trades such land as a public good and receives public funds for its protection. The Yasuní-ITT plan's high-level negotiating team, moreover, consists exclusively of government ministers; its account will be administered by the minister of the economy (Amazon Watch 2007; *El Comercio*, November 27, 2007).[23] While the Ecuadorian government has cited the presence of "isolated" indigenous peoples in the area as a justification for the Yasuní-ITT plan, indigenous territorial and cultural *rights* are not part of the plan's framework, nor do indigenous movement representatives hold key positions in the plan design or administrative teams.[24] And as this proposal responded to a successful campaign by indigenous and environmental activists to build public support and awareness about oil development in Yasuní, the plan can be seen as a symbolic and material appropriation of indigenous territory by the Ecuadorian state and the international donors supporting it. Such top-down, state-led approaches to development and representation are something that grassroots development advocates *and* indigenous organizations have criticized regularly in the past.

Development thus continues to entail border crossing and to form complexes of inclusion and exclusion. Colonial patterns of trusteeship, models of progress, and subaltern demands for improved livelihoods have comprised strands of development thinking and practice for at least a century. The Andes have unevenly and unequally appropriated—and been affected by—these transnational connections. Today Ecuador and Bolivia sit at a crossroad of international governance and capitalist agendas, governmental anxieties about economic growth, popular demands for dignity and security, and civic action for change. In recent decades, development processes in these countries have changed, now comprising a multiethnic mix of transnational actors, a new status awarded to indigenous culture, and altered prisms of human rights. Within today's globalized landscapes of development, these Andean spaces represent arenas of struggle over meanings and resources, which illuminate not only development's ongoing embeddedness in markets and states, but also the seizure of opportunities for autonomy and empowerment by erstwhile marginalized subjects.

APPENDIX 1

Methodology and Research Design

Our methodology centers on an "inter-institutional ethnography" (Burawoy et al. 2000) of indigenous development networks and their "situated cultural practices" (Ong 1999, 17). For this study, such a methodology involved ascertaining the following four items:

- The history and role of key actors in the indigenous development network, and the rationales for indigenous development
- How these actors situate indigenous development within broader agendas of development policy, government-led reform, and indigenous movement politics
- Other organizations and agencies they interact with and in what fashion
- The class, racial, and gender dimensions of indigenous development and the organizations involved

Each chapter of this book incorporates all four points of the ethnography into its analysis.

The substantive material in the book draws on our extensive fieldwork in Ecuador, Bolivia, the United States, and the U.K. We combined over one hundred interviews (mostly in Spanish) with participant observation and primary-document analysis, including the analysis of web sites. Within the Andes, we researched in and around La Paz and Cochabamba, Bolivia, and Quito and Cuenca, Ecuador. We conducted interviews with leaders of local, national, and international indigenous organizations. From there we "followed" the network to interview members of organizations primarily oriented toward development that have worked with indigenous peoples' organizations by providing financial aid, training, and technical advice.

In a classic grassroots development context, these development organizations may have consisted exclusively of nongovernmental agencies. However, a notable feature of indigenous development is the growing involvement of official development agencies and educational institutions in project design, financing, and execution. We therefore interviewed personnel in bilateral agencies such as COSUDE (Switzerland), GTZ (Germany), and DANIDA (Denmark), multilateral organizations like the World Bank and the Inter-American Development Bank, and Ecuadorian and Bolivian government agencies, including indigenous ministries and development councils. Finally, we carried out interviews with students, professors, and administrators of higher education institutions such as the Universidad de San Simón in Bolivia and the Universidad Salesiana in Ecuador.

All of our interviews were designed to elicit viewpoints and information regarding each organization or individual's position within indigenous development. These interviews were transcribed, and we translated all quotations included in this book from Spanish into English.

We also analyzed primary documents and web sites of the organizations whose leaders and functionaries we interviewed. In addition, we attended workshops, meetings, and conferences as participant-observers, in which indigenous leaders, NGO members, government officials, and functionaries of official development agencies directly interacted. These events involved discussion and debate around the design and implementation of development or development-related policies, legislation, and projects in which indigenous peoples would be beneficiaries or otherwise affected. One example was a meeting to discuss implementing an indigenous development plan in Raqaypampa, Bolivia; another was a conference bringing together scholars, indigenous activists, and development practitioners in Princeton, New Jersey.

The challenge of multisited ethnography (Kearney 1999) is providing both depth (a rich description of a particular situation or place) and breadth (making the connections between sites). We addressed this challenge by examining both grounded experiences of indigenous development—albeit without the nuances and flavor of classic ethnography—and the networks that connect with these grounded experiences (see Massey 1984; Burawoy et al. 2000). Such an approach endeavors to avoid the "impact model" of globalization while recognizing that subaltern agency is located in specific historical and politico-economic junctures (see Hart 2004). It inevitably positions us between providing local detail and making global generalizations; but we hope that the tensions inherent in this methodology provide a distinct vantage point on indigenous development and transnationalism—far from an all-seeing one—and inspire others to comment from their own viewpoints.

APPENDIX 2

Development-Agency Initiatives for Andean Indigenous Peoples, 1990–2002

Multilateral Development Agencies

- The *World Bank* has an indigenous people's thematic team within the Social Development Department and has implemented indigenous peoples' development projects in Ecuador, Bolivia, and Peru.
- The *Inter-American Development Bank* (IADB) has an Indigenous Peoples and Community Development Unit and was a key initiator of the Latin American Indigenous Peoples' Development Fund.
- The *United Nations Development Programme* (UNDP) is a key member of the global-scale Indigenous Knowledge Programme and sponsored an indigenous development program in Bolivia via the National Subsecretariat of Ethnic Affairs.
- The *European Union* (EU) directly funded the Small Farmer Participatory Development Project in Bolivia, indirectly financed projects or programs through European NGOs, and passed various resolutions on Andean and Amazonian indigenous peoples.

Bilateral Development Agencies

- *Danish Official Cooperation* (DANIDA) and the Danish Embassy sponsored multiple programs in Bolivia with indigenous peoples through state and nonstate institutions and funded the Fundación Diálogo, a Bolivian NGO working with indigenous peoples.
- *The Dutch Embassy* has worked in both Bolivia and Ecuador, often with local support NGOs, especially in grassroots development and water and irrigation projects.
- *The Belgian government* has been a key sponsor of the Diploma in Indigenous Affairs program in FLACSO, Ecuador.

- *GTZ*, a German agency, has sponsored bilingual and multicultural education programs in the Andes, funding teacher training and curricular development. It also financed a program with the regional Fondo Indígena for project preinvestment.
- *Swiss Development Cooperation* (COSUDE) does agricultural development work (including irrigation projects) in Ecuador and participatory decentralization projects in Bolivia.
- *The government of Spain* is a key donor to the Latin American Fondo Indígena. It has also sponsored irrigation projects and CODENPE in Ecuador.
- The *French Foreign Ministry* sponsors European and national NGOs in the Andes.
- The U.K.'s *Department for International Development* (DfID) sponsored a technology-enhancement program with the Bolivian indigenous confederation CIDOB.
- *United States Agency for International Development* (USAID) has undertaken limited work with indigenous peoples, although it co-sponsored environmental projects with lowland Bolivian indigenous peoples.

International NGOs and Foundations

- *Oxfam America*'s South American office has focused on Andean indigenous peoples. It has been key in the formation of pan-Amazonian indigenous confederation COICA and is a long-term sponsor of confederations CONAIE in Ecuador, CIDOB, and CONAMAQ in Bolivia, and AIDESEP in Peru. It supports indigenous organizations and specific projects.
- The U.S.-based *Inter-American Foundation* (IAF) was a key funder of indigenous organizations in Ecuador; in Bolivia it emphasized economic production projects.
- *Centre International de Coopération pour le Développement Agricole* (CICDA), based in France, has irrigation projects in the Andean highlands and funds local grassroots development NGOs in Bolivia and Ecuador.
- *SNV*, a Dutch-based NGO, works in Ecuador and Bolivia. In Bolivia, it is directly involved with CIDOB in the lowlands and to some extent

with CSUTCB affiliates in the highlands. It also funds and supports Bolivian NGOs.

- *SWISSAID* sponsored CONAIE's water-law proposal and CONAIE's research into indigenous farm production.
- *IBIS*, a Danish NGO, has funded indigenous organizations and productive projects in Ecuador and lowland Bolivia since the early 1990s and recently funded a Bolivian highland indigenous federation. In Ecuador, it funds ECUARUNARI's Women's Training School and the Quichua pueblos' project.
- *Terra Nuova*, based in Italy, provided funds to CONAIE and affiliates, as well as to municipalities run by indigenous mayors. It works through its Ecuadorian affiliate NGO, Tierra Nueva.
- *Norwegian People's Aid* (APN) previously funded Ecuadorian indigenous ECUARUNARI's Women's Training School and now funds indigenous-run municipalities and CONAIE.
- The *Hanns Siedel Foundation*, affiliated with Germany's Christian Democratic Union, funds fellowships for indigenous students and the indigenous research center in Quito.
- *Plan International*, via Plan International Altiplano, sponsors the implementation of bilingual, intercultural education system in Bolivian highlands.
- *Swiss Worker Aid* (AOS) does agricultural development and institutional strengthening with indigenous movement federations in highland Bolivia.

APPENDIX 3

Professional Biographies of Teachers
in Interculturalism

Pamela Calla (Bolivia)

- Born in Bolivia, grew up in a mining area
- PhD in anthropology from Cornell University, with fieldwork in Nicaragua
- Has visited U.K. on British Council link exchanges
- Completed consulting work at the Center for the Study of Economic and Social Reality (CERES) research center (Cochabamba) on gender and environment
- Taught a course on gender in CESU's gender diploma program
- Taught at PROEIBANDES (language-led program) in Cochabamba, Bolivia
- Taught a course on gender and ethnicity in the Universidad de la Cordillera, La Paz, run by her brother Ricardo Calla, while based in Cochabamba
- Moved to La Paz and is now a core member of the faculty at the Universidad de la Cordillera

Fernando Garcia (Bolivia)

- Ecuadorian linguist, fluent in Quichua
- Worked in Cuenca, Ecuador, in bilingual linguistics program
- Worked for PROIEBANDES node in Ecuador and traveled to Cochabamba, Bolivia
- Met Pablo Regalsky (CENDA, Bolivia) at Bartolomé de Las Casas program in Cuzco, Peru
- Recruited to CENDA in 1999 to head up a popular education program in Raqaypampa

- Worked with CENDA on issues of territoriality and the promotion of indigenous development plans
- Taught on interculturalism on the CEIDIS program

Catherine Walsh (Ecuador)

- U.S. citizen, born there
- PhD from a U.S. institution in anthropology; has taught in a U.S. university
- Close affiliations to Oxfam America in Boston
- Moved to Ecuador permanently in the 1990s
- Taught intercultural modules in the Universidad Andina Simón Bolívar, Ecuador
- Supervised teaching staff at CEIDIS in Bolivia, obtaining a master's degree from the Universidad Andina
- Supervised staff teaching at the Universidad Salesiana undergraduate program in Ecuador
- Taught a module on the CEIDIS undergraduate and master's degree program

Maria Esther Pozo (Bolivia)

- Born in Cochabamba, Bolivia
- Sociologist with background in gender working for a gender NGO in Cochabamba
- Directed an undergraduate degree program at CESU, funded by the Dutch
- Has visited the U.K. on British Council link exchanges
- Ran a web-based gender program via FLACSO, with contacts in Argentina
- Codirected CEIDIS, which has transnational links in Latin America
- Worked in education and ethnicity (via CEIDIS) while completing a PhD in Spain part-time

Isidoro Quinde (Ecuador)

- Identifies as Quichua and Cañari, born in Cañar
- Worked as a lecturer at Catholic University in Quito, from 1984 to 1986,

as a researcher in Quichua language and as promoter of literacy training in Ecuador

- Founded a distance learning center (Corporación Educativa MAC),
  serving as rector, researcher, and promoter, and learned computer and
  textbook-production skills
- Directed a project by the Ecuadorian NGO Fundación Esquel in the
  Amazon region. Decided he needed knowledge about the environment
  and biodiversity
- Left bilingual education to work in development and natural-resource
  conservation as of 1992; studied geography
- Has worked in CODENPE. Worked initially in participatory development planning, then directed the Identity and Culture department to
  implement an intercultural development program

ACRONYMS AND ABBREVIATIONS

AME	Asociación de Municipalidades Ecuatorianas (Ecuadorian Association of Municipalities)
AOS	Ayuda Obrera Suiza, Swiss Worker's Aid
APN	Ayuda Popular Noruega (Norwegian People's Aid)
CADA	Centro Andino de Desarrollo Agrario (Andean Center for Agrarian Development)
CAFOD	Catholic Agency for Overseas Development
CAMAREN	Sistema de Capacitación para el Manejo de los Recursos Naturales Renovables, Ecuador (Training System for Management of Renewable Resources)
CAOI	Coordinadora Andina de Organizaciones Indígenas (Andean Coordinator of Indigenous Organizations)
CDIMA	Centro para el Desarrollo Integral de la Mujer Aymara, Bolivia (Center for the Integral Development of Aymara Women)
CEIDIS	Consorcio para la Educación Intercultural y Desarrollo Integral Surandino (Intercultural Education Consortium for Southern Andean Development and Integration)
CEJIS	Centro de Estudios Jurídicos e Investigación Social, Bolivia (Center for Legal Studies and Social Research)
CENDA	Centro de Comunicación y Desarrollo Andino, Bolivia (Center for Communication and Andean Development)
CERES	Central de Estudios de Realidad Economía y Social (Center for the Study of Economic and Social Reality)
CESA	Central Ecuatoriana de Servicios Agrícolas (Center for Ecuadorian Agricultural Services)
CESU	Centro de Estudios Superiores, Bolivia (Postgraduate Research Center)
CGIAB	Comisión para la Gestión Integral del Agua en Bolivia (Bolivian Integral Water Management Commission)

CGIAC	Comisión para la Gestión Integral del Agua en Cochabamba, Bolivia (Cochabamba Integral Water Management Commission)
CGLA	Coordinadora de Gobiernos Locales Alternativos (Coordinator of Alternative Local Governments)
CICDA	Centre International de Coopération pour le Développement Agricole, France, Ecuador, Bolivia (International Center for Agricultural Cooperation and Development)
CIDOB	Confederación Indígena del Oriente Boliviano (Indigenous Confederation of the Bolivian Lowlands)
CIPCA	Centro para la Promoción e Investigación Campesina, Bolivia (Center for Campesino Promotion and Research)
CNRH	Consejo Nacional de Recursos Hídricos, Ecuador (National Advisory Council for Hydraulic Resources)
CNTCB	Confederación Nacional de Trabajadores Campesinos de Bolivia (National Federation of Peasant Workers of Bolivia)
CODENPE	Consejo para el Desarrollo de las Nacionalidades y Pueblos del Ecuador (Development Council of Nationalities and Peoples of Ecuador)
COICA	Coordinadora de Organizaciones Indígenas de la Cuenca Amazónica, South America (Indigenous Coordinating Body for the Amazon Basin)
CONACNIE	Consejo Nacional de Coordinación de las Nacionalidades Indígenas del Ecuador (National Coordinating Council of Indigenous Nationalities of Ecuador)
CONAIE	Confederación de Nacionalidades Indígenas del Ecuador (Confederation of Indigenous Nationalities of Ecuador)
CONAMAQ	Consejo de Ayllus y Markas de Qollasuyu, Bolivia (National Council of Ayllus and Markas of Qollasuyu)
CONAMU	Consejo Nacional de las Mujeres, Ecuador (National Women's Council)
CONAUA	Coordinadora de Usuarios del Agua, Ecuador (National Coordinator of Water Users)
CONDESAN	Consorcio para el Desarrollo Sostenible de la Ecoregión Andina, Peru (Consortium for Sustainable Development of the Andean Eco-region)
CONFENIAE	Confederación de Nacionalidades Indígenas de la Amazonia Ecuatoriana (Confederation of Indigenous Nationalities of the Ecuadorian Amazon)
CONPLADEIN	Consejo de Planificación y Desarrollo Indigena y Negra (Development and Planning Council of Indigenous and Black People)

COSUDE	Cooperación Suiza para el Desarrollo (Swiss Development Cooperation)
COWI	Consultancy within Engineering Environmental Science and Economics
CREA	Centro para la Renovación Económica del Austro, Ecuador (Economic Restruction Center of Cañar, Azuay, and Morona Santiago provinces)
CSUTCB	Confederación Sindicál Unica de Trabajadores Campesinas de Bolivia (Sole Union Confederation of Bolivian Peasant Workers)
CTI	Circunscripción Territorial Indígenas, Ecuador (Indigenous Territorial Circumscription)
DANIDA	Danish International Development Cooperation Agency
DED	Deutscher Entwicklungsdienst (German Development Service)
DfID	Department for International Development (UK)
DINEIB	Dirección Nacional de la Educación Intercultural Bilingue, Ecuador (National Directorate of Bilingual Intercultural Education Program)
DMI	Distrito Municipal Indígena, Bolivia (Indigenous Municipal District)
ECLA/ECLAC	Economic Commission for Latin America and the Caribbean (United Nations), (Comisión Económica para América Latina y el Caribe)
ECUARUNARI	Ecuador Runacunapac Riccharimui (Awakening of Ecuadorian Indigenous People)
ETARE	Equipo Técnico de Apoyo a la Reforma Educativa, Bolivia (Technical Support Team for Educational Reform)
FACOPI	Federación de Ayllus y Comunidades Originarias de la Provincia de Ingavi, Bolivia (Federation of Ayllus and Original Communities of Ingavi Province)
FASOR	Federación de Ayllus del Sur de Oruro, Bolivia (Federation of Ayllus of Southern Oruro)
FDC	Fondo de Desarrollo Campesino, Bolivia (Campesino Development Fund)
FEINE	Federación Ecuatoriana de Indígenas Evangélicos (Federation of Ecuadorian Evangelical Indigenous People)
FENOCIN	Federación Nacional de Obreros Campesinos, Indígenas y Negras, Ecuador (National Federation of Peasant, Indigenous and Black Workers)
FEPP	Fondo Ecuatoriano Populorum Progressio, Italy, Ecuador (Ecuadorian People's Development Fund)

FLACSO	Facultad Latinoamericana de Ciencias Sociales (Latin American Faculty of Social Sciences)
FOIN	Federación de Organizaciones Indígenas de Napo, Ecuador (Federation of Indigenous Organizations of Napo)
FORMIA	Proyecto de Apoyo al Fortalecimiento de Municipios Indígenas Alternativos, Ecuador (Project to Support Strengthening of Alternative Indigenous Municipalities)
FTAA	Free Trade Area of the Americas (proposal)
GAD	Gender and Development
GIS	Geographical Information System
GTI	Gerencia Teritorial Indígena, Bolivia (Indigenous Territorial Administration)
GTZ	Gesellschaft für Technische Zusammenarbeit (German Technical Cooperation)
HIPC	Heavily Indebted Poor Countries
HIVOS	Humanistisch Instituut voor Ontwikkelingssamenwerking, Netherlands (International Humanist Institute for Cooperation with Developing Countries)
IADB	Inter-American Development Bank
IAF	Inter-American Foundation (United States)
IBE (EIB in Spanish)	Intercultural Bilingual Education
ICCI	Instituto Científico de Culturas Indígenas, Ecuador (Scientific Institute of Indigenous Cultures)
IDP	Indigenous Development Plan
IDRC	International Development Research Centre (Canada)
IEDECA	Instituto de Ecología y Desarrollo de las Comunidades Andinas, Ecuador (Institute for Development and Ecology of Andean Communities)
IEE	Instituto de Estudios Ecuatorianos, Ecuador (Institute of Ecuadorian Studies)
IFAD	International Fund for Agricultural Development
IGO	Intergovernmental Organization
ILO	International Labor Organization
IMF	International Monetary Fund
INGO	International nongovernmental organization
INERHI	Instituto Ecuatoriano de Recursos Hídricos (Ecuadorian Institute for Hydric Resources)

INRA	Instituto Nacional de Reforma Agraria, Bolivia (National Agrarian Reform Institute)
ISALP	Investigación Social y Asesoramiento Legal Potosí, Bolivia (Social Research and Legal Counsel of Potosí)
ITDG	Intermediate Technology Development Group
ITT	Ishpingo—Tambococha—Tiputini (Ecuador)
LPP	Ley de Participación Popular, Bolivia (Law of Popular Participation)
MAIPO	Ministerio de Asuntos Indígenas y Pueblos Originarios, Bolivia (Ministry of Indigenous and Aboriginal Peoples' Affairs)
MAS	Movimiento al Socialismo
NGO	Nongovernmental organization
NOVIB	Nederlandse Organisatie voor Internationale Ontwikkelings-samenwerking (Dutch Organization for International Aid)
OAS	Organization of American States
OD 4.20	Operational Directive 4.20, on Indigenous Peoples (World Bank)
OP/BP	Operational Procedure/Best Practice (World Bank)
OPIP	Organización de Pueblos Indígenas de Pastaza, Ecuador (Organization of Indigenous Peoples of Pastaza)
OSG	Organización de Segundo Grado, Ecuador (Second-Tier Organization): Local civil organization, one scale out from community level
OTB	Organización Territorial de Base, Bolivia (Territorial Grassroots Organization)
PADEM	Pragrama de Apoyo a la Democracia Municipal, Bolivia (Municipal Democracy Support Program)
PADER	Promoción al Desarrollo Económico Rural, Bolivia (Rural Economic Development Promotion Program)
PDCR	Programa de Desarrollo Comunitario Rural, Bolivia (Program for Rural Community Development)
PDL	Proyecto de Desarrollo Local, Ecuador (Local Development Project)
PRATEC	Proyecto Andino de Tecnología Campesina, Peru (Andean Peasant Technologies Project)
PRODEPINE	Proyecto de Desarrollo para los Pueblos Indígenas y Negros del Ecuador (Development Project for Indigenous and Afro-Ecuadorian Peoples of Ecuador)
PROEIBANDES	Programa de Capacitación en la Educación Intercultural Bilingue de los Andes, Bolivia (Training Program for Intercultural Bilingual Education for Andean Countries)

PROGENIAL   Program for Gender Innovation in Latin America

PRONADER   Programa Nacional de Desarrollo Rural, Bolivia (National Rural Development Program)

PRONAR   Programa Nacional de Riego, Bolivia (National Irrigation Program)

RIAD   Red Interamericana para la Agricultura y Democracia (Inter-American Network for Agriculture and Democracy)

SAPRI   Structural Adjustment Participatory Review Initiatives, Ecuador

SENALEP   Servicio Nacional para la Alfabetización y Educación Popular, Bolivia (National Service for Literacy and Popular Education)

SNAEGG   Secretaria Nacional de Asuntos Etnicos, de Género y Generacionales, Bolivia (National Secretariat for Ethnic, Gender and Generational Affairs)

SNV   Stichting SNV Nederlandse Ontwikkelingorganisatie (SNV Netherlands Development Organization)

TCO   Tierra Comunitaria de Orígen, Bolivia (Original Communal Land)

THOA   Taller de Historia Oral Andina, Bolivia (Andean Oral History Workshop)

UASB   Universidad Andina Simón Bolivar, Ecuador (Simón Bolivar Andean University)

UNCED   United Nations Conference on Environment and Development

UNDP   United Nations Development Programme

UNESCO   United Nations Educational, Scientific, and Cultural Organization

UNICEF   United Nations Children's Fund

UNIFEM   United Nations Fund for Women

UNORCAC   Unión de Organizaciones Campesinas e Indígenas de Cotacachi, Ecuador (Union of Peasant Organizations of Cotacachi)

UNWGIP   United Nations Working Group on Indigenous Peoples

UOCE   Unión de Organizaciones Campesinas de Esmeraldas, Ecuador (Union of Peasant Organizations of Esmeraldas)

USAID   U.S. Agency for International Development

VAIPO   Viceministerio de Asuntos Indígenas y Pueblos Originarios, Bolivia (Vice-Ministry of Indigenous and Aboriginal Peoples' Affairs)

NOTES

Introduction: Indigenous Development in the Andes

1 When we speak of international development agencies in this book, we are including official multilateral and bilateral agencies, as well as international NGOs with home bases outside of—or with spatial remits beyond—Ecuador or Bolivia. Likewise, when we speak of the Andes, we are referring usually to Ecuador and Bolivia, and not necessarily to countries like Peru, Colombia, and Chile, which are often identified as Andean.

2 Mato (2000) describes this process as the "infusion of outside issues and agendas into domestic or local contexts" (199). On governmentality and its application to development, see Burchell, Gordon, and Miller (1991); Escobar (1995); Watts (2003); and Li (2007). Later in this chapter we apply governmentality theory to indigenous development in the Andes.

3 There are of course exceptions to this trend, most notably in Venezuela.

4 Very recent developments suggest a distancing from neoliberalism in Bolivia and Ecuador. This will be addressed in the concluding chapter, but a thorough examination of this phenomenon is beyond the scope of our analysis. See Hershberg and Rosen (2006) for an overview of post-neoliberal issues in Latin America.

5 The count was for so-called second-tier organizations, which in Ecuador are representative of a series of community-scale (first-tier) organizations, whose leaders are chosen by community organization delegates. Third-tier organizations are federations at the provincial scale or beyond.

6 As Shore and Wright (1997) have argued, the influence of policy lies in part through the ways that language, expectations, and technology classify individuals and groups as objects of power.

7 As such, we extend Pottier, Bicker, and Sillitoe's (2003) examination of development knowledge to development paradigms and agendas more broadly.

8 Intellectually, the work of Amartya Sen (1990, 1992) has influenced social neoliberalism. This paradigm has also been driven by publications and conferences of the United Nations, International Labor Organization, and Economic Commission for Latin America and the Caribbean. NGO and social-movement critiques of neoliberal orthodoxy, and their complaints about the lack of participation and transparency in development practices, have also informed the social neoliberalism.

9 On dialogic partnerships between liberalism(s) and other forms of thought, see Weir (1996). Dean (1999) builds on Weir's discussion to explicate how liberalism and neoliberalism can be reformed and reinvented through such dialogues (48–59).

10 Additional perspective on advanced liberal government can be found in Rose (1996), Shore and Wright (1997), and Dean (1999, chap. 8).

11 The most frequent definition or interpretation of social capital in mainstream development thinking is Robert Putnam's (1993).

12 Simple mimicry or copying of Western modernities is unlikely given the anticolonial ideological roots of Ecuadorian and Bolivian indigenous movements. This conceptual continuum from alternative modernities to grassroots epistemology is adopted from Watts (2003, 28). Also see Rahnema (1997); Ganokar (2001); Edelman and Haugerud (2005).

13 Omi and Winant (1994) developed the terms *racial formations* and *racial projects* in analyzing race relations in the United States. We apply these concepts here to Latin America, as they dovetail with Wade's approach.

14 Such homogeneity is often projected into the future, while diversity often refers to past "primordial differences" (Wade 2004, 264).

15 While blacks were already familiar to colonial settlers and administrators, "native Americans were a conundrum" (Wade 1997, 26). As part of rigid colonial categories, Indians were given a special tributary status within communal land and governance structures and formally protected from physical abuses and slavery. In practice, abuses and exploitation were frequent, and the colonial state used indigenous tributaries as a key tax base. However, this status did provide indigenous peoples with a modicum of physical protection, land rights, and political autonomy that facilitated reproduction of distinctive cultural practices and authority structures on the local level. In some cases, the category of "Indian" was appropriated and resignified by social movements and armed rebellions who claimed Inca lineage or cultural practices that cut across more localized ethnic identities (e.g., Stern 1987; Silverblatt 1995). The colonial system of subject identities and land tenure was largely dismantled after independence due to individualist notions of citizenship and property within nineteenth century liberalism, as well as the expansion of large landholdings and haciendas (Platt 1987; Parekh 1995; Gabbert 2001). Also, see K. Brown (1999) on how the British had difficulty defining indigenous Americans due to their racial ideologies formed through previous encounters with African peoples.

16 This reference to learning traditions as an identity marker occurred in spite of the fact that language use has been a fundamental component of the indigenous movement concept of "nationalities" in Ecuador and Bolivia. It has also informed indigenous movement demands for bilingual multicultural education whose purpose is to continue indigenous cultures and enhance grassroots participation in education.

17 However, development has only recently been considered within a transnational social field, as the outcome of networks and nonstate actors linking practice, rep-

resentation, and institutions in new ways (Radcliffe 2001a; L. Smith 2002; Goldman 2007).

18 While crossing national boundaries would provide the minimum traversal for an interaction to be considered transnational, other boundaries of scale and identity are often involved and require joint analysis with national boundary crossings. On transgressive transnationalism, see Mitchell (1997a).

19 These illustrate how both geography and political science are expanding beyond state-centered approaches.

20 International relations, as a field of study, is a subdiscipline of political science. Recently it has become more interdisciplinary.

21 Graduated sovereignty is a segmentation of government by population group, "subjecting [such] groups to different regimes of value . . . where they enjoy distinct kinds of rights, discipline, caring and security" (Ong 1999, 217).

22 Our perspective therefore contrasts with interpretations of globalization that unbundle nation-states and erase local specificity. See, for example, Carnoy et al. (1993), and Ohmae (1995).

23 Feminist work on postcoloniality and globalization, for example, highlights the ways in which "globalization's subjects are embedded in gender, class, race" and other social divisions (Nagar et al. 2002, 269).

24 However, indigenous individuals, families, and communities—including some of those active in development networks—may simultaneously be engaged with globalized capitalism outside of these policy and political networks.

25 Unlike Ong's private business managerial class, these are public and nonprofit administrators. However, some private-sector management norms and practices are applied to indigenous development projects and organizations—just as they are to general NGOs—as efficiency and cost cutting are prioritized in a context of dwindling bilateral aid funds (Makoba 2002; Townsend, Porter, and Mawdsley 2002).

26 The book can be read through in its entirety or selectively sampled according to the interests of the reader. Academic themes are outlined in the introduction, chapters 1 and 2, and the conclusion. Indigenous social movement issues are highlighted in chapters 3, 4, 6, and the conclusion; they are addressed indirectly in parts of chapters 2 and 5. General development debates are explored furthest in chapters 1, 2, 6, and the conclusion, while specific policy areas (community, water, education) are covered in chapters 3, 4, and 5. Background on Andean indigenous movements can be found in chapter 1; methodological issues are covered in appendix 1.

Chapter 1: Development, Networks, and Indigenous Politics

1 For overviews of the extensive literature on Andean and Latin American indigenous movements, see Van Cott (1994), Urban and Sherzer (1991), Assies, Van der Haar, and Hoekema (2000), Brysk (1994), and Diaz Polanco (1997). On ventriloquism, see Guerrero (1997).

2 One of the provincial-level members of ECUARUNARI, the Union of Peasant-Farmer Organizations of Esmeraldas (UOCE), is from the Ecuadorian coast and consists of nonindigenous (mestizo and black) members.

3 The indigenous movement in Ecuador is multiple and includes national federations of evangelical Indians (FEINE) and the more class-based FENOCIN, as well as smaller groupings such as communist-founded FEI. However, CONAIE has created a hegemonic position within the indigenous movement, vis-à-vis the state and with respect to public opinion. In January 2000, public opinion polls granted greater legitimacy to the self-declared Indigenous Parliament, organized by CONAIE, than to the National Congress (*Hoy* [Quito], January 7, 2000).

4 Morales's political party, Movement Toward Socialism (MAS), won over a quarter of the legislative seats in Bolivia's lower house in 2002 and won over half in 2005.

5 This paragraph draws on Kleymeyer (1993).

6 This amount represented some 7 percent of total donations.

7 Ecuadorian confederation web sites are more extensive than Bolivian ones (compare www.conaie.org and www.ecuarunari.org with www.csutcb.org and especially www.conamaq.org). The U.S.-based academic and activist Marc Becker has been instrumental in setting up and maintaining the sites of Ecuadorian indigenous organizations. More of the web site work now goes on within ECUARUNARI and CONAIE, however. The two Bolivian sites mentioned above have recently been incorporated into the Red Indígena. Local indigenous peoples' organizations create web sites infrequently, compared to regional and national ones.

8 Field notes, second Indigenous Summit of the Americas, Quito, July 2004. The follow-up continental indigenous summit took place in Guatemala in 2006.

9 Forest Peoples Program, staff member, interview, July 2000. For information, see http://iaip.gn.apc.org/index.html.

10 For a copy of the declaration, see http://www.un.org/esa/socdev/unpfii/en/declaration.html. On the permanent forum, created in 2002, see http://www.un.org/esa/socdev/unpfii/. Governments have argued that the UN Working Group on Indigenous Populations duplicates the remit of the UN Permanent Forum on Indigenous Peoples. In response, indigenous leaders have asserted that the working group has a human-rights focus and thus merits continuation, since the permanent forum handles a wider range of issues related to indigenous peoples.

11 See http://www.oas.org/OASpage/Events/default_ENG.asp?eve_code=11; and "Negotiations resume at OAS on indigenous rights" *Caribbean Net News*, 23 January 2007, www.caribbeannetnews.com/.

12 C. Kleymeyer, former Ecuadorian specialist, Inter-American Foundation, interview, November 2000; K. Healy, former Bolivian specialist, Inter-American Foundation, interview, November 2000. See also Healy (2001a).

13 Established in 1970, Oxfam America's goals by the late 1990s included self-help development and working with southern partners. Its Central America office concentrates on the environment (confidential interviews in 1999 and 2000).

14 A. Schlegel, Hanns Seidel staff member, interview, April 2000.

15 D. Rothschild, Amazon Alliance, interview, March 2000.

16 Relatively small-scale efforts were common however, such as SWISSAID-sponsored exchanges between Ecuadorian indigenous and mestizo farmers and their Colombian counterparts (F. Gangotena, SWISSAID, interview, February 2000).

17 F. Arenz, Norwegian Popular Aid (APN), interview, March 2000.

18 I. Naveda, Oxfam America, interview, April 2000; H. Hoffmeyer, IBIS-Bolivia, interview, November 1999. CAOI's web site is http://www.minkandina.org.

19 Bank Information Center staff member, personal communication, March 2000.

20 Danish bilateral representatives in Bolivia suggested that Denmark's proindigenous policy grew out of postcolonial guilt and in response to the UN Decade for Indigenous Peoples (M. Viveros, interview, September 1999; K. Edinger, interview, November 1999).

21 See http://www.gtz.de/home/english/; http://www.aeciecuador.org; http://www.cosude.org.ec; and http://www.cosude.org.bo.

22 "In its development aid or other schemes of economic cooperation, it [the European Commission] has never supported projects which might adversely affect the local population and nor will it do so in future" (as cited in Van de Fliert 1994, 24).

23 World Bank, Operational Policy and Bank Procedure on Indigenous Peoples (OP/BP 4.10). This is a recent revision of OD 4.20.

24 The Inter-American Development Bank includes the Indigenous Peoples and Community Development Unit within the Social Development and Public Governance Sub-department of the Sustainable Development Department. The UN Permanent Forum on Indigenous Issues belongs to the Division for Social Policy and Development, while the World Bank's Cultural Diversity and Indigenous People's Thematic Team is housed within the Social Development Department.

25 On social development in the 1960s and early 1970s, see UNECLA (1970) and Gore (2003). On the period since 1990, see World Summit for Social Development (1995), ECLAC (1997), and UNDESA (2005).

26 In prevailing social development thinking, other "vulnerable" groups include women, youth, the elderly, the disabled, and migrants (see UNDESA 2005, 49).

27 One apparent exception was the Structural Adjustment Participatory Review Initiative (SAPRI) carried out by the World Bank in tandem with governments and civil-society organizations in eight developing countries. However, once the initiative reached conclusions critical of neoliberal structural adjustment, the World Bank distanced itself from SAPRI and largely ignored its findings (Engler 2004).

28 On audit cultures North and South, see Desai and Imrie (1998). On the technical de-politicization of social policy, see P. Nelson (1996, 629), Segarra (1997), and Chalmers et al. (1997).

29 Indicative of these trends is their employment by agencies such as the World Bank and the British Department for International Development (DFID). Between 1988 and 1990, for example, the number of DFID social-development advisers rose from

two to nearly sixty (Stirrat 2000, 32). Advisers to strengthen civil society–government dialogue have also been hired (e.g., DFID's appointment to such a post in Bolivia in 2002).

30 Hybrid development institutions are distinct from Segarra's (1997) welfare network, as they entail new institutional forms and hence new discourses and workplace cultures.

31 IEDECA staff, interview; CARE staff, interview, March 2000.

32 In addition to the discussion here, the reinscription of scales through indigenous development policies is examined in some detail in chapters 2, 3, and 4.

33 V. H. Cárdenas, ex-president of the Fondo Indígena, La Paz, interview, September 1999. According to a former director of IADB's Indigenous Peoples Unit, ratification of the Fondo Indígena was faster than that for ILO Convention 169 (A. Deruyttere, director, IADB Indigenous Peoples Unit, interview, March 2000.) Up-to-date information on this fund can be found at http://www.fondoindigena.org.

34 By mid-2000, the World Bank and European Union were providing funding, as were Latin American governments (Bolivia, Chile, Mexico, Ecuador, Panama, Peru, and Guatemala) and individual European countries (Spain [with $5 million], Belgium, Germany [$0.7 million], Sweden, and France [$2 million]). The ILO and UNESCO contributed smaller amounts.

35 V. H. Cárdenas, interview, September 1999. For more information, see http://www.iadb.org/sds/IND/site_401_e.htm#2.

36 Confidential interview, November 1999. IBIS is a Danish development NGO that has focused on indigenous peoples in the Andean region since the mid-1990s.

37 A. Karakras, indigenous consultant to Fondo Indígena, interview, June 1999.

38 A. Deruyttere, Director, IADB Indigenous Peoples Unit, interview, March 2000; http://www.fondoindigena.org/formacion.shtml.

39 PRODEPINE stands for Proyecto de Desarrollo de los Pueblos Indígenas y Negros del Ecuador—Indigenous and Afro-Ecuadorian Peoples Development Project.

40 J. Uquillas, World Bank Latin America social development group, interview, March 2000.

41 PRODEPINE directors and staff, various interviews, January–May 2000.

42 S. Andrango, former executive director of PRODEPINE, interview, February 2000.

43 G. Ramón, former technical director of PRODEPINE, interview, April 2000.

44 Van Nieuwkoop and Uquillas 2000; G. Ramón, interview, April 2000.

45 This decision was made at a CONAIE assembly, passing by majority vote rather than unanimity. We return to this in the concluding chapter.

46 D. Tuchschneider, Bolivia World Bank officer, interview, December 1999; Davis 2002. Also see chapter 2.

47 These professionals included social scientists, especially (though not exclusively) anthropologists (Postero 2000).

48 VAIPO came under the newly named Ministry of Sustainable Development and Planning (P. Avejera, adviser in VAIPO, interview, September 1999; M. Morales,

Political Directorate, VAIPO, interview, September 1999; E. Ditchburn, DfID Bolivia section, interview, September 1999). For more on this complex institutional history, see Paulson and Calla (2000), Lind (2000b), and Van Cott (2000a).

49 CODENPE stands for Development Council of the Nationalities and Peoples of Ecuador. CONPLADEIN stands for Development Planning Council of Indigenous and Black People. CODENPE retains largely the same composition and structure as in its 1998 founding, in part because of CONAIE's ability to fight off a takeover of appointment power by the Gutiérrez government in 2004.

50 These changes within state indigenous-affairs agencies in Ecuador entailed greater control over agencies by CONAIE appointees, relative to other national indigenous confederations. The tensions generated by this shift in control continue to the present day. On the other hand, prior to CODENPE state indigenous agencies gave equal voice to all national indigenous confederations, even though CONAIE has been acknowledged as the most representative and most potent. Lucero (2003; 2006) and Guerrero and Ospina (2003) explore these disputes in some depth.

51 G. Churuchumbi, CODENPE, interview, May 2000. One way CODENPE is different from Bolivian indigenous-affairs agencies is that CODENPE's executives are appointed by indigenous organizations rather than the president.

52 I. Quindé, CODENPE, interview, April 2000.

53 D. Iturralde, interview, April 1999. Part of the dispute mentioned in note 50 revolves around this juxtaposition of visions.

54 I. Quindé, interview, April 2000; http://www.codenpe.gov.ec/sidenpe.htm.

55 For a comparison of Colombian and Bolivian state reform and indigenous rights, see Van Cott (2000a).

56 In education, interculturalism refers to the awarding of equal validity to indigenous languages and Spanish and a pedagogic intention to convey cultural meanings and values rather than merely assist Spanish language acquisition.

57 D. Tuchschneider, World Bank representative, La Paz, interview, December 1999; Van Cott (2000a 203).

Chapter 2: Development-with-Identity

1 For critical examinations of development discourses and institutions, see Escobar (1995), Ferguson (1994), Scott (1995), Sikkink (1991).

2 By talking about race and culture we do not mean to equate the two but rather to recognize how "cultural difference" can be used in reactionary discourses to mask talk of racial difference (see Rivera 1999; Stolcke 1999).

3 The historian Jorge Basadre envisioned a multiethnic "deep" Peru as the basis for nationalism, while Mario Vargas Llosa viewed "deep Peru" as strictly indigenous, marked off from the rest of the nation by irreconcilable racial difference (Mayer 1991, 478).

4 D. Iturralde, interview, April 1999.

5 Oxfam America staff, confidential interview, Lima (n.d.).

6 *Riego andino* (Andean irrigation) is similar to eco-Andeanism, arguing for an Andean and environmentally beneficial method of irrigation (see chap. 4).

7 Ayllus are Andean indigenous communities of extended families, cargo-based leadership patterns, and occupation of specific territorial spaces. Cargo-based leadership entails moving stepwise form lower positions to higher ones; the latter are more prestigious and more burdensome. The chief post is usually called *mallku.*

8 These images are gendered as well: those waiting in the countryside include "our women" (Cussi, Calle, and Mamani 2000, 61; confidential interview, 25 November 1999).

9 Depending on the particular project and context in which Andeanism appears, it can have empowering or disempowering effects.

10 The first quote is from L. M. Calvo, former director, SNAEGG, interview, December 1999, and the second from I. Naveda, Oxfam America, interview, April 2000.

11 B. Callau and C. Edinger, DANIDA staff, interview, October 1999.

12 D. Arts, SNV, interview, July 2000.

13 In our interviews, development experts and indigenous activists talked about the lack of information on axes of difference within indigenous populations, such as gender, age, household structure, and generation.

14 In a number of agency reports, no sources are referenced for poverty statistics (e.g., Van Nieuwkoop and Uquillas 2000, 5; Encalada, García, and Ivarsdotter 1999).

15 Senior World Bank staff member, interview, March 2000.

16 A 2004 follow-up study covered Mexico, Ecuador, Peru, Guatemala, and Bolivia, highlighting the limited change in levels of indigenous poverty from the early 1990s to the early 2000s (Patrinos 2004; Patrinos and Skoufias 2007). Although it used more detailed questions about language use, the 2004 follow-up study in Bolivia did not utilize national household surveys, which included a direct question on ethnic self-identification.

17 However, (neo)colonial extraction of indigenous surplus and the damaging impacts of land privatization in the nineteenth and twentieth centuries are mentioned in a handful of consultants' reports.

18 Oxfam America, interview, n.d.; DANIDA staff, interview, October 1999.

19 A. Pero, UNDP, interview, March 2000; also Brysk (2000), Van de Fliert (1994).

20 In the words of the World Bank's indigenous thematic team, indigenous social capital provides a platform for ethnodevelopment (Van Nieuwkoop and Uquillas 2000, 18; Davis 2002).

21 On social capital's intellectual history, see Bourdieu 1984; Hyden 1997. Also see Putnam (1993). On social capital in development thinking, see Harriss and De Renzio (1997).

22 World Bank, web site 2002.

23 Ethnographic descriptions of reciprocity (*mink'a* or *minga*), fictive kinship, and syncretic Catholic-indigenous rituals fill the anthropological literature on the Andes.

Our argument is not that these forms of social interaction do not exist, but rather to question the conceptual framework that connects them with current development thinking.

24 COWI and Consulting Engineers and Planners (1999); see chapter 5 on indigenous knowledge.

25 Oxfam staff, interview 1999.25. F. Gangotena, SWISSAID representative, interview, February 2000.

26 F. Gangotena, SWISSAID representative, interview, February 2000.

27 Not all parishes were in Andean highland regions; some were found in the coastal and Amazonian regions.

28 World Bank staff member, personal communication, April 2000.

29 K. Berelowitz, World Bank, interview, April 2000.

30 World Bank Participatory Training web site 1998.

31 The model here is distinct from PRATEC's, which also sees indigenous culture as a solution to development problems, but in a very different way.

32 PRODEPINE regional director and staff, interview, May 2000.

33 On the image of the entrepreneur in neoliberal development, see Mayer and Rankin (2002), who found that the neoliberal entrepreneur is often a female figure (also see chapter 6).

34 Confidential interview, Bolivia.

35 World Bank representative, interview.

36 For example, the 1950 Ecuadorian census was concerned with measuring indigenous market participation as consumers of nationally produced goods (Larson and Harris 1995).

37 This policy has thereby distanced itself from what Raymond Apthorpe terms "ideal ruralism," whereby the rural poor are consistently described in terms of lack—wittily summarized as "landless, stockless, feckless" (Apthorpe 1997, 49).

38 "In the present era of globalization where trade and investment liberalization, deregulation and privatization are the policies followed by most governments, the face of poverty for many indigenous peoples has changed for the worse" (Tauli-Corpuz 2005, 6).

39 W. Rivero, former head of VAIPO, as cited in Postero (2000).

40 IBIS-Bolivia staff, interview, November 1999; also Grootaert and Narayan (2001, 42). Similarly, a private German foundation working with indigenous Ecuadorians suggested that preserving culture represented a "profoundly conservative" political agenda (A. Schlegel, Hanns Siedel Foundation, interview, April 2000).

41 The role of communal territory in fostering political resistance is not mentioned.

42 I. Naveda, Oxfam America staff, interview, April 2000; also H. Hoffmayer, IBIS representative, interview, November 1999.

43 An exception is the FENOCIN federation of black, indigenous, and mestizo campesino populations with an agenda of development-with-identity and interculturalism (FENOCIN 1999).

44 B. Callau and C. Edinger, DANIDA staff, interview, October 1999.

45 J. Strobele-Gregor, GTZ representative at Fondo Indígena, interview, September 1999.

46 DfID Bolivia office, personnel interview, September 1999.

47 SNV-Bolivia, interview, October 1999.

48 At the same time, Indians had to be comfortable with support groups and the media using Western modes of communication (talking to people directly, using eye contact, personal presentation) (Lloyd 1998).

49 S. Andrango, interview, February 2000.

50 G. Churuchumbi, Ecuadorian activist and CODENPE staff member, interview, May 2000.

51 Mayer (1991) asks why modernity and evangelism are more attractive to some Andeans than traditional cultures are, forgetting the pernicious impact of racism.

52 CONAIE statement. http://www.conaie.org, accessed December 2007.

53 B. Chancoso, CONAIE external affairs spokesperson, interview, May 2000.

54 F. Gangotena, SWISSAID representative, interview, February 2000.

55 L. M. Calvo, former SNAEGG official, interview, December 1999.

56 V. H. Cárdenas, interview, September 1999.

57 A CODENPE staff member said, "We are trying to establish . . . intercultural development" (I. Quinde, interview, April 2000).

58 J. Uquillas, World Bank, interview, March 2000.

59 THOA and Aymara Education Council staff, interview, September 1999. In reaffirming indigenous identities, only rarely do indigenous movements address questions of sexuality. When one indigenous man spoke about sexual rights at a U.S. conference, the remaining indigenous participants fell silent (field notes, March 2001).

60 M. Caguano, PRODEPINE southern highlands office, interview, May 2000.

61 L. M. Calvo, interview, December 1999.

62 T. Griffiths, Forest Peoples Program, interview, May 2002; Staff member, Bank Information Center, interview, March 2000.

63 Víctor Hugo Cárdenas, interview, September 1999.

64 On ethnic exclusion, see J. Fox (1996); on gender exclusion see Molyneux (2002) and Silvey and Elmhirst (2003).

65 Of course, local patterns of racial exclusion and segregation by mestizo elites obstruct proindigenous reforms in other areas.

Chapter 3: Development in Place

1 Place is a portion of occupied geographical space that combines a specific social and geographical setting with a sense of origin or destination (Johnston et al. 2000, 442).

2 Senior Oxfam America representatives, interview, May 2000. Government agen-

cies or specific personnel in them sometimes share these NGO views of the local (D. Tuchschneider, director of rural development for World Bank in Bolivia, interview, April 2000; also see J. Cameron 2005, 368–69).

3 Along with the factors noted here, O'Neill (2003) argued that electoral incentives of political parties have driven political interest in decentralization.

4 One exception would be rural hacienda owners, who were usually whites or mestizos and viewed as elites.

5 However, these processes occurred in tandem with the forging of local Andean spaces by an increasingly wide range of actors, including indigenous federations, NGOs, diverse churches, and local associations (Bebbington 2000; Salman and Zoomers 2003).

6 Remarkably, international donors gave Bolivian rural development NGOs "an amount equal to almost 15 percent of the government budget and to 30 percent of all social spending" (Duran 1990, as cited in Kohl 2003, 321).

7 DANIDA representative, interview, November 1999; Van Cott (2000a); GTZ (2001); Keese and Freire (2006, 117).

8 Territoriality refers to "the assignment of individuals and groups to discrete areas through the use of boundaries" and hence comprises a mechanism by which power is exerted (Johnston et al. 2000, 823–24).

9 Smaller political units such as provinces, cantons, and parishes, in contrast, had no tradition of challenge to centralized power (see Slater 2003, 624–26).

10 These powers, responsibilities, and entitlements were not extended to departmental governments, whose members were appointees from the central government and municipalities (see Kohl 2002, 457; Slater 2003, 622–23).

11 In Ecuadorian political parlance, "sectional" (*seccional*) refers generically to all administrative units below the central government.

12 During the 1980s, a large number of municipalities were created under the new Ecuadorian democratic regime, in part with the encouragement of GTZ, a German bilateral agency (GTZ 2000).

13 This precedent turned out to be important for the Patacocha irrigation project discussed in chapter 4.

14 Coastal provinces tend to be the most commercially productive and prosperous in Ecuador and contribute what they often consider to be an unfair share of tax revenue to national coffers. Also, Ecuador lost nearly half of its national territory to Peru and only in 1998 formalized a peace agreement conceding that loss. Finally, presidential decrees granting titles to indigenous territory in the Amazon, where most of Ecuador's oil reserves are located, were careful to limit title to the surface rights only (Sawyer 1997; Selverston-Scher 2001).

15 Keese and Freire have also pointed out that the central government often ignores municipal requests for transfer or responds with a rejection on grounds of lack of preparedness, without much explanation of its reasoning (also see Cameron 2005, 372).

16 Individual indigenous leaders sometimes took advantage of new possibilities for personal prestige as well.

17 J. Callau and K. Edinger, DANIDA, interview, October 1999. Similar criteria were expressed in documents and interviews of U.S., Swiss, and Spanish bilateral agencies; the World Bank and Inter-American Development Bank; and NGOs such as IBIS (Denmark) and CARE (U.S. and international).

18 Only in 2004 did legislation pass requiring Ecuadorian municipalities to submit cantonal (municipal) development plans.

19 Municipal governments had to submit a formal request to the national government for such funds, and include documentation of capacity. The first significant transfers were made only in 2003.

20 In the 2004 municipal elections, the number of Pachakutik municipal majorities and mayorships declined to twenty, but in a handful of additional municipalities, Pachakutik politicians held a plurality (Tribunal Supremo Electoral 2004). As noted in chapter 1, Pachakutik was created in 1996 by CONAIE and other social movement organizations looking for political and development alternatives.

21 G. Dávila, senior SNV staff member, interview, May 2000; Torres (1999b); Cameron (2005).

22 In most cases, this participatory body was authorized by municipal ordinance, which also provided the assembly with power to remove the mayor from office.

23 Interviews with key personnel in NGOs associated with the Democracy and Local Development Group, February and March 2000. This group included the Institute of Ecuadorian Studies (IEE), CIUDAD, Tierra Nueva, Comunidec, Sendas, and Red Cantaro. The last of these is actually a network connecting eight NGOs (see Grupo Democracia y Desarrollo Local 1999, 209–11).

24 A. Barrera, CIUDAD, interview, March 2000. Also see Keese and Freire (2006, 115). Some of these NGOs are international, including IBIS-Denmark, the Inter-American Foundation (United States), Norwegian People's Aid, CARE, and Plan International. The first three have an "empowerment" mandate that justifies their support of alternative, indigenous movement-led municipalities (Torres 1999a, 28–29; Keese and Freire 2006; A. Cevallos, IBIS-Ecuador, interview, February 2000).

25 G. Dávila, interview, May 2000.

26 G. Ramón, PRODEPINE, interview, April 2000.

27 D. Arts, SNV, interview, July 2000; J. Frank, GTZ, interview, May 2000; E. Lucero, Universidad Andina, interview, March 2000.

28 Also see http://www.codenpe.gov.ec/formia.htm. The second phase of this program (from 2005–2008), called FORMIA, greatly increased the budget to nearly US$2.5 million (http://aeciecuador.org/site/file/content/14/).

29 Twenty percent of the national budget would go to municipalities on a per capita basis, with 85 percent of each municipality's allotment earmarked for new expenditures on projects, leaving only 15 percent for maintenance and payroll (Kohl 2002, 464).

30 In fact, smaller municipalities with little independent revenue were often worse off after the LPP than before (Kohl 2003, 319).

31 To the extent that decentralization was publicly debated prior to passing the LPP, it was pushed by elite departmental civic committees, and this discussion assumed allocation of authority to department-scale governments (Slater 2003; Blanes 2004, 113; also discussed earlier in chapter).

32 This was, in part, due to pressure from their grassroots constituents, who wanted to access their share of municipal resources (Blanes 2000; J. Merz, AOS, interview, December 1999).

33 Albó (2002, 81); Kohl (2003, 322); I. Arias, COSUDE/PADER, interview, December 1999; C. Espinosa, CENDA, interview, November 1999.

34 Medina (2003) argued however that the DMI was a compromise between the original LPP and indigenous leaders' demands for "indigenous municipalities," which would be on a wider scale and have broader powers than a submunicipal district.

35 This law emerged out of massive popular mobilizations that removed President Sánchez de Lozada from office in 2003. Sixty-eight indigenous "nonparties" ran for municipal office in 2004, often using the names of their local social-movement organization as their electoral name. Many other indigenous candidates won office as candidates of political parties, as they had done in 1997 and 1999 (Albó 2002, 82), but we do not have specific data as to how many.

36 COSUDE Bolivia, PADEM. See http://www.cosude.org.bo/es/Pagina_principal/ressources/resource_es_24390.pdf. PADEM was a complement to COSUDE's work abetting "productive municipalities" through its Rural Development Support Program, PADER (mentioned earlier in chapter).

37 J. Merz, AOS, interview, December 1999. Also PADEM (2000). The German agency GTZ took a similar approach in its municipal and rural development programs (Ayo 2003, 93).

38 R. Calla, Fundación Diálogo, interview, August 1999; M. Castro, ISALP, interview, November 1999. In English, ISALP stands for Potosí Legal Support and Social Research.

39 D. Tuchschneider, World Bank Bolivia, interview, May 2000. Tuchschneider also said that local policy coherence was crucial for development, and, if achieved, then national policy coherence was not necessary.

40 Also, the Heavily Indebted Poor Countries (HIPC) Initiative of the World Bank and IMF required that Bolivia send 70 percent of debt-forgiveness funds, which came from bilateral and multilateral relief, to municipalities (de Grave 2007, 21).

41 Tituaña was reelected as mayor in the 2000 and 2004 municipal elections.

42 UNORCAC is affiliated with the national indigenous peasant organization, FENOCIN, while Mayor Tituaña has links with CONAIE, the larger and more powerful indigenous confederation. These distinct affiliations have caused some tension between UNORCAC and Tituaña but have not undermined their ongoing alliance since 1996.

43 Cotacachi adapted this model from Porto Alegre and other Brazilian cities controlled by the Worker's Party, but Cotacachi actually subjects a much greater portion of the municipal budget to popular control (71 percent) than does Porto Alegre's participatory budget system (15 percent) (Ortiz 2004, 134–35; Wainright 2003, 38). Also, the Cotacachi assembly may revoke the mandate of the mayor or councilors for corruption or severe incompetence. This power goes beyond Porto Alegre's model and exceeds the 1998 Ecuadorian constitution, which grants recall power of mayors only by popular referendum.

44 These indices show increased access to water, electricity, communications, sewage, garbage collection, cooking gas, and building materials.

45 In one case, a local aqueduct was built largely with the labor of indigenous communities.

46 Auki Tituaña, Mayor of Cotacachi, interview, August 2003. http://www.otavalosonline.com/killkaykuna/dialogo_alcaldes/cotacachi.htm, accessed 22 July 2007. Tituaña believes that this rural-urban coalition has formed, in part, around a commitment to participation and transparency and rejection of clientelist politics.

47 G. Dávila, SNV, interview, May 2000. According to one Ecuadorian NGO functionary, his organization decided to assist Cotacachi due to high expectations about Auki Tituaña's leadership skills and his urban-rural coalition building. On these grounds, this NGO was also able to acquire additional monies from the Ecuador-Swiss debt-for-equity swap fund. J. P. Muñoz, Tierra Nueva, interview, March 2000.

48 GTZ 2004b 68–70; http://www.cotacachi.gov.ec/htms/esp/eventos/info8va.htm#v. A list of thirty-four organizations that have supported Cotacachi in some form is posted at, http://www.cotacachi.gov.ec/htms/esp/asamblea/Asamblea.htm.

49 The latter event was one of a few organized and financed by NGOs associated with the Ecuadorian Local Democracy and Development Group. F. Larrea, Fundación Heiffer Ecuador, interview, February 2000; J. P. Muñoz, Tierra Nueva, interview, March 2000.

50 Auki Tituaña, mayor of Cotacachi, interview, August 2003. From http://www.otavalosonline.com/killkaykuna/dialogo_alcaldes/cotacachi.htm, accessed 22 July 2007. The subtropical zone is often referred to as "Intag."

51 In spite of promises to counterbalance zonal municipal expenditures by employing a livelihood index (Ortiz 2004), relative spending on the urban zone actually increased. Go to http://www.cotacachi.gov.ec/htms/esp/Municipio/municipio.htm and click the "Presupuesto" sidebar.

52 Former UNORCAC leader R. Guitarra, cited in Ortiz 2004, 157.

53 Some of these imbalances between ethnic, racial, and class groupings may have enhanced the numerical weight of women in the assembly vis-à-vis men. The 2000 cantonal assembly registered male delegates at 53 percent and female at 47 percent (Ortiz 2004, 156), a rough parity. However, it has been argued that many indigenous women (and perhaps other rural women) have not participated as actively as men have, in part because they are expected to care for the home while

men are gone (Cameron 2005, 383). In surveys in Cotacachi, 35 percent of rural Andeans agreed with the idea of women staying home instead of participating, while 25 percent of urbanites agreed (Ospina 2006, 301).

54 The atlas project was part of a longer-term development program called SANREM-Andes. SANREM is an acronym for Sustainable Agriculture and Natural Resource Management, and there are additional regional programs in West Africa and Southeast Asia. See http://www.lanra.uga.edu/sanrem/andes/english/.

55 N. Gomez 2003, interview, cited in Ortiz 2004, 162–63.

56 These exclusions are seen to reflect a broader trend, in which UNORCAC remains an active participant in local politics, but cantonal leadership has moved toward a new elite composed of the urban middle class, environmentalists, campesino leaders from Intag (the mestizo, subtropical zone), and NGO-supported technical teams (Ortiz 2004, 148).

57 D. Tuchschneider, World Bank Bolivia, interview, May 2000.

58 C. Espinosa, CENDA, interview, November 1999. In chapter 4, we discuss Raqay-pampa further in relation to water politics and policy.

59 Albó and Quispe (2004); Medina (2003). For example, proindigenous action on municipal councils was hampered by competition between the various political parties that indigenous councilors belonged to, and indigenous municipal districts have been limited in terms of both autonomy and scale.

60 I. Quindé, CODENPE, interview, April 2000. Interestingly, this would apply to relations between indigenous groups as well as between indigenous and nonindigenous people, in Ecuador and beyond.

61 ECUARUNARI regional workshop on Quichua pueblo reconstruction, Riobamba, Ecuador, field notes, February 2000.

62 This not only distinguishes between indigenous and mestizo people but also differentiates among various indigenous identity groups. One additional assumption of this model is that such autonomy and segmentation will allow each group to develop unique innovations that can be borrowed by others or that may improve and transform national politics and development (Medina 2003).

63 Despite growing support for indigenous reconfigurations of local space, some indigenous federations and development agencies have contested these movements. The large Ecuadorian NGO Fondo Ecuatoriano Populorum Progressio, Ecuadorian "Populorum Progressio" Fund (FEPP), for example, viewed pueblo reconstitution and ayllus as a distraction from production and livelihood issues (J. Tonnello, director of FEPP, interview, February 2000). For details on disputes between indigenous federations around ayllus and pueblos, see Lucero (2006).

64 Part of Qollasuyu territory was in what is today Peru, in the area around Lake Titicaca (see, e.g., Orta 2001).

65 For instance, through decision making, dispute settlement, and rituals invoking the favor of indigenous deities and predicting weather patterns (Cussi, Calle, and Mamani 2002, 63; Healy 2001a, chap. 13).

66 Mamani and Choque (2001, 213–14); S. Blanco, Jacha Carangas mallku, interview, November 1999. This survey is known in Bolivia as a *muyu*.

67 CONAMAQ (2000g) specified that "this consists of Articles 1 and 171 of the constitution, Article 3 of the Ley INRA, Law 1257 . . . and others" (5). Law 1257 is the Bolivian ratification of ILO Convention 169 on indigenous rights.

68 Leaders of Potosí ayllu council, interview, November 1999.

69 We do not know the precise number of indigenous communities that now identify as ayllus. However, Oxfam America (2004) stated, "CONAMAQ encompasses approximately 543 ayllus and 2,200 original authorities." Experts in Bolivia believe that ayllus are the predominant form of local indigenous organization in Oruro and Potosí departments and influential in more than ten provinces in La Paz department (Ticona 2003; confidential interviews, January 2004). The situation is also in some flux, and local ayllus and federations may try to affiliate with both CONAMAQ and CSUTCB, as in the case of the Ingavi province ayllu federation.

70 For more detailed histories of the ayllu movement and its relations to CSUTCB, see Hahn (1996); Strobele-Gregor (1996); Ticona (1996); Mamani and Choque (2001); Andolina, Radcliffe, and Laurie (2005); and Lucero (2006).

71 S. Ovando, INRA TCO director, interview, December 1999.

72 According to Plata, Colque, and Calle (2003), *residentes* are individuals who maintain communal membership through familial landholdings in the countryside but spend most of their time away, usually in cities. As a result, they often fail to fulfill customary responsibilities to their home communities. This increases burdens on those who remain and erodes community solidarity.

73 This state entity changed names over time, from the Subsecretary of Ethnic Affairs (1993–1997), to the Vice-ministry of Indigenous and Original Peoples Affairs (1998–2002), to the Ministry of Indigenous and Original Peoples Affairs (2003–2006). It is currently called the Vice-ministry of Lands but retains the structure and functions of the former indigenous ministries and secretariats (INRA 2006, 49).

74 INRA (2006, 42–58); DANIDA (2004b, 41–42). This commission includes all players mentioned except private contractors. International donors participate as observers; they cannot vote on resolutions.

75 S. Ovando, INRA TCO director, interview, December 1999. She also said that this commission helped INRA explain to indigenous representatives that budget constraints put limits on the number of TCO claims that INRA could realistically process. The Danish bilateral agency, which sat on the commission's sessions regularly, confirmed this commission's facilitation and reporting utility but also noted that it cannot override INRA's decisions (DANIDA 2004b, 41).

76 INRA has a category of TCO claims, admitted for processing and with "financing assured" to see the process through to the titling stage (INRA 2006).

77 However, less than 15 percent of TCO titles granted nationwide are in the highlands, in spite of the fact that a far greater number of indigenous people live there (INRA 2006, 20). Reasons given for the lowland bias in TCO titling include perceptions

of the lowlands as "more indigenous," as holding natural resources more valuable on the market, and as having more conflicts of interest over such resources
(R. Calla, Fundación Diálogo, interview, August 1999; S. Ovando, INRA TCO director, interview, December 1999; Urioste 2007, 230–31). In fact, TCO titling procedures
in the Bolivian highlands did not begin until 2001, five years after they started in
the lowlands.

78 DANIDA financed legal training of Jesús de Machaqa indigenous leaders on LPP
and Ley INRA from 1997 to 2000, implemented by the Bolivian NGO Fundación
Diálogo (R. Calla, Fundación Diálogo, interview, August 1999; E. Ticona, Fundación Diálogo, interview, August 1999).

79 Regarding participation, DANIDA saw possibilities for direct democracy and culturally appropriate citizenship. Regarding sustainability, it saw collective property as
creating a sense of responsibility for natural resources. Regarding gender equity,
it believed that women's activism in TCO titling might spill over to other areas of
sociopolitical life (DANIDA 2004b, 23–24).

80 DANIDA-Bolivia office director, interview, January 2004.

81 Although not allocated exclusively for TCOs, other assistance for the ayllu movement was justified on similar grounds. The Danish NGO, IBIS, supported ayllus
because "where ayllus exist and still survive, it's obvious that one should not
destroy their tradition, but tap their potential and articulate it with modernity"
(IBIS-Bolivia office director, interview, November 1999). The same theme is found
in long-time ayllu supporter Oxfam America: "The Ayllu. . . . maintain[s] principles
[of] reciprocity, cooperation and labor exchanges and a complementary relationship between the individual and the group" (Oxfam America 1999). See Andolina,
Laurie, and Radcliffe (2005) for a more detailed discussion of international connections with the Bolivian ayllu movement.

82 DANIDA (2004b 10); DANIDA (2004c 11).

83 M. Burgoa, former INRA functionary, interview, cited in Almaraz 2005.

84 See INRA (2006, appendix H). A handful of TCOs at the (multiayllu) scale of marka
have been titled or assured of title.

85 INRA (2006, appendix H); DANIDA (2004b, 22). The Jacha Karangas council submitted a "multiscalar" claim for 1.6 million hectares for Karangas suyu in northern
Oruro but subdivided the claim by the territory of its member markas (see map
6 for an outline of Karangas countergeography).

86 World Bank–Bolivia official, interview, January 2004; confidential interview, January 2004. According to an independent Aymara professional and a DANIDA officer,
the Spanish consultants had little familiarity with the area. Nonetheless, the World
Bank argued that its survey found that Pacajes indigenous locals were confused
about or opposed to the Pacajes Suyu TCO claim, thus supporting its decision to
terminate financing of the claim. The World Bank office in Bolivia did not make
the survey results available to us however.

87 To facilitate such integration, this project allocated funds to train indigenous leaders

in "the functioning ... of local governments" (DANIDA 2004c, 48), and for "strengthening the capacities of municipal governments to relate with TCOS" (51).

88 Confidential interview, December 1999.

89 The assumed location of nine of these pueblos is actually represented on map 8. While CODENPE initially listed twelve Quichua pueblos, it would appear that CODENPE later conformed more to ECUARUNARI's highland Quichua pueblo count, as map 8 was adapted from CODENPE's web site.

90 In this sense, the pueblo process mirrors the ayllu movement's subdivision of Aymara and Quechua identities, except that Ecuadorian Quichua pueblos are analogous to Bolivian suyu-scale identities such as the Karangas or Quillacas peoples.

91 In contrast to Bolivian ayllus, which had no legal recognition prior to the 1994–1995 Law of Popular Participation, the Ecuadorian Ley de Comunas of 1937 acknowledged indigenous cultural differences and permitted freeholding communities a modicum of self-governance, albeit under corporatist state tutelage. Legal registration of indigenous communities from the 1960s to the 1980s created the grassroots membership of Ecuadorian national indigenous organizations.

92 G. Churuchumbi, CODENPE, interview, May 2000.

93 I. Quindé, CODENPE, interview, April 2000. On gender issues, see chapter 6.

94 I. Quindé, interview, April 2000. ECUARUNARI regional workshop on Quichua pueblos reconstruction, Riobamba, Ecuador, field notes, February 2000; Pichincha Richarrimui workshop on Cayambi and Kitu Kara pueblos reconstitution, San Pablo Urcu, Ecuador, field notes, May 2000.

95 I. Quindé, interview, April 2000; Pichincha Richarrimui workshop on Cayambi and Kitu Kara pueblos reconstitution, San Pablo Urcu, Ecuador, field notes, May 2000.

96 ECUARUNARI regional workshop on Quichua pueblos reconstruction, Riobamba, Ecuador, field notes, February 2000.

97 Drawing development paradigms in to a local level, advocates perceived pueblos as bases for sustainable development with identity, providing for food security, economic planning, higher rural living standards, and the satisfaction of basic needs (I. Quindé, CODENPE, interview, April 2000; G. Churuchumbi, CODENPE, interview, May 2000. ECUARUNARI regional workshop on Quichua pueblos reconstruction, Riobamba, Ecuador, field notes, February 2000; Memoria 1998).

98 B. Chancoso, CONAIE director of international relations, interview, May 2000.

99 ECUARUNARI regional workshop on Quichua pueblos reconstruction, Riobamba, Ecuador, field notes, February 2000; Pichincha Richarrimui workshop on Cayambi and Kitu Kara pueblos reconstitution, San Pablo Urcu, Ecuador, field notes, May 2000.

100 ECUARUNARI regional workshop on Quichua pueblos reconstruction, Riobamba, Ecuador, field notes, February 2000.

101 G. Churuchumbi, CODENPE, interview, May 2000; Meeting of communal presidents: Cangaua, Ecuador, field notes, March 2000.

102 In order to facilitate incorporation of any smaller-scale CTIs into a pueblo terri-tory, CODENPE's proposal includes a stipulation that indigenous communities or *parroquias* who solicit a CTI should identify as part of a broader pueblo (Lozano 2000, 77).

103 Pichincha Richarrimui workshop on Cayambi and Kitu Kara pueblos reconstitu-tion, San Pablo Urcu, Ecuador, field notes, May 2000. The *mancomunidad,* or network of local governmental administrative units, is also permitted by the 1998 Ecuadorian constitution (Lozano 2000, 79).

104 ECUARUNARI worked on this with the assistance of CODENPE functionaries. It was intended as a reform and renaming of the 1937 Ley de Comunas.

105 G. Churuchumbi, interview, May 2000; ECUARUNARI 1999c; Pichincha Richar-rimui workshop on Cayambi and Kitu Kara pueblos reconstitution, San Pablo Urcu, Ecuador, field notes, May 2000. According to one Quichua CODENPE func-tionary, CODENPE will, in turn, maintain close links with the continental Fondo Indígena (see chapter 1).

106 Although not coined as such, the CTI administration is analogous to the GTI (Indigenous Territorial Administration) concept in Bolivia.

107 I. Quindé, interview, April 2000. This particular functionary was trained profes-sionally as a geographer. According to Lefebvre (1991), territorial ordering is a spatial organization technology that follows particular social priorities.

108 I. Quindé, interview, April 2000. See chapter 5 for details on the FLACSO program. In English, FLACSO stands for Latin American Faculty of Social Sciences.

109 ECUARUNARI regional workshop on Quichua pueblos reconstruction, Riobamba, Ecuador, field notes, February 2000. Chapter 6 discusses the ECUARUNARI wom-en's training school in greater depth.

110 A. Cevallos, IBIS-Ecuador, interview, February 2000. Working with a budget of US$376,000 and a four-year calendar, the project advanced according to a multi-scalar local strategy: its workshops began on a subregional level (north, central, and southern highlands), after which ECUARUNARI transferred some of the project funds to provincial federations to carry out intracommunal (second-tier) pueblo workshops and then workshops in individual *comunas* (ECUARUNARI 1999c; ECUARUNARI regional workshop on Quichua pueblos reconstruction. Riobamba, Ecuador, field notes, February 2000).

111 ECUARUNARI regional workshop on Quichua pueblos reconstruction, Riobamba, Ecuador, field notes, February 2000. CODENPE received financing for pueblo pro-motion from the Ecuadorian government and the World Bank (via PRODEPINE) (I. Quindé, interview, April 2000; J. Aulestia, PRODEPINE, interview, May 2000).

112 J. Frank, GTZ, interview, May 2000. Note that CODENPE's CTI proposal was drafted in that same year.

113 Also, ECUARUNARI's constituent provincial organizations in Loja and Imba-bura renamed themselves as federations of "Pueblos Kichwas," See http://www

.ecuarunari.org/es/organizacion/federaciones.html and http://www.ecuarunari
.org/es/organizacion/consejo_gobierno.html.

114   Follow the links from http://www.ecuarunari.org/es/organizacion/upccc_plan-
vida/p_upccco2.html.

115   One possible explanation for why IBIS gave more leeway and financing to
ECUARUNARI than DANIDA did to ayllu organizations is that IBIS viewed the
Ecuadorian organizations as "more advanced" than Bolivian ones in proposal
and negotiating abilities (Andolina, Radcliffe, and Laurie 2005) and perhaps also
in their administrative and managerial skills. IBIS and Oxfam America sponsored
exchanges between Bolivia and Ecuador in part on those grounds, and DANIDA
may have shared this viewpoint. While IBIS is formally independent of DANIDA,
the latter provides nearly 90 percent of IBIS's budget, and there is some coordination between the two agencies (H. Hoffmeyer, IBIS, interview, November 1999; K.
Edinger, DANIDA, interview, November 1999).

116   G. Churuchumbi, CODENPE, interview, May 2000.

117   The only relevant development agency that mentioned neoliberalism as a problem
for indigenous people was the NGO Ayuda Obrera Suiza (AOS n.d.).

118   In addition, these businesses have effectively blocked municipal efforts to regulate
their contamination levels or water use for irrigation, further depleting the relative
access to resources for indigenous farmers and possibly harming the health of the
local population (Cameron 2005, 380).

119   Auki Tituaña, interview, August 2003. http://www.otavalosonline.com/killkaykuna/
dialogo_alcaldes/cotacachi.htm, accessed 22 July 2007.

120   In Ecuador, some mestizo activists working with indigenous-led "alternative municipalities" noted tensions over interculturalism: "There are a series of issues that
we will face in the next decade ... [including] our concern about the resurgence of
a narrow *indigenista* tendency which can create obstacles for a more intercultural
project. (J. P. Muñoz, Tierra Nueva, interview, March 2000). In Bolivia, Wilfredo
Plata suggested that "indigenist essentialisms" in platforms like the ayllu movement
"converted the [lowland] elites into anti-indigenous segregationists" (*La Razon*,
July 14, 2007).

121   In Bolivia, the break of Jesús de Machaqa (a territory with eighteen ayllus) from
Viacha municipality in 2002 was eased by Viacha's willingness to "unburden"
itself of responsibility for largely indigenous districts (Blanes 2000, 78). While both
sides are apparently satisfied with this outcome, it hardly matches the predominant model of inclusive, harmonious, intercultural municipalities. They handled
their differences by local separation rather than local integration. In Ecuador,
Cayambi pueblo workshops acknowledged that "what to do about mestizos,"
and indigenous Cayambi relations with them, as insufficiently addressed in
concepts of pueblo territoriality (Pichincha Richarrimui workshop on Cayambi
and Kitu Kara pueblo reconstitution, San Pablo Urcu, Ecuador, field notes, May
2000).

122 Indigenous movements have also used complementaridad to frame Andean gender relations. In that respect, the term has been critiqued for obscuring subregional differences in gender, as well as for downplaying gendered power relations. Whether these critiques would also apply to complementaridad as a metaphor for ethnic and race relations is an open question.

123 Potosí department ayllu federation leaders, interview, November 1999.

Chapter 4: Neoliberalisms and Transnational Water Politics

1 J. Loor, leader of the Ecuadorian Campesino Social Security Federation, interview, April 2000.

2 Ibid.

3 Ibid.; J. Alvear, former member of CESA, interview, April 2000.

4 J. Alvear, interview, April 2000.

5 A. Veliz, secretary of the Syndical Federation of Campesinos, interview, January 2000.

6 See for example, ITDG (1991); Boelens and Hoogendan (2002); Boelens and Dávila (1998).

7 O. Sanchez, acting director, Institute for Development and Ecology of Andean Communities (IEDECA) interview, March 2000; F. Gangotena, director of SWISSAID-Ecuador, interview, February 2000; H. Zaharia, director of Ecuador Office of the Center for Agricultural Cooperation and Development (CICDA), interview, April 2000.

8 O. Sanchez, interview, March 2000; J. Alvear, interview, April 2000.

9 In this respect, CENDA and PRATEC are sometimes more radical than indigenous organizations themselves and draw criticism for romanticizing Andean culture and turning a blind eye to poverty. Their view is more influential in Peru and Bolivia than in Ecuador.

10 C. Biederbick, IEDECA member, interview, April 2000.

11 Also see Guaraní leader cited in Benton (1999, 76).

12 The same countries are thus funding small eco-agriculture and water and irrigation projects as in Ecuador, and CONDESAN is now interested in becoming involved in Ecuador (personal communication, CONDESAN director, December 2001).

13 M. E. Udaeta, CIPCA Water and Legislative Forum director, interview, November 1999.

14 IEDECA has received financial and technical support from bilateral aid agencies of Switzerland, Holland, Germany, and Spain. Its French NGO partner is the International Center for Agrarian Development Cooperation, which also operates in Peru and Bolivia.

15 This occurred after IEDECA director Ivan Cisneros visited Washington. O. Sanchez, interview, March 2000; A. Zappata, director of IEDECA's Quito office, interview, May 2000; also see http://www.worldbank.org/research/sapri.

16 International consulting companies such as Dames and More or Anderson were particularly important in the Latin American region.

17 O. Sanchez, interview, March 2000; also Acción Ecológica (2000, 3–4). The flower-export industry in Ecuador received strong financial support from USAID as part of multilateral and bilateral support for the Structural Adjustment Program in Ecuador (Coulson 1999).

18 See the discussion of indigenous knowledge "scaling" in chapter 5.

19 These presidential proposals were even more influenced by market economic criteria and less by social criteria than the Water Council's proposal was (Sánchez 2000, 6–8).

20 P. Lanchimba, CONAUA president, interview, May 2000.

21 Economic Affairs Committee of the Ecuadorian National Congress, workshop on water law proposals, Riobamba, Ecuador, field notes and transcript, April 2000.

22 Ibid.

23 Ibid.

24 Indeed, one eyewitness at the following workshop in Guayaquil reported that its methodology stressed picking the brains of professional experts and listening to the needs of regional development councils (personal communication, May 2000).

25 Economic Affairs Committee of the Ecuadorian National Congress, workshop on water law proposals, Riobamba, Ecuador, field notes and transcript, April 2000.

26 Development NGO strategy meeting called by IEDECA and hosted by CICDA on water law debate process, Quito, Ecuador, field notes, May 2000.

27 If it lay on private or communal land, the water was property of the owner(s). If it lay within public land the government owned it (CGIAB 2001).

28 The Adenauer Institute is a German policy agency. Most government proposals that followed the 1997 proposal made only minor revisions to it.

29 CEJIS is the Centre for Juridical Studies, located in Santa Cruz. It advises indigenous and campesino organizations on legal matters affecting them.

30 F. Fernandez, executive secretary of the Union Federation of Campesina Women of Cochabamba, interview, December 1999; A. Veliz, executive secretary of the Union Federation of Campesino Communities of Cochabamba, interview, December 1999.

31 Rodriguez was the indigenous adviser to the Confederation of Indigenous Peoples of the Bolivian Lowlands (CIDOB) (interview, October 1999). Indigenous campesino leaders in Potosí and Oruro departments also affirmed these goals (F. Santos, executive secretary of the Syndical Federation of Campesino Workers of Potosí, interview, November 1999; H. Morales, general secretary of the Syndical Union Federation of Campesino Workers of Oruro, interview, November 1999).

32 A 1996 attempt to privatize water in Bolivia had met with strong regional resistance. While a concession in La Paz/El Alto was granted to the French company Lynoise des Eaux, privatization was opposed in Cochabamba. Resistance there focused on defending Misicuni, a multiple-dam project that had historically been central to

regional modernization dreams and that many argued would not be built if the city's water utility were to pass into private hands (Laurie and Marvin 1999).

33 Between 14 and 30 percent of Cochabamba's water supply comes from alternative systems such as communal and private wells, tanks, and private water vendors. Many of these systems date back many years and operate through collective uses and customs in water management, which involves communal labor and cultural rituals (Crespo 2003).

34 Despite the translation of Tucayta as "Federation of Communities of Cañar," it does not encompass the entire province of Cañar. There are other second-tier organizations in Cañar province at the same scale as Tucayta. Tucayta and these others affiliate at the provincial scale with the Union of Peoples and Campesino Communities of Cañar (UPCCC).

35 Coordinator of Tucayta technical team, interview, May 2000.

36 A social-neoliberal approach focusing on issues of exclusion, as well as economic reform, was adopted widely by multilateral and bilateral development agencies at this time. The Swiss development agency was asked to support the last phases of the project (US$600,000), as the Ecuadorian state was reducing its own involvement.

37 W. Dueñas, cited in CESA and CREA (1998, 42); L. Heredia, cited in CESA and CREA (1998, 28).

38 L. Heredia, COSUDE-Ecuador Technical Team, interview, April 2000.

39 F. Quinde, coordinator of Tucayta technical team, interview, May 2000.

40 CESA felt confident that Tucayta would be able to continue to manage the Patacocha irrigation system as well, albeit because of follow-up training from the Irrigation System Transfer project funded by the World Bank (CESA and CREA 1998, 50). Tucayta's (1999) development plan, however, revealed ongoing problems with the irrigation system, citing natural problems, local communities without needed skills, and neglect by the local government.

41 *Ch'aky* is a Quechua word for "lagoon."

42 G. Camargo, PDCR, interview, December 1999.

43 F. Quinde, coordinator of Tucayta technical team, interview, May 2000; C. Espinosa, in meeting between World Bank, PDRC, FDC, CENDA, and leaders from Raqaypampa Ch'aky project: Cochabamba, Bolivia, field notes, December 1999.

Chapter 5: Transnational Professionalization

1 See the introduction and chapters 1 and 2 for a discussion of how we understand social neoliberalism and its political significance.

2 On the World Bank, UNESCO, and UNICEF, see Aikman (2000), and Cortina and Stromquist (2000). See Kane (2001) on Nicaragua.

3 A. Schlegl, director of the Fundación Hanns Seidel, interview, April 2000. Hanns Seidel is an important funder of indigenous scholarships in Ecuador. See table 3.

4 H. Hoffmeyer, director, IBIS, interview, November 1999.

5 PRODEPINE in Ecuador became emblematic of these large-scale decentralized projects requiring great numbers of indigenous professionals.

6 I. Quinde, CODENPE, interview, April 2000. Parish (*parroquia*) is the smallest-scale administrative unit officially recognized in Ecuador.

7 For example, in Ecuador and Peru, the Summer Institute of Linguistics was particularly influential in the lowlands (Aikman 1999). From the 1970s, this often-controversial North American–led program focused on developing alphabets for oral languages as part of literacy campaigns that formed the basis of its evangelical mission.

8 A. Merks, GTZ, intercultural bilingual education specialist, interview, May 2000. MACAC is the Quichua word for war cry. The program built on a number of experiences of indigenous literacy campaigns in the mid-1980s.

9 P. Regalsky, CENDA and CEIDIS, interview, January 2000.

10 DINEIB in Ecuador, and the Education Reform Law in Bolivia, paid most attention to these stages by focusing on issues of literacy and early learning processes for children, respectively.

11 This is largely defined to include women, indigenous people, and black communities.

12 F. García, FLACSO, interview, May 2000; L. Macas, Instituto Cientifico de Culturas Indigenas, Scientific Institute of Indigenous Cultures (ICCI), interview, May 2000; section 5(e), "Perfil del egresado," [graduate profiles] in the degree program handbook for the master's degree in social sciences, major in anthropology and sociology, and graduate degree in indigenous peoples' rights, 2000–2001, Universidad de la Cordillera (La Paz, Bolivia), funded by the Danish Embassy and UNICEF.

13 A. M. Varea, lecturer at La Universidad Salesiana Ecuador and negotiator of funding from PRODEPINE for courses, interview, May 2000. La Universidad Salesiana was founded by a Catholic religious order with a very strong propoor doctrinal position. Students in Salesiana's courses can receive scholarships from Catholic funders, PRODEPINE, and the Hanns Seidel Foundation.

14 F. García, director of the indigenous affairs degree program, FLACSO, interview, May 2000.

15 P. Calla, lecturer at PROIEBANDES, interview, December 2000.

16 V. Chuma, head of the women's section of ECUARUNARI, interview, May 2000.

17 Ibid.; E. Ipaz, FENOCIN, interview, May 2000.

18 V. Chuma, interview, May 2000.

19 L. Macas, CONAIE and ICCI, interview, May 2000.

20 Although interculturalism is largely Latin American, the approach is also common in mainland Europe; in contrast, multiculturalism has been dominant in the UK, North America, and Australia (Cushner 1998).

21 See, for example, COSUDE (2001), which attempts to establish a state-of-the-art

understanding of interculturalism for topics as widespread as history, local development, religion, indigenous rights, art, neocolonialism, and gender. COSUDE is the
bilateral Swiss funding agency with more than twenty-five programs in Bolivia on
development of local production, natural resource management, business promotion, and democratic reform. It also works in Ecuador, where some of its programs
involve indigenous professionalization. There is also evidence that donor support for
other approaches—such as antiracism—are competing with intercultural programs
in some contexts (see Laurie and Bonnett 2002).

22 The director of the Puno program, Luiz Enrique López, was subsequently invited
by the GTZ to establish the PROIEBANDES bilingual intercultural masters degree
for indigenous students from across Latin America in Universidad Mayor de San
Simón, Cochabamba (see table 3).

23 Despite its originality, this program did not gain academic recognition, as inter-
institutional conflicts with Peruvian universities meant that the qualifications it
offered were not validated (Regalsky, CENDA, and students in the course, interview,
January 2000). The program is now in the process of affiliating itself with FLACSO,
the continent-wide social science institute.

24 P. Calla, PROIEBANDES lecturer, interview, December 1999.

25 P. Guerrero, anthropologist, La Universidad Salesiana, interview, May 2000.

26 L. Macas in Seminario Andino: Conflictos y Políticas Interculturales: Territorios y
Educación, Cochabamba, Bolivia, field notes, October 1999.

27 Building on the legacy of Paulo Freire, popular education envisages alternatives to
modern education in Andean America (Puiggrós 1999) and challenges the socialization of indigenous people into a discriminatory nation (Luykx 1999; Regalsky
2001, Howard-Malverde and Canessa 1995). Schools have often occupied a central
geographical position in communities to underscore their powerful "civilizing"
mission (Rival 1996). Alternative visions focus on communities' specific needs where
literacy is a political tool for everyday life, not merely an education goal. Closely
tying politics and education, popular education comprises the view that education
is historically and socially situated, is dialogical, should not reproduce the dominant
power schema, and results from political and social struggles. Similarly, educator
and learner take flexible, open, and nonessentialist positions (Puiggrós 1999, 171).
Initially, the approach did not distinguish between meeting the class-based needs of
indigenous peasants and strengthening indigenous culture and indigenous peoples'
political voice (Kane 2001).

28 As part of an Andeanist strategy questioning development based on the Green
Revolution (which sought to replace local indigenous seed stock with new, nonnative
high-yield varieties), CENDA worked with Raqaypampa communities to document
indigenous innovation in agriculture in the 1980s. Indicating how experimentation
and community decision making produced excellent results in fragile environments
(Calvo, Espinoza, Hosse, and Regalsky 1994), CENDA and Raqaypampa aimed to

contest conventional modernization and promote autonomous grassroots sustainable development (P. Reglasky, CENDA, personal communication, September 1999).

29 CENDA and CESU (Centro de Estudios Superiores Universitarios, the postgraduate social science college of the Universidad Mayor de San Simón) form the Bolivian node in the Consorcio para la Educación Intercultural y Desarrollo Integral Surandino, Intercultural Education Consortium for Southern Andean Development and Integration (CEIDIS) transnational consortium, which aims to bring together NGOs and academic institutions to focus on indigenous issues of territory, education, and interculturalism.

30 Such methods focus on participative learning and dialogue in workshops where the boundaries between the learner and the teacher are blurred.

31 Consejo de coordinación de mujeres del ECUARUNARI (1998).

32 Classes attended at CEIDES, Cochabamba, Bolivia, field notes, October–December 1999 and March 2001. On the Raqaypampa development plans, see chapters 3 and 4.

33 The UNDP program was funded by the International Development Research Centre (IDRC) in Canada (A. Pero, Indigenous People's Focus Point, UNDP, interview). See also World Bank, "Indigenous Knowledge for Development," http://www .worldbank.org/afr/ik; and UNESCO, "Best Practices on Indigenous Knowledge," http://www.unesco.org/most/bpindi.

34 M. T. Hosse, director, CENDA, and P. Regalsky, founding member, personal communication, April 2002.

35 L. Macas, CONAIE and ICCI, interview, May 2000.

36 E. Ipaz, FENOCIN, interview, May 2000.

37 CEDLA in Bolivia coordinates short courses and postgraduate teaching with FLACSO in Quito. These include a focus on interculturalism. AGRUCO, Cochabamba, runs an intercultural program in the sustainable development of natural resources, and new courses have been developed at an undergraduate level, with a module on interculturalism operating from 2001, in the anthropology program at Universidad Mayor de San Andrés in La Paz.

38 F. Garcia, CENDA, interview, November 1999; C. Walsh, Universidad Andina Simón Bolívar (UASB), interview, November 2000; P. Regalsky, CEIDIS, interview, December 1999; P. Calla, PROEIBANDES, interview, December 1999.

39 UASB, CEIDIS, FLACSO, and PROIEBANDES all operate programs that attract both national and international students from within the Andean region (table 3).

40 F. Garcia, former employee, PROIEBANDES-Ecuador, working with CENDA, interview, November 1999; P. Calla, lecturer in the Cochabamba program, interview, December 1999. In 2002, there were forty-four students in PROIEBANDES.

41 P. Regalsky, CENDA/CEIDIS, interview, December 1999.

42 A. Merks, GTZ, intercultural bilingual education specialist, interview, May 2000.

43 E. Ipaz, FENOCIN women's committee, interview, May 2000.

44 Pachamama (2000); V. Suárez and E. Ipaz, FENOCIN, interview, May 2000; V. Chuma, ECUARUNARI, interview, May 2000.

45 A *licenciatura* is a common university qualification in Latin America, equivalent to an intermediary scale between an undergraduate and master's degree. It involves a yearlong thesis and usually marks the achievement of professional status in a subject.

46 A. Kowii, PRODEPINE, interview, March 2000.

47 Ibid.

48 A. M. Varea, lecturer at La Universidad Salesiana, Ecuador, who negotiated the PRODEPINE scholarships, interview, May 2000.

49 A. Kowii, interview, March 2000.

50 Ibid.

51 I. Quinde, CODENPE, interview, April 2000.

52 V. Chuma, head of the women's section of ECUARUNARI, interview, May 2000.

53 A. Kowii, interview, March 2000.

54 J. Botazo, founder of La Salesiana program, interview, May 2000.

55 F. García, former PROIEBANDES–Ecuador employee, working with CENDA, interview, November 1999.

56 In this program, eleven teachers were from the United States, Canada, and Europe; forty-seven were based in Latin America.

57 C. Walsh, interculturalism program director in the UASB, interview, February 2000.

58 G. Bustos, professor of history and coordinator of Latin American studies at UASB, interview, February 2000.

59 V. Chuma, ECUARUNARI, interview, May 2000.

60 E. Lucero, director of the open course on local development and management at the UASB, interview, March 2000.

61 For academics, the transnational curriculum is an opportunity to analyze comparative tendencies in indigenous politics and its engagements with the pluricultural state.

62 Several students worked closely with communities on the implementation of pro-indigenous reform such as the Bilingual, Intercultural Education Reform Law.

63 P. Regalsky, codirector, CEIDIS-CENDA, interview, January 2000.

64 L. Macas, CONAIE and ICCI, interview, May 2000.

65 Ibid., Macas was also a key proponent of the Indigenous University.

66 Ibid.; I. Quinde CODENPE, interview, April 2000.

67 I. Quinde, interview, April 2000.

68 Currently, this indigenous university is called Amawtay Wasi (High Knowledge House) in Quichua, and Universidad Intercultural de Pueblos y Nacionalidades Indígenas (Intercultural University of Indigenous Peoples and Nationalities) in Spanish. See http://www.amawtaywasi.edu.ec/.

69 L. Macas, interview, May 2000.

70 Instead of understanding indigenous identities in terms of pregiven ethnic traits, Watts (2003, 24) illustrated how indigeneity is constructed through complex and unstable processes of identification based upon diverse historical genealogies. Drawing on Foucauldian understandings of governmentality and notions of governable space (Rose 1999), he argued that governable spaces of indigeneity have emerged through local and national struggles over customary rights in an international climate where indigeneity as a category has received increasing support. These spaces are governed through processes that involve struggles over the invention and reinvention of tradition and knowledge, as well as processes of representation in relation to culture, territory, and resources. They have become crucial sites for the construction of indigenous subjects and vehicles for political action.

71 In a questionnaire survey of eighty-eight students undertaking professionalization programs at La Universidad Salesiana, more than sixty students indicated that they believed their new qualifications would help them obtain careers in government, NGO, (I)NGO, and donor development projects and institutions.

Chapter 6: Gender, Transnationalism, and Development

1 On Andean women's oppression in class, racial, and gender hierarchies, see Nash and Safa (1980), Bronstein (1982), Bourque and Warren (1981).

2 To present the multiple perspectives of Andean indigenous women, men, and development agency staff, we analyzed over fifty semistructured interviews, field notes taken at diverse meetings and workshops, indigenous women's writings, and the "gray literature" produced for internal circulation by NGOs, states, and multilateral agencies. Third-world feminists have argued that development interventions are largely—if contradictorily and incompletely—premised on North-South postcolonial relations; they have also claimed that white/Western feminists do not speak from a position of neutrality or innocence in these debates (Mohanty 1991; Shohat 1998). To tackle questions of essentialism, we draw on poststructuralist and postcolonial perspectives about gendered people and gender discourses. In this context, our chapter attempts "to enact political-intellectual projects across differences" (Mohanty 1998, 486).

3 V. Chuma, ECUARUNARI leader, interview, May 2000.

4 The historian Florencia Mallon has described how, in Andean and Mexican Indian settlements, "ethnic, gender and spatial hierarchies helped organize local life, and communal hegemony was constructed along gender and generational lines" (Mallon 1995, 225). She also noted, "While men of different generations collaborated in their control of women's labor, sexuality and reproductive potential, older women and men collaborated in the reproduction of generational authority and privilege" (70).

5 V. Chuma, interview, May 2000.

6 Ibid. A relative lack of material on Bolivia restricts us largely to Ecuadorian examples here.

7 J. Lema, ECUARUNARI, interview, May 2000.

8 On Bolivia, G. Villca, leader of the Bolivian indigenous women's organization "Bartolina Sisa," interview, November 1999; on Ecuador, M. Arboleda and G. Camacho, interviews, May 2000.

9 On the transnational mobility of gender and development theory, see discussion in Moghadam (2000).

10 In the early 1990s, the World Bank appointed gender co-coordinators to each major regional grouping, introducing a male-focused component in its Latin America Gender Unit (Chowdhry 1995). In development's constantly shifting "allocation of visibilities" (Escobar 1995, 172), policymakers have argued that men pay a high cost for traditional masculinities. Such arguments have not, however, underpinned the World Bank's indigenous development projects.

11 G. Dávila, senior Dutch development agency consultant; M. Arboleda and G. Camacho, gender consultants, interviews, May 2000.

12 World Bank staff, interviews, March 2000.

13 World Bank staff member, personal communication, March 2000.

14 Associating indigenous women with tradition reproduces the equation of third-world women and "tradition" long critiqued by postcolonial writers (Mohanty 1991). On culture, development, and women, see Nussbaum and Glover (1995) and Chua, Bhavnani, and Foran (2000).

15 By failing to recognize changing rural divisions of labor, in part prompted by male out-migration, social capital models tend not to acknowledge the profound shifts in women's responsibilities and workloads (Encalada, García, and Ivarsdotter 1999; senior staff at Oxfam America, interview).

16 World Bank gender development specialist, interview, March 2000.

17 Ibid.

18 I. Quinde, CODENPE, interview, April 2000.

19 CONAMAQ-Guatemalan Maya exchange, La Paz, Bolivia, field notes, November 1999. Rather than recognize a parallel system of male-female participation (e.g., *mama t'allas*, female indigenous authorities married to male mallkus, found in Bolivia), the speaker here viewed feminism as the problematic issue and identified no possible alliance between feminism and Maya peoples.

20 World Bank ethnodevelopment specialist, interview, March 2000.

21 A. Barrera, staff member, Ciudad, interview, March 2000.

22 Confidential personal correspondence, March 2000.

23 Personal communication (Washington D.C.), March 2000.

24 At the same time, however, she recognized that "the themes of gender and indigenous issues have [a lot] in common, I would say, being the result of a structure of domination" (L. M. Calvo, former employee of the Bolivian Secretariat of Ethnic, Gender, and Generational Affairs, interview, November 1999).

25 Washington-based staff dealt with matters falling outside "mainstream projects," where indigenous women are among the stated beneficiaries of education or land-titling projects (World Bank employee involved in gender and indigenous issues, Latin America and Caribbean region, interview, March 2000).

26 K. Berelowitz, interview, March 2000.

27 Personal communication, May 2000.

28 The project eventually had a budget of US$50 million (US$25 million from World Bank, US$15 million from International Fund for Agricultural Development, and US$10 million from the Ecuadorian government and project beneficiaries).

29 Over US$10 million was distributed among 648 local development projects (PRODEPINE staff, interviews, January–May 2000). PRODEPINE's record on female scholarships is stronger than other INGO initiatives; a private German foundation gave 35 scholarships to women out of a total of 107 awarded during 1997 (Hanns Seidel Foundation 1997).

30 G. Ramón, technical director, PRODEPINE, interview, May 2000.

31 Ibid.

32 World Bank, personal communication; Ecuador World Bank office gender team, interview, May 2000.

33 This appears to have been the case particularly during the 1997–1998 Ecuadorian constituent assembly (interview 2000).

34 Personal interviews, January–May 2000.

35 Personal interviews, January–May 2000. This kind of transnational activism reflects what Keck and Sikkink (1998) call "leverage politics" (e.g., the World Bank uses its project funding as leverage) and "accountability politics" (e.g., the World Bank tries to hold CODENPE accountable to its previously stated agenda of human rights).

36 PRODEPINE staff, interviews, January–May 2000.

37 This team consisted of mestiza women with career histories in Ecuador's national women's movements. In this comparative review, a rural project called Programa Nacional de Desarrollo Rural, National Rural Development Program (PRONADER) was evaluated as a positive example of gender in development.

38 Confidential interview, May 2000.

39 Personal communication, 2000.

40 C. Velásquez, interview, September 2000.

41 Such patterns reflect deeper issues in indigenous development, such as when indigenous men appropriate women's local projects. In Ecuador's Chimborazo province and among the Shuar ethnic group, men were granted funds to work with women, but they administered these projects on their own, often unsuccessfully. Such outcomes reflect men's experience of making project bids and women's relative inexperience in development administration. In a study of over three hundred Bolivian grassroots projects, three-quarters of women had no knowledge of local projects, compared with one-quarter of men (Tibán 2001, 8).

42 These features are constructed as masculine only in particular postcolonial and racialized dynamics and do not refer to specific gendered individuals. If we interpret gendered norms in a postcolonial frame, we challenge the argument that masculinities in development are all pervasive while simultaneously being unmarked and unacknowledged (Elson 1991; Kabeer 1994, 34–7; Parpart 1995; Kimmel 2000). By arguing that *racial* differences between masculinities matter in the latter's valuation, we highlight the intersection of gender with race and class.

43 D. Iturralde, interview, January 2000.

44 The racialization of masculine criteria has consequences for indigenous men in development, as their masculinity is relatively less secure in national and international spaces where white/northern men reflect the default definition of "real men" (Canessa 2002; Larrea and Larrea 1999). Northern development masculinities are associated with competition, solution of technical problems, and full market orientation, whereas third-world (male) beneficiaries are relatively "feminized" (Chowdhry 1995). With respect to international development, men in the global South lose status through the importing of global male experts who are presented in hypermasculine terms. Among Bolivian hydraulic engineers, for example, foreign consultants have increasingly questioned male nationals' expertise at the same time that Bolivian men's lead role in nationalist development projects was discarded in favor of global capitalism (Laurie 2005). In Ecuador's PRODEPINE, the project's model of development enrolled indigenous and Afro-Ecuadorian male staff into a racially unmarked, but masculine, embodiment (compare Kimmel 2000). This postcolonial interpretation arguably offers another reason why the PRODEPINE project was so reluctant to incorporate gender-equity policies.

45 Ecuadorian gender consultants and a northern European bilateral development worker, interview, May 2000.

46 ECUARUNARI regional workshop on Quichua pueblos reconstruction, Riobamba, Ecuador, field notes, February 2000; see also Chuma (1999).

47 V. Chuma, ECUARUNARI leader, interview, May 2000. "Beijing + 5" refers to an international women's meeting held in New York in 2000 as a follow-up to the 1995 UN conference on women in Beijing.

48 Unprompted, the same woman went on to assert, "These movements can't exclude each other easily; being indigenous and not taking on gender, and being [a] gendered [movement] and not taking on the pluricultural character" (interview, May 2000).

49 V. Chuma, interview, May 2000.

50 Confidential interview, April 2000.

51 V. Chuma, interview, May 2000. Uprisings refer to nationwide protests against neoliberal reforms and political corruption in the 1990s and early 2000s.

52 Community members, Pacajes province, interview, November 1999. Comparing unionist and ayllu-based organizing in terms of their openness to women's

empowerment, some Bolivian Indian women have opted to support union organizations (G. Villca, interview, December 1999; see chapter 3 on the Bolivian ayllu
movement).

53 B. Chancoso, CONAIE external affairs spokesperson, interview, April 2000.

54 Indigenous women's concerns include the controversial question of domestic violence, which is a submerged but significant issue among female indigenous leaders
and grassroots women. In northern Ecuador, young women confronted leaders,
saying, "Yes, we women suffer a lot . . . more than men. We have the problem of
violence, of having more work." Younger women have put this issue on the table,
at times generating tension between generations. All age groups seem to want to
address domestic violence on their own terms, not those of feminism or "Western" gender models. In one interview, after the recorder was switched off, a female
indigenous interlocutor was adamant that nonindigenous, feminist approaches to
violence were inappropriate for her cohort.

55 At this point, transnational networks around these issues are little understood. For
a preliminary discussion, see Radcliffe, Laurie, and Andolina (2004).

56 ECUARUNARI regional workshop on Quichua pueblos reconstruction, Riobamba,
Ecuador, field notes, February 2000.

57 V. Chuma, interview, May 2000.

58 Nina Pacari, indigenous leader and former national congressional representative,
was invited onto Ecuador's Women's Political Coordinator to debate these questions (interview, May 2000).

59 As illustrated here, transnational meetings engage not only different indigenous
groups but also international development agencies that are imbued with specific
gender patterns (Oxfam America staff member, interview).

60 CONSAQ seminar for Mama T'allas, El Alto, Bolivia, field notes, December 1999.

61 ECUARUNARI was the first Ecuadorian indigenous organization to establish a
women's organization, in 1979–1980 (Rodas Morales 2002). Later training programs specifically for women were reframed as a component of ethnic and cultural
strengthening programs, such as a project proposal where women's leadership was
presented as one of five key attributes of Ecuador's indigenous movement (IBIS
2004).

62 V. Chuma, founder of ECUARUNARI Women's Training School, interview, May
2000.

63 Female leaders of ECUARUNARI, interviews, May 2000; ECUARUNARI (1998;
1999b).

64 Female ECUARUNARI leader, confidential interview, May 2000; also, Pachamama
(2000) and IBIS and ECUARUNARI (1999).

65 ECUARUNARI regional workshop on Quichua pueblos reconstruction, Riobamba,
Ecuador, field notes, February 2000.

66 FENOCIN women's team, interview, May 2000.

67 Inter-American Development Bank, www.iadb.org, 2005.

68 Here again, however, neoliberal development works through—and in relation to—gendered subjects and their representation.

Conclusion: Transnationalism, Development, and Culture

1 Examples include Putnam's (1988) work on two-level games and Waltz's (1959) model of three distinct "images" of personal, national, and international in world politics.

2 S. Ovando, INRA TCO director, interview, December 1999.

3 This process really took off in 2003, however, after the removal of President Sánchez de Lozada in the wake of massive indigenous and popular uprisings. The interim president, Carlos Mesa, oversaw the creation of a national plan to improve TCO creation and implementation processes, which in turn garnered even more international development aid for TCOs (DANIDA 2004b).

4 León (2003) provided an in-depth study of hierarchical aspects of transnational development networks operating in and through Bolivia, focusing on how international, national, and local cultural norms and practices intersect.

5 ECUARUNARI regional workshop on Quichua pueblos reconstruction, Riobamba, Ecuador, field notes, February 2000.

6 D. Tuchschneider, World Bank Bolivia, interview, May 2000; G. Ramón, PRODEPINE, interview, April 2000.

7 Confidential interviews, August 1999 and April 2000.

8 N. Pacari, interview, May 2000.

9 Conceptualizations of social capital within ethnodevelopment would likewise need to become multiscalar. See Bebbington and Perreault (1999), who offer more flexible notions of social capital that might serve as a starting point (also see Bebbington 2004b).

10 Indigenous Leaders of the Americas, letter to World Bank president James Wolfensohn, 15 March 2002 (draft), http://www.bicusa.org, accessed June 14, 2005.

11 Eyben and Ferguson (2004) have pointed to examples of development assistance in Africa that have adopted an analogous model, except that the aid recipients or users contracting support are governments, not civil-society actors.

12 Former CONAIE president Leonidas Iza confronted U.S. trade secretary Robert Zoellick at the 2003 Free Trade Association of the Americas (FTAA) talks in Ecuador and was shot at after he returned to Ecuador from anti-FTAA strategy meetings in Cuba.

13 CONAIE adviser, confidential interview, June 2006.

14 S. de la Cruz, vice-president of CONAIE, interview, July 2006.

15 Ibid.; CONAIE adviser, confidential interview, June 2006.

16 M. A. Carlosama, former indigenous adviser to ECUARUNARI and CONAMAQ, interview, January 2004.

17 We cite Hale (2002), who first expressed this paradox as such.

18 While most European and Asian bilateral agencies are complying with these policies, USAID refused and asked for exception. This exception was not granted by Bolivia, which has told USAID that it is free to withdraw its assistance for Bolivia (*El Diario*, 19 November 2007).

19 MAS, Movimiento al Socialismo (Movement to Socialism), was appropriated by coca-growers and other indigenous leaders in the mid-1990s, who were organized at that time under the "Political Instrument for Peoples' Sovereignty" designation. Since then, MAS has gradually become the largest party in the country insofar as elected positions go. It has held a majority in the lower legislative chamber and won a majority of seats in Bolivia's 2007 constituent assembly. MAS politicians also hold many municipal council and mayor posts.

20 All of our information on this provisional constitution is gleaned from the Asamblea Constituyente de Bolivia (2007).

21 At the same time, indigenous territorial authorities would be required to follow national or international human rights and environmental standards.

22 At the time of writing (early 2008) Bolivia's constituent assembly, consisting of a MAS majority, produced and passed a provisional constitution. However, that constitution has been disputed by opposition parties and regions and is still subject to approval or rejection by popular referendum. Ecuador's constituent assembly is just underway and has yet to pass any constitutional reforms. The indigenous–social movement coalition's main party, Pachakutik, has only four representatives in an assembly of over one hundred members. But it has allied with the majority Acuerdo País party, affiliated with President Correa; some of Acuerdo País's assemblyists share Pachakutik's views on certain issues.

23 ITT stands for Ishpingo-Tiputini-Tambococha. It is the name of the oil field zone within Yasuní Park that will not be drilled if the plan for compensation is successful.

24 CONAIE adviser, confidential interview, April 2007.

BIBLIOGRAPHY

Abram, M. 1992. *Lengua, cultura e identidad: El proyecto EBI 1985–1990*. Quito: Proyecto EBI / Abya-Yala.

Acción Ecológica. 2000. Cronología de la lucha comunitaria por el agua. *Alerta Verde* 93:2–6.

Adam, B. 2002. The gendered time politics of globalization: Of shadowlands and elusive justice. *Feminist Review* 70:3–29.

Aikman, S. 1999. *Intercultural education and literacy: An ethnographic study of indigenous knowledge and learning in the Peruvian Amazon*. Amsterdam: John Benjamins Publishing.

———. 2000. Bolivia. In *World yearbook of education: Education in times of transition*, ed. D. Coulby, R. Cowen, and C. Jones, 22–39. London: Kogan.

Albó, X. 1987. From MNRistas to Kataristas to Katari. In S. Stern, 379–419.

———. 1994. And from Kataristas to MNRistas? The surprising and bold alliance between Aymaras and neoliberals in Bolivia. In *Indigenous peoples and democracy in Latin America*, ed. D.L. Van Cott, 55–81. New York: St. Martin's Press.

———. 1999. *Iguales aunque diferentes: Hacia unas políticas interculturales y linguisticas en Bolivia*. La Paz: CIPCA-UNICEF.

———. 2002. Indigenous political participation in Bolivia. In Sieder, 252–76.

———. 2004. Muchos de los municipios más débiles han quedado librados a su propia suerte. Interview. In *Voces críticas de la descentralización: Una década de participación popular*, ed. D. Ayo, 39–63. La Paz: FES-ILDIS.

Albó, X., and CIPCA. 1999. *Ojatas en el poder local: Cuatro años después*. La Paz: CIPCA-PADER.

Albó, X., and W. Quispe. 2004. *Quiénes son indígenas en los gobiernos municipales*. La Paz: Plural-CIPCA.

Alem Rojo, T. 2000. *Comunicación y viviencia: Interculturalidad?* Cochabamba, Bolivia: Ediciones RUNA.

Alexander, J., and C. Mohanty, eds. 2001. *Feminist genealogies, colonial legacies, democratic futures*. New York: Routledge.

Almaraz, P. 2005. *Las Tierras Comunitarias de Orígen, son un instrumento para recuperar el derecho sobre sus tierras*. CIPCA working paper. http://cipca.org.bo/, accessed July 11, 2007.

Almeida, I., ed. 1991. *Indios: Una reflexión sobre el levantamiento indígena de 1990.* Quito: Abya Yala.

Alvarez, S. 2002. Encountering Latin American and Caribbean feminism. *Signs: Journal of Women in Culture and Society* 28:537–79.

Alvarez, S., E. Dagnino, and A. Escobar, eds. 1998. *Cultures of politics, politics of cultures: Revisioning Latin American social movements.* Boulder, Colo.: Westview Press.

Amin, A. E. 1994. *Post-Fordism: A reader.* Oxford: Blackwell.

Amazon Watch. 2007. Ecuador's pioneering climate change plan announced at Clinton Global Initiative, press release. www.amazonwatch.org/, accessed December 14, 2007.

Amnesty International. 1992. *The Americas: Human rights violations against indigenous peoples.* London: Amnesty International.

Andolina, R. 1999. Colonial legacies and plurinational imaginaries: Indigenous movement politics in Ecuador and Bolivia. PhD diss., University of Minnesota, Twin Cities.

———. 2003. The sovereign and its shadow: Constituent assembly and indigenous movement in Ecuador. *Journal of Latin American Studies* 35:721–50.

Andolina, R., S. A. Radcliffe, and N. Laurie. 2005. Development and culture: Transnational identity making in Bolivia. *Political Geography* 24:678–702.

Anonymous. 1998. *Voces de los Andes: Testimonios de mujeres indígenas y campesinas.* Cuenca, Ecuador: Mujer, imágenes y testimonio.

AOS. n.d. Participación y democracia. Sectoral Strategy Paper. La Paz: AOS.

Apffel-Marglin, F. 1998. Introduction: Knowledge and life revisited. In Apffel-Marglin and PRATEC, 1–50.

Apffel-Marglin, F., and PRATEC, eds. 1998. *The spirit of regeneration: Andean culture confronting Western notions of development.* London: Zed Books.

Appadurai, A. 1996. *Modernity at large: Cultural dimensions of globalization.* Minneapolis: University of Minnesota Press.

Applebaum, N., A. Macpherson, and K. Rosemblatt, eds. 2004. *Race and nation in Modern Latin America.* Chapel Hill: University of North Carolina Press.

Apthorpe, R. 1997. Writing development policy and policy analysis plain or clear: On language, genre and power. In Shore and Wright, 43–58.

Arboleda, M. 1993. Mujeres en el poder local. In *El espacio posible: Mujeres en el poder local,* ed. M. Arboleda, and R. Rodríguez, 20–42. Santiago, Chile: ISIS International / Ediciones de las Mujeres.

Arcos, C., and E. Palomeque. 1997. *El mito al debate: Las ONG en Ecuador.* Quito: Abya-Yala.

Arellano-López, S., and J. Petras. 1994. Non-governmental organizations and poverty alleviation in Bolivia. *Development and Change* 25:555–68.

Arratia, M., and L. Sánchez. 1998. *Riego campesino y género.* Cochabamba, Bolivia: PRONAR.

Arratia, L. 2004. Informe de actividades período 2003–2004. Unpublished report, INRA-Cochabamba, Bolivia.

Arroyo, A., and R. Boelens. 1997. *Mujer campesina e intervención en el riego andino: Sistemas de riego y relaciones de género, caso Licto, Ecuador.* Quito: CESA / CAMAREN / SNV.

Asamblea Constituyente de Bolivia. 2007. *Constitución política del estado: Aprobada en grande, detalle y revisión.* La Paz: Presidencia de la República de Bolivia.

Assies, W., G. Van der Haar, and A. Hoekema. eds. 2000. *The challenge of diversity: Indigenous peoples and reform of the state in Latin America.* Amsterdam: Thela Thesis.

Atkins, A. and E. Rey-Maqueira. 1996. *Ethno-development: A proposal to save Colombia's Pacific Coast.* London: Catholic Institute for International Relations.

Aulestia, A. 2002. Estudio de caso sobre el impacto de la perspectiva de género en la planificación participativa aplicada al desarrollo local en pueblos y nacionalidades PRODEPINE: Estudio de caso COCIQ-Qusapincha. Unpublished manuscript.

Ayllu Sartañani. 1992. *Pachamamax tipusiwa la pachamama se enoja: I. Qhurqui.* La Paz: Aruwiyiri.

Ayo, D. 2003. *Municipalismo, participación popular: Apuntes de un proceso.* La Paz: Muela del Diablo.

Bank Information Center. 2004. Indigenous peoples and the World Bank. http://www.bicusa.org/bicusa/issues, accessed March 16, 2004.

Barragán, R. 2007. De la reforma agraria a las Tierras Comunitarias de Orígen. In *Los nietos de la reforma agraria: Tierra y comunidad en al altiplano de Bolivia,* ed. Fundación Tierra, 81–111. La Paz: Fundación Tierra.

Barsky, O. 1988. *La reforma agraria Ecuatoriana.* Quito: Corporación Editoria Nacional.

Basch, L., N. Glick Schiller, and C. Szanton Blanc. 1994. *Nations unbound: Transnational projects and deterritorialized nation-states.* Langhorne, Penn.: Gordon and Breach.

Bauman, G. 1999. *The multicultural riddle: Rethinking national, ethnic and religious identities.* London: Routledge.

Bebbington, A. 1997a. Social capital and rural intensification: Local organisations and islands of sustainability in the rural Andes. *Geographical Journal* 163:189–97.

———. 1997b. New states, new NGOs? Crises and transitions among rural development NGOs in the Andean region. *World Development* 25:1755–65.

———. 1999. Capitals and capabilities: A framework for analyzing peasant viability, rural livelihoods and poverty. *World Development* 27:2021–44.

———. 2000. Re-encountering development: Livelihood transitions and place transformations in the Andes. *Annals of the American Association of Geographers* 163: 189–97.

———. 2002. Sharp knives and blunt instruments: Social capital in development studies. *Antipode* 34:800–3.

————. 2003. Global networks and local developments: Agendas for development geography. *Tijdschrift voor Economische en Sociale Geografie* 94:297–309.

————. 2004a. Social capital and development studies 1: Critique, debate, progress? *Progress in Development Studies* 4:343–49.

————. 2004b. Livelihood transitions, place transformations: Grounding globalization and modernity. In Gwynne and Kay, 173–92.

Bebbington, A., and G. Thiele. 1993. *Non-governmental organizations and the state in Latin America.* London: Routledge.

Bebbington, A., S. Guggenheim, E. Olson, and M. Woolcock. 2004. Exploring social capital debates at the World Bank. *Journal of Development Studies* 40(5): 33–64.

Bebbington, T., and T. Perreault. 1999. Social capital, development and access to resources in highland Ecuador. *Economic Geography* 75:395–418.

Beckett, J. and D. Mato. eds. 1996. Indigenous peoples/global terrains. Special issue. *Identities: Global studies in culture and power* 3(1–2).

Beijing Platform for Action. 1995. Fourth World Conference on Women Beijing Declaration. www.un.org/, accessed August 17, 2005.

Beijing Declaration. 1998. The 1995 Beijing Declaration of indigenous women. In *Indigenous women: The right to a voice*, ed. D. Vinding, 316–26. IWGIA Document no. 88. Copenhagen: IWGIA.

Benton, J. 1999. *Agrarian reform theory and practice: A study of the Lake Titicaca region of Bolivia.* Aldershot, England: Ashgate.

Berg, R., O. Montero, and S. Montgomery. 1983. Inquest in the Andes. *New York Times Magazine*, sec. 6, p. 50.

Bernal, F., and O. Sanchez. 2000. *Relaciones socio-organizativas y legales en el páramo y zonas de altura.* Quito: CAMAREN.

Bessis, S. 2001. The World Bank and women: "Instrumental feminism." In *Eye to eye: Women practising development across cultures*, ed. S. Perry and C. Schenck, 10–24. London: Zed Books.

Betsill, M., and H. Bulkeley. 2004. Transnational networks and global environmental governance: The cities for climate protection program. *International Studies Quarterly* 48:471–93.

Bigenho, M., and H. Cajías. 1996. Participación popular en el centro y sudeste de Potosí: Una visión panorámica de las organizaciones territoriales de base, "OTBs." *Reunión Annual de Etnología* [1995]: 198–206.

Blackwell, M. 2006. Weaving in the spaces: Indigenous women's organizing and the politics of scale in Mexico. In *Dissident women: Gender and cultural politics in Chiapas*, ed. S. Speed, R. A. Hernandez, and L. M. Stephen, 115–54. Austin: University of Texas Press.

Blanes, J. 2000. *Mallkus y alcaldes.* La Paz: PIEB-CEBEM.

————. 2004. Fue una propuesta orientada desde arriba y que tuvo que ver con el carácter no dialogante del mismo presidente. Interview. In *Voces críticas de la descentralización: Una década de participación popular*, ed. D. Ayo, 111–37. La Paz: FES-ILDIS.

Blunt, A., and C. McEwan, eds. 2002. *Postcolonial geographies: Writing past colonialism.* London: Continuum.

Boelens, R., and G. Dávila, eds. 1998. *Buscando la equidad: Concepciones sobre justicia y equidad en el riego campesino.* Assen, The Netherlands: Van Gorcum.

Boelens, R., and P. Hoogendam. 2002. *Water rights and empowerment.* Assen, The Netherlands: Van Gorcum.

Boelens, R., and M. Zwarteveen. 2002. *Water, gender and andeanity: Conflict or harmony?* In *Imaging the Andes,* ed. A. Zoomers and T. Salman, 145–66. London: Zed Books.

Bojanic, A. 2001. Agricultural extension in Bolivia and the Popular Participation Law. *Currents* (Swedish University of Agricultural Sciences) 27:25–31.

Bourdieu, P. 1984. *Distinction.* London: Routledge.

Bourne, R. 2001. *Indigenous rights in the Commonwealth Project.* Position paper. www.cpsu.org.uk, accessed November 6, 2007.

Bourque, S., and K. Warren. 1981. *Women of the Andes: Patriarchy and social change in two Peruvian towns.* Ann Arbor: University of Michigan Press.

Brah, A., H. Crowley, L. Thomas, and M. Storr. 2002. Globalization. Special issue. *Feminist Review* 70(1).

Brennan, T. 1997. *At home in the world: Cosmopolitanism now.* London: Harvard University Press.

Bretón, V. 2001a. Capital social, etnicidad y desarrollo: Algunas consideraciones críticas desde los Andes ecuatorianos. *Boletín Rimai* 32. www.icci.nativeweb.org/, accessed November 20, 2002.

———. 2001b. *Cooperación al desarrollo y organizaciones indígenas de segundo grado en el marco del estado neoliberal.* Paper presented at the congress of the Latin American Studies Association, September 6–9, Washington, D.C.

Bronstein, A. 1982. *The triple struggle: Latin American peasant women.* London: War on Want Campaigns.

Brown, M. F. 1993. Facing the state, facing the world: Amazonia's native leaders and the new politics of identity. *L'homme* 33(2–4): 307–26.

Brown, K. 1999. Native Americans and early modern conceptions of race. In *Empire and others: British encounters with indigenous peoples, 1600–1850,* ed. M. Daunton, and R. Halpern, 79–100. Philadelphia: University of Pennsylvania Press.

Brown, L. D., and J. Fox. 2001. Transnational civil society coalitions and the World Bank: Lessons from project and policy influence campaigns. In Edwards, and Gaventa, 43–58.

Brysk, A. 1994. Acting globally: Indian rights and international politics in Latin America. In Van Cott, 29–51. New York: St. Martin's Press.

———. 1996. Turning weakness into strength: The internationalization of Indian rights. *Latin American Perspectives* 23(2): 38–57.

———. 2000. *From tribal village to global village: Indian rights and international relations in Latin America.* Stanford, Calif.: Stanford University Press.

Burchell, G., C. Gordon, and P. Miller, eds. 1991. *The Foucault effect: Studies in governmentality.* Chicago: University of Chicago Press.

Burawoy, M., M. Blum, S. George, Z. Gillie, T. Gowan, L. Haney et al. 2000. *Global ethnography: Forces, connections and imaginations in a postmodern world.* Berkeley: University of California Press.

Bustamente, R. 2000. El difícil camino de la formulación de una nueva Ley de Aguas para Bolivia. In *La gestión integral del agua en Cochabamba,* ed. CGIAC, 117–39. La Paz: CGIAC.

Butler, J. 1993. *Bodies that matter: On the discursive limits of sex.* London: Routledge.

Calla, P. 2000. Gender, ethnicity and intercultural education. Paper presented at workshop, Current challenges to the Bolivian state: Issues of gender, ethnicity and citizenship. November 11, 2000. University of Newcastle, England.

Calla, R. 2000. Indigenous peoples, the law of popular participation and changes in governance: Bolivia, 1994–1998. In Assies, Van der Haar, and Hoekema, 77–94.

Calvo, L., C. Espinoza, T. Hosse, and P. Regalsky. 1994. *Raqaypampa: Los complejos caminos de una comunidad Andina.* Cochabamba, Bolivia: CENDA.

CAMAREN. 2000. *Actores del sistema de capacitación.* Quito: CAMAREN.

Cameron, G. 2001. Taking stock of pastorlist NGOs in Tanzania. *Review of African Political Economy* 87:55–72.

Cameron, J. 2005. Municipal democratisation in rural Latin America: Methodological insights from Ecuador. *Bulletin of Latin American Research* 24:367–90.

Canessa, A. 2002. My husband calls me "India" when he beats me: Reproducing racial hierarchies in an Andean hamlet. Unpublished manuscript.

Cárdenas, V. H. 1992. Prólogo: Homenaje a los 60 años del tinku entre Avelino Siñani y Elizardo Pérez. In *Educación indígena: ¿Ciudadanía o colonización?* ed. R. Choque, and V. Soria, 5–15. La Paz: Ediciones Aruwiyiri—THOA.

Carney, D. ed. 1998. *Sustainable rural livelihoods: What contribution can we make?* London: DfID.

Carnoy, M., M. Castells, S. Cohen, and F. Cardoso. 1993. *The new global economy in the information age.* University Park: Pennsylvania State University Press.

Carrasco, T., D. Iturralde, and J. Uquillas. eds. 1999. *Doce experiencias de desarrollo indígena en América Latina.* La Paz: Fondo Indígena.

Carrión, F. 1998. La constitución de un estado descentralizado. *Ecuador Debate* 44: 67–87.

Castells, M. 2000. *Rise of the network society.* 2nd ed. Oxford: Blackwell.

Castro, J. E. 2007. Poverty and citizenship: Sociological perspectives on water services and public–private participation. *Geoforum* 38:756–71.

Cervone, E., ed. 1998. *Mujeres contracorriente: Voces de líderes indígenas.* Quito: ACDI.

CESA. 1991. *Campesinado y entorno ecosocial.* Quito: CESA.

———. 1993. *Mujer andina: Condiciones de vida y participación.* Quito: CESA.

CESA and CREA. 1998. *La construcción de los embalses patacocha: Más que una obra de ingenieria.* Quito: CESA.

CGIAB. 2000. Socios del CGIAB. *Todo sobre el agua* 1:2.

———. 2001. ¿De quién son las aguas? *Todo sobre el agua* 3:3–4.

CGIAC. 2000a. Finding common ground. Unpublished report.

———. 2000b. *La gestión integral del agua en Cochabamba*. La Paz: CGIAC.

CGLA. n.d. Coordinadora de Gobiernos Locales Alternativos. Unpublished report, Quito.

Chalmers, D. 1992. *The international dimensions of political institutions in Latin America: An internationalised politics approach.* Paper presented at the annual meeting of the American Political Science Association, September 3–6, Chicago.

Chalmers, D., C. Vilas, K. Hite, S. Martin, K. Piester, and M. Segarra. 1997. *The politics of inequality in Latin America: Rethinking participation and representation.* London: Oxford University Press.

Chambilla, J. 1994. Una mirada a la interculturalidad y la educación popular. In *Interculturalidad y educación popular,* ed. PROCEP, 72–96. La Paz: PROCEP.

Chancoso, B. 2000. Comentario. In F. García, 28–35.

Chase, J., ed. 2002. *The spaces of neoliberalism: Land, place and family in Latin America.* Hartford, Conn.: Kumarian Press.

Chekki, D. A. 1988. Transnational networks in global development: Canada and the Third World. *International Social Science Journal* 117:383–98.

Chiriboga, M. 1988. *El problema agrario en el Ecuador.* Quito: ILDIS.

———. 2001. Constructing a southern constituency for global advocacy: The experience of Latin American NGOs and the World Bank. In Edwards and Gaventa, 73–86.

Chirix Garcia, E. D. 2000. ¿Quienes son y como se forman los hombres nuevos? *Jotaytzij* 11.

Choque, M. E. 1999a. La identidad y liderazgo de la mujer indígena en la lucha por el territorio. Unpublished manuscript, Department of Native American Studies, University of California, Davis.

———. 1999b. El Ayllu: Una alternativa de decolonización. Unpublished manuscript, La Paz.

———. 2000. *La reconstitución del ayllu y los derechos de los pueblos indígenas.* In F. Garcia, 13–30.

Choqueticlla, V., J. Maraza, and N. Vázquez. 2000. Del fortalecimiento del ayllu a la reconstrucción de la nación Quillacas-Azanaques: Federación de Ayllus del Sur de Oruro. In Carrasco, Iturralde, and Uquillas, 83–102.

Chowdhry, G. 1995. Engendering development? Women in development WID in international development regimes. In Marchand and Parpart, 26–41.

Chua, P., K. Bhavnani, and J. Foran. 2000. Women, culture, development: A new paradigm for development studies? *Ethnic and Racial Studies* 23:820–41.

Chuma, V. 1999. Mujeres indígenas y desarrollo colectivo. In *¡Acción positiva!* ed. CONAMU, 184–85. Quito: CONAMU.

Chuma, V., and P. Palacios. 2000. Reconstruyendo la democracia. http://icci.nativeweb.org/, accessed September 13, 2000.

CIDOB. 1993a. *OYENDU.* Santa Cruz, Bolivia: CIDOB.

———. 1993b. *Proyecto de ley de pueblos indígenas del oriente, chaco y amazonia boliviana.* Santa Cruz, Bolivia: CIDOB.

CIDOB, CSUTCB, and CSCB. 1999. Propuesta sobre la Ley de Aguas. Unpublished discussion document Dewey no. CENDIC 348 01. http://www.cidob-bo.org/.

CIPCA, ed. 1991. *Por una Bolivia diferente.* La Paz: CIPCA.

Cisneros, I. 1995. Las politicas públicas de apoyo al riego. In *Propuestas de apoyo al riego campesino: Memorias del taller,* ed. IEDECA, CICDA, and OSTROM, 29–32. Quito: IEDECA.

Clark, A. M. 1995. NGOs and their influence on international society. *Journal of International Affairs* 48:507–25.

Clark, K. 1998. Racial ideologies and the quest for national development: Debating the agrarian problem in Ecuador 1930–1950. *Journal of Latin American Studies* 30:373–93.

Clarke, P. 1998. Water, food security and livelihoods. In *Water Projects and Livelihoods—Poverty Impact in Drought Prone Environments,* ed. A. Nicol, PP–PP. SCF Workshop Report. London: Save the Children Fund.

Clifford, J. 1998. Mixed feelings. In *Cosmopolitics,* ed. P. Cheah, and B. Robbins, 362–71. Minneapolis: University of Minnesota Press.

CNRH. 1996. Propuesta de reforma a La Ley de Aguas. Unpublished working proposal, Quito.

CODENPE. 2001. PRODEPINE informe de monitoria, 1 de febrero 2000 a 31 de enero 2001. Quito: CODENPE.

———. n. d. Mapa interactivo. www.codenpe.gov.ec/, accessed December 13, 2005.

Cohen, R., and S. E. Rai. 2000. *Global social movements.* London: Athlone.

Colque, G. 2005. *La lucha por un gobierno local participativo: El caso de los aymaras de Jesús de Machaqa.* Working Paper 069/05. La Paz: Fundación Tierra.

———. 2007. Normas consuetudinarias y formales sobre la tierra. In *Los nietos de la reforma agraria: Tierra y comunidad en el altiplano de Bolivia,* ed. Fundación Tierra, 137–56. La Paz: Fundación Tierra.

Collins, J. 2000. A sense of possibility: Ecuador's indigenous movement takes center stage. NACLA *Report on the Americas* 33(5): 40–49.

Colloredo-Mansfeld, R. 1999. *The native leisure class: Consumption and cultural creativity in the Andes.* Chicago: University of Chicago Press.

———. 2000, March. *Undoing multiculturalism: Towards a relational autonomy in the Ecuadorian Andes.* Paper presented at the congress of the Latin American Studies Association, Miami.

Comaroff, J., and Comaroff J. L. 2001. *Millennial capitalism and the culture of neoliberalism.* Durham, N.C.: Duke University Press.

Conaghan, C., and Malloy, J. 1994. *Unsettling statecraft: Democracy and neoliberalism in the central Andes.* Pittsburgh: University of Pittsburgh Press.

CONAIE. 1989. *Las nacionalidades indígenas en el Ecuador: Nuestro proceso organizativo.* Quito: Abya Yala / CONAIE.

————. 1994a. *Memorias de las Jornadas del Foro de la Mujer Indígena del Ecuador.* Quito: CONAIE / UNFPA.

————. 1994b. *El proyecto político de la* CONAIE. Quito: CONAIE.

————. 1996a. *Memoria del taller sobre "Ley de Aguas" y sistema de riego comunitario: Perspectivas de las organizaciones.* Quito: CONAIE.

————. 1996b. *Propuesta de Ley de Aguas.* Quito: CONAIE.

————. 2000a. *Propuesta de ley de nacionalidades y pueblos indígenas del Ecuador.* Quito: CONAIE.

————. 2000b. *Estratégias situacionales de las nacionalidades y pueblos indígenas para el año 2000.* Quito: CONAIE.

————. 2007. *Constitución política del estado del Ecuador: Propuesta de la Confederación de Nacionalidades Indígenas del Ecuador.* Quito: CONAIE.

CONAMAQ. 2000a. Propuesta de diálogo indígenas–estado y gobierno. Unpublished working proposal, La Paz.

————. 2000b. El poncho del indio: Obstáculo para los intereses económicos. Unpublished press release, La Paz.

————. 2000c. Manifiesto del CONAMAQ. Unpublished report, La Paz.

————. 2000d. Propuestas y demandas de los ayllus, markas, y suyus de la república. Unpublished working proposal, La Paz.

————. 2000e. CONAMAQ Presentara al gobierno boliviano demanda de tierras comunitarias de orígen, propuesta de diálogo pueblos indígenas-estado/gobierno, la inmediata conclusion del camino Cotapata Santa Barbara y realizara su tercera reunión anual en la ciudad de La Paz. Unpublished press bulletin, La Paz.

————. 2000f. El derecho de los pueblos originarios al territorio. Unpublished working proposal, La Paz.

————. 2000g. Desarrollo del ayllu. Unpublished working proposal, La Paz.

CONAMU. 1999a. *Acción positiva: Memoria del seminario regional de mecanismos gubernamentales de género.* Quito: Consejo Nacional de Mujeres / Embajada Real de Países Bajos / UNICEF-UNIFEM.

————. 1999b. Mujeres del área rural: Derechos sexuales y reproductivas, experiencias productivas. In *Memoria: Taller "Mujeres del área rural,"* ed. CONAMU. Quito: CONAMU / IICA / UNFPA.

Congreso del Ecuador. 1994. *Ley de Aguas y reglamento.* Quito: CEP.

Conklin, B., and L. Graham. 1995. The shifting middle ground: Amazonian Indians and ecopolitics. *American Anthropologist* 97:695–710.

Connell, R. W. 1995. *Masculinities.* Berkeley: University of California Press.

————. 2005. Change among the gatekeepers: Men, masculinities and gender equality in the global arena. *Signs* 30:1801–25.

Consejo de Coordinación de Mujeres del ECUARUNARI. 1998. *I Seminario Taller de la Escuela de Formación de Mujeres Lideres del ECUARUNARI, Baños, Ecuador.* Training course handbook. Quito: ECUARUNARI.

Cooke, B., and U. Kothari. 2001. *Participation: The new tyranny?* London: Zed Press.

Cornwall, A., E. Harrison, and A. Whitehead. eds. 2004. Repositioning feminism in development. *IDS Bulletin* 35:4.

Corporación de Estudios y Publicaciones. (1994). *Ley de aguas y reglamento.* Quito: CEP.

Correia, M., and B. Van Bronkhorst. 2000. *Ecuador gender review: Issues and recommendations.* Report No. 20830-EC. Washington, D.C.: World Bank.

Cortina, R. 2000. Global priorities and local predicaments in education. In Cortina and Stromquist, 179–200.

Cortina, R., and N. Stromquist. eds. 2000. *Distant alliances promoting education for girls and women in Latin America.* London: Routledge.

Cortina, R., and H. Porter. 2000. Restructuring bilateral aid for the twenty-first century. In Cortina and Stromquist, 219–38.

COSUDE. 1998. *Estrategia del COSUDE en el Ecuador para el sector agrícola y de gestión de recursos naturales.* Quito: COSUDE.

———. 2001. *La encrucijada cultural: Anuario COSUDE 2001.* La Paz: COSUDE.

———. 2006. PADEM: Programa de apoyo a la democracia municipal. www.cosude .org.bo/, accessed June 27, 2007.

———. n.d. *Penipe* Brochure—Development Project Information. Quito: COSUDE.

Coulson, J. 1999. A study of female flower workers in Ecuador. PhD diss., University of Newcastle, England.

COWI and Consulting Engineers and Planners. 1999. *Diagnóstico de las oportunidades económicas de los pueblos indígenas de Bolivia para acceder a mercados, tecnologías y recursos nuevos.* Executive report. Washington D.C.: World Bank.

Cox, K. 1998. Spaces of dependence, spaces of engagement and the politics of scale: Or, looking for local politics. *Political Geography* 17:1–23.

Crang, P., C. Dwyer, and P. Jackson, eds. 2004. *Transnational spaces.* London: Routledge.

Craske, N. 1998. Remasculinisation and the neoliberal state in Latin America. In *Gender, politics and the state,* ed. G. Waylen, and V. Randal, 100–20. London: Routledge.

Craske, N., and M. Molyneux, eds. *Gender and the politics of rights and democracy in Latin America.* Basingstoke: Palgrave Macmillan.

Crespo, C. 2003. Water privatisation policies and conflict in Bolivia: The water war in Cochabamba 1999–2000. PhD diss., Oxford Brookes University, England.

Crush, J. 1995. *Power of development.* London: Routledge.

CSUTCB. 1992. *El Pututu: Vocero oficial de la CSUTCB.* La Paz: CSUTCB.

Cushner, K. 1998. *International perspectives on intercultural education.* London: Lawrence Erlbaum Associates.

Cussi, S., D. Calle, and A. Mamani. 2000. Nayaruxa chuymaxa ususkakituwa: Historia de la Federación de Ayllus y Comunidades Originarias de la Provincia Ingavi. In Carrasco, Iturralde, and Uquillas, 59–81.

DANIDA. 2004a. *Programa sectorial de apoyo a los derechos de los pueblos indígenas: Bolivia, Fase II, 2005–2009.* La Paz: Ministerio de Relaciones Exteriores.

———. 2004b. *Componente 2: Saneamiento y titulación de Tierras Comunitarias de Orígen. Programa sectorial de apoyo a los derechos de los pueblos indígenas—Bolivia, Fase II, 2005–2009.* La Paz: Ministerio de Relaciones Exteriores.

———. 2004c. *Componente 3: Gestión territorial indígena en Tierras Comunitarias de Orígen. Programa sectorial de apoyo a los derechos de los pueblos indígenas—Bolivia, Fase II, 2005–2009.* La Paz: Ministerio de Relaciones Exteriores.

Davis, S. 1994. The World Bank and indigenous peoples. In *Indigenous peoples and international organizations,* ed. L. Van de Fliert, 75–83. Nottingham: Spokesman.

———. 2002. Indigenous peoples and participatory development: The experience of the World Bank in Latin America. In Sieder, 227–51.

Davis, S., and W. Partridge. 1999. *Promoting the development of indigenous people in Latin America.* September 13, 2000. http://siteresources.worldbank.org/, accessed November 1, 2008.

De Filippis, J. 2002. Symposium on social capital: An introduction. *Antipode* 34: 790–95.

De Grave, J. 2007. Estado boliviano y cooperación internacional: Malestar, responsibilidades, aperturas. Working Paper, United Nations Development Programme, La Paz.

De la Cadena, M. 1998. Silent racism and intellectual superiority in Brazil. *Bulletin of Latin American Research* 17:143–64.

———. 2000. *Indigenous mestizos: The politics of race and culture, Cuzco, Peru, 1919–1991.* Durham, N.C.: Duke University Press.

De la Fuente, M., ed., Participación popular y desarrollo local: La situación de los municipios rurales de Cochabamba y Chuquisaca. Cochabamba, Bolivia: UMSS.

De la Torre, C. 1999. Everyday forms of racism in contemporary Ecuador: The experiences of middle-class Indians. *Ethnic and Racial Studies* 22:92–112.

De Lauretis, T. 1987. *Feminist studies/Critical studies.* Basingstoke, England: Macmillan.

De Waal, A. 2001. The moral solipsism of Global Ethics Inc. *London Review of Books,* August 23, 15–18.

Dean, M. 1999. *Governmentality: Power and rule in modern society.* London: Sage.

Deere, C. D., and M. León. 2001. Institutional reform of agriculture under neoliberalism: The impact of the women's and indigenous movements. *Latin American Research Review* 36(2): 31–63.

Deere, C. D., M. León, E. García, and J. César Trujillo. 1999. *Género y derechos de las mujeres a la tierra en Ecuador.* Quito: CONAMU / UNICEF / Embassy of the Netherlands.

Defilippis, D. 2001. El código civil y el recurso agua. *Todo Sobre el Agua* 4:2–3.

Degregori, C. I. 1998. Ethnicity and democratic governability in Latin America: Reflections from two Andean countries. In *Fault lines of democracy in post-transition Latin America,* ed. F. Agüero, and O. Stark, 203–34. Miami: North-South Center Press.

Delaney, D., and H. Leitner. 1997. The political construction of scale. *Political Geography* 16:93–97.

Deruyttere, A. 1997. *Indigenous peoples and sustainable development: The role of the Inter-American Development Bank.* Washington, D.C.: Inter-American Development Bank.

Desai, V., and R. Imrie. 1998. The new managerialism in local government: North-South dimensions. *Third World Quarterly* 19:635–50.

Díaz Polanco, H. 1997. *Indigenous peoples in Latin America: The quest for self-determination.* Boulder, Colo.: Westview Press.

Drainville, A. 2004. *Contesting globalization: Space and place in the global economy.* New York: Routledge.

Durán, J. 1990. *Las nuevas instituciones de la sociedad civil.* La Paz: Huellas SRL.

Dunn, K. 2001. Identity, space, and the political economy of conflict in Central Africa. *Geopolitics* 6(2): 51–78.

ECLAC. 1997. *The equity gap: Latin America, the Caribbean and the Social Summit.* Santiago, Chile: ECLAC.

———. 2004. *A decade of social development in Latin America, 1990–1999.* Santiago, Chile: ECLAC.

ECUARUNARI. 1998. Testimonios de la mujer del Ecuarunari. Quito: ECUARUNARI/IBIS-Dinamarca.

———. 1999a. *Constitución política de la República del Ecuador: Derechos y garantías fundamentales. Convenio 169 sobre pueblos indígenas OIT. Ley de comunidades indígenas del Ecuador.* Quito: ECUARUNARI.

———. 1999b. *III Seminario Taller, 20 nivel Escuela de Mujeres Lideres Indígenas Ecuarunari.* Quito: ECUARUNARI.

———. 1999c. Información básica: La reconstrucción de los pueblos, camino a la conformación del parlamento Quichua. Unpublished project proposal document, Quito.

———. 1999d. *Ley de Comunidades.* Quito: ECUARUNARI.

———. 2000a. *Rikcharishun: Periódico bilingüe de ECUARUNARI* 28(1).

———. 2000b. *Escuela de Formación de Mujeres Lideres "Dolores Cacuango."* http://mujerkichua.nativeweb.org, accessed September 13, 2000.

———. 2001. 1er encuentro del sistema nacional de formacion de líderes índigenas. http://ecuarunari.nativeweb.org/, accessed October 12, 2001.

Edelman, M., and A. Haugerud, eds. 2005. *The anthropology of globalization: From classical political economy to contemporary neoliberalism.* Malden, Mass.: Blackwell.

Edwards, M. 2001. Introduction. In M. Edwards and J. Gaventa, 1–14.

Edwards, M. and J. Gaventa, eds. 2001. *Global citizen action.* London: Earthscan.

Egan, K. 1996. Forging new alliances in Ecuador's Amazon. *SAIS Review,* Summer-Fall, 123–42.

Elson, D. 1991. *Male bias in the development process.* Manchester: Manchester University Press.

Encalada, E., F. García, and K. Ivarsdotter, eds. 1999. *La participación de los pueblos indígenas y negros en el desarrollo del Ecuador.* Washington, D.C.: Inter-American Development Bank.

Engler, M. 2004. SAPRIN: No prescription needed. *New Internationalist* 365:24.

Escobar, A. 1995. *Encountering development: The making and the unmaking of the Third World.* Princeton: Princeton University Press.

———. 2001. Culture sits in places: Reflections on globalism and subaltern strategies of localization. *Political Geography* 20:139–74.

Escobar, A., and S. Álvarez, eds. 1992. *The making of social movements in Latin America: Identity, strategy and democracy.* Boulder, Colo.: Westview Press.

Escobar, M. 2002. Sistematización de las experiencias de género en el PRODEPINE. Unpublished manuscript, Quito.

Espinosa, M. F. 2000. Ethnic politics and state reform in Ecuador. In Assies, van der Haar, and Hoekema, 47–56.

Eyben, R. 2000. Development and anthropology: A view from inside the agency. *Critique of Anthropology* 20:7–14.

Eyben, R., and C. Ferguson. 2004. How can donors be accountable to poor people? In Groves and Hinton, 164–80.

Fabian, J. 1983. *Time and the other: How anthropology makes its object.* New York: Columbia University Press.

Falk, R. 2000. *Human rights horizons: The pursuit of justice in a globalizing world.* London: Routledge.

FENOCIN. 1999. *Hacia el nuevo milenio: Porque el campo está la fuerza del desarrollo, de la identidad y la vida.* Quito: FENOCIN / Agriterra The Netherlands.

———. 2000. Confederación Nacional de Organizaciones Campesinas, Indígenas y Negras—FENOCIN. www.fenocin.org, accessed Dec. 15, 2000.

Ferguson, J. 1994. *The Anti-politics machine: "Development," depoliticization and bureaucratic power in Lesotho.* London: University of Minnesota Press.

Fernández, O., and C. Crespo. 2004. *Estado, movimientos sociales y recursos hídricos: Presión social y negociación luego de la guerra del agua de Cochabamba,* Informe Final. Cochabamba, Bolivia: IDRC / CESU.

Fine, B. 1999. The developmental state is dead. Long live social capital? *Development and Change* 30:1–19.

———. 2001. *Social capital versus social theory: Political economy and social science at the turn of the millennium.* London: Routledge.

Finnegan, W. 2002. Letter from Bolivia: Leasing the rain. *New Yorker,* April 8, 43–53.

Finnemore, M., and K. Sikkink. 2001. Taking stock: The constructivist research program in international relations and comparative politics. *Annual Review of Political Science* 4:391–416.

Flora, J., C. Flora, F. Campana, M. García, and E. Fernández. 2006. El capital social y las coaliciones de convencimiento: Ejemplos de temas ambientales en Ecuador. In Rhoades, 435–50.

Fondo Indígena. 2007a. XXVII reunión del consejo directivo. *Boletín Indígena* 5(2): 2.

———. 2007b. Estar informados es construir el poder: Nace el Sistema de Información de Pueblos Indígenas SIPI. *Boletín Indígena* 5(2): 8–9.

————. 2007c. Participación y politicas públicas para pueblos indígenas. *Boletín Indígena* 5(2): 5.

Foucault, M. 1991. Governmentality. In Burchell, Gordon, and Miller, 87–104.

Foweraker, J. 1998. Social movements and citizenship rights in Latin America. In Vellinga, 271–97.

Fox, D. 1998. *An ethnography of four non-governmental development organizations.* Lewiston, N.Y.: The Edwin Mellen Press.

Fox, J. 1996. How does civil society thicken? The political construction of social capital in Mexico. *World Development* 24:1089–1103.

Fox, R., and O. Starn. 1997. *Between resistance and revolution: Cultural politics and social protest.* New Brunswick, N.J.: Rutgers University Press.

Freeman, C. 2001. Is local:global as feminine:masculine? Rethinking the gender of globalization. *Signs* 26:1007–33.

Friedman, E., and K. Hochstetler. 2001. Sovereign limits and regional opportunities for global civil society in Latin America. *Latin American Research Review* 36(3): 7–35.

Fundación Solón. 1999. *Consulta nacional para discutir y fortalecer la propuesta de ley de aguas.* La Paz: Fundación Solón.

————. 2000. ¿Que hemos conseguido? *Tunupa* 5:12.

Fundación Tierra, ed. 2007. *Los nietos de la reforma agraria.* La Paz: Fundación Tierra.

Fuss, D. 1990. *Essentially speaking: Feminism, nature and difference.* London: Routledge.

Gabbert, W. 2001. Social categories, ethnicity and the state in Yucatán, Mexico. *Journal of Latin American Studies* 33:459–84.

Gandarillas, H., L. Salazar, L. C. Sánchez, and P. de Zutter. 1994. *Dios da el agua. ¿Que hacen los proyectos? Manejo de agua y organización campesina.* La Paz: Hisbol / PRIV.

Ganokar, D. 2001. On alternative modernities. In *Alternative modernities,* ed. D. Ganokar, 1–23. Durham, N.C.: Duke University Press.

García, F., ed. 2000. *Sociedades interculturales: Un desafío para el siglo XXI.* Quito: FLACSO.

Gardner, K., and D. Lewis. 2000. Dominant paradigms overturned or "business as usual"? Development discourse and the White Paper on International Development. *Critique of Anthroplogy* 20:15–29.

Garland, A. 2000. The politics and administration of social development in Latin America. In Tulchin and Garland, 1–14.

Garrard-Burnett, V. 2000. Indians are drunks and drunks are Indians: Alcohol and indigenismo in Guatemala, 1890–1940. *Bulletin of Latin American Research* 19:341–56.

Gathorne-Hardy, F. 1999. Professionalisation. In *A feminist glossary of geography,* ed. L. McDowell, and J. Sharp, 220. London: Arnold.

Gelles, P. 2000. *Water and power in highland Peru: The cultural politics of irrigation and development.* New Brunswick, N.J.: Rutgers University Press.

Gianotten, V., and T. de Wit. 1985. *Organización campesina: El objectivo político de la educación popular y la investigación participativa.* Amsterdam: Centrum voor Studie en Documentatie van Latinjins America.

Gibson-Graham, J. K. 1996. *The end of capitalism as we knew it.* Oxford: Blackwell.

Ginsburg, F. 1997. "From little things, big things grow": Indigenous media and cultural activism. In *Between resistance and revolution,* ed. O. Starn, 118–44. New Brunswick, N.J.: Rutgers University Press.

Godenzzi, J. 1996. Educacion bilingue e interculturalidad en los Andes y la Amazonia. *Revista Andina* 28:559–81.

Goldman, M. 2005. *Imperial nature: The World Bank and the making of the "green" neo-liberalism.* New Haven, Conn.: Yale University Press.

———. 2007. How "Water for All!" became hegemonic: The power of the World Bank and its transnational policy networks. *Geoforum* 38:786–800.

Gordon, C. 1991. Government rationality: An introduction. In Burchell, Gordon, and Miller, 1–52.

Gore, M. S. 2003. *Social development: Challenges faced in an unequal and plural society.* Jaipur, India: Rawat Publications.

Gorjestani, N. 2000. *Cultural diversity in the 21st century: The role of indigenous development.* Kuala Lumpur: World Bank Global Knowledge Fair.

Grenier, L. 1998. *Working with indigenous knowledge: A guide for researchers.* Ottawa: IDRC.

Grewal, I., and C. Kaplan, eds. 1994. *Scattered hegemonies: Postmodernity and transnational feminist practices.* Minneapolis: University of Minnesota Press.

Grillo, E. 1998. Development or decolonization in the Andes? In Apffel-Marglin and PRATEC, 193–243.

Grindle, M. 2000. The social agenda and the politics of reform in Latin America. In Tulchim and Garland, 17–52.

Grootaert, C., and D. Narayan. 2001. *Local institutions, poverty and household welfare in Bolivia.* Washington, D.C.: World Bank.

Grosz, E. 1994. *Volatile bodies: Towards a corporeal feminism.* Bloomington: Indiana University Press.

Groves, L., and R. Hinton, eds. 2004. *Inclusive aid: Changing power and relationships in international development.* London: Earthscan.

GTZ. 2000. *Portfolio actual de la GTZ en el Ecuador* Quito: GTZ.

———. 2004a. Services of the promotion of good governance. Eschborn, Germany: GTZ.

———. 2004b. Estudio sobre la cooperación alemana con nacionalidades y organizaciones indígenas en Bolivia, Ecuador y Guatemala. Eschborn, Germany: GTZ.

———. 2004c. Estudio sobre la cooperación alemana con nacionalidades y organizaciones indígenas en Bolivia, Ecuador y Guatemala: Tomo II, Estudio de países. Eschborn, Germany: GTZ.

Guerrero, A. 1997. The construction of a ventriloquist's image: Liberal discourse and the 'miserable Indian race' in late 19th century Ecuador. *Journal of Latin American Studies* 29:555–90.

Guerrero, F., and P. Ospina. 2003. *El poder de la comunidad: Ajuste structural y movimiento indígena en los Andes ecuatorianos.* Buenos Aires: CLACSO.

Gupta, A., and J. Ferguson, eds. 1997. *Culture, power, place: Explorations in critical anthropology.* Durham, N.C.: Duke University Press.

Gwynne, R., and C. Kay. 2004a. The alternatives to neoliberalism. In Gwynne and Kay 2004b, 253–67.

Gwynne, R. and C. Kay, 2004b. *Latin America transformed: Globalization and modernity.* 2nd ed. London: Arnold.

Haas, P. 1990. *Saving the mediterranean: The politics of international environmental cooperation.* New York: Columbia University Press.

———. 2002. Introduction: Epistemic communities and international policy coordination. *International Organization* 46:1–35.

Hahn, D. 1996. The use and abuse of ethnicity: The case of the Bolivian CSUTCB. *Latin American Perspectives* 23(2): 91–106.

Hajer, M. 1995. *The politics of environmental discourse: Ecological modernization and the policy process.* Oxford: Oxford University Press.

Hale, C. R. 2002. Does multiculturalism menace? Governance, cultural rights and the politics of identity in Guatemala. *Journal of Latin American Studies* 34:485–524.

Hall, S. 1989. The toad in the garden: Thatcherism among the theorists. In Nelson and Grossberg, 35–57.

———. 1996. Introduction: Who needs identity? In *Questions of cultural identity,* ed. S. Hall, and P. de Gay, 1–17. London: Sage.

Halpern, A., and F. Winddance Twine. 2000. Antiracist activism in Ecuador: Black-Indian community alliances. *Race and Class* 42(2): 19–31.

Hanagan, M., L. Moch, and W. te Brake, eds. 1998. *Challenging authority: The historical study of contentious politics.* Minneapolis: University of Minnesota Press.

Hans Seidel Foundation. 1997. Special issue on Mujer. *Yamaipacha* (Quito) 2.

Harris, O. 2002. The myth of conquest. Paper presented at seminar of the Centre for Latin American Studies, January 21, University of Cambridge.

Harriss, J., and P. De Renzio. 1997. "Missing link" or analytically missing? The concept of social capital. *Journal of International Development* 9:919–37.

Harriss, J. 2002. *Depoliticising development: The World Bank and social capital.* London: Anthem Press.

Harvey, D. 1989. *The condition of postmodernity.* Oxford: Blackwell.

———. 2000. *Spaces of hope.* Edinburgh: Edinburgh University Press.

Havemann, P. 2000. Enmeshed in the web? Indigenous peoples' rights in the network society. In *Global social movements,* ed. R. Cohen, and S. Rai, 18–32. London: Athlone.

Healy, K. 1994. *The recovery of traditional cultural resources for development in Bolivia.* Paper presented at the congress of the Latin American Studies Association, 10–12 March, Atlanta, Ga.

———. 1996. Ethnodevelopment of Bolivia's indigenous communities: Emerging paradigms. In *Tiwanaku and its hinterland,* ed. A. Kolata, 241–63. Washington, D.C.: Smithsonian Institution Press.

———. 2000. *Building networks of social capital for grassroots development among indigenous communities in Bolivia and Mexico.* Paper presented at Conference on Social Capital, April, Middlebury College.

———. 2001a. *Llamas, weavings and organic chocolate: Multicultural grassroots development experience from the Andes and Amazon of Bolivia.* South Bend, Ind.: University of Notre Dame Press.

———. 2001b. *Federations and foreign aid in Bolivia: Four pathways to prominence in grassroots development.* Paper presented at the congress of the Latin America Studies Association, September 6–8, Washington, D.C.

Heijdra, H. 1996. *Particpación y exclusión indígena en el desarrollo.* Santa Cruz, Bolivia: APCOB.

Hentschel, J., and W. Waters. 2002. Rural poverty in Ecuador: Assessing rural realities for the development of anti-poverty programs. *World Development* 30:33–47.

Hershberg, E., and F. Rosen, eds. 2006. *Latin America after neoliberalism: Turning the tide in the 21st Century?* New York: New Press.

Hickey, S., and G. Mohan, eds. 2004. *Participation: From tyranny to transformation?* London: Zed Books.

Hidalgo, M., ed. 1999. *Ciudadanías emergentes: Experiencias democráticas de desarrollo local.* Quito: Abya-Yala.

Hinton, R. 2004. Enabling inclusive aid: Changing power and relationships in international development. In Groves and Hinton, 210–20.

hooks, b. 1984. *Feminist theory: From margin to center.* Boston: South End Press.

Hooper, C. 2000a. Disembodiment, embodiment and the construction of hegemonic masculinity. In *Political economy, power and the body: Global perspectives,* ed. G. Youngs, 31–51. Basingstoke, England: Palgrave-Macmillan.

———. 2000b. Masculinities in transition: The case of globalization. In Marchand and Sisson Runyan, 59–73.

Howard-Malverde, R., and A. Canessa. 1995. The school in the Quechua and Aymara communities of highland Bolivia. *International Journal of Educational Development* 15:231–43.

Hudson, A. 1999. Beyond the borders: Globalization, sovereignty and extra-territoriality. In *Boundaries, territory and postmodernity,* ed. D. Newman, 89–105. London: Frank Cass.

Huntington, S. 1996. *The clash of civilizations and the remaking of the world order.* New York: Simon and Schuster.

Huntington, S., and E. Harrison. 2000. *Culture matters: How values shape human progress.* Cambridge, Mass.: Harvard University Press.

Hurtado, J. 1986. *El Katarismo.* La Paz: Hisbol.

Hyatt, S. B. 1997. Poverty in a post-welfare landscape: Tenant management policies, self-governance and the democratization of knowledge in Great Britain. In Shore and Wright, 217–38.

Hyden, G. 1997. Civil society, social capital and development: Dissection of a complex discourse. *Studies in Comparative International Development* 32(1): 3–30.

Hyndman, J. 2001, *Re-stating feminist geography.* Paper presented at annual meeting of American Association of Geographers, Feb. 27–March 3, New York.

Ibarra, A. 1992. *Los indigenas y el estado en el Ecuador.* Quito: Abya-Yala.

IBIS. 2004. Organizational development of the indigenous movement in Ecuador. Application for development funding. Unpublished report.

IBIS and ECUARUNARI. 1999. Grant proposal for reconstruction and strengthening of the Kichua *Pueblos* of Ecuador. Quito: IBIS-Dinamarca—representación Ecuador / ECUARUNARI.

IEDECA, CICDA, and OSTROM. 1995. Propuestas de apoyo al riego campesino: Memorias del taller, Quito.

INRA. 2006. *Plan nacional de saneamiento y titulación.* La Paz: Viceministerio de Tierras.

Inter-American Development Bank. 1998. *Strategy for integrated water resources management.* Washington, D.C.: IADB.

———. 2004. *Gender mainstreaming plan, 2003–5.* Washington, D.C.: IADB.

———. 2005. Empowering indigenous women. http://www.iadb.org/, accessed June 22, 2005.

———. 2006. *Operational policy for indigenous peoples and strategy for indigenous development.* Washington, D.C.: IADB.

ITDG. 1991. *Manejo de agua y adecuación de tecnología en la región Andina.* Lima: Intermediate Technology-ITDG.

Izko, X. 1992. *La doble frontera: Ecología, política y ritual en el altiplano central.* La Paz: Hisbol.

Jacomé, R. 1998. *Promover la equidad entre hombres y mujeres: Una necesidad sentida en el campo agropecuario.* Quito: INIAP / COSUDE.

Jameson, F. 1991. *Postmodernism, or the cultural logic of late capitalism.* Durham, N.C.: Duke University Press.

Jelin, E., and E. Hershberg. 1996. *Constructing democracy: Human rights, citizenship, and society in Latin America.* Boulder, Colo.: Westview Press.

Johnston, R., D. Gregory, G. Pratt, and M. Watts. 2000. *The dictionary of human geography.* Oxford: Blackwell.

Jokisch, B., and J. Pribilsky. 2002. The panic to leave: Economic crisis and the "new emigration" from Ecuador. *International Migration* 40:75–102.

Jolly, S. 2002. *Gender and culture change.* Brighton, England: Institute of Development Studies.

Joseph, G., and D. Nugent, eds. 1994. *Everyday forms of state formation: Revolution and the negotiation of rule in modern Mexico.* Durham, N.C.: Duke University Press.

Kabeer, N. 1994. *Reversed realities: Gender hierarchies in development thought.* London: Verso.

Kaghram, S., J. Riker, and K. Sikkink. 2002. From Santiago to Seattle: Transnational advocacy groups restructuring world politics. In *Restructuring world politics: Transnational social movements, networks, and norms,* ed. S. Kaghram, J. Riker, and K. Sikkink, 3–23. Minneapolis: University of Minnesota Press.

Kane, L. 2001. *Popular education and social change in Latin America.* London: Latin America Bureau.

Kaplan, C. 1995. A world without boundaries: The Body Shop's Trans/National Geographic. *Social Text* 43:45–66.

Katz, C. 2001. On the grounds of globalization: A topography for feminist political engagement. *Signs* 26:1213–34.

Kähkönen, S. 1999. *Does social capital matter in water and sanitation delivery? A review of literature.* Washington, D.C.: World Bank.

Kearney, M., and S. Varese. 1995. Latin America's indigenous peoples: Changing identities and forms of resitance. In *Capital, power and inequality in Latin America,* ed. S. Halensky, and R. Harris, 207–31. Boulder, Colo.: Westview Press.

Keck, M., and K. Sikkink. 1998. *Activists beyond borders: Advocacy networks in international politics.* Ithaca, N.Y.: Cornell University Press.

Keese, J., and M. Freire. 2006. Decentralisation and NGO-municipal government collaboration in Ecuador. *Development in Practice* 16:114–27.

Kelly, P. 1997. Globalization, power and the politics of scale in the Philippines. *Geoforum* 28:151–71.

Kimmel, M. 2000. *Men, masculinities and development.* Bahia: O Desafio da Diferenta / UFBA.

Klarén, P., and T. Bassert, eds. 1986. *Promise of development: Theories of change in Latin America.* Boulder, Colo.: Westview Press.

Kleymeyer, C. 1993. *La expresión cultural y el desarrollo de base.* Quito: Inter-American Foundation / Abya-Yala.

Kofas, J. 2001. The IMF, the World Bank, and U.S. foreign policy in Ecuador, 1956–1966. *Latin American Perspectives* 28(5): 50–83.

Kohl, B. 2001. ONGs y participación popular en las areas rurales de Bolivia. In de la Fuente, 73–107.

———. 2002. Stabilizing neoliberalism in Bolivia: Popular participation and privatization. *Political Geography* 21:449–72.

———. 2003. Nongovernmental organizations as intermediaries for decentralization in Bolivia. *Environment and Planning C: Government and Policy* 21:317–31.

Komvives, K. 1999. *Designing pro-poor water and sewer concessions: Early lessons from Bolivia.* Washington, D.C.: World Bank Private Sector Development Division.

Kondo, D. 1999. Fabricating masculinity. In *Between woman and nation: Nationalisms, transnational feminisms and the state*, ed. C. Kaplan, N. Alarcon, and M. Moallem, 296–319. Durham, N.C.: Duke University Press.

Korovkin, T. 2001. Reinventing the communal tradition: Indigenous peoples, civil society and democratization in Andean Ecuador. *Latin American Research Review* 36(3): 37–67.

Kothari, U. 2005. Authority and expertise: The professionalisation of international development and the ordering of dissent. *Antipode* 37:425–46.

Kowii, A. 1992. El derecho internacional y el derecho de los pueblos indios. In *Pueblos indios, estado y derecho*, ed. CEN, 213–27. Quito: CEN.

Krainer, A. 1996. *Educación intercultural bilingue en el Ecuador*. Quito: Abya-Yala.

Kyle, D. 1999. The Otavalo trade diaspora: Social capital and transnational entrepreneurship. *Ethnic and Racial Studies* 22:422–46.

Lander, E. 2001. Los derechos de propiedad intelectual en la geopolítica: El saber de la sociedad global del conocimiento. *Revista del Centro Andino de Estudios Internacionales* 2:79–112.

Larrea, A. M., and F. Larrea. 1999. Participación ciudadana, relaciones interétnicas y construcción del poder local en Saquisilí. In Hidalgo, 129–52.

Larrea, F. 1999. Frontera étnica y masculinidades en el ejercicio del gobierno local. *Iconos* 8:87–102.

Larrea, F., J. Cervantes, and N. Viedma. 1999. *Desarrollo social y gestión municipal en el Ecuador*. Quito: CODEPLAN / Presidencia de la República.

Larrea, M. 2002. Proyecto de desarrollo de pueblos indigenas de Ecuador PRODEPINE. Consultoria "Incorporacion del enfoque de genero en metodologia de inversiones publicas": Informe Final. Unpublished document, Quito.

Larreamendy, P. 2003. Indigenous networks: Politics and development interconnectivity among the Shuar in Ecuador. PhD diss., University of Cambridge.

Larson, B., and O. Harris, with E. Tandeter, eds. 1995. *Ethnicity, markets and migration in the Andes: At the crossroads of anthropology and history*. Durham, N.C.: Duke University Press.

Latour, B. 1993. *We have never been modern*. London: Harvester Wheatsheaf.

Laurie, N. 2004. Dams. In *Patterned ground: Entanglements of nature and culture*, ed. S. Harrison, S. Pile, and N. Thrift, 157–59. London: Reaktion.

———. 2005. Establishing development orthodoxy: Negotiating masculinities in the water sector. *Development and Change* 36:527–49.

———. 2007. Introduction: How to dialogue for pro-poor water. *Geoforum* 38:753–55.

———. forthcoming. Gendered urban waters: Gender intersections in private sector participation. *International Journal of Urban and Regional Research*.

Laurie, N., and A. Bonnett. 2002. Adjusting to equity: The contradictions of neoliberalism and the search for racial equality in Peru. *Antipode* 34:28–53.

Laurie, N., with P. Calla. 2004. Development, post-colonialism and feminist political geography. In *Mapping women, making politics: Feminist perspectives on political geography*, ed. L. Staeheli, E. Kofman and L. Peake, 99–122. London: Routledge.

Laurie, N., and C. Crespo. 2003. *An examination of the changing contexts for developing pro-poor water initiatives via concessions.* London: DFID.

———. 2007. Deconstructing the best case scenario: Lessons from La Paz-El Alto. *Geoforum* 38:841–54.

Laurie, N., and S. Marvin. 1999. Globalisation, neoliberalism and negotiated development in the Andes: Water projects and regional identity in Cochabamba, Bolivia. *Environment and Planning A* 31:1401–16.

Laurie, N., R. Andolina, and S. A. Radcliffe. 2002. The excluded "indigenous"? The implications of multi-ethnic policies for water reform in Bolivia. In Sieder, 252–76.

———. Indigenous professionalization: Transnational social reproduction in the Andes. *Antipode* 35:464–91.

———. 2005. Ethnodevelopment: Social movements, creating experts and professionalising indigenous knowledge in Ecuador. *Antipode* 37:470–96.

Lefebvre, H. 1991. *The production of space.* Oxford: Blackwell.

Leftwich, A. 1996. *Democracy and development: Theory and practice.* Cambridge: Polity.

Lehmann, D., and A. Bebbington. 1998. NGOs, the state and the development process: The dilemmas of institutionalization. In Vellinga, 251–69.

Leitner, H. 2003. The politics of scale and networks of spatial connectivity. In *Scale and geographic enquiry: Nature, society and method*, eds. E. Sheppard and R.McMaster, 236–55. Blackwell, Oxford.

León, R. 2003. *Guess who's coming to dinner?* Cochabama, Bolivia: CERES / DFID.

Li, T. M. 2007. *The will to improve: Governmentality, development and the practice of politics.* Durham, N.C.: Duke University Press.

Lind, A. 2000a. Negotiating boundaries: Women's organizations and the politics of restructuring in Ecuador. In Marchand and Sisson Runyan, 161–75.

———. 2000b. Negotiating the transnational: Constructions of poverty and identity among women's NGOs in Bolivia. Paper presented at the congress of the Latin American Studies Association, Miami.

———. 2003. Gender and neoliberal states: Feminists remake the nation in Ecuador. *Latin American Perspectives* 30:181–207.

———. 2005. *Gendered paradoxes: Women's movements, state restructuring and global development in Ecuador.* University Park: Pennsylvania State University Press.

Lipschutz, R. 1996. *Global civil society and global environmental governance: The politics of nature from place to planet.* Albany: State University of New York Press.

Little, J., and O. Jones. 2000. Masculinity, gender and rural policy. *Rural Sociology* 65:621–39.

Llorens, J. 1999. El sitio de los indígenas en el siglo XXI: Tensiones transculturales de la globalización. In *Cultura y globalización*, ed. C. Degregori, and G. Portocarrero 139–62. Lima, Peru: Universidad Católica del Perú/Instituto de Estudios Peruanos/Universidad del Pacífico.

Lloyd, J. 1998. *The politics of indigenous identity in Ecuador and the emergence of transnational discourses of power and subversion.* PhD diss., University of Liverpool.

Lozano, A. 2000. Propuesta: Circunscripciones territoriales indígenas y afro-ecuatorianas. Unpublished working paper, CODENPE. Quito.

López, A. 1993. La demanda indígena de la pluriculturalidad y multietnicidad: El tratamiento de la prensa. In *Los indios y el estado-país. Pluriculturalidad y multietnicidad en el Ecuador: Contribuciones al debate*, ed. E. Albán, 21–59. Quito: Abya-Yala.

López, L. 2000. *Status of health and education in indigenous communities: Indigenous peoples and social sector projects in Latin America*. Paper presented at joint workshop of the World Bank, Inter-American Development Bank, and Pan American Health Organisation, April 11–12, Washington, D.C.

Lucas, K. 2000. *La rebelión de los indios*. Quito: Abya-Yala.

Lucero, J. A. 2001. Crisis and contention in Ecuador. *Journal of Democracy* 12(2): 59–73.

———. 2002. Arts of unification: Political representation and indigenous movements in Bolivia and Ecuador. PhD diss., Princeton University.

———. 2003. Locating the "Indian Problem": Community, nationality and contradiction in Ecuadorian indigenous politics. *Latin American Perspectives* 30:23–48.

———. 2006. Representing "real Indians": The challenges of indigenous authenticity and strategic constructivism in Ecuador and Bolivia. *Latin American Research Review* 41:31–56.

Lucero, J.A., and M.E. Garcia. 2007. In the shadows of success: Indigenous politics in Peru and Ecuador. In *Highland Indians and the modern state in Ecuador*, eds. K. Clark and M. Becker, 234–47. Pittsburgh, Penn.: University of Pittsburgh Press.

Luoma, J. 2002. Water for profit. *Mother Jones*, November-December, 34–37 and 88.

Luykx, A. 1999. *The citizen factory: Schooling and cultural production in Bolivia*. Albany: State University of New York Press.

Macklem, P., and Morgan, E. 2000. Indigenous rights in the Inter-American system: The Amicus brief of the Assembly of First Nations in Awas Tingni v. Republic of Nicaragua. *Human Rights Quarterly* 22:569–602.

Minsterio de Agricultura y Ganadería. 2000. *Programa de transferencias de los sistemas de riego*. Quito: World Bank.

Makoba, J. W. 2002. Nongovernmental organizations and Third World development. *Journal of Third World Studies* (Spring): 53–63.

Mallon, F. 1995. *Peasant and nation: The making of postcolonial Mexico and Peru*. Berkeley: University of California Press.

Mamani, C., and M. E. Choque. 2001. Reconstitución del ayllu y derechos de los pueblos indígenas: El movimiento indio en los Andes de Bolivia. *Journal of Latin American Anthropology* 6:202–24.

Marchand, M., and J. Parpart, eds. 1995. *Feminism/Postmodernism/Development*. London: Routledge.

Marchand, M., and A. Runyan. 2000. *Gender and global restructuring*. New York: Routledge.

Marcus, G. 1995. Ethnography in/of the world system: The emergence of multi-sited ethnography. *Annual Review of Anthropology* 24:95–117.

Marston, S. 2000. The social construction of scale. *Progress in Human Geography* 24: 219–42.

———. 2003. A long way from home: Domesticating the social production of scale. In Sheppard and McMaster, 170–91.

Martin, P. 2003. *The globalization of contentious politics: The Amazonian indigenous rights movement.* New York: Routledge.

Martínez Flores, A. 1999. *Ecuador: Consultations with the Poor. A study to inform the World Development Report 2000/1 on poverty and development.* Washington, D.C.: CEPLAES / World Bank Poverty Group.

———. 2000. *El enfoque de género, las mujeres y los organismos no gubernamentales en el desarrollo local.* Quito: CEPLAES.

Martinez, L. 2003. Endogenous peasant responses to structural adjustment: Ecuador in comparative Andean perspective. In *Rural progress, rural decay: Neoliberal adjustment policies and local initiatives,* ed. Liisa North and John Cameron, 85–105. Bloomfield, Conn.: Kumarian Press.

Marvin, S., and N. Laurie. 1999. An emerging logic of urban water management, Bolivia. *Urban Studies* 36:341–57.

Massey, D. 1984. Introduction: geography matters. In *Geography matters! A reader,* ed. D. Massey, and J. Alle, 1–11. Cambridge: Cambridge University Press.

Massey, D., and P. Jess, eds. 1995. *A place in the world? Places, cultures and globalization.* Oxford: Oxford University Press.

Mato, D. 1997. Globalización, organizaciones indígenas de América Latina y el "Festival of American Folklife" de la Smithsonian Institution. *Revista de Investigaciones Folklóricas* 12:112–19.

———. 1998. The transnational making of representations of gender, ethnicity and culture: Indigenous peoples' organizations at the Smithsonian Institution's Festival. *Cultural Studies* 12:193–209.

———. 2000. On global and local agents and the social making of transnational identities and related agendas in "Latin" America. *Identities* 4:167–212.

Mawdsley, E., J. Townsend, G. Porter, and P. Oakley. 2002. *Knowledge, power and development agendas: NGOs north and south.* Oxford: INTRAC.

Mayer, E. 1991. Peru in deep trouble: Mario Vargas Llosa's "Inquest in the Andes" re-examined. *Cultural Anthropology* 6:466–504.

Mayer, M., and K. Rankin. 2002. Social capital and community development: A North/South perspective. *Antipode* 34:804–8.

McCall, C. 2005. The complexity of intersectionality. *Signs* 30:1771–1800.

McDowell, L. 2001. Linking scales: Or, how research about gender and organizations raises new issues for economic geography. *Journal of Economic Geography* 1:227–50.

McNeish, J. 2001. Pueblo chico, infierno grande: Globalisation and the politics of participation in highland Bolivia. PhD diss., University of London, Goldsmith's College.

Medina, J. 2001. Cultura, civilización e interculturalidad: Algunas definiciones básicas. *La encrucijada cultural. Anuario COSUDE 2001.* La Paz: Plural Editores.

———. 2003. Municipio indígena: Historia de un concepto. In *Municipio indígena: La profundización de la descentralización en un estado multicultural,* ed. J. Medina, 13–31. La Paz: Ministerio de Participación Popular.

Mejia, M., and J. Hidalgo. 2006. Del mapa al Sistema de Información Geográfica SIG: La experiencia del atlas del cantón Cotacachi. In R. Rhoades, 451–56.

Memoria. 1998. *Memoria: Segundo taller consultativo de análisis de proyecto de ley de los pueblos y nacionalidades del Ecuador.* Quito: Instituto "El Inca."

Mitchell, K. 1997a. Transnational discourse: Bringing geography back in. *Antipode* 29:101–14.

———. 1997b. Transnational subjects: Constituting the cultural citizen in an era of Pacific Rim capital. In Ong, and Nonini, 228–58.

Mitchell, K., S. Marston, and C. Katz. 2003. Life's work: An introduction, review and critique. *Antipode* 35:415–42.

Moghadam, V. 2000. Transnational feminist networks: Collective action in an era of globalisation. *International Sociology* 15(1): 57–85.

Mohanty, C. 1991. Cartographies of struggle: Third World feminism and the politics of feminism. In *Third world women and the politics of feminism,* ed. C. Mohanty, A. Russo, and L. Torres, 1–47. Bloomington: Indiana University Press.

———. 1998. Crafting feminist genealogies: On the geography and politics of home, nation and community. In *Talking visions: Multicultural feminism in a transnational age,* ed. E. Shohat, 485–500. New York: MIT Press.

Molyneux, M. 2002. Gender and the silences of social capital: Lessons from Latin America. *Development and Change* 33:167–88.

Molyneux, M., and N. Craske. 2002. The local, the regional and the global: Transforming the politics of rights. In Craske and Molyneux, 1–31.

Moreiras, A. 1998. Global fragments: A second Latinamericanism. In *The cultures of globalization,* ed. F. Jameson, and M. Miyoshi, 81–102. London: Duke University Press.

Morris, A., and S. Lowder. 1992. *Decentralization in Latin America: An evaluation.* New York: Praeger.

Moncayo, P. 2004. Ecuador: El reto de la descentralización. *Tendencia* 1:85–97.

Moser, C. 1993. Adjustment from below: Low-income women, time and the triple role in Guayaquil, Ecuador. In *"Viva": Women and popular protest in Latin America,* ed. S. A. Radcliffe and S. Westwood, 173–96. London: Routledge.

Mujer y Ajuste. 1996. *El ajuste estructural en Perú: Una mirada desde las mujeres.* Lima: Ediciones Mujeres y Ajuste.

Muñoz, J. P. 1999. Indígenas y gobiernos locales: Entre la plurinacionalidad y la ciudadanía cantonal. In Hidgalgo, 39–62.

Muratorio, B., ed. 1994. *Imágenes e imagineros: Representaciones de los indígenas ecuatorianos, siglos XIX y XX.* Quito: FLACSO.

Murra, J. 1956. *The economic organization of the Inca State.* Chicago: University of Chicago Press.

Murray, W. 2006. *Geographies of globalization.* New York: Routledge.

Mychalejko, C. 2007. Ascendant Copper risks losing mining project in Ecuador. *ZSpace,* http://www.zmag.org/zspace/, accessed December 14, 2007.

Nagar, R., V. Lawson, L. McDowell, and S. Hanson. 2002. Locating globalization: Feminist (re)readings of the subjects and spaces of globalization. *Economic Geography* 78:257–84.

Narayan, D. 1999. *Bonds and bridges: Social capital and poverty.* Washington, D.C.: World Bank Poverty Group.

Narayan, D., and L. Pritchett. 1999. Cents and sociability: Household income and social capital in rural Tanzania. *Economic Development and Cultural Change* 47:871–897.

Nash, J., and H. Safa, eds. 1980. *Sex and class in Latin America.* New York: J. F.Bergin.

Nederveen Pieterse, J. 2001. *Development theory: Deconstructions/reconstructions.* London: Sage.

Nelson, C., and L. Grossberg, eds. 1988. *Marxism and the interpretation of culture.* London: MacMillan.

Nelson, D. 1999. *A finger in the wound: Body politics in quincentenial Guatemala.* Durham, N.C.: Duke University Press.

Nelson, P. 1996. Internationalising economic and environmental policy: Transnational NGO networks and the World Bank's expanding influence. *Millennium: Journal of International Studies* 25:605–33.

———. 2001. Information, location and legitimacy: The changing bases of civil society involvement in international economic policy. In Edwards and Gaventa, 59–72.

New York Declaration. 2005. Indigenous women speak out on development: Pre-Beijing+10 meeting declaration. Unpublished statement, New York.

Nielsen, E. H., and K. Simonsen. 2003. Scaling from below: Practices, strategies and urban spaces. *European Planning Studies* 11:911–27.

Nickson, A. 2001. Tapping the market—Can private enterprise supply water to the poor? *Id21 Insights* 37:1–4.

Nickson, A., and C. Vargas. 2002. The limitations of water regulation: The failure of the Cochabamba concession in Bolivia. *Bulletin of Latin American Research* 21:99–120.

Nicol, A. 2000. *Adopting a sustainable livelihoods approach to water politics: Implications for policy and practice.* London: Overseas Development Institute.

Nieto, S. 1993. El problema indígena. In *Los indios y el estado-país,* ed. E. Albán, 61–86. Quito: Abya-Yala.

Nonini, D., and A. Ong. 1997. Chinese transnationalism as an alternative modernity. In Ong and Nonini, 3–33.

North, L., and J. Cameron. 2000. Grassroots-based rural development strategies: Ecuador in comparative perspective. *World Development* 28:1751–66.

Núñez del Prado, J., and D. Pacheco. 2001. *Visiones sobre desarrollo rural.* Quito: Friedrich Ebert Stiftung—ILDIS.

Nussbaum, M., and J. Glover, eds. 1995. *Women, culture and development: A study of human capabilities.* Oxford: Clarendon.

Oaxaca Declaration. 2002. *Declaration from the First Summit of Indigenous Women of the Americas.* www.reddesalud.org/english/, accessed June 22, 2005.

OED Evaluations. 2003. *Implementation of Operational Directive 4.20 on Indigenous Peoples: An evaluation of results.* Washington, D.C.: World Bank.

Ohmae, K. 1995. *The end of the nation-state: The rise of regional economies.* London: HarperCollins.

Oliart, P. 2001a. *University life and masculine identities among education students in Ayacucho.* Paper presented at a workshop of the Development Studies Institute, Copenhagen.

———. 2001b. *Vida universitario e identidades masculinas en Ayacucho después de la guerra.* Lima: Fundación Carlos Chagas.

———. 2004. *The World Bank state reforms and their implications for indigenous cultures of Latin America.* Paper presented at a workshop of the *Americas Research Group Dialogue,* April, University of Newcastle, England.

Olowaili Declaration. 2000. Olowaili Declaration: Third Meeting of Indigenous Women of the Americas. Third Continental Meeting of the Indigenous Women of the First Nations Abya Yala, March 5–8, Panama City. www.afn.ca/, accessed September 27, 2002.

Omi, M., and H. Winant. 1994. *Racial formations in the United States.* London: Routledge.

O'Neill, K. 2003. Decentralization as an electoral strategy. *Comparative Political Studies* 36:1068–91.

Ong, A. 1996. Cultural citizenship as subject-making: Immigrants negotiate racial and cultural boundaries in the United States. *Current Anthropology* 37:737–51.

———. 1999. *Flexible citizenship: The cultural logics of transnationality.* London: Duke University Press.

———. 2000. Graduated sovereignty in South-East Asia. *Theory, Culture and Society* 17(4): 55–75.

Ong, A., and D. Nonini, eds. 1997. *Ungrounded empires: The cultural politics of modern Chinese transnationalism.* London: Routledge.

Orlove, B. 1993. Putting race in its place: Order in colonial and postcolonial Peruvian geography. *Social Research* 60:302–36.

Orellana, R. 2000. Municipalization and indigenous peoples in Bolivia: Impacts and perspectives. In Assies, van der Haar, and Hoekema, 181–96.

Orta, A. 2001. Remebering the ayllu, remaking the nation: Indignous scholarship and activism in the Bolivian Andes. *Journal of Latin American Anthropology* 6:198–201.

Ortiz, S. 1999. Participación ciudadana y desarrollo local: Algunas pistas de reflexión. In Hidalgo, 63–83.

———. 2004. *Cotacachi: Una apuesta por la democracia participativa.* Quito: FLACSO.

Ospina, P. 2006. *En las fisuras del poder: Movimiento indigena, cambio social y gobiernos locales.* Quito: IEE.

Oxfam America. 1999. Grant BOL/85–99. Unpublished proposal, Lima.

———. 2000. *1999 Annual Report.* Boston: Oxfam America.

———. 2004. CONAMAQ: Consejo Nacional de Ayllus y Markas de Qollasuyu news brief. www.oxfam.org/, accessed December 4, 2004.

Pacari, N. 1996. Taking on the neoliberal agenda. *NACLA Report on the Americas* 29(5): 23–32.

———. 1998. El régimen de aguas en el Ecuador desde el punto de vista indígena-campesino. In Boelens and Dávila, 298–305.

———. 2002. La participación politica de la mujer indígena en el congreso ecuatoriano: Una tarea pendiente. In *Mujeres en el parlamento*, ed. M. Mendez and J. Ballington, 45–60. Stockholm: International Institute for Democracy and Electoral Assistance.

Pachamama. 2000. La Escuela de Formación de Mujeres de ECUARINARI. Special issue. *Boletín de las Mujeres de la Confederación de Pueblos de la Nacionalidad Kichwa del Ecuador ECUARUNARI*, April.

PADEM. 2000. *Empoderamiento de las comunidades campesinas e indígenas.* La Paz: PADEM.

Palenzuela, P. 1999. Etnicidad y modelos de auto-organización económica en el occidente de Guatemala. In *Construcciones étnicas y dinámica sociocultural en America Latina*, ed. K. Koonings and P. Silva, 53–76. Quito: Abya-Yala.

Pallares, A. 2002. *From peasant struggles to Indian resistance: The Ecuadorian Andes in the late twentieth century.* Norman: University of Oklahoma Press.

Parekh, B. 1995. Liberalism and colonialism: A critique of Locke and Mill. In *The decolonization of imagination: Culture, knowledge and power*, ed. J. Nederveen Pieterse and B. Parekh, 81–98. London: Zed Books.

Parpart, J. L. 1995. Deconstructing the development "expert": Gender, development and the "vulnerable groups." In Marchand and Parpart, 221–43.

Parry, B. 2002. Cultures of knowledge: Investigating intellectual property rights and relations in the Pacific. *Antipode* 34:670–706.

Patiño, A. 1996. Repotencialización de la identidad para un desarrollo comunitario alternativo. *Identidad* 1(1): 30–35.

Patrinos, H. A. 2004. *Indigenous people, poverty and human development in Latin America, 1994–2004.* Washington, D.C.: World Bank.

Patrinos, H. A., and E. Skoufias. 2007. *Economic opportunities for indigenous peoples in Latin America.* Conference edition. Washington, D.C.: World Bank.

Patzi, F. 1998. *Insurgencia y sumisión: Movimientos indígenas-campesinos 1983–1998.* La Paz: Comuna.

Paulson, S. 2002. Placing gender and ethnicity on the bodies of indigenous women and in the work of Bolivian intellectuals. In *Gender's place: Feminist anthropologies of Latin America*, ed. R. Montoya, L. J. Frazier, and J. Hurtig, 135–54. London: Palgrave Macmillan.

Paulson, S., and P. Calla. 2000. Gender and ethnicity in Bolivian politics: Transformation or paternalism? *Journal of Latin American Anthropology* 5:112–49.

Peet, R., and M. Watts. 1996. *Liberation ecologies: Environment, development, social movements*. London: Routledge.

Peredo, E. 2004. *Una aproximacion a la problematica de género y etnicidad en America Latina*. Santiago: CEPAL Unidad Mujer y Desarrollo Secretaria Ejecutiva.

Perreault, T. 2003. Changing places: Transnational networks, ethnic politics, and community development in the Ecuadorian Amazon. *Political Geography* 22:61–88.

Perry, G., and S. Burki. 1998. *La larga marcha: Una agenda de reformas para la próxima década en América Latina y el Caribe*. Washington, D.C.: World Bank.

Phillips, L. 1987. Women, development and the state in rural Ecuador. In *Rural women and state policy in Latin America*, ed. C. D. Deere and M. León, 105–23. Boulder, Colo.: Westview Press.

Piori, M., and C. Sabel. 1984. *The second industrial divide: Possibilities for prosperity*. New York: Basic Books.

Plant, R. 1998. *Issues in indigenous poverty and development*. Washington, D.C.: Inter-American Development Bank.

———. 2002. Latin America's multiculturalism: Economic and agrarian dimensions. In Sieder, 208–26.

Plata, W., G. Colque, and N. Calle. 2003. *Visiones de desarrollo en comunidades Aymaras*. La Paz: PIEB.

Platt, T. 1982. *Estado boliviano y ayllu andino*. Lima, Peru: Instituto de Estudios Peruanos.

———. 1987. The Andean experience of Bolivian liberalism, 1825–1900: Roots of rebellion in 19th Century Chayanta Potosí. In S. Stern, 280–323.

Portes, A., L. Guarnizo, and P. Landolt. 1999. The study of transnationalism: Pitfalls and promise of an emergent research field. *Ethnic and Racial Studies* 22:217–37.

Portes, A., and P. Landolt. 2000. Social capital: Promise and pitfalls of its role in development. *Journal of Latin American Studies* 32:529–48.

Portocarrero, G., and P. Oliart. 1989. *El Perú desde la escuela*. Lima, Peru: IAA.

Postero, N. G. 2000. *Bolivia's indígena citizen: Multiculturalism in a neoliberal age*. Paper presented at the congress of the Latin American Studies Association, March 15–18, Miami.

Pottier, J., A. Bicker, and P. Sillitoe. 2003. *Negotiating local knowledge: Power and identity in development*. London: Pluto.

Power, M. 2003. *Rethinking development geographies*. London: Routledge.

Prieto, M. 1998. El liderazgo de las mujeres indígenas: Teniendo puentes entre género y étnia. In Cervone, 6–14.

Prieto, M., C. Cuminao, A. Flores, G. Maldonado, and A. Pequeño. 2004. Las mujeres indígenas y la búsqueda del respeto. In *Mujeres ecuatorianas: Entre las crisis y las oportunidades 1990–2004*, ed. M. Prieto, 155–94. Quito: FLACSO.

PRODEPINE. 1997. *Consejo Nacional de Planificación de los Pueblos Indígenas y Afroecuatorianas, CONPLADEIN: Documento de Proyecto*. Quito: CONPLADEIN / PRODEPINE.

————. 1999. *Manual de seguimiento y evaluación del Prodepine, MASEP-PRODEPINE.* Quito: PRODEPINE.

————. 2001. *Informe de monitoria: Préstamo 4277-EC y 464-EC.* Quito: PRODEPINE.

————. n.d.a. *Etnicidad y pobreza en el Ecuador, población indígena y negra. Proyecciones 2000 y matriz de selección de las parroquias de intervención de PRODEPINE.* Quito: PRODEPINE.

————. n.d.b. *Informe final de la consultoria para la incorporación del enfoque de género en las metodologías de trabajo de PRODEPINE.* Quito: PRODEPINE.

————. n. .d.c. *Preparación y evaluación de proyectos de inversión.* Quito: PRODEPINE.

Pscharaopoulos, G., and H. Patrinos. 1994. *Indigenous peoples and poverty in Latin America: An empirical analysis.* Washington, D.C.: World Bank.

Puiggrós, A. 1999. *Neoliberalism and education in the Americas.* Boulder, Colo.: Westview Press.

Putnam, R. 1988. Diplomacy and domestic politics: The logic of two-level games. *International Organization* 42:427–60.

————. 1993. *Making democracy work: Civic traditions in modern Italy.* Princeton, N.J.: Princeton University Press.

Radcliffe, S. A. 1996. Gendered nations: Nostalgia, development and territory in Ecuador. *Gender, place and culture* 3(1): 5–21.

————. 1999. Latina labour: Restructuring of work and renegotiations of gender relations in contemporary Latin America. *Environment and Planning A* 30(2): 1–13.

————. 2001a. Development, the state and transnational political connections: State and subject formation in Latin America. *Global Networks* 1:19–36.

————. 2001b. *Indigenous movement representations in transnational circuits: Tales of social capital and poverty.* Paper presented at the annual conference of the American Association of Geographers, Feb. 27–March 3, New York.

————. 2002. Indigenous women, rights and the nation-state in the Andes. In Craske and Molyneux, 149–72.

————. 2004. Geography of development: Development, civil society and inequality—social capital is almost dead? *Progress in Human Geography* 28(4): 517–27.

————, ed. 2006. *Culture and development in a globalizing world: Geographies, actors and paradigms.* London: Routledge.

Radcliffe, S. A., and N. Laurie. 2006. Indigenous groups, culturally appropriate development, and the socio-spatial fix of Andean development. In Radcliffe, 2006, 83–106.

Radcliffe, S. A., and S. Westwood. 1996. *Remaking the nation: Place, identity and politics in Latin America.* London: Routledge.

Radcliffe, S. A., N. Laurie, and R. Andolina. 2002a. Re-territorialized space and ethnic political participation: Indigenous municipalities in Ecuador. *Space and Polity* 6:289–305.

―――. 2002b. Indigenous people and political transnationalism: Globalization from below meets globalization from above? Unpublished working paper, ESRC Transnational Communities Programme, WPTC-02–05.

―――. 2004. The transnationalization of gender and reimagining Andean indigenous development. *Signs* 29:387–416.

Rahnema, M., ed. 1997. *The post-development reader.* London: Zed Books.

Rai, S. 2003. *Mainstreaming Gender, Democratizing the State? National Machineries for the Advancement of Women.* Manchester: Manchester University Press.

Ramón, G., ed. 1992. Actores de una década ganada: Tribus, comunidades y campesinos en la modernidad. Quito: COMUNIDEC.

Ramos, A. 1998. *Indigenism: Ethnic politics in Brazil.* Madison: University of Wisconsin Press.

Rao, V., and M. Walton. 2004. Culture and public action: Relationality, equality of agency and development. In *Culture and public action: A cross-disciplinary dialogue on development policy,* ed. V. Rao and M. Walton, 3–36. Stanford, Calif.: Stanford University Press.

Rappaport, J., and D. Gow. 1997. Cambio dirigido, movimiento indígena y estereotipos del indio: El estado colombiano y la reubicación de los Nasa. In *Antropología de la modernidad,* ed. V. Uribe and E. Restrepo, 361–99. Bogotá, Colombia: Instituto Colombiano de Antropología.

Rasnake, R. 1989. *Autoridad y poder en los Andes: Los kuraqkuna de Yura.* La Paz: Hisbol.

Razavi, S., and C. Miller. 1995. *Gender mainstreaming: A study of efforts by the UNDP, the World Bank and the ILO to institutionalise gender issues.* UNRISD occasional paper no. 4. Geneva: UNRISD.

Regalsky, P. 2001. Ethnicity and class: The Bolivian State and Andean space management. M.Phil thesis, University of Newcastle, England.

Regalsky, P., and N. Laurie. 2007. "The school, whose place is this"? The deep structures of the hidden curriculum in indigenous education in Bolivia. *Comparative Education* 43(2):231–51.

Revesz, B., and C. Blondet. 1984. *Educación, asesoria y organizaciones populares.* Lima, Peru: Centro de Estudios de y Promoción del Desarrollo.

Rhoades, R., ed. 2006. *Desarrollo con identidad: Comunidad, cultura y sustentabilidad en los Andes.* Quito: Abya-Yala.

Risse-Kappen, T., ed. 1995. *Bringing transnational relations back in.* Cambridge: Cambridge University Press.

Rival, L. 1996. *Hijos del sol, padres del jaguar: Los Huaorani de ayer y hoy.* Quito: Abya-Yala.

Rivera, S. 1987. *Oppressed but not defeated: Peasant struggles among the Aymara and Qhechwa in Bolivia, 1900–1980.* Geneva: UNRISD.

―――. 1990. Liberal democracy and ayllu democracy in Bolivia: The case of northern Potosí. *Journal of Development Studies* 26(4): 97–121.

Rivera, F. 1999. Las aristas del racismo. In *Ecuador racista: Imágenes e identidades*, ed. E. Cervone, and F. Rivera, 19–44. Quito: FLACSO.

Rivera, T. 1999. *Mujeres peruanas, mujeres indígenas: Diferentes rostros, el mismo problema y la misma esperanza.* www.mujeresyhombressigloxxi.perucultural.org.pe, accessed April 2, 2005.

Rivero, F. 2001. Desarrollo rural en el escenario de la participacion popular: El caso de Mizque. In de la Fuente, 39–72.

Rogers, M. 1996. Beyond authenticity: Conservation, tourism and the politics of representation in the Ecuadorian Amazon. *Identities* 3:73–125.

Rodas Morales, R. 2002. Muchas voces, demasiadas silencios: Los discursos de las lideresas del movimiento de mujeres en Ecuador. Working paper no. 4. Quito: Fondo para la Igualdad de Género de ACDI.

Rodriguez, G. 2007. Ecuador: Uprising in demand of a country free from large-scale mining. *WRM Bulletin* 119. www.wrm.org.uy/, accessed December 14, 2007.

Rose, N. 1996. Governing "advanced" liberal democracies. In *Foucault and political reason: Liberalism, neo-liberalism and rationalities of government*, ed. A. Barry, T. Osborne, and N. Rose, 37–64. London: University College London Press.

Rosenau, J. 2000. Change, complexity and governance in globalizing space. In *Debating governance*, ed. J. Pierre. 167–200. Oxford: Oxford University Press.

Rostow, W. 1968. *Stages of economic growth: A non-communist manifesto.* Cambridge: Cambridge University Press.

Said, E. 1978. *Orientalism.* New York: Vintage.

Salman, T., and A. Zoomers, eds. 2003. *Imaging the Andes: Shifting margins of a marginal world.* Amsterdam: CEDLA.

Sánchez, L., D. Tuchschneider, P. de Zutter, and R. Zelada, eds. 1994. *Del paquete al acompañamiento? Experiencias del PRIV en extensión agropecuaria.* La Paz: Hisbol / PRIV.

Sánchez, O. 2000. Resumen del proceso de discusión de la ley de aguas y la participación ciudadana. Unpublished report. Cayambe, Ecuador.

Sandoval, G. 1993. *Las ONGs y los caminos del desarrollo.* La Paz: Centro de Estudios y Proyectos.

Santana, R. 1995. *Ciudadanos en la etnicidad.* Quito: Abya-Yala.

Satish, S. 1999. *The World Bank policy on indigenous peoples: India consultations on the Approach Paper for revision of Operational Directive 4.20.* Report No. 30438. New Dehli: World Bank.

Sawyer, S. 1997. The 1992 Indian mobilization in lowland Ecuador. *Latin American Perspectives* 24(3): 65–82.

Schech, S., and J. Haggis. 2000. *Culture and development: A critical introduction.* Oxford: Blackwell.

Schild, V. 1998. New subjects of rights? Women's movements and the construction of citizenship in the "new democracies." In Alvarez, Dagnino, and Escobar, 93–117.

Scott, D. 1995. *Gender and development: Rethinking modernization and development theory.* Boulder, Colo.: Lynne Reinner.

Scott, J. 1998. *Seeing like a state.* New Haven, Conn.: Yale University Press.

Secretaria Técnica del Frente Social. 1998. *Retrato de mujeres: Indicadores sociales sobre la situación de las indígenas y campesinas del Ecuador rural.* Quito: SIISE.

Segarra, M. 1997. Redefining the public/private mix: NGOs and the Emergency Social Investment Fund in Ecuador. In Chalmers, Vilas, Hite, Martin, Piester, and Segarra, 489–515.

Selverston, M. 1997. The politics of identity reconstruction: Indians and democracy in Ecuador. In Chalmers, Vilas, Hite, Martin, Piester, and Segarra, 170–91.

Selverston-Scher, M. 2001. *Ethnopolitics in Ecuador: Indigenous rights and the strengthening of democracy.* Miami: North-South Center Press, University of Miami.

Sen, A. 1990. Development as capability expansion. In *Human development and the international development strategy of the 1990s,* eds. K. Griffin and J. Knight, 41–58. London: Macmillan.

———. 1992. *Inequality reexamined.* Cambridge, Mass.: Harvard University Press.

———. 2000. *Social exclusion: Concept, application and scrutiny.* Manila: Office of Environment and Social Development, Asian Development Bank.

Sending, O. J., and I. Neumann. 2006. Governance to governmentality: Analyzing NGOs, states, and power. *International Studies Quarterly* 50:651–72.

Sheppard, E., and R. McMaster. 2003a. Scale and geographic inquiry. In Sheppard and McMaster, 256–67.

Sheppard, E., and R. McMaster, eds. 2003b. *Scale and geographic inquiry.* Oxford: Blackwell.

Shohat, E., ed. 1998. *Talking visions: Multicultural feminism in a transnational age.* New York: Massachussets Institute of Technology.

Shore, C., and S. Wright, eds. 1997. *Anthropology of policy: Critical perspectives on governance and power.* London: Routledge.

Siddarth, V. 1995. Gendered participation: NGOs and the World Bank. *IDS Bulletin* 26(3): 31–37.

Sieder, R., ed. 2002. *Multiculturalism in Latin America: Indigenous rights, diversity and democracy in Latin America.* Basingstoke: Palgrave Macmillan.

Sikkink, K. 1991. *Ideas and institutions: Developmentalism in Brazil and Argentina.* Ithaca, N.Y.: Cornell University Press.

———. 1993. Human rights, principled issue networks, and sovereignty in Latin America. *International Organization* 47:411–41.

Sillitoe, P. 1998. The development of indigenous knowledge. *Current Anthropology* 39:223–56.

Silva, P. 1998. Neoliberalism, democratization and the rise of the technocrats. In Vellinga, 73–92.

Silverblatt, I. 1995. Becoming Indian in the central Andes of seventeenth century Peru. In *After colonialism: Imperial histories and post-colonial displacements,* ed. G. Prakesh, 279–98. Princeton, N.J.: Princeton University Press.

Silvey, R., and R. Elmhirst. 2003. Engendering social capital: Women workers and rural-urban networks in Indonesia's Crisis. *World Development* 31:865–79.

Slater, D. 1997. Geopolitics and the postmodern: Issues of knowledge, difference and north-south relations. In *Space and social theory: Interpreting modernity and post-modernity*, ed. G. Benko, and U. Strohmayer, 324–35. Oxford: Blackwell.

———. 1998. Rethinking the spatialities of social movements: Questions of borders, culture and politics in global times. In Alvarez, Dagnino, and Escobar, 380–401.

———. 2003. On the spatial dynamics of democratic politics: Analyzing the Bolivian case. *Development and Change* 34:607–32.

Smith, J., C. Chatfield, and R. Pagnucco, eds. 1997. *Transnational social movements and global politics: Solidarity beyond the state*. Syracuse, N.Y.: Syracuse University Press.

Smith, J., R. Pagnucco, and C. Chatfield. 1997. Social movements and world politics: A theoretical framework. In Smith, Chatfield, and Pagnucco, 59–77.

Smith, L. 2002. The search for well being: Placing development with indigenous identity. *Thamyris: Intersecting Place, Sex and Race* 9:87–108.

Smith, N. 1990. *Uneven development: Nature, capital and the production of space*. Oxford: Blackwell.

———. 1993. Homeless/global: Scaling places. In *Mapping the futures: Local cultures, global change*, ed. J. Bird, 87–119. London: Routledge.

———. 2003. Scale bending and the fate of the national. In Sheppard, and McMaster, 2003b, 192–212.

Solanes, M., and D. Getches. 1998. *Prácticas recomendables para la elaboración de leyes y regulaciones con el recurso hídrico*. Washington, D.C.: IADB.

Solón, P. 2000. Acuerdo Gobierno-CSUTCB, CSCB sobre el agua. *Todo Sobre el Agua* 2:3.

———. 2001. Entre la constitución y las leyes del modelo neo-liberal. *Todo Sobre el Agua* 4:4–6.

Somers, M., and G. Gibson. 1994. Reclaiming the epistemological "other": Narrative and the social construction of identity. In *Social theory and the politics of identity*, ed. C. Calhoun, 37–99. Cambridge, Mass.: Blackwell.

Sorenson, G. 2004. *The transformation of the state: Beyond the myth of retreat*. New York: Palgrave MacMillan.

SNV. 2004. *Participatory local development planning: A guide for municipalities in southern Ecuador*. The Hague: SNV.

Speed, S., A. Hernandez, and L. Stephen. eds. 2006. *Dissident Women: Gender and cultural politics in Chiapas*. Austin: University of Texas Press.

Spivak, G. 1988. Can the subaltern speak? In Nelson and Grossberg, 271–313.

Stamatopoulou, E. 1994. Indigenous peoples and the United Nations: Human rights as a developing dynamic. *Human Rights Quarterly* 16:58–81.

Starn, O. 1991. Missing the revolution: Anthropologists and the war in Peru. *Cultural Anthropology* 6:63–91.

Stavenhagen, R. 1996. Indigenous rights: Some conceptual problems. In *Constructing democracy: Human rights, citizenship and society in Latin America*, ed. E. Jelin and E. Hershberg, 141–59. Boulder, Colo.: Westview Press.

———. 1998. Indigenous peoples: Emerging international actors. In *Ethnic diversity and public policy*, ed. C. Young, 133–52. London: Macmillan.

———. 2002a. Indigenous people and the state in Latin America: An ongoing debate. In Sieder, 24–44.

———. 2002b. The return of the native: The indigenous challenge in Latin America. John Brookes Memorial Lecture, March 15, University of London.

Steinmetz, G. 1999. Introduction: Culture and the state. In *State/culture: State formation after the cultural turn*, ed. G. Steinmetz, 1–37. Ithaca, N.Y.: Cornell University Press.

Stephen, L. 1991. Culture as a resource: Four cases of self-managed indigenous craft production in Latin America. *Economic Development and Cultural Change* 40(1): 101–30.

Stern, A. 2004. From mestizophilia to biotypology: Racialization and science in Mexico, 1920–1960. In Applebaum, Macpherson, and Rosemblatt, 187–210.

Stern, S., ed. 1987. *Resistance, rebellion, and consciousness in the Andean peasant world, 18th to 20th centuries*. Madison: University of Wisconsin Press.

Stirrat, R.L. 2000. Cultures of consultancy. *Critique of Anthropology* 20(1): 31–46.

Stolcke, V. 1999. New rhetorics of exclusion in Europe. *International Social Science Journal* 51(1): 25–36.

Strobele-Gregor, J. 1996. Culture and political practice of the Aymara and Quechua in Bolivia: Autonomous forms of modernity in the Andes. *Latin American Perspectives* 23(2): 72–90.

Stutzman, R. 1981. El mestizaje: An all-inclusive ideology of exclusion. In *Cultural transformation and ethnicity in modern Ecuador*, ed. N. Whitten, 45–94. Urbana: University of Illinois Press.

Sub-Alcaldia del DMI Calcha. 1998. *Estatuto del Distrito Municipal Indígena Calcha*. Calcha, Bolivia: Sub-Alcaldia del DMI Calcha.

Taller de Historia Oral Andina. 1995. *Ayllu: Pasado y futuro de los pueblos originarios*. La Paz: Aruwiyiri.

Tauli-Corpuz, V. 2005. *Indigenous peoples and the Millennium Development Goals*. Paper presented at the 4th session of the UN Permanent Forum on Indigenous Issues, May 16–27, New York.

Tene, C., G. Tobar, and D. Bolaños. 2004. *Programas de microcredito y capital social entre mujeres indígenas*. Working paper no. 18 on Sustainable Development, Indignous Peoples Series. Quito: World Bank Latin American and Caribbean Region.

Tennant, C. 1994. Indigenous peoples, international institutions and the international legal literature from 1945–1993. *Human Rights Quarterly* 16:1–57.

Tibán, L. 2001. Género y sustentabilidad: nuevos conceptos para el mundo indigena. *Boletín ICCI-Rimai* 29. http://icci.nativeweb.org/, accessed April 2, 2005.

Ticona, E. 1996. CSUTCB: *Trayectoria y desafios*. La Paz: CEDOIN.

———. 2003. El *Thakhi* entre los Aymara y Quechua o la democracia de los gobiernos comunales. In *Los Andes desde los Andes*, ed. E. Ticona, 125–46. La Paz: Ediciones Yachaywasi.

Ticona, E., and X. Albó. 1997. *La lucha por el poder comunal*. La Paz: CIPCA / CEDOIN.

Tilly, C. 1998. *Durable inequality*. Berkeley: University of California Press.

———. 1999. From interactions to outcomes in social movements. In *How social movements matter*, ed. M. Guigni, D. McAdam, and C. Tilly, 253–70. Minneapolis: University of Minnesota Press.

Torres, V. H. 1999a. El desarrollo local en el Ecuador: Discursos, tendencias y desafíos. In Hidalgo, 15–38.

———. 1999b. Guamote: El proceso indígena de gobierno municipal participativo. In Hidalgo, 87–112.

———. 2004. Innovando la institucionalidad local: La experiencia de los municipios alternativos en Ecuador. In *Capital social e institucionalidad local: Estudios de caso en Bolivia y Ecuador*, ed. K. Andersson, D. Pacheco, R. León, P. Uberhuaga, and V. H. Torres, 45–101. Montebello, Guatemala: Red Internacional de Participación para el Manejo Sostenible de los Recursos Naturales.

Torzano, C., and J.L. Exeni, eds. 1994. *Las IPDS y la descentralización*. La Paz: ILDIS.

Townsend, J., G. Porter, and E. Mawdsley. 2002. The role of the transnational community of non-government organisations: Governance or poverty reduction. *Journal of International Development* 14:829–39.

Treakle, K. 1998. Ecuador: Structural adjustment and indigenous and environmentalist resistance. In *The struggle for accountability: The World Bank, NGOs and grassroots movements*, ed. J. Fox, and D. Brown, 219–59. Cambridge, Mass.: MIT Press.

True, J., and M. Mintrom. 2001. Transnational networks and policy diffusion: The case of gender mainstreaming. *International Studies Quarterly* 45:27–57.

Tribunal Supremo Electoral. 2004. *Resultados electorales 2004*. Quito: Tribunal Supremo Electoral.

Tsing, A. 2005. *Friction: A global ethnography of connection*. Princeton, N.J.: Princeton University Press.

Tucayta. 1999. *Plan de desarrollo local de Tucuy Canar Ayllucanapac Tantanacuy— Tucayta*, Quito: PRODEPINE.

Tulchin, J., and A. Garland, eds. 2000. *Social development in Latin America: The politics of reform*. Boulder, Colo.: Lynne Rienner.

UNDESA. 2005. *The Social Summit: Ten years later*. New York: United Nations.

UNECLA. 1970. *Social change and social development policy in Latin America*. New York: United Nations.

Uquillas, J. 2002. *Fortalecimiento de la capacidad de autogestión de las organizaciones indígenas en el Ecuador: El caso de PRODEPINE*. Paper presented at the first Latin American Studies Association conference on Ecuadorian Studies, July 18–20, Quito, Ecuador.

Urban, G., and J. Sherzer, eds. 1991. *Nation-states and Indians in Latin America.* Austin: University of Texas Press.

Urioste, M. 1987. *Segunda reforma agraria: Campesinos, tierra y educación popular.* La Paz: Centro de Estudios para el Desarrollo Laboral y Agrario.

———. 2007. Conclusiones y algunas recomendaciones. In *Los nietos de la reforma agraria: Tierra y comunidad en al altiplano de Bolivia,* ed. Fundación Tierra, 225–35. La Paz: Fundación Tierra.

VAIPO. 1998. *Desarrollo con identidad: Política nacional indígena y originaria.* La Paz: VAIPO.

Valentine, G. 2007. Theorizing and researching intersectionality: A challenge for feminist geography. *The Professional Geographer* 59:10–21.

Van Cott, D. L., ed. 1994. *Indigenous peoples and democracy in Latin America.* New York: Inter-American Dialogue / St. Martin's Press.

———. 2000a. *The friendly liquidation of the past: The politics of diversity in Latin America.* Pittsburgh: University of Pittsburgh Press.

———. 2000b. Explaining ethnic autonomy regimes in Latin America. Paper presented at the congress of the Latin American Studies Association Congress, March 15–18, Miami.

———. 2002. Constitutional reform in the Andes: Redefining indigenous-state relations. In Seider, 45–73.

———. 2003. Andean indigenous movements and constitutional transformation: Venezuela in comparative perspective. *Latin American Perspectives* 30:49–69.

———. 2006. Radical democracy in the Andes: Indigenous parties and the quality of democracy in Latin America. Working paper 333, Kellogg Institute, University of Notre Dame.

Van de Fliert, L. 1994. *Indigenous peoples and international organizations.* Nottingham, England: Spokesman / Russell Press.

Van Nieuwkoop, M., and J. Uquillas. 2000. *Defining ethno-development in operational terms: Lessons from the Ecuador indigenous and Afro-Ecuadoran peoples development project.* Washington, D.C.: World Bank.

Van Schaik, L. 1994. The Netherlands government policy on indigenous people. *IWGIA Documents* no. 76. Amsterdam: IWGIA.

Vellinga, M., ed. 1998. *The changing role of the state in Latin America.* Boulder, Colo.: Westview Press.

Vertovec, S. 1999. Conceiving and researching transnationalism. *Ethnic and Racial Studies* 22:447–62.

———. 2001. *Transnational social formations: Towards a conceptual cross-fertilization.* Working paper, Transnational Communities Programme, WPTC-01–16.

Viceministerio de Tierras [Bolivia]. n.d. Resumen de propuestas de los pueblos indígenas y orignarios para la asamblea constituyente [unofficial]. La Paz: Viceministerio de Tierras.

Vilas, C. 2006. The left in South America and the resurgence of national-popular regimes. In *Latin American after neoliberalism: Turning the tide in the 21st century?* eds. Hershberg and F. Rosen, 232–51. New York: New Press / NACLA.

Vinding, D. 1998a. *Indigenous women: The right to a voice.* Copenhagen: International Work Group on Indigenous Affairs.

———. ed. 1998b. Indigenous women: The right to a voice. IWGIA Document no.88, Copenhagen.

Visweswaran, K. 1998. Race and the culture of anthropology. *American Anthropologist* 100:70–83.

Wade, P. 1997. *Race and ethnicity in Latin America.* London: Pluto.

———. 2004. Race and nation in Latin America: An anthropological view. In Applebaum, Macpherson, and Rosemblatt, 263–81.

Wainright, H. 2003. Making a people's budget in Porto Alegre. NACLA *Report on the Americas* 36(5): 37–42.

Walby, S. 2005. Introduction: Comparative gender mainstreaming in a global era. *International Feminist Journal of Politics* 7:453–70.

Waltz, K. 1959. *Man, the state and war: A theoretical analysis.* New York: Colombia University Press.

Warren, J. 1998. The state of Indian exorcism: Violence and racial formation in eastern Brazil. *The Journal of Historical Sociology* 11:492–518.

Warren, K. 1998. *Indigenous movements and their critics: Pan-Maya activism in Guatemala.* Princeton, N.J.: Princeton University Press.

Warren, K., and J. Jackson, eds. 2002. *Indigenous movements, self-representation and the state in Latin America.* Austin: Texas University Press.

Warren, M. 1991. *Using indigenous knowledge in agricultural development.* Discussion Paper 127. Washington, D.C.: World Bank.

Watts, M. 2002. Alternative modern—development as cultural geography. In *Handbook of cultural geography*, ed. K. Anderson, M. Domosh, S. Pile, and N. Thrift, 433–53. London: Sage.

———. 2003. Development and governmentality. *Singapore Journal of Tropical Geography* 24(1): 6–34.

Weir, L. 1996. Recent developments in the governance of pregnancy. *Economy and Society* 25:372–92.

Weismantel, M. 2001. *Cholos and pishtacos: Stories of race and sex in the Andes.* Chicago: University of Chicago.

Weismantel, M., and S. Eisenman. 1998. Race in the Andes: Global movements and popular ontologies. *Bulletin of Latin American Research* 17:121–42.

White, S. 2002. Thinking race, thinking development. *Third World Quarterly* 23: 407–20.

Whitten, N. 2003. *Millennial Ecuador: Critical essays on cultural transformations and social dynamics.* Iowa City: University of Iowa Press.

Woolcock, M. 2000. Social capital: Implications for development theory, research and policy. *The World Bank Research Observer* 15:225–49.

World Bank. 1993. *Water resources management.* Washington, D.C.: World Bank.

———. 1995. *Meeting infrastructure challenges in Latin America and the Caribbean. Directions in development.* Washington D.C.: World Bank.

———. 1997. *Project appraisal document on a proposed loan in the amount of US$25.0 Million to the Republic of Ecuador for an indigenous and Afro-Ecuadorian peoples development project.* Report No. 17217-EC. Washington, D.C.: World Bank.

———. 1998a. *Demand responsive approaches to community water supply: Moving from policy to practice.* Washington, D.C.: World Bank.

———. 1998b. Participatory training of indigenous peoples in Latin America. www.worldbank.org, accessed June 21, 2000.

———. 1999b. *Bolivia: Indigenous peoples development: Conditions, policies and program strategy.* Washington, D.C.: World Bank.

———. 1999c. *Bolivia: Plan de desarrollo indígena. Diagnóstico nacional informe final.* La Paz: World Bank / Viceministerio de Asuntos Indígenas y Pueblos Originarios.

———. 1999d. *Food for thought: Proceedings from Brown Bag Lunch Series.* Washington, D.C.: World Bank.

———. 2000a. *Ecuador gender review issues and recommendations: A World Bank country study.* Washington, D.C.: World Bank.

———. 2000b. Indigenous knowledge for development. http://www.worldbank.org/, accessed April 3, 2000.

World Summit for Social Development. 1995. *The Copenhagen Declaration and Programme of Action.* New York: United Nations, Department of Public Information.

Wray, N. 1989. La constitución del movimiento étnico-nacional indio en Ecuador. *América Indígena* 49(1): 77–99.

Yashar, D. 1999. Democracy, indigenous movements and the postliberal challenge in Latin America. *World Politics* 52:76–104.

———. 2005. *Contesting citizenship in Latin America: The rise of indigenous movements and the postliberal challenge.* Cambridge: Cambridge University Press.

Yudice, G. 1998. The globalization of culture and the new civil society. In Alvarez, Dagnino, Escobar, 353–74.

Zamosc, L. 1994. Agrarian protest and the Indian movement in the Ecuadorian highlands. *Latin American Research Review* 21(3): 37–69.

INDEX

■

Robert Andolina is an assistant professor of international studies at Seattle University. His research publications on Andean indigenous movements and development policy appear in English and Spanish in various journals and edited volumes, including the *Journal of Latin American Studies*.

Nina Laurie is a professor of development and environment in the School of Geography, Politics, and Sociology at Newcastle University, U.K. She works on neoliberalism, water politics, and gender and identity in the Andes. She is coauthor of *Geographies of New Femininities* (1999) and coeditor of a special issue of *Antipode*, "Working the Spaces of Neo-liberalism: Activism, Professionalization and Incorporation" (2005).

Sarah A. Radcliffe is based at the Department of Geography, University of Cambridge, U.K. Her work has focused on postcolonial patterns of governance and identity in the Andes, especially issues of race, gender, state formation, and citizen-state relations. She is coauthor of *Re-making the Nation* (1996), editor of *Culture and Development in a Globalizing World* (2006), and coeditor of *Viva! Women and Popular Protest in Latin America* (1993).

Library of Congress Cataloging-in-Publication Data

Andolina, Robert, 1968–
Indigenous development in the Andes : culture, power, and
transnationalism / Robert Andolina, Nina Laurie, and Sarah A. Radcliffe.
p. cm.
Includes bibliographical references and index.
ISBN 978-0-8223-4523-7 (cloth : alk. paper)
ISBN 978-0-8223-4540-4 (pbk. : alk. paper)
1. Indigenous peoples—Andes Region—Politics and government.
2. Social movements—Andes Region.
I. Laurie, Nina.
II. Radcliffe, Sarah A.
III. Title.
F2212.A6155 2009
307.1'40890098—dc22
2009029300